ANTIQUE
GARDEN
ORNAMENT
Two Centuries of American Taste

by Barbara Israel

with a Preface by Mark Hampton
Photographs by Mick Hales

ANTIQUE
GARDEN
ORNAMENT

Two Centuries of American Taste

Harry N. Abrams, Inc., Publishers

To my grandmothers,

Emily Brewster Frelinghuysen

and

Margaret Dix Lawrance,

whose love of gardens

and their ornament

captured my imagination.

Editor: Elaine M. Stainton
Designer: Judith Hudson
Photo Research: Alexandra Truitt and Jerry Marshall

Library of Congress Cataloging-in-Publication Data
Israel, Barbara.
   Antique garden ornament : two centuries of American taste / by
Barbara Israel ; with a preface by Mark Hampton ; photographs
by Mick Hales.
      p.   cm.
   Includes bibliographical references (p.   ) and index.
   ISBN 0-8109-4203-8
   1. Garden ornaments and furniture—United States—History.
   I. Hales, Michael. II. Title.
   SB473.5.I76   1999
   717'.0973—dc21   99-11145

PAGE 2: Urns. c. 1928. Granite. 6'8" wide. Peapack Gate, St. Joseph's
Villa (formerly Blairsden), Peapack, New Jersey.

PAGE 6: Urns. English. c. 1830. Carved stone. 37" with base x 25".
Middleton Place, Charleston, South Carolina.

PAGES 8–9: Busts. c. 1899. Marble. 9' high. St. Joseph's Villa (formerly
Blairsden), Peapack, New Jersey.

PAGES 10–11: Wall fountain and water cascades. c. 1898–1900.
American. Carved stone. St. Joseph's Villa (formerly Blairsden),
Peapack, New Jersey.

PAGE 12: *Autumn.* Eighteenth century. French.
Terra cotta. 31 x 39". Belcourt Castle, Newport, Rhode Island.

Printed and bound in Hong Kong

Harry N. Abrams, Inc.
100 Fifth Avenue
New York, N.Y. 10011
www.abramsbooks.com

CONTENTS

PREFACE

There are numerous books on garden ornament that have been widely read over the years. Gertrude Jekyll's *Garden Ornament,* first published in 1918, immediately comes to mind. The vast majority of these works, however, deal with England and the Continent. The subject of American garden ornament through history has suffered from neglect. So it is enormously rewarding to read Barbara Israel's beautiful and scholarly book, *Antique Garden Ornament: Two Centuries of American Taste,* which will surely become an immediate resource for architects, landscape architects, interior designers, dealers, collectors, and students.

The range of material Mrs. Israel deals with is very broad, introducing the reader to a wide variety of historic American gardens, the quality of which is remarkable. Mick Hales, a well-known and extraordinarily sensitive photographer, has captured the haunting beauty of these gardens and their ornaments. In many cases, the gardens chosen have a rare and undiscovered quality that adds greatly to the interest of the book.

Mrs. Israel's accompanying text, endowed with lively historical details and important research, provides an appropriate framework within which to view these original images. While her discussion leaves the more academic points of design to the landscape architects, it does present and explain the key elements behind the chronicled use of ornament in relation to the landscape.

On the practical side, the catalogue of black-and-white photographs identifies many objects that are seen today and that benefit from categorization. Moreover, the importance of the directory of foundries, the examples of their marks, and their dates of operation cannot be emphasized enough and should serve for many years to come as a significant aid for both the budding collector and the connoisseur. It will also assist in protecting the integrity of the cast-iron market by creating an educated public who will know how to assess the essentials of an object before acquiring it. The same consumers will appreciate further answers provided in the section on authenticating and maintaining ornaments. And for the more studious, the extensive bibliography will serve as a guide and starting point for research into the history of decorations for the garden.

This definitive work should enliven an already exciting garden ornament market, inspiring collectors through the remarkable examples presented herein, in addition to providing an excellent foundation for further consideration of American garden ornament.

Mark Hampton
June 5, 1998

INTRODUCTION

The two hundred years between 1740 and 1940 witnessed the creation of many important American gardens. This book will discuss the origins and development of American taste in terms of the ornament that decorated the grounds of these historic estates. We will consider not only the styles, techniques, materials, and ornaments themselves that were transported to America from Europe and elsewhere, but also domestic products emerging from the growing sophistication, confidence, and technical abilities of the new nation.

In 1926, writing for *The Studio,* an art-oriented periodical, Percy Cane observed that "[i]nstead of originating the national arts she [America] has searched the world and fed aesthetically from those of other countries."[1] While the tastemakers and creators of great estates did turn to Europe for guidance and example in the period discussed, inevitably, many of the imported styles were transformed when absorbed into the new and challenging environment of the New World, with its immense tracts of land, severe climatic conditions, and vast regional differences. This book will address the history of garden design only as it pertains to ornament, inasmuch as the appropriateness of garden ornament is intrinsically linked to that of landscape design in general. It will not attempt to discuss the full range of design movements that affected American gardens, but will consider the relationship of ornament to the basic principles of these movements.

Broadly speaking, American gardens have been laid out according to one of two opposing schools of landscape design: the formal or Italianate, originating in Renaissance Italy; and the picturesque or English garden style, claiming its origin in the Romantic period of the late eighteenth century. The Italian style was based on symmetrical, terraced beds and straight pathways, generally including classical statuary, furniture, and urns. Later, the architects of such seventeenth-century French Baroque gardens as Versailles reinterpreted the formal garden style of Italy on an extraordinary scale, using a multitude of ornamental details. Geometry and ornament dominated the actual plantings in schemes of this sort. In contrast, the second school of landscape design, which found its genesis in a variety of influences, including Romantic paintings, while no less contrived, emphasized the plantings and the true contours of the land. Such terms as "natural," "picturesque," "informal," "English landscape garden," and *"jardin anglais"* refer to this style, which is characterized by a sparsely ornamented, yet judiciously engineered, landscape that resembled nature as closely as possible. Any artistic improvement was calculated to appear to be part of the landscape. Because straight lines did not exist in nature, serpentine lines were *de rigueur*. Classical allusions were permitted in the form of temples, busts, urns, obelisks, or curved walls and seats, called exedrae. Urns and furniture in the rustic style, a decorative conceit using designs based on twigs, branches, and stumps, were associated with picturesque gardens.

In the eighteenth and nineteenth centuries, American taste was strongly influenced by literature – from both home and abroad – that planted the seeds of interest in landscape and its decorations. Design books, critical commentaries, and garden publications all contributed to the knowledge and helped form the preferences of American homeowners and garden professionals. At the beginning of the nineteenth century these texts fostered an awareness of the aesthetics of landscape design and ornament. Later, profits from industry had created a prosperous middle class in America, which responded enthusiastically to the advice of tastemakers. One such authority was the British author Humphrey Repton, a strong supporter of the English picturesque garden. In 1803 he wrote *The Art of Landscape Gardening*, a book that was widely read in America. Another popular source was Bernard McMahon's *The American Gardener's Calendar* of 1806, which contributed significantly to the available garden commentary by providing month-by-month advice on all aspects of gardening. In 1834, John Claudius Loudon, the English proponent of a landscape style called "gardenesque," a combination of Italianate and picturesque styles, published the *Encyclopedia of Gardening*, which proved a popular reference for American gardeners.

In the nineteenth century, one native voice came to supplant all others as the ultimate authority on American garden taste. Andrew Jackson Downing, a Hudson valley landscape specialist, who, often drawing on the words of both McMahon and Loudon, communicated specific directives to garden owners. While not necessarily the originator of all the ideas he propounded, he was the foremost influence on American garden ideas from the 1840s until the 1890s. Still held in high regard today, Downing's particular interest was determining how to create an American interpretation of the English "picturesque" garden. In 1841 he published *A Treatise on the Theory and Practice of Landscape Gardening*, the first American book of its kind. Five years later he followed up with the first issue of *The Horticulturist*, his illustrated monthly magazine. Its aim was to

report on "the zeal and enthusiasm which the last five years have begotten in American Horticulture."[2] Nineteenth-century enthusiasm for home and garden also found expression in other periodicals, such as *Godey's Lady's Book* and *Peterson's Magazine*, both of which touched on the benefits of gardens for families.[3]

The historic houses of America are young compared to those of Europe, but much information can be extracted from their brief histories. For the colorplates of this book, I have selected a number of houses and properties to illustrate the tastes of colonial landholders, Victorian homeowners, and the proprietors of the great country estates of the early twentieth century. In order to refine the scope of this survey, I have included only intact pieces from the original garden plans of private residences. Most of these ornaments are traditional in subject matter and form. A one-of-a-kind object specially commissioned for a garden may be considered, but on the whole the objects discussed will be pieces made in large numbers to be sold specifically for outdoor decoration. An important point to remember, often made in any discussion of garden history, is that gardens are ephemeral. Their ornament is less so, although still threatened by war and weather. What was preserved of American gardens and their ornament has been invaluable to this study.

While my original intent was to include a wide geographical sampling of historic houses with fine gardens, most that I have finally chosen are located near a coastline. The reason for this is largely historical. In brief, the first gardens of note in America were laid out in the Northeast and in Virginia; soon thereafter, others were established in the South. Finally, toward the end of the nineteenth century, some fine gardens were laid out in the West. I have only noted a few of the regional aspects of gardens and their ornament, as regional differences are too broad a topic for this survey. Collecting garden ornament, historically, has been a luxury for the rich, a passion of the elite. The houses and gardens I have pictured across the country, for the most part, are large estates of wealthy landholders. Wherever possible I have attempted to discuss smaller properties, although, in general, it is the larger gardens that have been preserved.

The black-and-white photographic catalogue of garden ornament illustrates period styles, makers, exemplary forms, and, in some cases, artists' works. For this purpose, I have opted for important and representative examples in each category; the captions to the photographs provide historical and other pertinent background information. Appendix 1 contains a list of manufacturers of garden ornament and their marks compiled from city directories and other period sources. It does not presume to be more than a thorough sampling of late-nineteenth- and early-twentieth-century companies that produced garden ornament in America and abroad; however, the addresses, dates, and makers' marks should make it possible to identify and date a good proportion of marked pieces. Appendix 2, devoted to maintenance, identification, and security, is designed to answer questions that I am often asked by collectors. Appendix 3 offers a list of selected historic gardens in America.

What would entice a person to pursue a career in garden ornament? In my case it was one magnificent estate: Blairsden, in Peapack, New Jersey, renamed St. Joseph's Villa in the 1950s – a Louis XIII-style house and garden that, more than any other playground, had an irresistible attraction for me. A few times as a child, I secretly circumnavigated the locked entrance gates and scaled the clifflike hills surrounding the house to peek through the trees at Blairsden's formal garden.

Only years later did I discover that I had not been alone in my admiration. In 1911, Wilhelm Miller, the horticultural editor of *Country Life in America,* wrote an ardent appeal to the owners of large gardens to create a landscape style that would be uniquely American. He implored, "Let every country use chiefly its own native trees, shrubs, vines and other permanent material, and let the style of gardening grow naturally out of necessity, the soil and new conditions. When we stop imitating and do this, America will soon find herself." Very few formal gardens earned Miller's respect. He continued: "I have seen only one other large garden that seems to me to have made important contributions toward an American style of formal garden. That is Blairsden, at Peapack, N.J., the home of Mr. and Mrs. C. Ledyard Blair. It has the real Italian 'garden magic,'

i.e., the charm that is not dependent upon flowers. And it is not a copy. The real spirit has been transported and actually adapted to American conditions."[4]

What I had seen at Blairsden was an early-twentieth-century American landscape born not of imitation but of an inspired fusion of inherited tradition and indigenous character. It is something of that spirit of cultivated invention, so characteristic of the best American gardens, that I hope to capture in this book.

Barbara Israel
September 1, 1998

NOTES

1. Cane, 16.
2. *The Horticulturist* 1 (July 1846): 10.
3. Mac Griswold, "American Artists, American Gardens," in *Keeping Eden,* 173.
4. W. Miller, v, vi, 21.

CHAPTER 1

FOUNTAINS

Fountains are the most compelling of garden ornaments. Grand or modest, their unique charm lies not only in the beauty of their architecture but also in the musical sound of splashing water, the play of light on shimmering surfaces, and the viewer's fascination with how they work. Fountains in American gardens have a briefer history than their ancestors in Europe and in the eighteenth century. When the emphasis was initially on survival rather than splendor, they occupied a place of less importance in the eyes of estate owners. In the agrarian society of eighteenth-century America, an owner's principal concern regarding water was to provide enough to irrigate his crops and to supply his farm animals – not sourcing, storing, and piping it for fountains. Necessity thus forced the English colonists to adopt a practical approach to water use, one that favored utility rather than display. Even where fountains were installed, their owners preferred uncomplicated mechanics and simplified treatments far removed from the complex systems and ornamental forms that had developed in Europe.

Most European fountain types were derived from ancient Greek and Roman models and their Renaissance revivals, especially those in the gardens of Italian villas of the sixteenth century.[1] In this golden age of fountains, their designers created magnificent tiers of basins, majestic sculptural wall arrangements, and fantastic cavelike grottoes. In the next century French garden planners turned to these Renaissance precedents for inspiration, copying and reinterpreting Italian examples and creating vast geometric gardens studded with fountains. The water displays in the gardens of Versailles, far more numerous originally than today, were considered some of the finest and most elaborate in the world.[2] Together, the ornate fountains of sixteenth-century Italy and seventeenth-century France became the prototypes for most later forms.

FIG. 1

Fountain. After Carlo Bizzaccheri. c.1915.
Carved stone. Italian. 72 x 62" diam.
Cranbrook House, Bloomfield Hills, Michigan.

This fountain is a copy of an original designed by Carlo Bizzaccheri for the Piazza of Santa Maria in Cosmedin in Rome. In around 1718, when Pope Clement XI Albani called on Bizzaccheri, an architect, to remodel the long-neglected piazza, the fountain was the centerpiece of his design. Bizzaccheri based elements of the piece, particularly the octagonal basin, on the principal feature of the Albani coat of arms, an eight-pointed star.[1] The rock-work base and crouching figure of Triton are clearly derived from Gianlorenzo Bernini's fountains, which dominate several Roman squares.

1. Sanfilippo, 182.

Ornamental fountains exist in many variations. The most common types are the freestanding tazza-form, or shallow, bowl, the wall-mounted or semiattached water ensemble, and the fountain figure, used either alone or in combination. Another variation, the grotto, a cavelike structure set into a wall with a fountain in its interior, is relatively rare (see fig. 2). Originating in Renaissance Italy, the grotto merits mention as an accessory to the natural garden, albeit one of exceptional expense.[3] Here, we will consider primarily private garden fountains in traditional styles: freestanding examples that are not, for the most part, integrated into architecture. In certain cases, however, public fountains that have served as models for those in private gardens also will be mentioned.

A tazza-form fountain consists of at least one circular basin mounted on a decorative pedestal. Frequently, there are several basins repeated in graduated tiers. Water is carried to the top level by an internal pipe and released through a decorative spout. As the top bowl fills, the water spills over its sides into the larger basin below. The entire structure is mounted in a ground-level basin or pool. At times, coping – a molded edging of stone or marble – surrounds the edge of the pool.

The classic design and versatility of the tazza form has led to its nearly universal acceptance in Europe and North America. A fountain of this type, used singly or in combination, can be plain or decorated, with or without sculptural additions. A large architectural treatment suits the

FIG. 2
Grotto fountain. 1915–21. American. Limestone. Approx. 9'8" x 6'8" opening. Vizcaya Museum and Gardens, Miami, Florida.

In keeping with the Italian Renaissance theme of the gardens at Villa Vizcaya, James Deering, a cofounder of the International Harvester Company, and his Colombian landscape architect, Diego Suarez (1888–1974), included a pair of rustic grottoes with indoor fountains like the Italian examples found at the Villa Farnese at Caprarola, the Villa Gamberaia at Settignano, and the Boboli Gardens in Florence. Vizcaya's grottoes were carved in place by stonecutters following models made by an Italian sculptor, Edoardo Camilli. The extraordinary openings, flanked by male atlantes and female caryatid figures, lead to cool, wet interiors, with walls and ceilings inset with shells.[1]

1. Davidson, 19.

FIG. 3

Fountain. Sixteenth century. Italian. Marble.
42 × 20". Vizcaya Museum and Gardens,
Miami, Florida.

This fountain, originally a holy water
font from a chapel in a palace in Urbino,
Italy, occupies a central location in the
extensive gardens of Vizcaya at the top of
a "mount" built to suggest an Italian hillside. The mount was a conceit that served
to shield the house from the intense
reflection of the nearby ocean. Vizcaya,
the Miami estate of James Deering, features a strong axial plan and abundant
garden ornament, including a large
number of fountains. Jets shooting from
the basin, in a style typical of Italian
water gardens, increase the effect of
splashing water.

requirements of a formal garden whereas a modest tazza
can serve as an informal fountain or even a birdbath.
Often, large tazza fountains are decorated with a central
figure plumbed to spout water, either from itself or from an
accessory animal or object. The subjects for these figures
were usually chosen from Greek and Roman mythology,
particularly those deities relating to water or the sea.
Renaissance figural fountains, such as the *Putto with
Dolphin* of circa 1470 by Andrea del Verrocchio (1435–88),
provided influential models for later centuries (cat. 1.33).

Wall fountains require a massive surface for support.
The wall not only carries the weight of basin and figure but
also houses the supply pipes. Water may flow directly into
a catch basin or through a decorative feature, such as a
grotesque or animal mask, the face of a cherub or nymph,
or another figure in relief. These not only add visual interest but also conceal the mechanism of the fountain. Wall
fountains generally release water through spouts in gentle

streams; however, occasionally, when water pressure per-
mits, they feature ornamental sprays called jets. More commonly used on tazza-form fountains, jets are produced by
nozzles that control the shape, pattern, and intensity of
the stream of water. These *jets d'eau,* as they are called in
France, were seen in vast numbers in formal European gardens, and served as precedents for late-nineteenth- and
early-twentieth-century American fountain usage. American garden ornament trade catalogues of the period offered
nozzles in various sizes and shapes, described as "French
Rose," "Brass," "Tulip," and "French Fountain" jets.[4]

We know only a little about the early forms of fountains in America, since the few period accounts that exist
make no specific mention of ornamental fountains. According to an account of 1770, an imaginative Thomas Jefferson,
one of the first Americans to adopt the ideas of the informal, or picturesque, English landscape designers, once considered a plan for a naturalistic grotto at Monticello, his

home in Virginia (see fig. 36, p. 55). This plan included a piped water feature in the grotto's interior, which was fed by "water from the spring [that, after being] guided into the grotto, [would] empty into a basin and then run off down the hill."[5]

While specific descriptions such as that of Jefferson's design are uncommon, eighteenth-century references do also note the presence of fountains outside Virginia. In a letter written in the early nineteenth century, Miss Elizabeth Mifflin noted her appreciation of "the gardens, [and] the fountains" of the Grange, her grandfather's estate in Haverford Township, Pennsylvania, which had been laid out in 1770 by John Cruikshank.[6] A recent study of early gardens of the Chesapeake Bay region found that fountains also had been set up in a number of formal terraced sections of eighteenth-century Maryland gardens. In the 1790s, William Gibson, the Baltimore county clerk, created an eight-bed symmetrical garden whose central feature was

"a fountain or water basin."[7] A painting of approximately 1816 by Charles Willson Peale (1741–1827) of his own garden at Belfield in Germantown, Pennsylvania, shows a circular fountain pool with a single jet of water. Supposedly, the eccentric Peale had an amusing feature on top of this ten-foot-high spout of water, a gilded ball that danced above it in the air, supported only by the pressure of the jet.[8]

Although properties in the North tended to be smaller and less elaborate than in the South, New England gardens also included fountains. The diary of the Reverend William Bentley, the pastor of the East Church in Salem, Massachusetts for more than thirty years beginning in 1784, provides insight into the existence of and even the mechanics of fountains of his time. In 1792, Bentley noted a fountain in his friend Mr. Brattle's parterre garden in Cambridge.[9] Years later, in June 1798, he described visiting a former classmate, Mr. Bangs, whose grounds boasted a

FIG. 4
Wall fountain. c. 1925. Italian. Various marbles. 9'6" x 6'3" x 39". The John and Mable Ringling Museum of Art, Sarasota, Florida.

Composed of many varied elements, this wall fountain, with its lushly carved colossal shell, foliate scrolls, and youths supporting a jug, exemplifies Baroque extravagance. The use of different marbles, a specialty in Italy, contributes to the richness of the composition and to the fountain's almost theatrical flamboyance, which appealed to the taste of the Ringling family. The flower baskets sitting on the volutes may be later additions.

fountain with water supplied from a millpond.[10] A few months later he reported on a carefully planned water-works in the garden of another friend, General Hull, in Newton: "His Aqueduct is led a mile . . . [i]t supplies the fountains in front of the house."[11] Bentley's interest in the water supply to Hull's and Bangs's fountains is illuminating since it provides an idea, albeit sketchy, of late-eighteenth-century supply and transportation by aqueduct of water for fountains. Since sculptural forms are not mentioned in any of these references, it seems likely that early American fountains were uncomplicated setups, perhaps a spray and a pool, with water supplied by siphon or gravitational pull.

In the early nineteenth century, the materials, design, and accessibility of fountains and other outdoor ornaments were altered by the development of systems of mass production in the cast-iron industry. The demand for cast-

FIG. 5

Apollo Fountain. John Massey Rhind. Marble carved by Pietro Faitini (in Italy), bronze cast by John R. Williams, Inc., New York. 1900–02. Istrian stone and bronze. Approx. 13 × 20 × 9'. Georgian Court College, Lakewood, New Jersey.

Surrounded by sea nymphs and putti, Rhind's fountain depicts the chariot of Apollo rising from the sea at the start of a new day. A birthday present from George Gould to his wife, Edith, this fountain featured an early form of electric illumination, perhaps influenced by the fountains at the Paris Universal Exposition of 1889 and the Chicago World's Columbian Exposition of 1893.

FIG. 6 AND FIG. 7

Fountain. Janes, Beebe & Co., New York. c. 1858. Cast iron. Fencing. New York Wire Railing Company, New York. c. 1860. Wire and cast iron. Forsythe Park, Savannah, Georgia. Fountain marked: *JANES, BEEBE & CO.*

In 1851 J. P. V. André, a French founder from Val d'Osne, France, installed a colossal, bronzed, cast-iron fountain in the east nave of the Crystal Palace Exhibition hall in London. Its illustration in the exhibition catalogue clearly inspired the Forsythe Park fountain.[1] Indeed, Janes, Beebe & Co. offered a replica of the Crystal Palace fountain in its 1858 catalogue. Like the original, this version featured four tritons set close to its immediate base.[2] In the Forsythe Park example, however, the tritons stand apart from the central element and are piped to provide individual water jets. The addition of piped swans brought the number of freestanding figural spouts in the pool to eight. The mixture of naturalistic, classical, and Renaissance themes in this fountain typifies Victorian extravagance in garden ornament. The juxtaposition of a gently curving scalloped upper bowl with a larger architectural lower bowl was a popular device, probably calculated to lighten the appearance of such large pieces. Also of note is the wire and cast-iron fence surrounding the pool, which was sold to the city of Savannah by John Wickersham of the New York Wire Railing Company.[3]

1. London, 1229.
2. Janes, Beebe & Co., no. 5.
3. Gayle, 9.

iron products, including decorative objects, broadened, encouraging the expansion of the cast-iron trade, first in England, following the American War of Independence; then in Prussia, following the Napoleonic Wars;[12] and later in America, following the establishment of the iron industry and the discovery of anthracite coal deposits.

In England, improvements in iron manufacture by the end of the eighteenth century were such that ". . . the multiplication of cast-iron products from the foundries was made possible."[13] The development of coal-fired smelters and the demand for iron for military use during the American War of Independence created the modern iron industry in England. After the war, English manufacturers sought new uses for their improved cast iron, and expanded to produce items of architecture and ornament.[14]

America was slower to produce significant amounts of ornamental work, as it lagged behind English and Continental technical advances well into the nineteenth century. In the eighteenth century, the American colonies had been forbidden to make iron products, but were encouraged to make pig iron for English manufacturers. In fact, even with the restrictive Act of 1750, the colonies, particularly Massachusetts and Pennsylvania, continued to create objects for local use, most notably stoves and firebacks. In spite of the stimulus given to iron manufactures by the Revolutionary War, the American iron industry continued to rely largely on charcoal smelting, devastating forests in the process. Even the discovery of the largest deposit of anthracite coal in the world, a 480-square-mile area in Eastern Pennsylvania, in the first quarter of the nineteenth century did not immediately inspire a change in smelting methods.[15]

It was not until after 1830 that new techniques encouraged a noticeable growth in large-scale American iron manufacture, including products of ornamental iron. Firms such as Robert Wood of Philadelphia, which had begun as a blacksmith shop in 1840, by 1850 claimed a large iron factory devoted to producing rails for railroads in addition to decorative cast iron. Objects for the garden became affordable and widely available for the first time from firms such as Wood's. As one twentieth-century writer characterized this innovation, ". . . the most stubborn portion of the min-

eral kingdom has been annexed to the realm of taste."[16] Although American cast-iron production took more time to establish than Great Britain's had, it became the most important American industry of the mid-nineteenth century, and was valued as such. In 1853 a writer in *Appleton's Mechanics' Magazine* stated flatly that "We regard this [the iron industry] as the great interest of the country, and superior in real value to our gold mines a thousand times."[17]

By the second half of the nineteenth century the versatility of cast iron offered designers new options to feed the Victorian desire for decorative diversity. The malleability of the metal permitted numerous combinations of decorative motifs, waterspouts, fountain figures with various balusters, basins, and molded edges. The New York–based companies of J. W. Fiske Iron Works and J. L. Mott Iron Works, two of the most prolific and important foundries in the country, offered acanthus leaf designs, Islamic patterning, and Moorish styles, as well as the traditional egg-and-dart edging on fountain pans. Popular subjects for fountain spouts were fish, rams' and lions' heads, and water plants. Many figures were used, too, including Neptune, draped nymphs, maidens, and sentimentalized children, as well as cherubs, cupids, alligators, serpents, swans, cranes, egrets, ducks, and dolphins, either alone or in combinations. More often than not, these were supported by tiers of bowls or basins.

The freestanding tazza form dominated all others in catalogue offerings. An architectural baluster for a tiered fountain could be chosen with applied water birds, dolphins, botanical specimens, or lions' heads. Shapes of bowls varied and could be ordered to simulate shells, acanthus leaves, or other features of nature. In 1853 a writer reported in *Godey's Lady's Book* that the "Robert Wood Ornamental Iron-Works" (later Wood & Perot) had used more than a hundred pieces in producing a large fountain.[18] In 1875, Wood & Perot, a Philadelphia foundry known for its fine casting, offered an ornate tazza-form fountain with full-sized standing lions at the corners.[19] The broad range of figures that might be added permitted a buyer to satisfy his or her need to customize a design, even though the components themselves were mass produced.

Andrew Jackson Downing (1815–52), a native of New York, was America's first landscape expert and proponent of the natural style of garden. In his seminal 1841 work, *A Treatise on the Theory and Practice of Landscape Gardening,* he wrote: "Fountains are highly elegant garden decorations, rarely seen in this country," explaining that the scarcity was not on account of expense or "any want of appreciation of their sparkling and enlivening effect" but as a result of a lack of artisans equipped to construct "architectural and other jets d'eau."[20]

Downing would have been surprised by Belmont, an 1853 Italianate mansion in Nashville, Tennessee, the city home of Joseph and Adelicia Acklen. The geometric, villa-style garden was profusely decorated with nineteenth-century cast-iron and marble ornaments. Even though she had a complete 1855 volume of Downing's didactic periodical, *The Horticulturist,* Mrs. Acklen's exuberant arrangements did not resemble the prudent, natural style of gardening promoted therein. Moreover, Belmont featured a most impressive 105-foot-high water tower that generated enough hydraulic pressure to pump water to numerous fountains and to one of the earliest underground irrigation systems.

FIG. 8

Fountain. c. 1850, with additions before 1867. Marble and cast iron. Approx. 7'6" x 48" diam. Belmont Mansion, Nashville, Tennessee.

Purchased by Adelicia Acklen around the time her house, Belmont, was completed in 1853, this simple marble fountain initially had a single tier. A painting of the house and gardens in 1867 shows the additional tier already in place, along with its cast-iron baluster. The result is a classical treatment similar to an example illustrated in the 1848 volume of *The Horticulturist.*[1]

1. *The Horticulturist,* 2, 42.

FIG. 9

Fountain. c. 1897. Italian. Marble. 24' diam., 7' high. Canyon Ranch (formerly Bellefontaine), Lenox, Massachusetts.

The curved, segmented Renaissance-style fountain basin echoes the waisted form of late-sixteenth- and early-seventeenth-century Venetian wellheads.[1] Elsewhere on this property the architects Carrère & Hastings placed an Italian wellhead of similar form (cat. 7.8). The fountain features several Romanesque elements: stiff acanthus leaves on the support beneath the upper bowl and grotesque masks that spout water into both basins. The coping, or edging, of the pool — matched pieces of semicircular stone — adds a finished rim, which serves as a secure boundary.

1. Rizzi, 65.

The survival of the period ornament in this antebellum garden, including the simple two-tiered circa 1850 marble fountain, can be credited to the determination of Adelicia Acklen (fig. 8). A woman of extraordinary business acumen, Mrs. Acklen was one of the few Southern landowners whose extensive real estate holdings survived the Civil War. Her most startling commercial exploit took place during the war, in 1863, in the eight months after her husband's death. Mrs. Acklen and a female cousin, outwitting both Confederate and Union generals, managed to export and sell the cotton produced on the Acklen plantation in Louisiana. This unbelievable sale reaped a staggering $960,000 in gold.[21]

Downing's landscape style was not as influential in the South as it was in the Anglophile North. However, an essay by H. Noel Humphreys in an 1851 issue of *The Horticulturist* not only suggests the formality of a garden such as Belmont but also forecasts the taste of early-twentieth-century gardens in America. Humphreys, one of Downing's spokesmen, recommended the same terraced style of the Italian villa gardens that had inspired the eighteenth-century Virginians. His article was illustrated with engravings of the famous Roman gardens at the Villa Belvedere and the Villa Doria-Pamphili, both of which included conspicuous tazza-form fountains with water flowing copiously from numerous jets. Humphreys praised these fountains as "excellent model[s] for the careful examination of the modern student . . ."[22]

In the second half of the nineteenth century, a number of changes took place that altered tastes and therefore the forms and subjects of fountains. One change was that as garden owners, particularly in the North, accepted the Downing interpretation of the informal English garden, they began to buy fountains that incorporated natural forms and to place them in ways that harmonized with the environment. This new tendency toward informality in the garden encouraged the use of simple fountains. New homeowners with small suburban or town gardens could now enjoy the sound of flowing water while showing an appreciation for decorative tradition. In the May 1848 issue of *The Horticulturist,* Downing published a plan for a symmetrical "small arabesque flower garden" that allowed for a vase or a fountain in the center.[23] Soon thereafter *Godey's Lady's Book,* another important periodical of the day, noted that "fountains, when they are now introduced, must be of

a comparatively simple nature, or they will look incongruous and out of place."[24] In 1868 the affordability of fountains was documented by F. R. Elliott: "The fountain is the second available item of ready construction within a moderate cost. . . . The cost is little more than the introduction and placing of pipes."[25]

The appropriate use and placement of ornament were a major concern to nineteenth-century tastemakers, who recognized the potential for abuse by coarse, uncouth *arrivistes*. Proponents of the natural garden advised against placing a fountain in an open space, where it would be an eyesore when silent and a distraction when operating. The recommended location was either in a conservatory or at the center of an Italian [that is, formal] garden.[26] In responding to the purists of the picturesque or romantic school, who wanted a minimum of formality, H. Noel Humphreys again wrote in 1850 that fountains were "among the most refined of all garden ornaments" and that if an architectonic fountain were placed in harmony with its equally architectural surroundings, it would legitimize even an ostentatious artistic display.[27]

The Victorian taste for opulence affected the subject matter of many nineteenth-century fountains. Designers covered every edge and surface with leaves and flowers, satisfying the period's passion for horticultural and botanical specimens. A "drooping" fountain, where water spilled over the side of the basin, was offered in a style to complement "a Gothic or Elizabethan house."[28] Mythological and allegorical themes, never totally out of fashion, were joined in the 1840s by rustic forms with branches and twigs and later, between 1860 and 1880, by such sentimental subjects as children and animals. A fountain on the grounds of the Andrus estate in Ithaca, New York, typifies the Victorian tendency to combine styles. A photograph taken around 1865 shows the fountain with a scantily dressed youth carrying a large bird spouting water, all supported on a rockwork base; the effect, as one writer notes, "was not purely classical, nor sentimental, nor rustic, but a conservative combination of three themes."[29] Common fountain figures were mythological deities, cherubs, and animals. Often these statues were freestanding, mounted on or attached to architectural supports in the center of a bowl or pool. Water jets spouted from the mouths of birds, serpents, frogs, or fish but rarely from a human figure.

By the mid-nineteenth century the prestige of fountains was significantly increased by the ambitious displays at the international and domestic exhibitions of the new products of industry. An 1842 description of an award-winning cast-iron fountain at the fair of the American Institute in Albany extolled American craft: "This superb article might be said to form the climax of garden ornaments . . . in a style which would do honor to any country . . . displaying a taste and skill which richly entitles [the makers] to patronage." The writer further explained that "the cost of such a fountain would be but trifling."[30] The most pivotal of the great industrial shows was the Crystal Palace Exhibition of 1851 in London, where the variety of materials used for fountains included terra cotta from Minton (United Kingdom), artificial limestone from John Seely (United Kingdom), carved stone from Lechesne Brothers of Paris, and cast iron from E. March (Prussia) and J. P. André and Lesler of Paris, among others.[31] A central fountain display by the Coalbrookdale Company of Shropshire assured its international influence, a fact that was confirmed by the presence of numerous replications of the English firm's nineteenth-century designs in later American catalogues.

At the Philadelphia Centennial Exhibition of 1876 the designer of the Statue of Liberty, Frédéric-Auguste Bartholdi, and the Durenne Foundry of Sommevoire, France combined forces to produce and display a thirty-foot-high cast-iron fountain that included gas lanterns on the edge of the bowl. Other, quite different fountains that received awards were a formal marble example carved in Rome by the American sculptor Margaret F. Foley (1827–77) and a cast-iron, Renaissance-revival-style tiered example from J. L. Mott Iron Works of New York.[32] Visitors, on occasion, purchased the fountains at these expositions. At the 1876 Philadelphia Exhibition Edward Steves, a lumber businessman from San Antonio, Texas, bought a cast-iron and stone fountain by the otherwise unknown artist Henry Debiller. The fountain was shipped home first by sea to Galveston and then

Fountain. c. 1930. French. Cast iron and concrete. Height of figure, approx. 40", pool approx. 14 x 16'. Nemours Mansion, Wilmington, Delaware.

A playful baby faun sits amid six tortoises in this exuberant fountain at Nemours. The two jugs that the boy carries, presumably for wine, give the piece a bacchanalian touch. The frogs at each corner of the pool join the tortoises in spraying numerous jets of water. Cast in iron, this fountain group is painted to resemble bronze, and exemplifies the du Ponts' taste for ornament of the highest quality and craftsmanship.

by "mule drag" to San Antonio. The fountain, a tazza with a putto holding a large fish, still stands in the garden of the Steves homestead (cat. 1.5).[33] Another American exhibition, the renowned World's Columbian Exposition held in Chicago in 1893, brought changes that would signal a shift to a more formal garden ornament style.

The Columbian Exposition, in celebration of the four hundredth anniversary of Columbus's discovery of America, deeply affected the artistic tastes of the country. Many of the architects and landscape architects who designed the exposition had studied in Europe. Some of them became part of the Beaux-Arts movement that would guide the country toward more formal design. The focal point of the entire "White City," so called for its many white buildings, was a series of enormous and complicated classically inspired fountains, whose tumultuous reception by visitors ensured the reputations of their creators. Frederick W. MacMonnies (1863–1937), who sculpted the central fountain ensemble, an immense ship with figures called the "Barge of State,"

was especially acclaimed for his work. The adjoining fountains incorporated one product of recent technology, electrical power, in extraordinary displays of light and water. The twenty-three-year-old Pierre S. du Pont made an unforgettable trip to the Columbian Exposition in Chicago. He attributed his later creation of the formal gardens and elaborate fountains at Longwood Gardens in Kennett Square, Pennsylvania, to his enthusiasm as a young man for the fountains not only at the Columbian Exposition in Chicago but also at the Philadelphia Centennial and the Paris Universal Exposition of 1889 (fig. 59, p. 73).[34]

The last quarter of the nineteenth century witnessed the beginnings of the American Renaissance movement. The proponents of this revival saw parallels between American culture and that of the Italian Renaissance, and the garden specialists among them sparked interest in Italianate gardens and their ornament. Charles A. Platt (1861–1933), an architect who lived in Cornish, New Hampshire, fully absorbed the formal garden vernacular when he traveled in Italy, and shared his observations in his book *Italian Gardens,* published in 1894. Platt, although trained as an architect, became one of the leading landscape designers of the day, planning such notable private gardens as Weld and Faulkner Farm in Brookline, Massachusetts, Gwinn in Bratenahl, Ohio, and Maxwell Court in Rockville, Connecticut.[35] American garden designers were further informed by the 1904 book *Italian Villas and Their Gardens* by Edith Wharton (1862–1937). Wharton described and praised the formal Italian garden especially for its "[i]ntricacy of detail, complicated groupings of terraces, fountains, labyrinths and porticoes."[36]

By the end of the century new factors were introduced that significantly changed the character of American garden fountains. The National Sculpture Society, founded in 1893, was dedicated to "upgrade the status of American sculptors and to increase public awareness and subsequent sales of work by Americans."[37] The establishment of the American Association of Landscape Architects in 1899 legitimized landscape design as a serious profession. At the beginning of the twentieth century, in a departure from the classical style then in vogue, a new type of fountain came into being. Practicing fine-art sculptors were drawn into creating cherubic and nymphic fountain figures in bronze specifically for the garden, not only to support themselves but also to fulfill the needs of garden designers. The intimate scale of many of these sculptures suited smaller gardens.

A great many such artists, including Frederick W. MacMonnies, Janet Scudder (1875–1940), Edward McCartan (1879–1947), and, later, Paul Manship (1885–1966), and Gaston Lachaise (1882–1935), produced original designs that defined a specifically American character in garden statuary. Inspired by classical and Renaissance precedents, their fountain figures featured engaging, sinuous forms that complemented and harmonized with the natural environment.[38] The sculptures were also designed to interact with water and to express its "emotional effect." The artistic approach of this group was heralded in *House and Garden* in 1925: *But, what has become of Neptune and his company? Here is a change in sculpture that is most significant, for the fountain figure is the most important statue in garden art. Instead of the classical reference to the sea's presiding deity with his tritons and nereids, dolphins and sea-horses, the modern sculptor seeks to express the very spirit of the water.*[39] Fountain sculptures by fine artists from this period were reproduced for American gardens throughout the remainder of the twentieth century. Other artists who worked on garden figures included Elie Nadelman (1885–1964) and John Gregory (1879–1958), as well as a number of women, such as Gertrude Vanderbilt Whitney (1877–1942), Anna Hyatt Huntington (1876–1973; see fig. 34), Malvina Hoffman (1887–1966), Rachel Hawks (1879–1953?), and Harriet Frishmuth (1880–1979). As noted by Michele H. Bogart in *Fauns and Fountains,* the catalogue of an exhibition of early-twentieth-century garden statuary, the large number of women sculptors can be attributed to the categorization of garden sculpture as a decorative art. As such, the sculptors were required to design and execute statues in which content was secondary to the needs of the architect and the garden. Not surprisingly, this left the field in the hands of women artists who, in the early part of the twentieth century, were only beginning to break into the male-dominated field of sculpture.[40]

FIG. 11

Fountain. Charles Platt. 1911. American.
Carved stone. Approx. 16 x 8'. Gwinn,
Bratenahl, Ohio.

The focal point at the crossing of two
paths, this fountain sits in the "Wild
Garden" of Gwinn. William Mather,
the owner of the estate, hired Charles
Platt and Warren Manning to serve as
landscape architect and horticulturist,
respectively. Mather asked the two
men – each of whom had very different approaches to landscape design –
to submit drawings for a fountain.
Manning planned a free-form rock-
work spring while Platt offered a more
classical invention, which appears to
have been influenced by a fountain in
the sixteenth-century gardens of the
humanist Agostino Giusti in Verona,
which Platt may have seen on his travels. The Giusti fountain has a baluster
and bowl identical to the same features
in Platt's design, shown here.[1] Mather
chose Platt's two-tiered architectural
fountain, demonstrating the extent
to which popular taste, in this case for
formality, can guide the choices of a
discerning patron.

1. Listri and Cunaccia, 66–68.

Notwithstanding the prolific work of these American sculptors, in the years between 1895 and 1940, the vast majority of ornaments for the garden were still produced by artisans in Europe and America. Indeed, the classical theme required by the 1893 Columbian Exposition's organizers suggested formal subject matter to a receptive public. Finely carved fountains, statues, urns, and seats became popular examples of the formal style, primarily made of the favored materials, marble and bronze. The vogue for cast-iron ornament slowed at the turn of the century as hand-craftsmanship came to be preferred to mass production. Moreover, the First World War interfered with the making of decorative cast iron, particularly in Europe, as metal objects of all sorts were regarded as potential munitions.

Many Americans in the early twentieth century who wished to import garden ornament hired agents to buy for them. Others traveled to Italy in person so that they could buy both Greek and Roman antiquities, as well as reproductions of Renaissance fountains. The American collector/travelers of this era often went to Florence and stayed at either the Excelsior or the Grand Hotel on the Arno, near many galleries and studios, particularly those of Antonio Frilli and Pietro Barzanti, two Florentine sculptors who produced marble ornament for export. Their galleries carried reproductions of classical statuary and decorations and arranged shipping through English-speaking representatives.[41]

At the same time that Americans were buying ornamental garden accessories abroad, domestic marble carvers began to produce decorative objects that rivaled the forms and craftsmanship of Italy. New methods of quarrying and cutting blocks increased marble output in America. The wire saw came into use in Europe around 1890, allowing the slow but accurate extraction of blocks. In America, where the architectural use of marble predominated, a

FIG. 12

Bacchante with an Infant Faun, with earlier base. Frederick W. MacMonnies (1863–1937). Statue, originally cast 1893; bowl, c. 1925; pedestal originally erected 1570, restored 1790. Bronze and marble. Approx. 11 x 5' diam. The Huntington Library, Art Collections, and Botanical Gardens, San Marino, California.

This fountain unites two disparate elements with shared classical connotations into a single composition. The heavily carved base, with its Roman-inspired grotesque masks and garlands, dates to the sixteenth century, with some later eighteenth-century "improvements." In the early twentieth century, when Henry Huntington acquired a cast of Frederick MacMonnies's famous bronze *Bacchante* group, he had it mounted on the base. The life-sized original of MacMonnies's statue, now at The Metropolitan Museum of Art, was denounced in 1893 for its "wanton nudity and drunkenness."[1]

1. Janson, 262.

technique called channeling provided a speedy, thorough quarrying of larger blocks.[42] Another change that supported the domestic market was then Congressman (later president, in spite of this unpopular legislation) William McKinley's 1890 fifty percent import tariff on new, sculpted marble – a direct attack on European imports. This tariff was successful in improving the market for domestic marble. Except for antiquities, which could be imported duty free, there are few records of imported worked marble in 1909.[43] In determining the accuracy of the dates of antique objects, however, it is important to remember that a fifty percent duty would provide considerable incentive to falsify a date.

Concurrent with a change in materials, a wider variety of fountain forms was introduced by landscape architects to satisfy the eclectic tastes of the early twentieth century. Wall fountains appeared as principal elements in smaller gardens and as subordinate features in large gardens.[44] As early as the mid-1890s, in the immense garden at Biltmore in Asheville, North Carolina, Frederick Law Olmsted (1822–1903) placed a series of wall fountains in a retaining wall (see fig. 13). In the late 1920s a wall fountain was installed in the small rose garden at the Edsel Ford House in Grosse Pointe, Michigan (see cat. 1.18). At Vizcaya, the Miami home and garden of James Deering, a grotto fountain with ornate surface decoration was installed around 1921 (fig. 2). Also in the twenties Charles Platt designed a distinctive wall fountain for William Mather, the owner of Gwinn, a house on the Lake Erie shore in Bratenahl, Ohio.

During the early part of the twentieth century the "City Beautiful" movement, an effort to improve the appearance of American cities, grew out of the influence of both the Columbian Exposition and the Beaux-Arts architects. As a result, imposing, monumental fountains were installed in cities across the country.[45] The owners of private gardens followed suit, ordering large-scale, carved stone or marble replicas of Italian originals, some in imitation of public fountains.

The fountains purchased to decorate the grand, private country house gardens between 1890 and 1930 were extravagant beyond anything seen in America to this point.[46] The vast wealth accrued around the turn of the century by some American financiers provided the means

FIG. 13
Wall fountain. c. 1899. American. Carved stone. Approx. 15' x 8'8". Biltmore Estate, Asheville, North Carolina.

This fountain is one in a series that Frederick Law Olmsted (1822–1903) designed for a retaining wall at Biltmore, the 125,000-acre estate of George W. Vanderbilt begun in 1888. Olmsted's plans for the grounds of this expansive property were inspired by a trip to Europe that he had taken shortly before. This intimate niche, with its surface decoration suggesting stalactites, recalls the grotto style of the Italian Renaissance. Although Olmsted was best known for his naturalistic style, at Biltmore, a work of his later career, he designed classical formal gardens enhanced by a multitude of ornaments.[1]

1. MacKay, Baker & Traynor, 317.

Oceanus and the Three Rivers. After Giovanni Bologna (called Giambologna; 1529–1608). 1914. Italian. Marble and granite. Approx. 30 × 20' diam. Kykuit, National Trust for Historic Preservation, Pocantico Hills, New York.

The Kykuit fountain, like the smaller version at Cà d' Zan, is based on Giambologna's *Oceanus* fountain now in the Boboli Gardens in Florence. While it represents Oceanus, the god of the world-encircling sea, it is hard to distinguish the figure from statues of Neptune.[1] In Florence, the statue's ideally long viewing distance was compromised by its placement in a limited space. Fortunately, this American setting overlooking the Pocantico Hills north of New York City restores its proper spatial relationship to the viewer and thus increases its overall impact. Americans would have found this fountain desirable because it suggested something of the cultural sophistication of the Medici, the legendary Florentine family that had commissioned the original.

1. Lazzaro, 195.

FIG. 15

Fountain. 1931. English. Lead and wrought iron. 9'7" × 7' diam. Longwood Gardens, Kennett Square, Pennsylvania.

This large, circular English lead cistern, manufactured by Henry Hope & Sons for Pierre S. du Pont, is characterized by a pair of dolphin waterspouts. Originally designed as a sample lead enclosure to hide the lights and nozzles in the canals of the main fountain garden, it was later adapted by du Pont as a drinking fountain.

to install gardens, fine ornament, and, especially, exceptional fountains. The development of major gardens took place not only on the East Coast but also on the coast of California. In the 1930s William Randolph Hearst built his impressive Hearst Castle in San Simeon, California. Around the same time, Henry Huntington was creating the magnificent gardens at his estate, later called The Huntington Library and Gardens, in San Marino, California. Both East and West shared the same devotion to Italian styles and workmanship, using traditional materials such as bronze, marble, granite, and terra cotta. Particular styles of fountains, especially those imitating Renaissance originals, were almost compulsory for the mansions of the enormously wealthy estate owners.

The following account brings to light the unusual circumstance that a number of these acquisitive collectors, in their quest for the best for their gardens, ordered identical versions of the same fountain. Copies of the large Fontana delle Tartarughe (Fountain of the Tortoises) in the Piazza

Fountain of the Tortoises. After Giacomo della Porta, Taddeo Landini, and Gianlorenzo Bernini. J. Chiurazzi & Fils, Naples, Italy. Early twentieth century. Marble and bronze. 10' x 18'3" x 18'3". The John and Mable Ringling Museum of Art, Sarasota, Florida.

John Ringling ordered this fountain from J. Chiurazzi & Fils in Naples, a foundry known for producing excellent bronze reproductions of antique and Renaissance sculpture. One of the numerous versions in this country, this monumental piece was modeled after the Fontana delle Tartarughe by Taddeo Landini in the Piazza Mattei in Rome. Furthermore, another Fountain of the Tortoises at Villa Blanca, the former estate of Amory S. Carhart in Tuxedo Park, New York, bears four inscriptions, one in each of the four cartouches interspersed with the large shell basins, that translate to "Ornamented and restored in the fourth year of Alexander VII's reign." In that year, 1658, Bernini enlarged the basins, remodeled the supports of the four shells, and added the tortoises to the original fountain.[1]

1. Brizzi, 40.

Mattei in Rome were imported and are still found in a number of American gardens. This Mannerist-style fountain basin is named after the tortoises that are held by four full-sized bronze figures. One replica was installed at the Elms in Newport just after the turn of the century while another, imported around 1908 for Amory S. Carhart's Villa Blanca in Tuxedo Park, New York, stands on a portion of the original estate. On the West Coast the Crocker estate in Hillsborough, California, imported another copy in 1909 from an Italian foundry. In the 1910s George Booth ordered yet another for his garden at Cranbrook in Bloomfield Hills, Michigan. Around the same time John Ringling purchased the same Roman fountain directly from the Chiurazzi foundry in Naples for Cà d' Zan, meaning "John's house," his estate in Sarasota (fig. 16). Whether these men were aware of the duplication is unknown. They were either completely unsuspecting or, on the other hand, totally conscious of the exalted status of the Fontana di Tartarughe.

By the early twentieth century American estate owners stimulated makers to a new level of fountain art that began to rival some of their European counterparts. The demand for ornamental fountains was such that both fine and decorative artists were enlisted to furnish gardens. In contrast to the eighteenth century, when political leaders and estate owners such as Thomas Jefferson respected the garden as a horticultural and design project, the financial tycoons of the early twentieth century wanted their fountain gardens to rival the scope and ostentation of such superb Italian gardens as that of the Villa D'Este in Tivoli near Rome. Further changes and refinements came in the 1930s as such landscape architects as Fletcher Steele combined neoclassicism with new, modernist approaches. At Naumkeag, the Choate garden in Lenox, Massachusetts, Steele introduced pools "as extensions of the ground surface. . . . Four low pools with upright jets," thereby removing sculptural ornament altogether from fountains.[47] Jefferson would certainly have appreciated the simplicity of Steele's plan, and he would have admired the respect shown for the natural configuration of the landscape. Thus, fountains had come full circle, from an eighteenth-century simplicity by necessity to twentieth-century simplicity by design.

CHAPTER 2
STATUES

This figure represents Ganymede, the
object of Zeus's desire. According to
Greek mythology, Ganymede, a Trojan
prince of extraordinary beauty, was
abducted by Zeus, who had assumed the
form of an eagle. The suggestive position of the bird's wing and the lan-
guorous pose of the youth hint at the
homoerotic subject of the tale. The
estate's owner, James Deering, collected
a number of mythological statues of
such figures as Bacchus, Neptune, and
Leda and the Swan.

With their unrivaled variety and versatility, statues introduce not only a narra-
tive theme but also an artistic presence into a garden. In 1936 Richardson Wright,
the editor of *House and Garden,* succinctly traced their history: "Mankind has
advanced up a garden path. Sometimes it leads tortuously from the totems of primitive gardens to the host of garden goddesses and gods imaged in Roman times
and down through the revival of garden statuary in Renaissance eras to the precise
or wistful location of sculpture in gardens today."[1]

Compared to other countries and cultures, America has had a short garden
history and a more limited experience with the use of statuary. In the early years
of the eighteenth century, American patrons and craftsmen found inspiration
in the forms and use of English and Continental garden statuary. English taste
and traditions were understandably the primary influence on colonists in North
America. However, the installation of an Italian garden allied its owner with all
the knowledge of classical culture, a suggestion that appealed to a particular American elite, the creators of the Tidewater gardens on the James River in Virginia.

The earliest large American gardens, especially those in Virginia, openly imitated the refined English interpretation of the formal, terraced Italian villa garden.
The accessories of this style of garden were allegorical and symbolic statues,
which were placed at the terminations of straight pathways and at junctions of
intersecting axes of formal, symmetrical sections.[2]

Westover, a plantation in Charles City County, Virginia, is a rare extant, if
not fully preserved, example of an early Tidewater garden. The estate was inherited
in 1705 by William Byrd II (1674–1744), who in 1726 began planning extensive
gardens inspired by contemporary English formal design. In his own words Byrd

acknowledged his leanings toward English ways, which always had "too strong an influence on me."[3] We know that Westover's garden included statuary since a visitor in the 1780s reported seeing "very lovely statues" in a formal arrangement there.[4]

Although little physical evidence remains of privately owned early American gardens and their ornament, some information can be found in eighteenth- and early-nineteenth-century diaries and household inventories. These sources mention the existence of statues in early gardens, but give limited information about them. Philip Vickers Fithian, a diarist of the day, wrote of an April 7, 1774 visit to Colonel John Tayloe's plantation, Mount Airy, near Warshaw, Virginia, that Tayloe had ". . . a large well formed, beautiful Garden, as fine in every Respect as any I have seen in Virginia. In it [stood] four large beautiful Marble Statues. . . ."[5] These four were probably an imported grouping and may well have

represented some aspect of nature, such as the Elements or the Seasons, in accordance with prevailing European tastes. By choosing marble statues, early American garden owners reflected an appreciation of Continental gardens, since marble had extensive use in Italy and France, but only a limited one in England during the eighteenth century.[6]

Inspired by travels in Europe, many Americans chose garden statues that specifically imitated or interpreted antique Greek and Roman sculpture. The statues at Cliveden, the Philadelphia estate of the Chew family, were, according to family tradition, wedding presents in 1757 from the wealthy merchant, Joseph Turner, to his niece, the second Mrs. Benjamin Chew.[7]

Only twenty years later, in 1777, the Battle of Germantown raged through the house and grounds of Cliveden, serving up a tragic and humiliating military loss for George Washington. Various accounts recorded the

FIG. 18 AND FIG. 19
Statues. c. 1760. Italian. Carved stone.
Fig. 18: 60"; fig. 19: 63". Cliveden, Philadelphia, Pennsylvania.

Cliveden, the 1767 house of Judge Benjamin Chew, is home to a number of statues reputed to have been wedding gifts to the second Mrs. Chew from her uncle, the shipping merchant Joseph Turner. According to period documents these statues were on-site when the 1777 Battle of Germantown was fought on the grounds of Cliveden (see above). Their damaged condition notwithstanding, there has been some question whether or not the examples remaining on the property are the same statues that were noted in early references to the battle. An April 1791 letter concerning the disposal of ornaments at Wilton Plantation (the former home of Joseph Turner) was written to the new owner, Henry Hill, by Mrs. Chew's sister, Margaret Smyth: "I never entertained presence of the statues during the battle, and a medal struck in 1780 to commemorate the battle for the British victors actually showed the statues knocked off their pedestals.[8] Two of the four marble statue fragments that remain at Cliveden appear to be eighteenth-century interpretations of the antique. One is a classically draped female figure, reminiscent of Hellenistic sculpture; the other, a body and leg fragment of a once-intact male figure, recalls a well-known Greco-Roman torso of Pan (right).[9]

Also affected by Italian garden traditions, Governor John Eager Howard built Belvedere, his house and garden in Baltimore, Maryland, between 1783 and 1786. Howard modeled the gardens after the formal courtyard of the same name in the Vatican Palace commissioned by Pope Julius II in 1504. The Vatican Belvedere became the sixteenth century's most influential garden, affecting the establishment and design of others both in Italy and abroad.[10] This early

a doubt but that the decayed statues & pieces of marble at Wilton house would be included in the sale of the house, especially as the things of that sort given by my late uncle to Mr. & Mrs. Chew went to the purchaser of their house near Germantown."[1] Mrs. Smyth was referring to the September 1779 sale of a battle-scarred Cliveden from Benjamin Chew to Blair McClenachan, a young Irish privateer. It is clear from this letter that Joseph Turner had been a collector of garden ornament, some of which he had given to his niece, Mrs. Chew, and some of which had remained on his estate until his death. Turner's collection, referred to in Mrs. Smyth's letter as "decayed," probably from exposure, was sold by his executors in 1791 independently from the Wilton house and property, much to the dismay of his niece, Margaret Smyth, and the new owner.[2] However, as to the pieces given to Mr.

and Mrs. Chew, after eighteen years at Cliveden, McClenachan resold the house, grounds, and presumably the statues in April 1797 back to Benjamin Chew.[3] Thus, it seems that the statues in the garden at Cliveden survived not only the Battle of Germantown but also the sale and resale of the property to become perhaps the only extant garden ornament in America to have been silent witnesses to a battle of the American Revolution.

1. Chew, Box 248, on disposal of marble ornaments at Wilton Plantation, Margaret Smyth to Henry Hill, 15 April 1791 (copy sent to Benjamin Chew). For this information I thank Mark Reinberger of the University of Georgia.
2. See Richards. I thank the curatorial staff of Cliveden for sharing this unpublished research.
3. Chew, Box 248, Benjamin Chew to Henry Hill, 28 April 1791.

Renaissance garden popularized the ancient Roman practice of exhibiting sculpture in a garden or other outdoor setting.[11] At his own Belvedere, Howard paid particular attention to the arrangement and display of grand statues modeled after the antique.[12]

In order to re-create the style of classical gardens, Americans selected statuary with mythological themes. The multitude of subjects included in the Greek and Roman pantheon cannot be covered here,[13] but we should note that figures of the gods and goddesses of the sun, the earth, the woodland, love, poetry, and the arts and their associated allegorical representations have a long history in the gardens of Europe and America. For William Byrd II, who rose many mornings before dawn to read Thucydides and Homer, the presence of mythological statues in his garden reflected his knowledge of Greek history and epic poetry, reminding the visitor of his cultural and intellectual achievements.[14] Moreover, while the inclusion of allegorical sculpture in the garden confirmed the owner's taste, apt placement, such as situating satyrs in a woodland setting, would indicate the breadth of his knowledge. One source notes that John Custis, the former father-in-law of George Washington's wife, as early as 1740 set up suitable lead statues to allude to Roman mythology in his four-acre garden in Williamsburg, Virginia.[15] A very specific later mention of allegorical statues was made in the 1762 diary of a female visitor to Belmont, the home of William Peters outside of Philadelphia: "In the middle stands a statue of Apollo. In the garden are statues of Diana, Fame and Mercury. . . ."[16]

Lead statues had been introduced to England by Huguenot artisans from the Netherlands who immigrated during the reign of William and Mary (1689–1702). Some represented the subjects of mythology, but others depicted themes of everyday life. Since the English eighteenth-century landscape garden required natural and rustic decoration made of branches and twigs, appropriate statues included pastoral or Arcadian themes such as shepherds and shepherdesses or hunters and huntresses (see figs. 21–22).[17]

The Custis garden is the sole instance in this study of the presence of lead statues in American eighteenth-century gardens. Other than the eagle finials at Westover, in Charles City County, Virginia, the home of William Byrd II, no extant examples of eighteenth-century lead statuary in America are known. This fact alone, however, does not disprove its possible, or even probable, use. In times of war, lead was frequently melted down for munitions. Furthermore, lead is an inherently fragile material due to its flexible nature and characteristic heavy weight, and it could deteriorate when subjected to the fluctuating and harsh weather conditions of the United States.

An English company, the Coade manufactory of Lambeth, made a significant contribution to garden ornament when it produced a well-priced and finely designed stoneware that could withstand the weather.[18] Founded in 1769 by Eleanor Coade, the company made classically inspired architectural details and garden ornaments often marked with the company name and date of production. The factory's high-grade, durable, clay-based artificial stone was made according to a formula that was for many years reported to have been scrupulously guarded from

FIG. 20

Augustus of Primaporta. J. Chiurazzi & Fils, Naples, Italy. Early twentieth century. Marble. 11'. Cà d' Zan, Sarasota, Florida.

This piece is a copy of a first-century A.D. statue in the Vatican collection. It accurately reproduces the original form of the statue before the restoration of the broken fingers on both hands. Cà d' Zan ("John's House") was owned by John and Mable Ringling, avid collectors of all varieties of art, who installed a well-furnished sculpture garden, where the Ringlings assembled many reproductions of antique and Renaissance sculpture, as well as pieces from the early twentieth century. The location of the Ringling *Augustus of Primaporta* in front of a natural seascape is particularly successful, as it gives this vigorous, athletic statue ample visual space.

FIG. 21

Shepherdess. After John Cheere. c. 1900.
English. Lead. Approx. 58". Vizcaya Museum
and Gardens, Miami, Florida.

This figure, outfitted in eighteenth-
century informal country attire, is paired
with a lead shepherd (fig. 22) in the
gardens of Vizcaya. The two provide a
lively counterpoint to the more restrained
classical Italianate sculptures placed
throughout Vizcaya's extensive formal
gardens.

FIG. 22

Shepherd. After John Cheere. c. 1900.
English. Lead. Approx. 58". Vizcaya Museum
and Gardens, Miami, Florida.

This statue was crafted after John Cheere
(1709–1787), an important maker of
garden statuary during the second half
of the eighteenth century in England.
Cheere, whose range included both
pastoral and classically derived figures,
often is considered the most prolific and
influential rococo garden sculptor. The
character of his figures was in keeping
with the ebullient style associated with
the paintings of Jean-Honoré Fragonard
(1732–1806) and other masters of the
rococo idiom. The figure shown here
was often reproduced; an identical
figure stands in the garden of the early-
twentieth-century Cranbrook House
in Bloomfield Hills, Michigan.

competitors. Following lead in the early century, Coade stone gained acceptance in the late eighteenth century as a material for garden ornament in England.[19]

Marketed through their gallery in London with a catalogue of offerings, Coade stone had limited sales success in America.[20] Nevertheless, an 1830 lithograph documents a pair of Coade stone statues in the garden of the Pickman-Derby-Brookhouse House on Washington Street in Salem, Massachusetts. Today, these regrettably vandalized figures are in the collection of the Peabody-Essex Institute. Catalogue comparisons suggest the subject matter of the statues as the muses Clio and Urania.[21] Many English companies attempted to imitate the buff color and durability of Coade stone, the most successful being the nineteenth-century firms J. M. Blashfield of Stamford, Pulham's Terra-Cotta of Broxbourne, Doulton & Watts of Lambeth, and a later company, M. H. Blanchard, the founder of which actually had apprenticed at Coade & Sealy and allegedly bought the casting molds of the Coade manufactory both in 1839 and in 1843. A 1796 advertisement in the *Pennsylvania*

Packet implies that perhaps Americans were not so far behind their former fatherland. The listing described a local sale of statues in a similar material: "six elegant carved figures, the manufacture of an artist in this country, and made from materials of clay dug near the city, they are used for ornaments for gardens . . . and will stand any weather. . . ."[22] The Philadelphia sculptor William Rush (1756–1833) worked in clay and wood, producing allegorical statues for civic locations.

Imported ornament maintained its cachet in spite of a healthy trade in American-made statuary that existed at the end of the eighteenth century. The gardens at the exceptional Rosedown Plantation in St. Francisville, Louisiana, were created by the owners, Daniel and Martha Turnbull. The formal garden, begun in the 1830s, was inspired by French, English, and Italian examples admired by the estate's owners on numerous trips to Europe. The Turnbulls' daughter, Sarah, recorded an 1851 family trip that included visits to the English gardens of Chatsworth, Hampton Court, and Windsor Castle. She also described touring

FIG. 23

Satyr. c. 1900. Italian. Marble. 48". St. Joseph's Villa (formerly Blairsden), Peapack, New Jersey.

This statue is one of four satyrs that stand guard on the southeast garden wall of St. Joseph's Villa, overlooking one of the last remaining unspoiled views in New Jersey. Italianate in inspiration, the figures have been in place since the property was known as Blairsden in the early 1900s, distracting visitors with a note of merriment and humor while they admire the breathtaking landscape. Originally set on the wall without any greenery behind them, these carousing woodland deities can be identified as satyrs by the symbols they carry, the pipes of Pan and the fruits of their other favorite mentor, Bacchus.

the grounds of the Palace of Versailles and specifically noted statuary in both the gardens of the Grand Duke of Tuscany near Florence and the garden of the Villa Albani, an eighteenth-century garden in Rome. Another document in the Rosedown archives, an August 18, 1851, invoice from the statuary house of F. Leopold Pisani in Florence, lists the purchase of four statues, namely, a copy of the Medici Venus and the figures of Diana, Mercury, and Zeus (listed on the invoice as "Jove").[23] To this day these four statues line the Rosedown's oak-shaded entrance drive, along with marble personifications of the Four Seasons and the Four Continents. The Turnbulls' selection of statues illustrates the extent to which European taste influenced elite Americans in the South. Rosedown escaped the destruction suffered by so many Southern gardens during the Civil War and has survived today with its original ornament largely intact, offering a rare opportunity to study a well-documented antebellum collection.[24]

After the Revolution, the historical portrait bust, a classical form, took on a deeper meaning for Americans. An accessory of the English landscape garden, which relied on classical allusions, such busts immortalized historical heroes or honored contemporary events of particular note. Stonecarvers' advertisements frequently offered busts; one notice in the *Federal Gazette* of Philadelphia in 1796 offered for sale "busts of Gen. Washington, Marquis La Fayette, Doctor Franklin."[25] An observer who visited the Van Rensselaer mansion in Albany during her youth noted later in the 1860s that she had once seen "larger-than-life busts, one of Washington and the other of Lafayette."[26] The garden at Lansdowne, a late-eighteenth-century house along the Schuylkill in Philadelphia that was host to many a distinguished guest, reportedly "was ornamented with busts and statues."[27] The adoption of the portrait bust form in itself points to a certain identification with and veneration of the ideals of ancient Rome. Busts of American heroes effectively likened these great leaders to those of the past.

The young Republic enthusiastically embraced the

This statue is one of four at Rosedown representing the continents Asia, Africa, Europe, and America. In this piece, which stands with eleven other marble statues along the plantation's oak-lined drive, *Africa* is shown wearing an elephant headdress, with a lion at her feet and carrying harvested fruits. The figure's dress, attributes, and physiognomy reflect nineteenth-century European stereotypes of the African continent.

forms of antiquity. In 1803 the newly formed Society of Fine Arts in New York (later the American Academy of the Arts) purchased and exhibited sixteen casts of antique statues from the Louvre for artists to study and emulate. So as to avoid affronting the sensibilities of the ladies some of the casts had "fig leaves . . . affixed and a separate day set aside for female viewing." Four years later, the Pennsylvania Academy of Fine Arts in Philadelphia organized a similar display of fifty casts from France.[28] The nineteenth century's obsession with the classical, in sculpture as well as garden ornament, led the artist William Wetmore Story (1819–1895) to jest, "Where is the voice that in the stone can speak / In any other language than the Greek?"[29]

By the mid-nineteenth century, large marble studios and cast-iron foundries began to be established in America. The arrival of significant numbers of immigrant stone and marble carvers in the early nineteenth century brought European traditions of quality craftsmanship to North America. In the 1850s, for instance, marble carver Ottaviano

Gori modeled "marble mantles [sic], statuary, fountains, vases, [and] monuments."[30] Gori, whose shop was located at 893 and 897 Broadway in New York City, "procur[ed] marble in the rough, direct from the quarries," in order to be carved into his own "original designs."[31] In 1856 *The Independent,* a Northeast weekly newspaper, advertised for the price of one dollar a comprehensive marble workers' manual translated from the French.[32] From this information, and the fact that Gori had "recently made large additions to his Marble Works, by extending them across the rear of his old established stand,"[33] we may assess that there was, indeed, a growing market for American-made marble ornaments in the early 1850s.

In the Italian tradition, marble and stone continued as favored materials for garden statues, but the development that most changed the nineteenth-century garden ornament landscape was the introduction and proliferation of the mass-produced cast-iron statue. Although well established in Europe, the cast-iron industry did not really

FIG. 25

America. c.1851. Italian. Marble. 58" high. Rosedown Plantation and Gardens, St. Francisville, Louisiana.

Another of Rosedown's four continents, this figure bears many of the attributes conventionally associated with the native inhabitants of America, including a feathered headdress and skirt and a bow and arrows. At her feet is a large lizard of some variety, perhaps a salamander or a strangely rendered alligator. All of these characteristics correspond to the representation of America in the 1758–60 edition of Cesare Ripa's emblem book *Iconologia,* which was primarily based upon the writings of Jesuit missionaries who had traveled to the New World.[1] An identical statue of the American continent, along with Asia, Europe, and Africa, stands in the garden at Godington Park, Kent, England.[2]

1. Ripa, pl. 105.
2. Plumptre, 58.

FIG. 26

Statue. Rudolf Schadow (1786–1822). c. 1810.
Marble. 46 x 16 x 24". Middleton Place,
Charleston, South Carolina.

This statue, named locally at Middleton
Place as the *Wood Nymph,* was sculpted
by the German artist Rudolf Schadow
in the first decade of the nineteenth
century. An identical statue, also by
Schadow, is in Munich. An 1815 painting
by Wilhelm Schadow, Rudolf's brother,
now in the collection of the Staatliche
Museen, Nationalgalerie in Berlin, shows
Wilhelm, Rudolf, and their compatriot,
Bertel Thorvaldsen, sitting in front of
this or a similar statue.[1] This restrained,
classical figure, almost asexual in appearance, was cited in the March 7, 1840,
edition of the *Charleston Courier* as
having an "exquisite softness and
delicacy of finish . . . [displaying] such
perfection of feminine beauty."[2]

1. For this information I thank Barbara
Doyle and the staff of Middleton Place.
2. *Charleston Courier,* March 7, 1840, from
the archives of Middleton Place.

develop in America until the 1830s. Foundries were set up in most of the large coastal cities: New York, Philadelphia, Boston, and New Orleans, to name only a few. Cast-iron components for transportation, commerce, and the military came first but were soon followed by an expansion into decorative ornament. The proliferation of parklike cemeteries increased the demand for new cast-iron ornaments and inspired private homeowners to "embellish" their own grounds. The subject of ornament in nineteenth-century cemeteries is a study unto itself that will be briefly touched upon in a later chapter on furniture.

Satisfying the extremely varied tastes of the Victorians, cast iron and other metals allowed for the easy replication of known sculptural groups modeled after both ancient and contemporary sources. Interest in classical figural statues made of traditional materials, in addition to cast iron, continued in this period. The collector Horatio Hollis Hunnewell (1810–1902) in the 1860s chose a statue of Flora by the artist Martin Milmore (1844–83) for the conservatory over-looking his garden in Wellesley, Massachusetts.[34] But for the most part, classical figures were upstaged by the proponents of the natural garden, such as Andrew Jackson Downing, who preferred rustic or naturalistic ornament.

Enthusiasm rather than thoughtful planning often dictated the arrangement and number of statues in a nineteenth-century garden, inspiring the following 1855 quotation from Downing's influential periodical, *The Horticulturist:* "To see a lawn filled with statuary, and vases . . . parading like the ware of a tradesman to catch the eye of the public, – how can one help feeling disgust at such vanity and corrupt taste!"[35] Such sentiments reflected *The Horticulturist*'s naturalistic mantra, which carried on even after Downing's 1852 death. These visual sore spots, the products of industry that were now offered at a price that many could afford, came on the market in many forms; some of the most popular were likenesses of animals.

While it is difficult to associate the use of cast-iron animal figures in general to any special trend, there does

FIG. 27

Flora. 1875–1900. Probably French. Terra cotta. Approx. 75". Vizcaya Museum and Gardens, Miami, Florida.

This terra-cotta statue, representing Flora, is reminiscent of similar figures produced by such French manufacturers as Gossin Frères and F. & A. Jacquier. Although exhibiting the surface wear associated with many terra-cotta statues, the piece is nonetheless remarkably intact. The pedestal with which the figure itself is paired is ornamented by an unusual variation of a foliate wreath, a classical motif commonly used for the decoration of plinths.

FIG. 28

Flora. Attributed to F. & A. Jacquier, Caen, France. After Antoine Coysevox (1640–1720). c. 1900. Terra cotta. Approx. 60 x 29". Biltmore Estate, Asheville, North Carolina.

This statue representing Flora is one of a group of four that were copied after originals by Antoine Coysevox, a prolific sculptor who completed several commissions for Louis XIV at Versailles. All four statues were offered in a catalogue published around 1900 by F. & A. Jacquier of Caen, France.[1] There, they are identified as being after Coysevox, and indeed, this statue is actually marked *Coysevox*, in reference to the original work. The loss of the statue's right arm, although hardly detrimental to the artistic form, is a reminder of the fragile nature of terra cotta.

1. Jacquier, nos. 38, 40, 41, and 43.

seem to be an explanation for the popularity of deer statues. In England, Victoria's beloved Prince Albert took pride in and received significant attention for his tender-hearted deer-watching excursions at Balmoral Castle, the Queen's Scotland retreat. Albert's intense devotion to the animals inspired many followers (both in Britain and in the United States), who, if unable to tramp the countryside in pursuit of a glimpse of natural beauty, could at least buy and display deer-related objects around their homes. Wishing to "memorializ[e] the prowess of the Prince,"[36] and thereby respond to a growing fashion for cervine ornament, iron manufacturers went so far as to produce cast-iron stag heads to hang indoors, as well as full-sized beasts for the garden.[37] An 1857 public notice of the New York–based founder, Janes, Beebe & Co. stated, "DEER – Beautiful specimens reclining . . . and one standing, the attitudinal effect of which is so good, and the antlers so natural, that on a lawn, or among shrubbery, the figure has a wonderfully life-like appearance" (cat. 2.36).[38] This passion for cast-iron deer took hold in the late 1840s and continued well beyond the close of the nineteenth century.

Deer statues, among the most ubiquitous and important of cast-iron animals in American gardens, came to the American market from France as well as England. The stylized, embattled French versions of deer were generally modified into gentle, amiable beasts by American makers. While French animal sculpture has been traditionally known for its expressive design and execution, American statues tended to reflect a simpler, more peaceful aesthetic. Possibly responding to the French interpretation, one American writer proposed for statuary that "a severe line [be] drawn at 'death agonies' and the like."[39]

Since the eighteenth century statues of lions have had particular appeal to American homeowners. One of the earliest known pairs are the heavily weathered marble examples that flank the doorway at Cliveden in Philadelphia. Holding armorial shields, they recall the heraldic lions of Tudor England, symbolic representations of family lineage.[40] The Italian Neoclassical sculptor Antonio Canova (1757–1822) created a pair of traditional marble reclining lions that were completed in Rome in 1792 for the tomb of Pope

Clement XIII. These mourning lions were later adapted as independent sculptures and widely copied in marble, stone, and cast iron.[41] In one case, the Canova lions were copied for the 1929 Caproni Monument in the Forest Hills Cemetery in Roxbury, Massachusetts. The design was laid out by the architect Ralph Adams Cram (1863–1942) and executed by the craftsman Andrew Dresselly after the 1792 originals.[42] Another sculptor, the Dane Bertel Thorvaldsen (1768/70–1844), who worked in Rome some thirty years later in a similar Neoclassical style, carved a single mourning lion for a tomb and, later, a second to make up a pair that has been frequently reproduced.[43] Replicas of the Thorvaldsen lions were offered in American catalogues of garden ornament as late as 1930 (cat. 2.32).[44] The Thorvaldsen model often has been confused with the similar Canova lions, whose renown is so pervasive that practically any reclining lion is attributed, frequently incorrectly, to Canova. Copies of the acclaimed and unusual Medici lions, which stand with opposing front paws balanced on balls, origi-

FIG. 29

Lion. c. 1897. Continental. Marble. 35 × 56 × 15½". Georgian Court, Lakewood, New Jersey.

George Jay Gould, railroad magnate, broke ground at Georgian Court, his extensive estate, in 1896. Included in the building scheme were formal Italianate gardens, decorated with masterfully carved statues, fountains, urns, and benches. This statue is one of a pair that flanks the entrance to a sunken garden. The standing lion statue replicates a design by the French sculptor Antoine-Louis Barye (1796–1875). A fiercely expressive creature, the lion was perhaps intended to remind the viewer of Gould's substantial financial power. J. W. Fiske Iron Works offered a seven-foot zinc version of the work around 1901.[1] The Barye lion also appears in stone in F. & A. Jacquier's c. 1900 statuary catalogue.[2]

1. Fiske [1901–1907], 13, no. 427.
2. Jacquier, nos. 64, 65.

FIG. 30

Sphinxes. c. 1910–20. French. Bronze.
38 x 63 x 22". Old Westbury Gardens,
Old Westbury, New York.

In the early twentieth century, pairs
of sphinxes often were used to flank
entrance walks to act as symbolic
guardians of the house and keepers of
paths and passages. The figured saddlecloths, carefully defined locks of hair
tied in a band, and small tiaras charac-
terize this pair as Renaissance-style
sphinxes. The design of these sphinxes
follows the form of those attributed to
the eighteenth-century English sculptor
John Cheere that decorate the Corona-
tion Avenue at Anglesey Abbey in
England. In another English garden,
that of Syon House near London
(1760–61), a lead pair of this same form
stand on either side at the Lace Gate.[1]

1. Weaver, fig. 288, 179.

nally in the loggia of the Villa Medici, have not been found
in America in the course of this study. They would have
been, however, important inspirations to Americans who
may have admired them while on the Grand Tour. One of
the originals is considered antique and thought to date to
the second century A.D.; the other is a late-sixteenth-cen-
tury companion carved by the Renaissance sculptor
Flaminio Vacca (1538–1605).[45]

A relative of the lion statue, the sphinx combines a
leonine body with a woman's head and torso, and occasionally was adorned with a variety of headdresses, breastplates, or saddlecloths. Egyptian inspired, they were
produced in marble in seventeenth-century France, in lead
in eighteenth-century England, in stoneware by Coade in
the company's catalogue of circa 1784, and in artificial
limestone by another English maker, Austin's Artificial
Stone Works, in its 1835 catalogue.[46] The passion for Egyptian design began with the appreciation of an unfamiliar
culture after Napoleon's Egyptian campaign of 1798 and
continued to flourish throughout the nineteenth century.
The Horticulturist of February 1851 encouraged the fashion,
". . . let us pass into Egypt . . . here is the Sphinx . . . and it
shows the *grand* taste of the Egyptians to have converted
it into the wonderful figure which still remains."[47]

While lions or sphinxes were normally placed in formal gardens or in close proximity to a house, other wild
animal statues with less regal associations were set in more
natural gardens. Indeed, the picturesque gardens of
America invited the use of bird, rabbit, turtle, and frog
statues. These smaller animal figures were made by numerous foundries in the nineteenth century. J. L. Mott Iron
Works, the renowned New York founder, for example,
offered a rabbit, a frog, and a squirrel in its 1890 catalogue.
The period of popularity of cast-iron lawn animals, according to a 1949 writer, Mrs. Chetwood Smith, was approximately 1830 to 1890.[48]

European precedents repeatedly paved the way for the
designs of the American makers, and statues of dogs were no
exception. By 1860 cast-iron and zinc terriers, setters, and
greyhounds, among others, made their way into American
gardens and homes. An antique Roman statue from Italy,
the *Dog of Alcibiades,* had been made in singles and pairs,
one example being in the Uffizi in Florence. Although these

dogs inspired many copies in marble and stone in England,[49] this was not so in America. Joseph Winn Fiske, one of the most important founders of New York City, owned one of the few firms to offer a zinc version in 1893.[50] In another case, the English sculptor Matthew Cotes Wyatt (1777–1862) was commissioned to portray Lord Dudley's favorite Newfoundland, Bashaw. This work, executed in marble and bronze in 1831–34, was later displayed at the Crystal Palace Exhibition of 1851.[51] Although the statue was ridiculed in England in the 1870s, the dog's posture, with its head and tail raised, was echoed in a standing spaniel in J. L. Mott Iron Works' 1875 catalogue.[52]

One of the most well liked canine figures, the iron Newfoundland statue, was produced by a variety of firms in America. An unusual story about this statue originated at Hayward, Bartlett & Company, a Baltimore foundry, which in the late 1850s made cast-iron portraits of their dogs, Sailor and Canton, later known as ancestors of the Chesapeake Bay retrievers: "In producing the replicas carefully modeled in true conformation of the Newfoundland breed, the partners added to the statuary fame of their Monumental City [Baltimore], but further the mascots before their door became the symbols of the Hayward, Bartlett & Company, and also worthy talismans of its prosperity."[53] In 1899 when interest in cast iron had waned, the statues were discarded, and soon thereafter the financial health of the company went into decline. When the Hayward and Bartlett families realized their turn of luck, they replaced their mascots in their original spot flanking the entrance doorway and witnessed the return of their good fortune.

While cast-iron animals were certainly pervasive around the turn of the century, critical reviews were not always favorable. Indeed, in 1903, Samuel Swift, a tastemaker and frequent contributor to *House and Garden* magazine, attacked the use of such ornaments – which by then had been long established – citing "the lurking dogs, the frightened deer and other fauna imperishably preserved in this merciless substance, whose coats were freshened once a year with new paint."[54] Swift went on to argue that the improvement of the American garden rested, in part, on the elimination of such cast-iron creatures from the landscape!

FIG. 31

Dog. c. 1860. American. Cast iron. 26 × 50 × 11". Rosedown Plantation and Gardens, St. Francisville, Louisiana.

Although unmarked, this figure of an Irish setter is similar to a number of dog statues offered in American trade catalogues. A closely related version appeared in a Robert Wood & Co. catalogue of around 1875,[1] and later J. W. Fiske Iron Works of New York pictured a zinc "New Foundland" in its catalogue published between 1892 and 1907.[2] Hayward, Bartlett & Company of Baltimore also produced models of Newfoundlands (fig. 32) that are remarkably similar to Rosedown's Irish setter.[3] This dog's pose, standing with its tail raised, is one example of the dozens of cast-iron and zinc animals that were manufactured by domestic foundries in the last half of the nineteenth century as garden ornaments.

1. Wood, 157, no. 571.

2. Fiske [1892–1907], 11, no. 387.

3. Latrobe, 41.

FIG. 32

Dog. c. 1850. American. Cast iron. 38 x 12 x 44". Belmont Mansion Association, Nashville, Tennessee.

This cast-iron Newfoundland is identical to the design first produced by Hayward, Bartlett & Company, a Baltimore firm, in the 1850s. Many foundries used and reproduced their popular design, which led to the sculpture's fairly common appearance in American gardens. In the 1880s, Hayward, Bartlett & Company went further and adopted this particular dog, the ancestor of the Chesapeake Bay breed, as the symbol of their enterprise and placed statues like this one in front of their building (see p. 51).

When fountain figures were transformed by fresh ideas in the twentieth century, so likewise were garden statues, in a movement that was mostly fueled by a small group of fine-art sculptors, many of them women. But, one critic has credited the sculptor Frederick W. MacMonnies (1863–1937) with the initiation of "garden sculpture as a fine art . . . [since] [u]p to this time it had existed as a commercial enterprise with a stock of copies from the antique."[55] The 1893 Columbian Exposition in Chicago began a trend toward original designs for and fine execution of garden statues. At this exposition, where the landscape architect Frederick Law Olmsted turned "a big, barren swamp into a palatial pleasure-ground . . . ," the emphasis was on innovation, despite the Beaux-Arts architectural setting.[56]

The introduction of bronze garden statuary coincided at the turn of the twentieth century with a diminishing interest in the previously popular figures of iron and zinc. The Arts and Crafts movement inspired an appreciation for handcrafted objects to the detriment of manufactured goods. Moreover, along with a shift in material and mode of craftsmanship came a change of subject matter. Now eighteenth- and nineteenth-century classical goddesses were joined by exuberant idealized maidens and youths.[57] The whimsical, attenuated forms of the new figures ex-

FIG. 33

Statue. A. Olivetti & Co. 1930. Italian. Carved stone. 60" without base. Longwood Gardens, Kennett Square, Pennsylvania.

This peasant genre statue, carved in Italy by Piero Morseletto for A. Olivetti & Co., exhibits one of the Arcadian themes associated with the much-copied work of the Flemish-born, later English garden sculptor John Van Nost the Elder (d. 1710). The piece is paired with a shepherdess, one of the more commonly depicted characters of the Arcadian idiom. The two works, which are displayed in architectural niches flanking a wall fountain, overlook the pool of a formal garden. The juxtaposition of these elements results in an unusual combination of the Romantic ideals of pastoral statuary and the formal regularity of classical architecture.

pressed a love of life in marked contrast to the civic monuments of the day, which tended to be "tedious modern statues of course, commemorating public men."[58] The vast collection of sculpture at Brookgreen Gardens in Georgetown County, South Carolina, originally intended to display the work of Anna Hyatt Huntington, presented the sculpture of many of these artists in a garden environment. Brookgreen Gardens is, however, a setting where fine art predominates; it is essentially an outdoor museum rather than a garden where art and nature have equal importance.

The late nineteenth and early twentieth centuries saw American innovations in methods of marble trade and production. Improvements in marble quarrying and cutting methods accompanied by a fifty percent tariff on "imported worked marble, other than works of antiquity" furthered "the immense development which has taken place in all branches of the [American marble] industry."[59] Converging with these developments was the re-emergence of the popularity of the formal Italianate garden and its requisite marble ornament. The taste for the traditions of the classical world, spurred on by the writings on Italian gardens by Edith Wharton and Charles A. Platt (see p. 28), was perpetuated in the subject matter of the new bronze sculpture as well as in finely carved marble statues.

A standard form, the ever-popular historical bust, achieved an unparalleled importance at Blairsden in Peapack, New Jersey. C. Ledyard Blair, a successful financier, and his designers, James Greenleaf and Carrère & Hastings, lined the dramatic entrance avenue with nine-foot-high marble busts of the first twelve Roman emperors (pp. 8–9). The impact was reminiscent of the multiple busts in the Emperor's Walk designed by William Andrews Nesfield (1793–1881) for the gardens at Grimston in Yorkshire, England. Another form, the cherub statue, ever present as a fountain figure, did not immediately earn a place as a sculpture in its own right in the American garden. In the early twentieth century, figural groups such as copies after eighteenth-century European models were installed at Middleton Place in South Carolina (fig. 38) and Rosecliff in Newport, Rhode Island (fig. 37).

FIG. 34

Dog. Anna Hyatt Huntington. c. 1910. American. Granite. 46". Huntington Library, Art Collections, and Botanical Gardens, San Marino, California. Signed: *A. Hyatt.*

The Huntington estate, built between 1910 and 1914, is home to many important statues. This finely carved piece was executed by Anna Hyatt before she married Henry Huntington's son Archer and became her patron's daughter-in-law. It was purchased in 1910 by Henry Huntington's wife Arabella as a gift for him. Notable for its projection of the dog's noble character, the work has been displayed continuously outdoors since that time.

FIG. 35

Otho. c. 1899. Statuary and figured marbles. 9'2" x 42". St. Joseph's Villa (formerly Blairsden), Peapack, New Jersey.

This bust is one of a suite of portraits of the first twelve Roman emperors that still stands regally along the driveway entrance next to the reflecting pool on the property once known as Blairsden (pp. 8–9). Each bust is marked with the emperor's name and the dates of his reign and are arranged, for the most part, chronologically. The display of forms from classical antiquity in a garden was thought to demonstrate the owner's appreciation of ancient culture, and the practice also may have derived in part from the Roman tradition of keeping ancestors' portraits to commemorate the importance of the family. For a collector, incorporating a set of emperors' portraits in the garden not only suggested a familiarity with history but also intimated to the *cognoscenti* that the collecting family was of a rank and mettle comparable to that of the Roman nobles preserved in stone. The Italian subject also reinforced the architecture designed by Carrère & Hastings and the goal of C. Ledyard Blair to re-create a perfect simulacrum of an Italian hillside villa in America.

FIG. 36

Cleopatra. Also known as *Dido,* or *Ariadne.* Frederick George Richard Roth (1872–1944). After the antique. c. 1920. Italy. Marble. Approx. 60" x 6'6" x 20". Kykuit, National Trust for Historic Preservation, Pocantico Hills, New York.

The model for this figure was a second-century A.D. Roman copy of a Hellenistic sculpture. The figure served at first as part of a fountain in the garden of the Vatican Belvedere; later, its niche was decorated to resemble a grotto.[1] *Cleopatra,* the statue's currently preferred designation, came to be thought of as a standard reclining figure for a grotto. In America, Thomas Jefferson, who once contemplated using a "reclining nymph" in his grotto plan for his garden (see pp. 19–20), was possibly inspired by this form.[2] Indeed, he owned a smaller version of the same figure, which is still in the collection of Monticello. The arched backdrop shown here for the figure at Kykuit, the John D. Rockefeller estate, may have been intended as an allusion to its Roman predecessor's carved niche.

1. Haskell and Penny, 184.

2. Beiswanger, 310.

FIG. 37

Earth. c. 1902. French. Carved stone. 7'2".
Rosecliff, Preservation Society of Newport
County, Newport, Rhode Island.

According to tradition, this figural
group *Earth* and its companion, *Air,*
were bought from Jules Allard (1832–
1907) et Fils, a decorator and retailer
based in Paris. They were apparently
sculpted after seventeenth-century
models. However, three putti holding a
dog hardly seem to represent "Earth."
Further research has suggested another
possible interpretation. A number of
seventeenth-century Baroque painters,
inspired by a 1553–54 painting by Titian,
showed an interest in the depiction of
Venus and Adonis. Titian's painting
represents the moment when Venus
tries to stop Adonis from leaving to hunt
the Calydonian Boar. At Venus's side, a
group of putti, often used to represent
Cupid himself, is shown restraining
Adonis's dogs.[1] The figural group at
Rosecliff may be an interpretation of a
seventeenth-century Baroque painting
or sculpture representing this detail of
Titian's painting.

1. Aghion et al., 16–17, 100.

FIG. 38

Putti Musicanti. c. 1850. Italian. Marble. 29 x 40 x 10". Middleton Place, Charleston, South Carolina.

This cheerful group adorning a shady corner of the Middleton Place garden has thematic roots in Italian quattrocento sculpture. Luca della Robbia's marble *Cantoria* of the late 1430s, made as a choir loft for the Cathedral of Florence, is decorated with figural plaques on which youths carved in relief appear to make joyful music. This group at Middleton Place seems ready to entertain a more secular audience. The boys' heavy eyelids, which emphasize their sweet expressions, and their shocks of hair are infused with the sentimentality designed to satisfy Victorian taste.

Unusual manifestations of the classical repertoire inhabited early-twentieth-century American gardens. The Roman god Janus was represented in art by double-headed statues that faced in two directions. Originally set in place to guard a building from both directions, the Janus figure was later accorded the honor of giving its name to the first month of the year in the Roman calendar.[60] The Roman Janus figure made its appearance in America at the turn of the twentieth century as a classical addition to Italianate gardens (fig. 39).

Terminus, the Greek god of boundaries, was represented in the ancient world by his likeness in a bust supported by a tapering pillar. When such a post was topped with the head of Hermes and given male genitals, it was called a *herma,* or herm. Roman interpretations, which were not phallic, became popular as property dividers and garden ornaments.[61] Prevailing language does not distinguish these differences and calls any square pillar surmounted with a bust a herm, herma, term, or terminus.

In the twentieth century the purpose of these pillars also was decorative: "once used . . . to define limits of land, [they were] now freed from that dull task, to be set up . . . wherever found desirable, as to accent a terrace, or to flank a flight of steps."[62] Guy Lowell's 1901 *American Gardens* illustrated such statues in the garden of Green Hill in Brookline, Massachusetts, Faulkner Farm, the Sprague garden also in Brookline, and Box Hill, Stanford White's garden in St. James, New York.[63]

By the turn of the century a taste for exotic imagery had taken hold and awareness of foreign cultures was at an all-time high. The dominant taste of the first quarter of the twentieth century in America was extremely diverse.[64] In 1902 *House and Garden* published a series of articles on the gardens of Persia, Algeria, Holland, Spain, Italy, and England.[65] Egypt, Korea, China, and Japan also became important design influences.[66] West Coast gardens led the way with Foo dogs from China, bronze cranes from Japan, and temple figures from the Orient. In 1904 the Paris firm

FIG. 39

Herm. c. 1915. Italian. Marble. 62". Vizcaya Museum and Gardens, Miami, Florida.

Herms or *Hermae* began as guardians of Greek crossroads in the early fifth century B.C. The Romans introduced them into their gardens as decoration. The herm or term (see above) shown here belongs to the Roman rather than the Greek tradition.[1] The designer of this piece eschewed the more customary form of a single bust on a post and instead adapted a Janus-like head combining back-to-back male and female faces. Twentieth-century American garden owners such as James Deering, the owner of Vizcaya, chose statues that reconfigured traditional forms to create new compositions that maintained a link to their artistic heritage.

1. Radice, 131.

FIG. 40

Foo Dog. Early twentieth century. Probably
Chinese. 6'3" x 26" x 19". Longwood Gardens,
Kennett Square, Pennsylvania.

Traditionally used as temple guardians,
this fearsome creature is a blend of lion
and dog. Foo dogs usually appear in
pairs, one male and one female. The
male, who generally holds an orb or ball
under a paw, flanks the female – the
example illustrated – who instead holds
a surly cub underfoot. As symbolic
watchdogs, the pair protects the *Foo,*
or fortune, of the structure whose
entrance they adorn.

FIG. 41

Dwarves. Late nineteenth century.
Continental. Carved stone. Approx. 36".
Ganna Walska Lotusland, Santa Barbara,
California.

The tradition of placing figures of
dwarves in the garden originated in central Europe. The estate's owner, Ganna
Walska, a famous beauty of Polish
descent, imported these from her French
property, the Château de Gallius, to be
placed in the Theatre Garden at Lotusland in California.[1] Sculptures of
dwarves appeal to garden owners who
appreciate them as caricatures of a range
of human follies and foibles. For example,
Walska chose a hunchbacked merchant,
a quadruple-bonneted matron, and a
figure of staunchly aristocratic bearing,
which, through their diminutive size,
their accurate costumes, and their proud
bearing, make a gentle mockery of com-
placency and pretension.

1. Crawford, 31.

of Emile Muller offered cast-iron sphinxes in the styles of ancient Egypt, the Italian Renaissance, and France during the reigns of Louis XIV and Louis XV. Meanwhile, the English firm of J. P. White, one of the largest suppliers of garden ornament in the early twentieth century, retailed two models of Egyptian-style marble sphinxes in various sizes.[67] Although American collectors were still buying in Europe, domestic firms, such as J. L. Mott Iron Works, did offer sphinxes in their catalogues as early as 1890.

American gardens devoted to statuary occasionally included images of the grotesque. The tradition of displaying distorted figures in gardens originated in Germany in the seventeenth century. Despite a lively following in Italy during the eighteenth century, grotesques did not find general acceptance in America, perhaps owing to their darkly humorous character.[68] Lotusland in California, the home and garden of Ganna Walska, a Polish immigrant and stage performer, does, however, boast a collection of twelve hunchback dwarves dressed in theatrical costumes appropriately arranged on the seats and stage of an out-

door theater (fig. 41). Dwarf statues were included in the early-twentieth-century gardens of Boxly, owned by Mrs. Frederick Winslow Taylor in Philadelphia; Weld, the Brookline, Massachusetts, garden of Mr. and Mrs. Larz Anderson; and The John and Mable Ringling Museum in Sarasota, Florida.[69]

In the early twentieth century, garden statues in America gained the prominence that they had only known in the colonial eighteenth century as they again came to represent impeccable taste, superior intellect, and ample resources. F. W. Ruckstuhl, the vice president of the Municipal Art Society, epitomized the serious-mindedness of his era when he listed the purposes of outdoor statuary in 1902: "[they are] only four in number, but very important, morally. They are: *to delight, to refine, to console, to stimulate.*"[70] Thus, in the early twentieth century, the appreciation of the multitude of styles inculcated by Victorian eclecticism united with a sense of design fostered by skilled artists and designers to produce an informed, cultivated, openminded audience for statues of the finest quality.

FIG. 42

Hero. c. 1910. American. Carved stone. 36 x 54 x 22". Old Westbury Gardens, Old Westbury, New York.

This sculpture of the Hellenistic maiden Hero illustrates the perfect harmony of a garden statue with its surroundings. The figure gazes into the water, imagining the Hellespont and mourning the death of her lover Leander, who drowned in the straits on a stormy night after he lost sight of her beacon. This statue extended over a pond presents an image of sorrow and introspection for visitors to discover as they walk through the garden.

FIG. 43

Time. Seventeenth century. Italian. Carved stone. 10'5" with pedestal. The Huntington Library, Art Collections, and Botanical Gardens, San Marino, California.

The ancient, ravaged countenance, the wings, the scythe, and the hourglass leave no doubt that this figure represents Time. Time's passage and its persistent reduction of all things were a popular subject in literature and visual culture of Baroque Europe. An educated and sophisticated collector such as Henry Huntington would have understood the sculpture's significance, and he may have incorporated it into his collection to show his knowledge of allegory and to testify to life's fleeting impermanence.

FIG. 44

Hercules and the Hydra. Attributed to Orazio Marinali (1643–1720). c. 1700. Italian. Carved stone. Approx. 7'5" x 30" x 30". Kykuit, National Trust for Historic Preservation, Pocantico Hills, New York.

The statue illustrates the story of the Lernean Hydra, the second of Hercules's Twelve Labors. The figure has the burly musculature of other gods and heroes, but the attributes belong specifically to Hercules: a lionskin mantle, a club, and the nine-headed hydra. The theme of the Labors of Hercules appealed to many collectors; it was especially significant for a man like John D. Rockefeller, whose phenomenal success in the business world would have taught him to appreciate the power of human ingenuity and endurance.

CHAPTER 3

URNS

FIG. 45

Warwick Vase. Emil Siebern (1889–1942).
c. 1920. American. Istrian stone. 6'2" high.
Kykuit, National Trust for Historic
Preservation, Pocantico Hills, New York.

In 1770 Sir Gavin Hamilton, then
English ambassador to the Court of
Naples, unearthed parts of an enormous
white marble vase from the bottom of a
lake at Hadrian's Villa, east of Rome.[1]
Indeed, the procurement of what came
to be known as the Warwick Vase was a
triumph of eighteenth-century British
collecting in Italy. After the recovered
marble pieces of this ancient work were
reassembled, the restored vase was sold
to George, Earl of Warwick, who transported it to Warwick Castle. Today it
stands in the Glasgow Museum in
Scotland.[2] In the 1850s, both Coade
and J. M. Blashfield offered copies of
the Warwick Vase in artificial stone,
and Handyside Co. exhibited it in cast
iron at the 1851 Crystal Palace Exhibition. The Galloway & Graff replica
shown at the Philadelphia Centennial
Exhibition of 1876 added to its renown
in America and perhaps encouraged
J. L. Mott to offer it in his 1893 vase
catalogue in zinc and cast iron.[3]

1. Warwick Castle, 25.

2. Haskell and Penny, 67.

3. Mott 1893, pl. 19–L, 3.

Urns have probably been used more consistently than any other form of garden
ornament. Despite the ever-capricious fashions of historic garden design, the
acceptance of urns by champions of various garden styles has been remarkably
constant. Indeed, in the minds of even the most fervent proponent of naturalistic
design (in which ornament was severely limited), the urn was admired as an
object of taste and refinement. While their purpose, function, and, certainly,
ornamentation have undergone changes, the basic forms of urns have varied
little since antiquity.

The terms commonly used to describe the two traditional forms of garden
urns are Italian: "tazza," or cup, and "campana," or bell. Both of these forms are
related to vases produced in the fifth to sixth centuries B.C. in Greece. Like the
fountain of the same name, a tazza-form urn has a low bowl shape and a width
that exceeds its height. The tazza corresponds to the kylix, a low, wide-mouthed,
footed Athenian drinking cup (fig. 46). The campana echoes the Greek calyx
krater, a wide, footed vase resembling an upturned bell used in the ancient world
to dilute strong wine with water (fig. 47).[1] In their earliest forms, these two Attic
vases traditionally had handles, but later versions are occasionally seen without.
In the popular vocabulary of garden ornament the words "urn" and "vase" have
become virtually interchangeable and will be used as such in this study.

In the late sixteenth century, antiquarians learned of the decorative use of
urns in the gardens of antiquity when marble neo-Attic vases of the second half of
the first century A.D. were unearthed in Italy.[2] Following this discovery, it became
fashionable to display urns of marble, stone, or terra cotta that closely imitated
these antique forms. In Italian Renaissance gardens, urns were used either as

FIG. 46

Profile of a Greek kylix

FIG. 47

Profile of a Greek calyx krater

sculptural ornaments or adapted as fountains. These objects represented the owner's reverence for the highly sought treasures of antiquity. Classical styles continued and flourished into Baroque extravagance during the late seventeenth century at Versailles, and the unique bronze urns created by artists and sculptors for Louis XIV provided models for later generations. In the seventeenth century, Dutch and English lead urns were fashioned with classical motifs as decoration, including the standard repertoire of swags, garlands, masks, and stylized foliate scrolls. By the eighteenth century, however, the majesty associated with decorative urns was somewhat tempered by their association with death and mourning.

Despite the nearly universal acceptance of decorative urns in the nineteenth and twentieth centuries, there is little early record in diaries and other accounts of urns being used as garden ornaments in colonial or newly federated America. Although there are references to fountains and statues in eighteenth-century formal gardens, little or nothing is mentioned about urns, even in historical accounts about regions known for their love of formal gardens, such as Pennsylva-

FIG. 48

Pair of urns. c. 1850–60. American. Cast iron. 39½ x 31". Rosedown Plantation and Gardens, St. Francisville, Louisiana.

The cast-iron, tazza-form urn was a common nineteenth-century product offered in many trade catalogues. The examples shown here are of regular form, with the then standard egg-and-dart, semi-lobing, and fluted decoration serving as their only adornments. The wide, shallow bowls were designed to accommodate plantings in accord with the Victorian penchant for botanical cultivation. As seen here, the urns were placed on pedestals with classical wreath decorations of a type identified in the 1893 J. W. Fiske Iron Works vase catalogue as "Grecian" pedestals.[1] The same combination of urn and wreathed plinth was endorsed in 1848 by *The Horticulturist,* where it was used as an example of how to properly elevate and display ornamental vases.[2]

1. Fiske c. 1893, 62.
2. *The Horticulturist* 2, 40–41.

FIG. 49

Urn. c. 1900. Carved stone and cast stone.
6'2" × 41" × 38". Cà d' Zan, Sarasota, Florida.

This finely carved urn sits at the center
of a boxwood garden on the grounds
of John Ringling's Florida estate,
Cà d' Zan. Crowned with a cast stone
bouquet of flowers, the carved body is
crisply delineated with heavy garlands
and tiny bellflowers. This combination
of materials is occasionally seen in earlier
nineteenth-century examples. In the
early twentieth century urns with broad
mid-sections like this one were used in
garden placements as gatepost finials
or on the roofs of buildings.

nia, Maryland, and Virginia.[3] Is it possible that urns existed
in early American gardens but were not considered worthy
of note? Or were they simply absent? Further studies of the
period may answer these questions.

We do know that Thomas Jefferson and John Adams, in
a search of landscape inspiration, visited gardens in England
and France in 1786. In their diaries they reported their
admiration for a garden at the Leasowes, a country place
in Shropshire belonging to the poet William Shenstone.[4]
Years earlier in Shenstone's "Unconnected Thoughts on
Gardening" he had written: "Urns are more solemn if large
and plain; more beautiful if less ornamented. Solemnity
is perhaps their point, and the situation of them should
still co-operate with it."[5] In keeping with his sentiments,
Shenstone displayed a single urn in his "Lover's Walk"
garden dedicated to a mysterious Miss Dolman.[6]

In fact, during the eighteenth century the use of a
single commemorative urn became characteristic of the
English picturesque, or Romantic, garden style. The words
of the garden's founder would be eternally preserved,
inscribed into the carved marble of a monumental urn
and placed in the very center of the garden.[7] Because of
the time lag in transmission of styles from England to

America, it was not until the mid-nineteenth century that
Americans embraced this fashion. Nevertheless, it can be
assumed that the two famous gentlemen, Jefferson and
Adams, renowned for their politics more than for their
horticultural exploits, must have returned from their trip
aware of the use of decorative urns in Renaissance and
Baroque European gardens. In 1839, thirteen years after
Jefferson's death, a visitor to Monticello recorded a dilapi-
dated scene: "Around me I beheld nothing but ruin and
change . . . cattle wandering among Italian mouldering
vases."[8] Italian gardens decorated with terra-cotta oil jars
had probably inspired his choice of ornament.

As there is no physical evidence of urns in extant early
gardens,[9] one must rely on records, writings, and pictorial
renderings of the period. The inventories of the eighteenth-
century Governor's Palace in Williamsburg, Virginia, list
"lead vases" as ornaments in the formal palace gardens.[10]
Lead ornaments had a short life span in America as they
were often melted down during wartime or corroded by
severe weather. A rare entry in an 1802 diary describing the
garden of Elias Hasket Derby in Salem, Massachusetts
notes, "a full view of the garden below . . . The large marble
vases . . . gave it so uniform and finished [an] apperarance

[sic] that . . . everything appeared like enchantment."[11] The existence of urns in gardens also can be confirmed by a visual source. A painting by Augustus Weidenbach of the lawn of Belvedere, the 1786 Baltimore home of Governor John Eager Howard, shows no less than five urns on pedestals, interspersed with imported eighteenth-century statues. The 1858 date of the painting does not confirm the presumed early-nineteenth-century date for the urns unless it could be proved that they were imported along with the statues.[12]

Documentation also can be found in needlework pictures embroidered at the beginning of the nineteenth century depicting urns in the context of death and mourning. Although such images are not necessarily an accurate depiction, they are perhaps useful in establishing the use and typical placements of urns and in forecasting the importance of urns as an essential landscape feature in cemeteries at the beginning of the nineteenth century. One such embroidery, made by Hannah Clapp in 1809 to commemorate the death of her son, Abner Clapp, shows the tradi-

tionally close association of urns with funerary rituals.[13] The urn shown there, a simple two-handled form with a flame finial-topped lid, is supported by a stone plinth. Similar lidded urns in the Italian Renaissance style were popular ornaments for English gardens during the eighteenth century but only later came into fashion in America.[14]

Around 1850 a young woman, Miss Ellen Poore, wrote of her recollection of the garden at Indian Hill Farm in West Newbury, Massachusetts. The garden plan had been altered in 1833 by an unidentified gardener who may have been familiar with the English picturesque landscape tradition and its use of informal, sometimes makeshift containers. As Miss Poore noted: ". . . [there were] four flowerbeds with box edges. Where these met in the centre stood a rustic vase filled with flowers."[15] In a more formal vein the semicircular garden at Prospect, a house in Princeton, New Jersey, was laid out by the then fashionable Philadelphia architect John Notman (1810–65). A rare 1843 plan designates, in the words of the architect, the use of one central

FIG. 50

Urn. c. 1898. Italian. Marble. 54 x 42" diam.
Canyon Ranch (formerly Bellefontaine),
Lenox, Massachusetts.

Very little remains of the extensive collection of outdoor ornament that Mr. and Mrs. Giraud Foster amassed for the gardens at Bellefontaine, their palatial Lenox estate. One of the few survivors is this elongated version of a campana-form urn, decorated with female masks and swags. Possibly retailed by a firm such as J. P. White of Bedford, England, or the Italian equivalent, this urn would have originally been one of a pair. Indeed, just such a pair of identical marble urns can be seen near the main house at Rosecliff in Newport, Rhode Island. The architects of Bellefontaine, Carrère & Hastings, may have been responsible for the design and selection of the garden ornament, as Thomas Hastings, one of the two partners in the firm, was known to be interested in not only the house but also the disposition of the grounds.

Urn on pedestal. c. 1870–80. American. Cast iron. 37½ x 19". Melrose, Natchez, Mississippi.

Usually referred to in trade catalogues as the "Woodbury Vase," this urn and pedestal ensemble was manufactured by a number of American cast-iron foundries. It seems likely that this urn, which is one of a pair, was purchased from Robert Wood & Co., considering that many of the extant ornaments in Natchez match offerings in that firm's catalogues. Moreover, the vigorous flare of the upper section of the vase more closely matches the image of an urn pictured in the 1875 Wood catalogue than examples offered by other companies.[1]

Although the name Woodbury is most commonly associated with the urn, at least two manufacturers identify it as the "Venetian Vase."[2] In 1856, *The Horticulturist* devoted particular attention to Robert Wood's Woodbury Vase and deemed it in "every way suitable for a garden, terrace, or other situation."[3] J. L. Mott Iron Works of New York and Chase Brothers & Company of Boston also produced the less flared version of this model.[4]

1. Fiske c. 1893, 94.
2. Wood, 273, fig. G.
3. *The Horticulturist* 8, 90.
4. Mott 1893, 11, pl. 90–L; Chase Brothers, 1859, 21.

"urn" and seven "vases" at various corners of the garden.[16] The use of the two distinct words suggests that the designer may have specified vessels of two different forms. Indeed, an 1852 photograph of the garden at Prospect shows the "vases" to be tall planters on pedestals. Perhaps the "urn" was intended to be purely a sculptural focal point.[17]

Notman's commission reminds us that it was traditional to use architects with no specific training in garden design to lay out grounds as well as structures. It was not until the 1840s that Andrew Jackson Downing became the first self-styled specialist in landscape design in America. Beginning with the publication of his book *A Treatise on the Theory and Practice of Landscape Gardening* in 1841, he guided the taste of a country eager to read and absorb Romantic ideas about art and beauty and led them toward an appreciation of nature and art in the outdoors.[18] In his periodical, *The Horticulturist,* Downing cited a statement by J. C. Loudon, a noted English garden expert of the early nineteenth century, that "[t]he history of every country may be traced by its vases. . . ."[19] Downing, whose influence lasted well into the twentieth century, extolled the virtues and uses of ornamental vases, noting that, "There are few

objects that may, with so much good effect, be introduced into the scenery of pleasure grounds, surrounding a tasteful villa, as the *vase* in its many varied forms."[20]

Photographs of mid- to late-nineteenth-century gardens disclose how frequently the garden urn was included as part of the outdoor decoration.[21] Two 1891 pictures of the grounds of the Alexander estate in Staten Island show a single ornament, a large, probably cast-iron, unplanted urn with enormous rococo handles. It had been placed in a way to communicate its elevated stature on the lawn directly in front of the main entrance of the house.[22] For the smaller gardens of the Victorian period, those of workers and craftspeople, the urn was practically the single most popular choice for an ornament.[23]

In the mid-nineteenth century the cast-iron urn, a weather-hardy reservoir with decorative merit and a lower cost than stone, increased the popularity of urns in general. Cast iron came to be recognized as a remarkable substitute for stone or bronze. The mass production of urns permitted multiple orders, a choice of finishes, and prompt delivery. Ever-practical Victorian designers developed a self-watering urn with a minireservoir that could be filled with water on

FIG. 52

Urn. c. 1880. American. Cast iron. 39 × 19 ×
19". Ebenezer Maxwell Mansion, Philadelphia,
Pennsylvania.

During the nineteenth century, American cast-iron manufacturers experi-
mented with new urn forms that were
not based on those of antiquity. Fanciful
decoration, particularly on the handles,
abounded on such urns as this one.
Following Andrew Jackson Downing's
suggestion,[1] this urn is placed in the
center of the small plot of lawn on what
once was a suburban property.

1. Downing 1842, 233–234.

weekly trips to the cemetery; the plant could then soak
up the supply as needed (cat. 3.7).[24] Moreover, Victorian
custodial inclinations encouraged the use of classically
styled winter covers that protected the impenetrable cast-
iron urns from freezing (cat. 3.6)!

In July 1848, Downing, more concerned with aesthetics
than practicality, published two precepts for garden design
in *The Horticulturist*. The first was: "Looking at the vase in
an artistical point of view it is considered as performing the
office of uniting the architecture and the grounds of a complete country residence."[25] The second was: "To set down a
vase upon the earth, or the lawn, without any pedestal, is
to give it a temporary character, and to rob it of that dig-
nity and importance which it gains both to the eye and the
reason, by being placed on a firm and secure pedestal."[26]
The question of whether or not to plant garden containers
was a debate of constant interest to Victorians. Downing
suggested that "stone or pottery vases are . . . seldom filled
with plants of any kind," intimating that metal urns were
to be used for plantings.[27]

Stylistically, the variety of choices in cast-iron urns was
vast. In order to romanticize this basest of metals, makers
offered "vases" in artistic catalogues contrived "to erase its

[iron's] historically plebian connotations."[28] The catalogues
show that the versatility of the medium satisfied the Victorian fascination for the Gothic, the rococo, the Oriental,
and the exotic as designers could create elaborate handles,
fully decorated bowls, fanciful balusters, and coordinating
pedestals. Interchangeable parts permitted extraordinary
combinations, some of which were successful but many of
which seem now to lack aesthetic unity. The elaborate nature
of urns apparently attracted garden owners of this period
more than the simpler classical forms of the first half of the
nineteenth century.[29] The campana-form urns at Middleton
Place (see p. 6) represent the tall, slim, unadorned earlier
style while the tazza-form urn in the re-created garden at
the Ebenezer Maxwell house in Philadelphia exemplifies
the later Victorian ardor for lavish surface decoration and
elaborate handles (fig. 52).

The same makers who modeled statues after European
designs also chose antique and Renaissance precedents
for urns. Nineteenth-century designs by European artists
provided material to copy. J. W. Fiske Iron Works, one of
the largest and most prestigious cast-iron foundries in New
York City, offered as many as eight designs in its 1893 vase
catalogue that replicated offerings from the 1870 catalogue

of the Société Anonyme des Hauts-Fourneaux & Fonderies du Val d'Osne.[30] In another case, a pair of tall vases in Fiske's catalogue was embellished with applied oval copies of the 1824 plaques of "Night" and "Morning" made by the Danish sculptor Bertel Thorvaldsen.

At the turn of the twentieth century, as interest in cast iron waned, terra cotta returned to favor. Downing had forecast this trend by recommending terra-cotta pots as early as 1848. He particularly endorsed Garnkirk, a Scottish company, for its terra-cotta vases, stating that they "exhibit pleasing forms, and a soft mellow shade of colour . . ."[31] By 1903, the unabashed critic Samuel Swift observed this shift in taste, "[I]t is fair to assume that the terra-cotta vase or urn or tree tub is the immediate successor . . . of the cast-iron receptacle without which no man's garden was once complete."[32] Indeed, in the 1920s garden at Gwinn at Bratenahl, near Cleveland, Ohio, designed in collaboration by Charles A. Platt and Warren Manning,

the Galloway-made, glazed terra-cotta urns on the balustrade by the lakeside add a classical note, giving the distinct impression of an Italian waterscape (fig. 53).

Central and northern Italian gardens inspired the decorative use of large numbers of terra-cotta pots in gardens. During the Renaissance, and perhaps earlier, lemons and citrons were rare and commanded high prices. They were so precious that they were grown, most of the year, under carefully controlled conditions. In order to assume a full year of stable cultivation, the lemon trees, in their terra-cotta pots, were stored in *limonaia,* or lemon houses, until the first of May, when "these vases or tubs were either fixed on balustrades and pillars or, more often, movable so as to enable the gardener to arrange the trees into small groves or ornamental designs."[33] American garden owners of the early twentieth century, searching for Italian garden traditions, opted to fill their outdoor spaces with arrangements of planted terra-cotta pots. This practice was more com-

FIG. 53

Urn. William Galloway, Philadelphia. c. 1905. Glazed terracotta. 21½ x 25½ x 13" base. Gwinn, Bratenahl, Ohio. Marked: *WM. GALLOWAY / PHILADELPHIA.*

This marked urn was offered in the c. 1917 Galloway catalogue of terra cotta and pottery.[1] Its simple, classical shape sits at several points along the balustrade of Gwinn's lakefront terrace in imitation of an Italian coastline view. The placement of the urn, its integration into the architectural setting, and the variety of plant within it all conform to Andrew Jackson Downing's suggestions of 1841. He proposed that in order to decorate a terrace effectively, one should place "neat flower-pots on the parapet, or border and angles of the terrace."[2] The most suitable specimen that Downing recommended to occupy these vessels was the "American or Century *Aloe,* a formal architectural-looking plant,"[3] as shown here.

1. Galloway c. 1917, 7, no. 245.
2. Downing 1841, 423.
3. Downing 1841, 423.

FIG. 54
Urn. Glens Falls Terra Cotta Company, Glens
Falls, New York. c. 1895. Terra cotta. 39½ x 25
x 23". The Breakers, Preservation Society of
Newport County, Newport, Rhode Island.

Around the turn of the twentieth century, the American terra-cotta industry
enjoyed renewed success and, judging
from this piece, artistic vitality. This
urn, one of a pair, perfectly comple-
ments the Italianate style of the home of
Cornelius Vanderbilt II, The Breakers.
The fine detailing of the relief work
depicts a full range of ornament inspired
by the Renaissance, including *rinceaux*
(scrolling foliage), fruit garlands, a lion's
mask, and satyr heads at the bases of the
handles. The impeccable craftsmanship
of this piece reflects the attention to
detail seen throughout the decoration
of The Breakers.

mon in warmer states such as California and Florida but
was also found in gardens as far north as Maine.[34]

After 1900, smaller gardens continued along the lines
prescribed by Downing; however, the design of larger gardens shifted to a formal approach recalling the Italian villa
grounds that had so appealed to eighteenth-century Virginians. As in the case of fountains (see pp. 27–28), the taste
for classical formality evolved from the Beaux-Arts style of
the Chicago Columbian Exposition of 1893, as well as from
countless literary and artistic influences. Urns designed
after Greco-Roman and Renaissance models were admired
as sculptural ornament, alone or in groups, as paragons of
perfect classical form. Around 1902 the landscape architect
Bruce Price planned the gardens for Georgian Court in
Lakewood, New Jersey, the home of the financier George
Gould. Even the gardens of Versailles could not claim urns
as extravagant as those imported for Gould.

While representing the finest craftsmanship and materials, the urns at Georgian Court were also bought with an
eye to their historical importance. Many were purchased
through the art dealer Sir Joseph Duveen and were thought
to be actual Renaissance pieces. Four Istrian stone urns at
Georgian Court, one of which is illustrated in figure 55, are
identified as sixteenth-century examples in Sister M. Christina Geis's book on the house.[35] However, their crisp surfaces and edges do not indicate four hundred years of
weathering. Also, it is unlikely that four perfect examples
could have survived from the 1500s, implying that their true
date is probably around 1900. At the time of the purchase,
Duveen had an impeccable reputation as an art dealer;
nonetheless, recent studies have questioned the accuracy of
his scholarship in many instances. Moreover, the 1890
McKinley tariff, which required a fifty percent import duty
on newly worked marble, would have served as a strong
temptation for the purchaser to represent the Georgian
Court urns as Renaissance examples.

The great country house gardens of the early twentieth
century made use of classical urns as accompaniments.
Pierre S. du Pont, known for his success as an entrepreneur,
was deeply impressed by visits to Italian gardens and international expositions. Around 1925 he installed a long wall of
carved stone lidded urns in individual niches at his Longwood Gardens in Kennett Square, Pennsylvania (figs. 59–60).

FIG. 55

Urn on pedestal. c. 1900. Italian. Istrian stone. 8' x 31" square base. Georgian Court College (formerly Georgian Court), Lakewood, New Jersey.

The four magnificent urns on pedestals that flank the Apollo Fountain at Georgian Court College are examples of the finest nineteenth-century Italian stone carving (see p. 70). Purchased by the art dealer Sir Joseph Duveen, who collected such pieces for his elite clientele, the urns were probably carved by the same hand that made the copies of the seats from the Vatican garden for Georgian Court (see fig. 70). Refined in every detail, the example illustrated here combines classical elements, a processional relief around the bowl, mask and loop handles, a semi-lobed body, and mythical creatures that could bear the name "griffin" except for the unlikely addition of an Edwardian-style gentleman's head.

FIG. 56

Urn. After Claude Ballin. A. Durenne, Sommevoire, France. c. 1880. Cast iron. Approx. 22 x 14 x 11". Nemours Mansion, Wilmington, Delaware. Marked: *A. DURENNE/SOMMEVOIRE*.

Based on a seventeenth-century design for an urn at Versailles, this urn was produced by the prominent French founder A. Durenne. The original, designed in 1665 by Claude Ballin, the royal goldsmith to Louis XIV, was cast in bronze. The pensive putti that form the handles are seated on lion masks that look outward from the shoulder of the urn. Several other urns at Alfred I. du Pont's home, Nemours, were made by Durenne after Ballin designs at Versailles, in keeping with du Pont's predilection for French design.

FIG. 57

Urns. c. 1893. Italian. Carved stone. 50 x 25½".
The Breakers, The Preservation Society of
Newport County, Newport, Rhode Island.

These unique, irregularly shaped urns,
retailed by Olivetti & Co. in turn-of-
the-century New York, enter into the
realm of pure fancy. They are distinguished by their abundant swags of fruit
and foliage, serpentine curves, and shell-
like wave forms that are hallmarks of
rococo design. Perhaps the most expressive features are the grotesque masks,
which border on caricature. Here, the
mask, a standard classical motif, is reminiscent of the grotesque figures carved
into sixteenth-century Italian grottoes.

FIG. 58

Urn. c. 1910. Italian. Marble. Approx.
23 x 11". The Huntington Library, Art
Collections, and Botanical Gardens, San
Marino, California.

This exquisitely carved lidded urn is
notable for its profusion of ornament.
The craftsman used every available inch
of space to realize the design. This urn
is markedly similar to a model offered by
the Galloway Terra-Cotta Company of
Philadelphia around 1917.[1] The Galloway
design had handles, and, indeed, on
close examination, the Huntington urn
also shows traces of once having handles.

1. Galloway c. 1917, 14, no. 249.

Urns. A. Olivetti & Co. 1930. Italian. Carved stone. Longwood Gardens, Kennett Square, Pennsylvania.

This group of urns, carved by Piero Morseletto for A. Olivetti & Co., is installed within a traditional architectural form, the blind arcade. By framing individual urns under arches, the designer treated each one as a separate sculpture, showcasing their many different forms and shapes. Visually, the row of urns creates a sinuous line that carries the eye to the belvedere at the center of the arcade.

FIG. 60

Lidded urn. A. Olivetti & Co. 1930. Italian. Carved stone. Approx. 6'. Longwood Gardens, Kennett Square, Pennsylvania.

This urn is one of many lining the south wall of the Fountain Garden at Pierre S. du Pont's Longwood Gardens. The modified egg-and-dart decoration on the lid and lobes on the lower bowl derived from Italian Renaissance styles. The pedestal design, the olive branches, and the fruit finial add a note of vegetal imagery linking this otherwise formal urn to its verdant surroundings.

FIG. 61

Urn. c. 1920. American. Carved stone. 62 x
32 x 32". Gibraltar, Wilmington, Delaware.

This graceful urn is one of a pair set
at either end of a loggia. The classic
campana form is here accentuated by
four unusual handles. These features
are characterized by dramatic, sweeping
lines, not unlike the Art Deco forms
of the later 1920s. An identical urn was
displayed around the turn of the century
at Eugene Glaenzer's New York gallery
of fine and decorative art, which could
point to an earlier date of production.[1]
The same model is documented as having been manufactured by the Galloway
Terra-Cotta Company of Philadelphia.[2]

1. Glaenzer, 16.
2. Galloway c. 1920, 15, no. 548.

Although part of a collective formal statement, each urn
and pedestal was displayed as a work of art on its own. As
late as the 1940s the landscape designer Beatrix Farrand
placed classical-style urns on pedestals at the intersection of
the axes of the gardens at Dumbarton Oaks.

The geometric gardens of the early twentieth century
placed considerable attention on urns. Their forms were
developed in answer to the demand for flamboyant examples, handcrafted of exotic materials, and based on historic
motifs and models. In spite of their importance, urns were
adjuncts to the grandiose mansions and gardens they
adorned, eclipsed by the scale of the houses and grounds.

From the middle of the nineteenth century, the urn
was endowed with special significance in the garden. An art
form on its own that reflected changing tastes, singly or in
pairs, the urn imposed order on the landscape. The enthu-
siastic Downing was insistent on its correct use because
". . . so highly artificial and architectural an object as a
sculptured vase, is never correctly introduced unless it appears in some way connected with buildings, or objects of a
like architectural character."[36] Unlike most other garden
ornaments, the static form of urns does not allow them to
blend with or relate to nature. Downing wrote of them
with conviction, advising that they not be "accompanied
only by natural objects . . . [which] is in a measure doing
violence to our reason or taste, by bringing two objects so
strongly contrasted, in direct union."[37] By and large, gardeners, professional and amateur alike, were in accord with
Downing's thinking that the urn, or vase, had a consequen-
tial role in garden design. In Downing's own plans from
before the Civil War through the era of the great estates
ending with World War II, the urn, in all its variants,
served to extend the architecture of the house into the
grounds, offering a link between the contrasting worlds of
art and nature.

CHAPTER 4

FURNITURE

This impressive Florentine piece was probably made especially for the Huntington estate. The menacing lion arm supports are unusual in terms of the tastes of American garden owners and designers of ornament, who preferred lion statues of a more placid appearance. This chair is also remarkable for its simulation of textile patterns and trims; the seat is figured to resemble a woven brocade while numerous laces and fringes hang neatly from the edge. It is these features that make the chair a unique fusion of interior and exterior ornament, reflecting the lavish use of textiles within the house and evoking the classical solidity of the architecture itself.

Garden furniture provides a visitor with a sense of welcome and a promise of comfort. In the first century A.D., one of the letters of Pliny the Younger, an ancient Roman consul, described a sybaritic corner of his own villa garden. Under a pergola of vines, a semicircular marble seat was set above bubbling fountains, offering cool repose on hot days.[1] In medieval France garden seats were linked with a romantic tradition; numerous illustrations from this period depict courting couples "engaged in amorous discourse" on U-shaped turf seats.[2] Grandeur replaced intimacy in early Italian Baroque gardens such as the Villa Borghese in Rome, which displayed enormous carved half-round seats called exedrae, which echoed the curves of a nearby fountain pool.[3] In the 1750s English designers created rustic furniture of roots, twigs, and branches in response to the naturalistic requirements of "picturesque" gardens. Not until many years later did these extraordinarily rich decorative traditions affect American taste.

At variance with their European heritage, the pragmatic colonists of eighteenth-century America chose sensible seats made of wood. Furniture design books from England showed garden benches, chairs, and tables in fantastical rococo, Gothic, Chinese, rustic, and classical styles.[4] But simple, straight seats with arms and backs, often decorated with Chinese lattice designs, suited the practical-minded American populace. The diary of William Faris, a craftsman from Annapolis, included the author's 1790 advertisement of a garden seat made according to a design published by the London cabinetmakers Bowles and Carver. A wooden "chair," resembling a household settee, could be ordered "made and painted to particular directions."[5]

FIG. 63

Bench. c. 1900. Italian. Marble. 33 x 60 x 16".
St. Joseph's Villa (formerly Blairsden), Peapack,
New Jersey.

The form of this beautifully carved bench
is not often seen in this country. The
carved rams' heads with ribbon garlands
and fruit swags are nearly identical to the
motifs that ornament an ancient marble
altar at the Capitoline Museum in Rome.[1]
Such a formal, classical treatment is
appropriate to the bench's location on the
grounds near the main house. The piece
stands at the edge of an Italianate terrace
overlooking a magnificent view of the
mountains. Its elegance and refinement
are appropriate to the grandeur of the
scenery, the architecture of the house, and
the similarly formal interior furnishings.

1. Speltz, 73, 75.

The most significant find in recent years was the discovery of what is believed to be the oldest extant American
garden seat, dating to the last quarter of the eighteenth century. The eight-foot-long, yellow pine Almodington seat,
so called because it came from the Maryland plantation of
the same name, now resides in the Museum of Early Southern Decorative Art in Winston-Salem, North Carolina
(cat. 4.3).[6] Since outdoor wooden furniture is notoriously
short-lived, the Almodington seat probably owes its remarkable survival to having spent life on a porch rather than in
the exposed setting of a garden. The 1750 pattern book of
the English furniture designer William Halfpenny may
have provided the design for the four diagonal Chinese-
style sections of the back. These sections, two of which are
repeated, replicate Halfpenny's "Open Gates with Dutch
Battens Pannels and Chinese Barrs."[7] Here we should
note that the word "bench", in formal garden ornament
parlance, refers to a seat without a back; in this study, however, we will use "bench" and "seat" interchangeably as
they are used in conversation.

The Windsor chair is another wooden seat that was
commonly placed on a porch and, according to custom in
England,[8] often carried into the garden to seat guests. In the
years 1783–84 an Englishman, Mr. Vaughan, settled in Philadelphia and in the process of fixing up his garden arranged
for adequate seating: "Windsor settees and garden chairs
were placed in appropriate places . . ."[9] The best-known collection of these chairs was the thirty Windsors that graced
the east portico of Mount Vernon, the Virginia home of
George Washington. Twenty-seven of these presumably
painted – a common practice[10] – "ovel Back Chairs," also
called bow side chairs, were purchased by Washington from
the cabinetmakers Gilbert and Robert Gaw in 1796.[11]

Occasional references in early accounts of pre- and
post-Revolutionary gardens include mentions, but not
descriptions, of seats. William Byrd II of Virginia recorded
improvements at his Tidewater plantation, Westover, in
1720–21 when his staff "positioned seats" in the garden.[12]
An observer who recorded a trip from Boston to New York
in the summer of 1794 reported that "Most of the houses
have a large court before them, full of lilacs and other
shrubs, with a seat under them. . . ."[13]

In 1804 Thomas Jefferson made a list of "Planned Improvements" to Monticello in which he outlined a purposeful placement of "Temples or seats at those spots on the walks most interesting either for prospect or the immediate scenery."[14] Thus, his plan provided seating from which to admire the view, following an accepted tenet of the popular school of English picturesque gardening. In 1806 Bernard McMahon, one of the proponents of this movement, recommended placing "rural seats" in recesses of a pleasure ground.[15] These probably imitated the forms of English rustic furniture of the second half of the eighteenth century, which were neoclassical types embellished with branchlike additions.[16] Beyond that, the only conclusion possible is that the style of seats in eighteenth-century America, in all likelihood, conformed to the style of the gardens in which they were placed.

Wrought iron was used in addition to wood as a material for seating furniture. Originally made for English parks, Regency or Sheraton seats may have found their way into American gardens. At the end of the eighteenth century, these whimsical seats with scrolling decoration were "produced [and] assembled in simple forms from iron rod" in England. Fabrication in the States is, however, undocumented.[17] In Alice Lockwood's *Gardens of Colony and State,* a 1931 compendium of photographs and information compiled by the Garden Club of America, Mrs. Charles Biddle of Andalusia, the Biddle family estate near Philadelphia, reported and pictured an English Regency seat on the property. This simple seat of reeded strips of iron was reputed to have been recorded in the Biddle garden prior to 1800.[18] A balloon-back side chair with quatrefoil motifs made in Charleston, South Carolina, a wholly different example of early wrought-iron work, has been preserved at Davenport House in Savannah, Georgia (fig. 64). The King of Denmark presented this chair to the Barnsley family in thanks for a large shipment of cotton to his country in May 1819.[19]

In the northern states at the beginning of the nineteenth century a desire to preserve America's rural landscapes prompted the advent of public parks and cemeteries.

FIG. 64

Side chair. c. 1810. American. Wrought iron. 46 × 24 × 21". Davenport House, Savannah, Georgia.

According to the owners of Davenport House, this seat is known as the "Uncle John" chair and may have been part of a larger set. It is apparently an example of early wrought iron made in Charleston, South Carolina. Punctuated by several lively elements, it remains simple and elegant in form. The scrolls on the feet, along with the tulip, or lotus, motifs, are elements of classical revival vocabulary, yet their combination is anything but predictable. The wide rods forming the seat are seen in a few cast-iron furniture patterns, most notably those designed by Karl Friedrich Schinkel in the 1830s.

The opening of Mt. Auburn Cemetery in Cambridge, Massachusetts in 1831 provided a model of landscaping that inspired the parklike style of many later rural cemeteries.[20] Andrew Jackson Downing, interested in all landscape design, explained the appeal of cemeteries: "The true secret of the attraction lies in the natural beauty of the sites, and in the tasteful and harmonious embellishment of these sites by art."[21] As explained in chapter 1 (see pp. 21–23), cast-iron production in America developed after the 1830s and by midcentury was an established industry. Strength, durability, and low cost were the attributes of cast iron that made it an excellent material for outdoor benches, chairs, and tables. Graveyards were criticized if they failed to offer the common courtesy of space for mourners' benches, where visitors could spend quiet, meditative moments. Cemetery benches also served the morbid purpose of providing the necessary props to replay the deathbed scene of a loved one.[22] The need for seating in these emotionally charged surroundings resulted in the development of cast-iron chairs and benches in various and eclectic styles. Soon, owners of private gardens became aware of trends in the parks and cemeteries, and cast-iron seating became an integral part of the domestic environment as well.[23]

Even though the development of the cast-iron trade did not begin in earnest in America until after 1830, it was already well under way in Europe. In 1825, the Prussian architect Karl Friedrich Schinkel designed the first cast-iron garden seats for a royal commission in the Potsdam Parks. Another classically inspired Schinkel design was produced around 1835 exclusively for the Römische Bäder, the Roman Baths, and was then put into manufacture by other Prussian foundries (cats. 4.1 and 4.2).[24] The J. P. V. André foundry in Paris, established in 1833, began to produce ornate art castings shortly thereafter.[25] Around 1840 the Coalbrookdale Company of Shropshire, England, emerged as a leader in decorative and ornamental iron castings. Managed for many years by the Darby family and known for its preeminent use of cast iron in engineering projects, Coalbrookdale hired foreign designers to raise the aesthetic standard of a hitherto uninspired industry.[26]

The products of Coalbrookdale and other English cast-iron foundries can be identified by their makers' marks and encoded dates. For the years between 1842 and 1883 the British had a highly organized registration mark system for metals, not unlike their system of hallmarks for silver and gold.[27] In the 1840s Coalbrookdale was manufacturing and registering cast-iron garden seats.[28] Their registered designs, offered in catalogues from 1846 until the end of the nineteenth century, served as models for many American founders (see figs. 65 and 66). Despite precautionary measures taken by British ornamental cast-iron manufacturers, their designs were copied in America and elsewhere abroad. On

FIG. 65
Coalbrookdale registered design "Lily" S.36, published in the firm's 1875 catalogue.

FIG. 66
J. L. Mott's "Lily-of-the-valley" pattern, plate 15, as published in the firm's 1889 catalogue.

the other hand, many French and Prussian designs were pirated by the British. In America, the need for design protection was evident as early as 1847 when a patent was issued to the J. L. Mott Iron Works for a cast-iron, revolving outdoor "opera chair" (see drawing with cat. 4.65).

Among the important centers for ornamental cast-iron garden seat production were New York, Philadelphia, Baltimore, Boston, Dayton, and New Orleans. Other influential makers and many lesser producers of garden seats were located across the eastern seaboard and in the Midwest. American foundries responded to the demand for cast-iron furniture by picturing their offerings in decorative catalogues. Wood & Perot of Philadelphia (1858–66), one of the foremost foundries of the country, published a design book with approximately three thousand patterns.[29] The period trade catalogues of nineteenth-century foundries aid in identifying popular styles, finishes, materials, dimensions, intended use, and even original prices of this period. The Coalbrookdale Company in England offered its seats in a choice of green, chocolate, or bronzed finishes and its seat bottoms with either slatted wood or patterned iron.[30] Probably in imitation, some American ornamental cast-iron producers offered their seats in bronzed or galvanized finishes with a choice of similar seat bottoms. The patterned iron seat, however, is more commonly found on American chairs and benches.

Matching armchairs were frequently made along with matching side chairs, tables, and consoles in the same pattern. For example, by 1913 J. W. Fiske Iron Works of New York was offering the "rococo" or "Gothic" pattern in no less than five corresponding items in its trade catalogue: settee, bench, side chair, armchair, and table.[31] The eclectic tastes of the Victorians inspired combinations of classical, rustic, Gothic, rococo, Renaissance, and Oriental elements in garden seats of this period. The strength of cast iron allowed designers to eliminate traditional vertical supports in seat backs and feature a Victorian favorite – realistic botanical forms. Acanthus leaf legs, floral aprons, vine-encrusted arm supports, and branchlike back supports gratified the passion for horticultural designs.

In the 1858 painting by Augustus Weidenbach mentioned in chapter 3 (see p. 66), Governor John Edgar Howard's crowded Baltimore lawn was home to five garden seats.[32] One can be identified as a piece in the rustic style with twigs and branches, and four others are easily recognized as being in the cast-iron "grapevine" pattern, a design created by Charles Young in Scotland in 1850.[33] Another instance of the use of multiple seats is found in the garden of Richmond House in Natchez, Mississippi, which even today boasts nine exceptional Gothic-style seats (see fig. 67). As they are marked "Israel P. Morris, Philadelphia" and dated 1842, they can boast a rare survival of the Civil War, and they highlight a unique business and shipping relationship between the riverside cities of the South and the northern business center of Philadelphia.[34] Indeed, between 1859 and 1861, Wood & Perot, the top Philadelphia cast-iron firm, maintained a New Orleans foundry, Wood, Miltenberger & Co., further evidence of the commercial association between these distant cities. The garden at Lansdowne, another house in Natchez, contains a "lily-of-the-valley" bench made by the same company, renamed Robert Wood & Co. after Elliston Perot left. Since the bench's mark includes the ending "& Co.," it was made between 1866 and 1879 (see fig. 68).

The choice of appropriate furniture for particular landscape styles was the concern of Charles McIntosh of England, an eminent authority on gardens. In his 1853 London publication, *The Book of the Garden,* he reported on the use of new materials of the nineteenth century, cast iron and cast stone. About cast iron he wrote that "Metallic chairs are certainly . . . the most durable; and the only objection against them is oxidation, which is apt to soil ladies' dresses."[35] McIntosh's writings, which were extensively quoted in *The Horticulturist* during 1853, were influential not only in England but also in America. They discussed how the form of ornament should be dictated by the style of the gardens in which they would appear. In his chapter on "Geometrical Flower-Gardens" (or the formal, Italianate style), for example, McIntosh encouraged the use of the "Convulvus" (morning glory) pattern cast-iron chair,

FIG. 67

Seat. 1842. Israel P. Morris, Philadelphia, Pennsylvania. Cast iron. 35 x 55 x 17". Richmond Plantation, Natchez, Mississippi. Marked: *I. P. MORRIS, PHILA^D, 1842.*

The 1842 date on this garden seat establishes it as one of the earliest pieces of American ornamental cast-iron furniture. Even though the Philadelphia city directory listing of the Israel P. Morris company does not begin until 1850, the firm must have already been in production in 1842. Two sections of the house at Richmond Plantation had extensive alterations done during the period from 1830 up until the Civil War. Improvements to the garden might well have included the addition of an 1842 bench. Although it has been claimed that this Gothic pattern was first cast in Rotherham, England, by James Yates,[1] the mark on the bench shown here dates it at the same time as Yates's production, and therefore shows an early American awareness of European trends. Until recently, this pattern was thought to be original to the foundry of Val d'Osne, in business near Paris after 1833. The only American foundry known to have offered it was Janes, Kirtland & Company of New York in their 1870 catalogue.[2]

1. Himmelheber, 17, 26, pl. 83.
2. Janes, Kirtland & Co., no. 138.

stone or marble seats with ornate carved backs, and classical flat stone seats.[36] He followed with a chapter on the "Gardenesque Style of Flower Gardens" [a combination of geometric and picturesque styles], in which he advised the use of wrought-iron seats in a manner similar to the Regency style, or rustic chairs, Tyrolean thrones, and bent-iron tree surrounds.[37] For the "Picturesque Style of Flower Gardens" [the informal or English landscape style], he approved seats set against stumps and rustic benches of bent wood.[38]

In 1851, the Crystal Palace Exhibition renewed interest in all kinds of garden furniture and ornament. The Coalbrookdale Company displayed garden chairs with rustic ornament in bronzed cast iron.[39] Although the exact pieces displayed at the Crystal Palace may not have been copied for the American market, pattern books of exhibitors must have been available. The fact that copies of a number of registered Coalbrookdale garden seats turned up later in American cast-iron catalogues suggests a substantial influence. Many styles of garden seats were exhibited, many of which recalled a rustic theme. Other exhibitors entered chairs of wood; one in particular was constructed of knots of woods taken from trees grown in Sherwood Forest.[40] The rustic style, characterized by twigs, branches, or bark, was consistently drawn on for garden furniture from its beginnings in England in the second half of the eighteenth century to its mid-nineteenth-century interpretations by American cast-iron foundries.

In a different vein, John Reynolds of London exhibited an "ornamental wire flower table . . . supported by three serpents of wire," an indication of the emergence of wirework as a new material for furniture.[41] Nineteenth-century French companies were credited with being particularly proficient at producing the novel wire furniture. Using a framework of bent-iron rod, makers stretched and tied wire on chairs and settees by hand in a series of loops, scrolls, and basket weaves. In his 1853 catalogue John Wickersham, the head of the New York Wire Railing Company of New York City, showed chairs and tables entitled "French Wire Furniture" and recommended it as "exceedingly light and unique in appearance."[42]

Innovative materials and forms were the nineteenth-century furniture designer's forte. France led the way not only in wirework but also with other ingenious conceptions that appealed to American taste. Early in the century French companies produced garden furniture constructed of tubular iron rods and decorated with cast mounts. Gaudillot Frères & Roy, located in Besançon in Burgundy,

France, received two awards at French expositions in 1834 and offered elegant, durable, classically derived settees, chairs, tables, and flower stands made of bent-iron rods.[43] The midcentury park furniture of Paris, which was also of bent iron but followed the model of Michael Thonet's bentwood of the 1840s, offered the buyer easy-draining, flat, pierced seats, and a stylish look along with a surprising sturdiness and low cost. Matching tables, used for outdoor dining in the parks, also made their way into the gardens of private homes to complete the set.[44] Another French creation, the spring steel chair, used bent iron as a framework and thin steel straps that flexed at the ends to give cushioning as well as support. Shortly after François Carré filed his 1866 U.S. patent for this chair, Lalance & Grosjean, French émigrés themselves, purchased the rights to it.[45] This firm marked its chairs with a distinctive brass button located in the center of the seat (cat. 4.47). J. W. Fiske Iron Works carried a nearly identical chair in its 1865–70 catalogue, adding a jaunty rocker to increase its appeal.[46] The spring steel chair, produced in various models, retained its popularity in the twentieth century, having a particular spell of success in the 1920s.[47] This may have been because one version had a sunburst back, a pattern that was fashionable in the period.

FIG. 68

Settee. Robert Wood & Co., Philadelphia, Pennsylvania. c. 1870. Cast iron and wood. 33 x 49 x 16". Lansdowne, Natchez, Mississippi. Marked: *ROBERT WOOD & CO. PHILA.*

This "lily of the valley" settee (see also fig. 66 and cat. 4.21) follows a design registered by the Coalbrookdale Company of England, with one minor change in the leaf configuration on the front legs. The settee incorporates a conventionally British wooden slatted seat; American manufacturers generally preferred a pierced, iron one. This piece was produced by Robert Wood & Co.; its presence at Lansdowne illustrates the wide reach of northeastern retailers of garden ornaments throughout the South.

The Arts and Crafts movement of the early twentieth century encouraged the reintroduction of hand-wrought iron for garden seats. Some companies expanded their normal production to include wrought-iron furniture while others specialized in it. The Leinfelder Company in La Crosse, Wisconsin, made graceful, airy chairs and benches with handwoven seats when their industrial factory had slow days (cats. 4.57 and 4.58).[48] Florentine Craftsmen of Long Island City, New York went into business in 1918 and soon thereafter became a leader in ornamental wrought iron. The firm maintained a full-time blacksmith, who hand-forged the leaves, tendrils, and berries that decorated the distinctive patterns that the company made famous.[49] Soon after his arrival from Italy in the 1920s John B. Salterini set up a competing factory in Brooklyn that stayed in business until approximately 1950, offering a line of wrought-iron garden furniture of botanically inspired designs.[50]

The late nineteenth and early twentieth centuries saw a revival of interest in historical forms, particularly the classical, along with American modernization in methods of trade and production. Aluminum, an innovative metal introduced at the Paris Exposition of 1855, became industrially viable after 1886 when an American and a Frenchman simultaneously discovered a method that could be used to manufacture it.[51] This metal, which today carries an unfortunate reputation for looking "cheap," has been used in a highly refined and artistic manner in the manufacture of garden seats. The elegant 1920s hand-hammered aluminum chairs now at Casa del Herrero in Montecito, California, were designed and made by the house's owner, George Steedman, as outdoor furniture in the traditional Spanish style (see below).

Improvements in marble quarrying and cutting methods in America accompanied by a fifty percent tariff enacted in 1890 to restrict importation of worked marble, excluding works of antiquity, furthered a tremendous expansion in all areas of the domestic marble industry (see p. 31).[52] Thus, when marble and stone benches re-emerged to satisfy the need for seating in formal Italianate gardens, they were found readily available at reasonable prices from American

FIG. 69

Armchairs. George F. Steedman, Montecito, California. c. 1930–35. Aluminum. Large chair: 48 x 27". Small chair: 38 x 25". Casa del Herrero, Montecito, California.

George F. Steedman, the original owner of Casa del Herrero and a silversmith by trade, designed and constructed these exceptional chairs of aluminum. While not entirely a new material by the 1930s, aluminum was still an experimental product. In these chairs, Steedman used lightweight, malleable metal to simulate embossed leather. The overall form and ornamentation of the chairs are in keeping with Casa del Herrero's Spanish colonial revival style.

FIG. 70

Garden seat c. 1900. American. Istrian stone.
44" x 74" x 26". Georgian Court College
(formerly Georgian Court), Lakewood,
New Jersey.

When George Gould wanted to convert
two hundred acres of pine forest into a
lush estate with a mansion at the center,
he hired Bruce Price, one of "America's
most able and best known architects during the last quarter of the nineteenth
century."[1] Knowledgeable in both house
and garden structure, Price transformed
the raw land into classical Italianate gardens in keeping with the perfect symmetry
of the house. To find garden ornament,
Gould hired Sir Joseph Duveen to search
Europe's formal gardens firsthand, not
only for objects but also for design ideas,
which he was then to pass on to Price.
With the help of workshops in the United
States, Price ordered copies of what was
not available in Europe. The bench shown
here is one of six imported Istrian stone
benches at Georgian Court that were
modeled after late Renaissance designs
from the Vatican Gardens.[2] All are placed
near the sunken garden near the lagoon
and the bridge in the formal garden.

1. Geis, 99.

2. Geis, 141.

retailers. Samuel Swift writing in *House and Garden* in 1903
complimented "the comparative excellence of honest reproductions . . . such as the familiar bench from the Tiffany
Studios, New York, with winged lion end pieces. . . ."[53]
The seats he referred to were solid architectural pieces, less
ornate but similar in feeling to those in George Gould's
gardens at Georgian Court in Lakewood, New Jersey. The
carved examples imported for the Georgian Court garden
were the most elaborate imaginable (see above). These six
straight-backed, garden seats of Istrian stone – a dense
stone from the northeast of Italy that resembles marble –
with finely carved classical motifs demonstrated some of the
finest craftsmanship to be found. An extraordinary chair at
The Huntington Library and Gardens in San Marino, California, installed in approximately 1910, proved that marble
carvers could even imitate a luxurious fringe (fig. 62).

The regal formal gardens of the country estates of the
early 1900s called for important large-scale garden furniture.
Virtually a work of architecture, the semielliptical exedra in
the 1900 garden at the Elms in Newport, for example,
rivaled its Baroque ancestor in the Villa Borghese garden in
Rome (see fig. 71). Impressive exotic pieces, such as the
"Etruscan" chairs at Naumkeag, the Fletcher Steele garden
in Stockbridge, Massachusetts, satisfied the diverse tastes of
garden owners of the early twentieth century (fig. 72).

In stark contrast, a standard seat for smaller, although
still elite, gardens was a plain, flat stone bench with carved

FIG. 71

Seat (exedra). 1910–20. American. Marble.
55" x 11'2" x 32". The Elms, a property
of the Preservation Society of Newport
County, Newport, Rhode Island.

The revival of historic styles in the late
nineteenth and early twentieth centuries influenced architects and patrons
who built summer homes in Newport.
The Elms (1899–1901), designed by
Horace Trumbauer for Pennsylvania
coal magnate Edward J. Berwind,
was no exception. The grandeur of
the Elms, which was modeled after

the Château d'Asnieres outside Paris,
extends into its impressive gardens. The
monumental seat shown here is one of a
pair, whose style and setting help to unite
visually the interior of the house and the
gardens. Such a permanent outdoor
bench with a semicircular form and a high
back is called an exedra. The Beaux-Arts
style, which favored the ornamental preferences of Louis XIV, XV, and XVI, was
brought to America both by Parisian dec-
orators and by proponents of French
styles, such as Trumbauer and the architect and decorator Ogden Codman.[1]

1. Hewitt, 72–73.

supports. In 1903 a "tiny formal garden" was laid out at the Briars on Mt. Desert Island, Maine, for Mrs. Montgomery Sears with just such a simple "carved marble bench . . . among the tall phloxes. . . ."[54] Perhaps in imitation of the light appearance of marble, a vogue for enameled, white, wooden furniture also emerged in the 1920s: "[I]t is effective at a distance, its lines are good, and it wears well."[55] In addition, during the early part of the century, benches of cast stone made in imitation of carved stone proliferated, "designed with a view of meeting the demand for a simple yet artistic piece of lawn furniture."[56]

The introduction of concrete was not welcomed by such advocates of the picturesque as William Robinson (1838–1935), the British author of *The English Flower Garden* in 1883. He wrote, "As to private gardens . . . one sees cement showing its ugly face."[57] In another outspoken opinion, this time against the seats themselves, he stated, "It is rare to see a garden seat that is not an eyesore."[58] Instead, Robinson recommended old tree stumps or the bole of the tree to "[make] a very good rustic seat."[59]

In the eighteenth century, the young Republic espoused simplicity and practicality in garden seating. After the mid-nineteenth century, however, Americans developed an insatiable thirst for a variety of styles and materials for garden furniture. Inspired by the new products of industry, Victorians decorated their gardens by choosing from a vast selection of patterns and forms. After 1895 cast-iron interpretations of rustic, botanical, and Renaissance revival subjects gave way to intricately carved seats depicting classical themes. Amelia Leavitt Hill, a writer in the June 1921 *Arts & Decoration,* summed up the twentieth-century move toward dignified accessories that compliment Mother Nature: "[A]ppropriateness is the keynote of successful decoration. Nothing too much. . . . And when we introduce our handiwork among hers, we must bring her of our best if harmony is to be the result of our efforts."[60]

FIG. 72

Armchair and ottoman. c. 1930. American. Cast stone. Chair: 35 x 34 1/2 x 29". Stool: 9 x 20 x 11 1/2". Naumkeag, Stockbridge, Massachusetts. Collection of The Trustees of Reservations.

Naumkeag unites the architecture of Stanford White with the garden design of Nathan Barrett and Fletcher Steele. Barrett, the initial landscape designer, created a formal European garden. Later, Mabel Choate, daughter of the estate's original owners, Joseph and Caroline Choate, made improvements to the garden of her summer home with the help of the modernist Fletcher Steele. On the terrace of the house sits this Etruscan-derived "throne" and its footstool, made of pink cast stone. When Miss Choate commented to Steele on how uncomfortable the armchair and the footstool were, he replied, "You're not supposed to sit in them, you are supposed to look at them."[1]

1. Karson 1989, 117.

FIG. 73

Table. c. 1900. Italian. Bronze and various
marbles. 38 x 22" diam. Eagle's Nest,
Centerport, New York.

The eclectic taste of William K. Vanderbilt,
Jr., is reflected in this elegantly proportioned marble and bronze table recalling
ancient classical forms. The triform
bronze base with splayed legs terminating
in paw feet is supported by a twisted
rope stretcher. The top, a mosaic of
colorful marbles typical of Italian *pietra
dura,* is set into a bronze framework.

FIG. 74

Bench. c.1910. Italian. Marble. 21 x 60 x 15".
Stan Hywet Hall and Gardens, Akron, Ohio.

This formal bench is strategically placed
on the west terrace at Stan Hywet,
which opens onto a grand vista that
creates a feeling of visual continuity.
The bench's classical forms, such as the
egg-and-dart motif on the seat and the
rams' heads on the legs, contrast with
the English Tudor style of the mansion
and its nearby traditional walled garden.
Given the stylistic eclecticism that
prevailed in early-twentieth-century
American country houses, however,
the inclusion of this Italian bench is
entirely appropriate.

FIG. 75

Table. Italian. Late sixteenth century. Marble.
38" x 6'3" x 42". Villa Vizcaya, Miami, Florida.

Grand marble tables were part of
the standard repertoire of large early-
twentieth-century American estates.
James Deering's Villa Vizcaya, built in
the manner of a centuries-old Italian
villa, seems a particularly suitable
home for this robust late Renaisssance
table. The piece is comparable in overall form, but not style, to an ancient
Roman marble table dated to before
A.D. 79, also in the collection of Villa
Vizcaya.[1] The quality and variety of
Italian objects at the estate are a testament to Deering's interest in creating
an authentic Italian garden.

1. Vermeule, 269, fig. 227.

CHAPTER 5

SUNDIALS AND ARMILLARY SPHERES

This unusual multifaced sundial was carved from local sandstone, as was much of Stan Hywet Hall. The estate, owned by Goodyear Tire and Rubber magnate Frank A. Sieberling, was built on an old sandstone quarry, which accounts for the substantial use of the material. The sundial serves as the focal point of one end of the West Terrace. It is surrounded on one side by a sandstone exedra, or permanent semicircular garden bench, which acts as a visual framing device. The four dial faces were probably calibrated according to the position of the sun at different times in the year. The use of multiple faces recalls a tradition of Scottish multifaced dials and is in keeping with the estate's predominantly English Tudor architectural style. Surmounting the piece is a celestial globe.

A sundial is not only a garden ornament but also a mathematical instrument. Indeed, the calculations necessary to make an accurate dial require mathematical information. For example, Thomas Jefferson, a devotee of arithmetic puzzles, confined by rheumatism on August 23, 1811, amused himself by determining the hour lines of "an horizontal dial for the latitude of this place. . . ."[1]

A traditional sundial records the hour of the day using a slanted indicator called a *gnomon,* the Greek word for "pointer." The gnomon, or style, is mounted on a flat surface, or table, marked with hour numerals and directionals. "The gnomon that indicates the time of day must slope to the horizontal plane at an angle equal to the latitude of the place, and must also lie due north and south."[2] As the sun passes overhead the gnomon's shadow falls on the plate, registering the hour.

Sundials have been documented in practically every country and century for thousands of years. Histories of these devices have, in general, focused on operational rather than decorative aspects.[3] In her comprehensive chronicle published in 1872, Mrs. Alfred Gatty, an English artist who devoted her life to recording different varieties of sundials did mention the beauty of antique dials by Greek artists, the ornamental features on Roman examples, and the unusual designs of the concave Renaissance dials of Charles I in England.[4] She noted that the complex, decorative seventeenth-century Scottish dials "form a unique and remarkable series, delightful alike to the artist, the architect, and the mathematician . . . [and] were designed with a view to the adornment of the house and garden. . . ."[5] At Glamis Castle near Forfar, Scotland, a monumental Scottish sundial included such artistic features as rampant lions, barley twist columns, and a sculptural finial on a baluster-form multiple dial.[6]

A sundial plate can be mounted vertically, horizontally or inclined. If it is supported by architecture, it is said to be "attached"; if freestanding, "detached." In eighteenth-century America "when only men in easy circumstances carried a watch," vertical dials were inscribed on walls, within gables or over doors, to enable passers-by to check the time.[7] Inclined dials, often used in multiples on multi-faced stone blocks to correspond simultaneously to many locations, were complicated conceits for mathematicians.[8] A horizontal dial, where a flat plate is mounted on the top of a post or baluster, partly owing to its portable nature, is the most commonly used form in gardens. The term "sun-dial" originally referred only to the dial, but in current usage it has come to mean the base and the dial together.

Another device, the armillary sphere, used by ancient astronomers, is made up of a series of intertwining metal rings. Originally these rings represented the celestial equa-tor, the tropics, and other cosmic reference lines to form a skeletal celestial sphere. A simplified version of the armil-lary sphere was later known and used in navigation as the astrolabe.[9] Eventually armillary spheres were adapted to work as sundials, and as such can be classified as equinoctial dials, which can be used to calculate the equinoxes. A metal rod placed through the center of the sphere worked as a gnomon, casting its shadow on a wide hour ring with nu-merals.[10] Although less common than a horizontal dial, the armillary sphere has also become a valued decorative object for the American garden.

Sundials of differing forms were the principle time-keepers in Europe until the thirteenth century, when mechanical clocks were introduced. Surprisingly, in the early days of clocks sundials served as guides to their precise setting. Centuries later, the sundial's former role as an aid to clocks was forgotten and even denigrated as an American writer cautioned in 1902, ". . . a dial is never an instrument by which to catch a train."[11] Seeming to cast aspersions on its once-trusted accuracy, this statement also served as a reminder not to rely on a sundial on a cloudy day. Progressively the sundial became a garden object of predominantly decorative rather than practical or scientific interest on both sides of the Atlantic.[12]

Initially in the American colonies sundials functioned as necessary timekeepers, but gradually their use became more and more symbolic and decorative. By the end of the American Revolution relatively accurate clocks and watches permitted the new Americans to accept sundials solely as ornaments. American sundials never rivaled the European models in stylistic diversity.[13] On the whole, horizontal sundials occupied the central spots in American colonial gardens. They were not, however, well docu-mented, possibly because they were so numerous that they seemed unremarkable.[14]

Typically, the inhabitants of the American colonies perpetuated English sundial traditions, even transporting London-made dials specially calculated for the latitudes of their New World homes. John Endecott (1588/89–1665), for example, a governor of the Bay Colony, lived in Salem, Massachusetts, in the early seventeenth century. In 1630, Endecott imported a rare pear tree from England, and shortly thereafter, a brass sundial bearing the date 1630 and calibrated for forty-two degrees, the latitude of his new home.[15] Years later, between 1796 and 1810, the Reverend William Bentley, a chronicler and pastor of East Church in Salem, visited and recorded the condition of Governor Endecott's sundial and its companion, the 160-year-old pear tree, which had never ceased producing exceptional fruit. Bentley's concern for their historical importance and con-tinued survival peaked in 1810, when he bought the sundial for three dollars from a profligate heir of Endecott's and sent propagation twigs from the pear tree to former president John Adams. Adams was both a friend of Bentley's and a pomologist, a specialist in fruit production. Finally, in 1867, the small dial was donated to the Essex Institute, now the Peabody-Essex Institute in Salem (cat. 5.1). It is generally accepted as the oldest existing sundial used in America.[16]

Where and how was the Endecott dial used? Was it set on a base, on a sill, or operated as a hand-held timekeeper by a gentleman before the advent of pocket watches?[17] The eight holes in the edge of the 5¼-inch-wide plate suggest that it was attached to a surface, probably a wooden post in a centrally located place.[18] Another similar dial plate with five holes punched outside of the ring of numerals, dated 1650, belonged to Jonathan Fairbanks of Dedham, Massachusetts.[19] Since both dials lack a compass, a necessity for a portable dial, and have bolt holes around their edges, they were almost certainly set in permanent situations.[20] Although some eighteenth-century sundial pedestals were made of stone, it is likely that the Endecott and Fairbanks dials were originally secured to now-deteriorated wooden bases.

While horizontal sundials are presumed to have been widely used in early American gardens, few have survived. One exception is an eighteenth-century bronze horizontal sundial that stands outside the main door of Mount Vernon, George Washington's Virginia home (fig. 77). It is presumably the one that Washington purchased in November 1785 and prominently displayed in the circle in front of his house.[21] Washington's mother, Mary, also owned a sundial, located at her home in Fredericksburg, Virginia.[22] The brass sundial plate currently there dates to the mid-nineteenth century, but the stone of the pedestal was cut from a local quarry that was in operation as early as the mid-eighteenth century. Thus, there may have been an earlier dial that was lost or did not survive the Civil War.[23]

Historical accounts provide further information about early American sundials. Another horizontal dial, which in 1906 had reportedly been *in situ* for at least a century, stood within a circular driveway facing the entrance of Wye, an eighteenth-century estate in Wye River, Maryland. Like the device at Mount Vernon, it was probably located by the entrance for the convenience of travelers.[24] A mid-nineteenth-century memoir describes the "old moss-covered sundial" in a turf circle in front of Vaucluse, the Portsmouth, Rhode Island, residence of the Honorable Samuel Elam, built in 1803.[25] A 1931 photograph documents a finely carved square stone pillar as "[t]he sun-dial at Vaucluse."[26] The plain style and central placement of this timekeeper suggest that it was original to the garden, which had been laid out around the same time that the house was built.

This rare survival, a fixed, eighteenth-century American sundial, stands in a turf circle outside the main door of Mount Vernon, George Washington's Virginia home. The simple, octagonal dial rests on a wooden support that conforms to its shape, and both are mounted on a plain round post. Since a 1902 *House and Garden* article on the grounds and gardens of Mount Vernon featured photographs of the sundial with a different pedestal, it can be assumed that the current post is a replacement.[1] In the eighteenth century, gentleman homeowners often owned a portable hand-held dial as well as a fixed one. In her 1902 book, *Sun-Dials and Roses of Yesterday,* Alice Morse Earle asserted that Washington carried "a silver pocket-dial which was given him by Lafayette."[2]

1. Bibb, 461–462.
2. Earle 1902, 143.

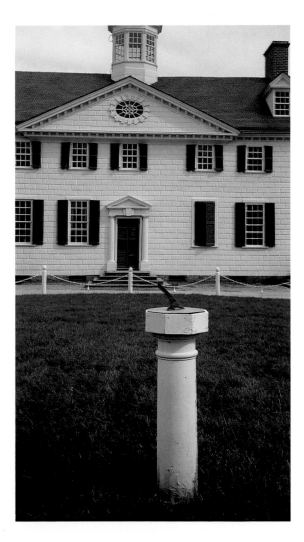

FIG. 78

Sundial. W. W. Wilson. 1844–50. American. Cast iron and bronze. 36 x 9" diam. Rosedown Plantation and Gardens, St. Francisville, Louisiana. Marked: *MANUFAC-TURED/BY/W.W.WILSON/PITTSBURGH/PA.*

American cast-iron sundials are rare. The columnlike base of this example achieves a functional, yet elegant simplicity. The relatively plain dial face, signed by the little-known clockmaker W. W. Wilson of Pittsburgh, is punctuated by a small, circular mirror that reflects the clouds above. The unusual dome cover enhances the overall architectural appearance of the instrument.

The formal ornamental gardens of the larger houses of the colonies and the new republic had geometric layouts, which often incorporated a single central walkway at the end of which would be a sundial or armillary sphere.[27] One such example is the garden at Ashland, the 1806 Lexington, Kentucky, home of Henry Clay. This garden possesses a sundial with a plain round pedestal, which is believed "by tradition" to date from the garden originally laid out in the early nineteenth century by Lucretia Clay.[28] The extant dial was pictured in 1934 at the center of the formal garden on a turf circle at the intersection of radiating paths.

Another well-preserved garden at Rosedown Plantation in Feliciana Parish, Louisiana, contains an unusual cast-iron sundial both with a winter cover and an inset mirror that reflects the course of the clouds (fig. 78). Placed to the side of a central lawn and marked by the maker, "Manufactured/by/W. W. Wilson/Pittsburgh/Pa," this rare American piece dates prior to 1850. Cast-iron sundials are seldom found, but another, thought to be circa 1845, stands in the garden at

the ante-bellum house, Richmond, in Natchez, Mississippi (cat. 5.9). Both these examples are set up in what appear to be random locations, haphazard installations that indicate that their purposes were functional rather than aesthetic. These odd situations are difficult to judge in terms of design, as they may not be original, but the result of tree growth eclipsing the sun, requiring the relocation of the sundial. Later in the second half of the nineteenth century, asymmetrical placements of sundials were deliberately chosen, following the tenets of the English picturesque garden school.

As the English landscape expert J. C. Loudon, who was less rigid than the picturesque garden purists, stated in his publication of 1853, "A sundial is one of the most agreeable and useful of architectural appendages, and in this country is become venerable, as a piece of garden furniture." He recommended a traditional formal placement: "Its situation should always be central, and where it can be walked round and viewed on every side."[29] The sundial would have a different fate in the hands of strict interpreters of the

English picturesque garden. In 1931 a garden expert reported ". . . no English garden was complete without this ornamental time-keeper, but when picturesque landscape gardening came into fashion and the enclosing walls demolished, these interesting relics were no longer the center of the parterre, but were placed on any expanse of lawn."[30]

Indeed, Andrew Jackson Downing, an ardent disciple of Loudon's, showed ambiguity in his treatment of sundials. In his own garden along the Hudson he situated a sundial informally, where it could be "glimpse[d] through the trees."[31] On the other hand, he must have favored the surprisingly formal placement of a sundial centered on a pathway flanked by two cast-iron urns shown in a painting from the 1840s of Blithewood, another Hudson River valley estate,[32] as he used it as the frontispiece of his 1849 edition of *A Treatise on the Theory and Practice of Landscape Gardening.*[33]

If the placement of sundials was a matter of style before 1850, their relocation to the margins of gardens reflected waning interest in them during the second half of the nineteenth century, a period of Victorian exuberance in the use of ornaments. Although the dials were never totally out of favor, they were overshadowed by the popularity of "reclining stags, garden vases" and other garden ornamentation.[34]

In 1864, long after Downing's death in 1852, the periodical he had founded, *The Horticulturist,* suggested a location for a sundial "by the side of some walk well retired from other objects. . . ."[35] In the mid-nineteenth century the owners of American gardens sometimes chose the informal style, and sometimes the formal. The proprietor of an 1856 garden in Cazenovia, New York, Ledyard Lincklaen, did both. Showing an appreciation for the naturalistic style, he mounted a sundial plate on a boulder in his garden, then compromised its informality by placing it to "mark the intersection of the principal paths."[36]

Not until the years after the 1876 Philadelphia Centennial Exhibition when a new sense of colonial history inspired the creation of old-fashioned gardens did the sundial re-emerge as "an icon of the Colonial Revival garden."[37] By the beginning of the twentieth century, entire books, such as Alice Morse Earle's *Old-Time Gardens* (1901) were devoted to the re-creation of colonial gardens, and articles in periodicals specifically encouraged homeowners to erect sun-

dials: "The sundial is an old garden feature, which can well be used in any ordinary American garden, although more particularly suited to the English and Colonial types."[38] To these new followers of American traditions, the horizontal sundial represented the timekeeping choice of their Founding Fathers. The desire to preserve the country's history inspired the formation of many organizations to preserve and improve historic houses and gardens.[39] In 1900, supporters of the Moffat-Ladd house in Portsmouth, New Hampshire, chose to embellish the eighteenth-century house by adding a carved stone and bronze English sundial (see fig. 79). In some cases enthusiasm to unearth historic roots inspired exaggeration. In 1901, Helen Hamilton Shields Stockton, the owner of Morven, the eighteenth-century house of her ancestor Richard Stockton in Princeton, New Jersey, installed a sundial on the grounds of the property. The dial was inscribed "Two hundred years of Morven I record," implying that it had been in place since 1701, when in fact the house itself was built closer to 1754.[40] Clearly, Mrs. Stockton took liberties with the foundation date of the house in order to emphasize its connection with the colonial past.

Starting in the late nineteenth century the influential contemporary English proponent of tasteful gardening, Gertrude Jekyll, brought about major changes in American flower bed design. At the same time, she firmly dictated sundial installations that incorporated a substantial base and transported them from their haphazard locations, ". . . lost in an expanse of grass . . . without any vestige of the stone step or platform,"[41] to more formal placements. The sundial in the 1916 Claude Bragdon garden at the George Eastman House in Rochester was set on a step that would have perfectly satisfied Jekyll's requirements. This is not suprising, as the west garden was based on the garden at Hestercombe House in England, designed by Jekyll in collaboration with the architect Edward Luytens.[42]

Although American taste was primarily derived from England, early-twentieth-century garden designers found sundials well suited to formal placements in Italianate gardens of this period.[43] They were to be sited far from any sign of "modernity," at the mid-point of intersecting paths or in a "small enclosure of close-shaven turf."[44] Photo-

FIG. 79

Sundial on pedestal. c. 1900. English. Bronze and lead. 36 x 14". Moffat-Ladd House, Portsmouth, New Hampshire.

Although the pedestal of this sundial bears a strong resemblance to the Englishman James Gibbs's early-eighteenth-century designs, the piece probably dates to the early twentieth century.[1] The dial exhibits several hallmarks of Colonial Revival pieces, for example, the sentimental inscription, *I stand among ye summer flowers/And tell ye passing of ye hours/When winter steals ye flowers away/ I tell ye passing their day,* rendered in a manner that imitates cursive script. True eighteenth-century dials occasionally do include inscribed mottoes, but they have a more refined presentation than this and are often in Latin. Mottoes of the sort seen on this piece, which reflect the romantic ideals associated with eighteenth-century American life, appealed to proponents of the Colonial Revival. The high angle of the gnomon could mean that the dial was made for a location more northerly than Portsmouth.

1. Strange, 47, no. 9.

graphs of early-twentieth-century gardens record many horizontal sundials in central locations in formal garden plans.[45] In 1921, their ubiquitous use prompted Amelia Leavitt Hill to comment, "The sundial shows danger of becoming, like the pergola, a garden commonplace, but it is one that can hardly be dispensed with."[46]

While the horizontal dial was the most common type in many early twentieth-century gardens, the armillary sphere was also popular. The famous turn-of-the-century gardens of Larz and Isabel Anderson at Weld, in Brookline, Massachusetts, displayed an armillary sphere on a Louis XV pedestal.[47] In the 1920s Caroline Sinkler, the owner of The Highlands, a Greek Revival house in Fort Washington, Pennsylvania, employed Wilson Eyre, a renowned architect

of the day, to redesign the garden. Eyre's new plan altered the picturesque garden installed in the mid-nineteenth century, which had so caught Downing's attention that he illustrated it in his 1841 publication, *A Treatise on the Theory and Practice of Landscape Gardening.* The formalization of the grounds at The Highlands included the installation of a bronze armillary sphere set on a marble post (fig. 80 and cat. 5.19).[48]

In 1928 Phillips Academy in Andover, Massachusetts, installed an extraordinary armillary sphere, significant as a mathematical instrument, an artistic statement, and perhaps as a message to students to appreciate the passage of time. The architect Charles Platt, author of the influential 1894 *Italian Gardens,* commissioned the sculptor Paul Manship to create this enormous sphere for the front lawn

FIG. 80

Armillary sphere and pedestal. c.1920.
English. Bronze and marble. 7' x 22". The
Highlands, Fort Washington, Pennsylvania.

The architect Wilson Eyre re-designed the
grounds of The Highlands in the 1920s.
This armillary sphere (cat. 5.19) is the focal
point of the present herb garden, and is
thus elevated on a stepped brick platform.
The garden itself is surrounded by an
ancient-looking crenelated wall, which
might have pleased Andrew Jackson
Downing. The garden's restoration in
the 1920s incorporated both formal and
in-formal features typical of early twentieth-century American gardens.

of the school (cat. 5.21).[49] The great size of the Andover
example (it measures thirteen feet six inches across), not to
mention its considerable cost, its prominent location, and
the fact that it was created by an artist of the first rank, all
suggest the sphere's significance as a decorative object, as
well as its importance to an academic community.

Eclectic tastes of the same period inspired the creation
of some unusual sundials. The Atlas figure at Old Westbury Gardens, the 1905–07 Phipps estate on Long Island,
was depicted as struggling, eternally bent by the weight of a
ball sundial with hour lines encircling it (fig. 81). Figural
sundials, a form that had been popular in England in the
late seventeenth and early eighteenth centuries, usually
consisted of a cast or sculpted figure supporting a sundial
plate. In an example at Georgian Court in Lakewood, New
Jersey, a bronze dial plate balances in the hands of three

FIG. 81

Sundial. c. 1920. American or English. Carved stone. 6'2" x 21" x 24". Old Westbury Gardens, Old Westbury, New York.

This piece, which represents Atlas supporting the Earth on his shoulders, is a rare example of a figural sundial. It is situated in a densely shaded area near the Boxwood Garden at Old Westbury. The globe dial is marked by lines and numbers that refer to the hours of the day. The now-missing gnomon that once protruded from the globe allowed for an accurate measurement of time. A similar figure of Atlas is found at the Villa Aldobrandini at Frascati in Italy.[1]

1. Masson, pl. 117.

satyrs encircling a leafy post (cat. 5.13). The expanding market for garden ornament convinced such serious artists such as Paul Manship to create whimsical sundials interpreted from traditional forms. The sculptor Abastenia St. L. Eberle (1878–1942) made a true original: a cherub standing on an oval disk leading a tortoise on a string. The string served as the gnomon by casting a shadow that falls along the hour lines on the supporting plate (cat. 5.16).[50] Two examples of a type rarely seen in America, the multiple-sided sundial, were placed both at Old Westbury Gardens, designed in 1905, and in the 1911 garden at Stan Hywet in Akron, Ohio (fig. 76). An audible form, the cannon dial, was the only sundial type that would unfailingly attract attention. It sounded its blast at a specified time, usually high noon, when the sun's rays shone through a glass lens and ignited the gunpowder in a small cannon. In 1906 Walter Dyer, a writer for the periodical *Country Life in America*, reported that the Tomlinson estate in Goshen, New York, possessed a cannon dial that exploded a "two-pound charge of powder."[51]

Early sundial plates used in America were made of a variety of materials: brass, pewter, copper, lead, stone, stoneware, bronze, silver, and wood. Thomas Jefferson preferred "[s]late, . . . less affected by the sun, [which] is preferable to wood or metal."[52] On the other hand, sundials of cast iron were not often recommended, as their accuracy was questioned "due to the lack of precision in iron casting."[53] Possibly the least costly dial plates to make were of pewter as they were cast in molds, and the metal itself, known as "poor man's silver," was available and affordable (cats. 5.4 and 5.5). There are few surviving early examples in any material,[54] but if there were many in pewter or lead, both soft metals, these may have been severely corroded by weather, or melted down to be used for some other purpose.

Early sundial makers came from a variety of professions, which underscored the fact that almost anyone could make a sundial. Guided by extant examples, we know that early manufacturers might be instrument makers, engravers, or metalsmiths in pewter, copper, or silver. Others were clockmakers.[55] Even as late as 1925 an optical instrument maker, E. B. Meyrowitz, offered brass and slate dial plates in his catalogue.[56] Not until well into the twentieth century were sundials no longer made by technicians, but retailed by such garden ornament makers as the firm of Kenneth Lynch in Wilton, Connecticut, indicating the end of the era of the sundial as a functional object and recognizing its true emergence as a decorative symbol.

In the seventeenth century, although gnomonics, the study of dial calculation, was a serious academic subject, the English engravers of the bronze dials of the period beautified an otherwise mathematical presentation with decorative makers' marks, ornate directionals, armorial crests, attractive numerals, signs of the zodiac, and philosophical sayings. Sundials in America essentially copied these English traditions. On a philosophical level, because of its particular duty as a measurer of time, the sundial is traditionally regarded as an eternal presence relative to the viewer, whose hours are numbered. Latin quotations or their English translations on sundial plates have been the subject of numerous books and, in spite of their ominous overtones, contain a particular appeal to many.[57] One fine Latin example reads, *Vidi nihil permanere sub sole* – "I have seen nothing last forever under the sun."[58]

The tortoise, a symbol of eternity, shares the sundial's reputation for immortality. The association, moreover, stems from the ancient beliefs of the Hindu religion, as well as a Chinese belief that the lines on the animal's back symbolize the Elements and a lunar calendar.[59] A now lost sundial in the garden at Ophir Farm, the late nineteenth-century home of the Honorable Whitelaw Reid in Purchase, New York, included a life-sized bronze tortoise supporting the dial plate. The whole piece was set on a hexagonal marble base decorated with bronze zodiacal signs.[60] The signs of the zodiac, from the Greek word *zodios* meaning "figure of an animal," represent the twelve "constellations crossed successively by the sun . . . [and] are valued in gnomonics for decorations of the dials or to indicate pictorially the positions of the sun in the sky. . . ."[61]

While the designs of dial plates were fairly consistent, their pedestals varied according to changes in furniture and architectural styles. Colonial sundial pedestals, when found, are remarkably simple. In the Friends' burial ground in Germantown, Pennsylvania, a London-made brass sundial dated 1778 was mounted on a severely plain granite pedestal.[62] Although the austerity of this particular pedestal's design might be attributable to Quaker taste, which favored unadorned forms, eighteenth-century Americans in general seem to have preferred less elaborate pedestal designs than those seen in James Gibbs's English pattern book of 1728. His "Pedestals for Sundials" were formal, classical forms decorated with swags, ribbons, and other motifs.[63] The designs of pedestals were selected to accord with the styles of the gardens in which they were placed. Thus, simple, unadorned posts of the eighteenth century gave way to the Gothic and the Rococo Revival styles of the nineteenth century. In the early 1900s it came to be understood that "[w]here there is stone garden furniture the sundial pedestal should of course be in the same period style, and such incongruities as a Louis XV pedestal in a formal Dutch garden should be avoided."[64] In 1912 Virginia Robie, a garden writer, recommended an old-fashioned garden as "the ideal setting for a Colonial dial – just as a formal garden with it[s] architectural symmetry is the true background for a dial of carved bronze or marble."[65]

Reverence for the past and an ability to adopt the established cultural traditions of others as their own are natural for a young country without its own ancient traditions. Thus, although the particular aspect of the sundial that appealed to Americans initially was its timekeeping capability, in later centuries its aesthetic qualities and historical associations became the primary focus. As early as the eighteenth century the Reverend Bentley showed an instinct to preserve history evidenced by his enthusiasm for the Endecott sundial. Indeed, the later Colonial Revival gardens of the early twentieth century openly imitated traditions of the country's early years, making sundials a focal point and at the same time appreciating their decorative and associative appeal. In 1906, the garden writer Walter A. Dyer noted that "the sundial is too venerable to be a fad," remarking that "it is a changeless symbol of eternity in the midst of things that live and die."[66]

CHAPTER 6

GATES, FENCING, AND FINIALS

FIG. 82
Detail of gates. 1916. Samuel Yellin,
Philadelphia. Wrought iron. Gate: 8' high.
Stan Hywet Hall and Gardens, Akron, Ohio.

The handwrought works of Samuel
Yellin's studio achieved imaginative
results that were never overly reliant
on pre-planned architectural drawings.
Relatively understated and lacking
an arched overthrow, these gates are
energized by their use of sculptural,
undulating floral motifs, scrolls,
and spears.

Richardson Wright, the editor of *House and Garden,* wrote in 1936, "No matter how elaborate garden walls and hedges are made, they still are lineal descendants of those first barriers set up by primitive man to protect his patch."[1] When actual defense of property was no longer needed, defining its limits was still considered necessary. In early colonial America, such concerns as marking boundaries, protecting crops and gardens from predators, and confining livestock all provided an impetus to install fences. The earliest enclosed spaces in the colonial period were dooryards, informal courtyards extending from the door of the house. Most fences in the seventeenth and eighteenth centuries were of fieldstone, or of wood, whether Virginia rail (a zigzag, stacked-log fence also known as "worm"or "snake"), pale (or stockade), picket, horizontal board, or post and rail.[2] In 1783 a European traveler reported that "[f]ences certainly are nowhere else to be found of so many varieties as in America."[3]

Guardianship, proof of possession, and privacy were of paramount importance to colonists.[4] Fencing was thus considered a significant feature of property, one that was overseen and administered in New England by inspectors known as Viewers of Fences. These officers regulated the existence and maintenance of fences, and fined any landowner who failed to enclose his property adequately.[5] In Williamsburg, the political and cultural capital of Virginia after 1699, fences were considered so practical that many town houses were required by an act of the General Assembly of 1705 to "inclose the said lots, or half acres, with a wall, pales, or post and rails [to a minimum height of four and a half feet] within six months after the building . . . shall be finished."[6] In most parts of the colonies fencing was also respected as a civilized method of establishing ownership of land. Fencing did not develop an ornamental character until there was considerably more time, money, and craftsmanship available for it.

In seventeenth-century America an early ironworking venture known as Hammersmith was undertaken on the Saugus River in Lynn, Massachusetts. Trained ironworkers were brought in from Scotland to produce wrought and cast iron from the 1640s until the 1670s. For the most part, however, the Hammersmith ironworks only produced household necessities, not fencing. In spite of its ultimate failure as a business in the 1670s this operation sowed the seeds of future ironworking enterprises, both by teaching valuable lessons from the economic challenges it had faced and by disseminating the knowledge of its skilled workers. Indeed, throughout the 1700s ironwork furnaces were set up in other parts of the country where iron ore deposits were plentiful.[7]

It was not until the eighteenth century, however, that hand-wrought ironwork for gates and fencing was produced to any degree at all, and even then it proved too expensive for any but the finest properties, public or private.[8]

Ornamental gates in America can trace their roots to English examples, which themselves have Continental precedents. After William and Mary began their reign in 1689, Jean Tijou, a Huguenot refugee, immigrated from the Netherlands to England, bringing with him the knowledge and skills to motivate generations of iron craftsmen. The repoussé ironwork that he was known for, produced by hammering thin sheets of iron from the back to create an embossed relief decoration, was of unparalleled quality. Tijou refined some of the characteristic features of the Dutch garden, namely wrought-iron pierced grills and gates, and introduced them to English parks and private residences.[9]

FIG. 83

Finial. c. 1916. Italian. Carved stone. 20 × 14 × 10". Gibraltar, Wilmington, Delaware.

The garden at Gibraltar was designed by the innovative landscape architect Marian Cruger Coffin between 1916 and 1925 for Hugh Rodney Sharp, Sr., and Isabella du Pont Sharp. This finial at Gibraltar is one of four that adorn the posts at the street and service entrance to the garden. It is exceptional for its high-relief carving and naturalistic display of fruit and foliage.

FIG. 84

Gates and finials. c. 1730–40. English. Lead and wrought iron. Gate: 10'; Eagle: 34". Westover, Charles City County, Virginia.

The wrought-iron gates and eagle gate-pier finials that William Byrd II imported from England were a standard, though refined, form for entranceways to smaller English country estates. An estate in England, Compton Beauchamp in Shrivenham, Berkshire, had a similar pair of gates leading to its Wild Garden, and, more surprisingly, a broad wrought-iron screen or fence like Westover's with alternating finials of lidded urns and acorns extending across the front of the courtyard.[1] Even if the Compton Beauchamp ironwork is not as early as Westover's, its forms reflect the taste that affected Byrd's selections. The monogram W. E. B. in the cresting identified the owner, as did the eagles, which may have been chosen as a play on his name. While English eighteenth-century wrought-iron work is exceptional and rare in this country, extant lead figures as early as these are almost unheard of in America.

1. Ayrton and Silcock, 144–145.

In the 1700s American iron gates, fences, and fence ornamentation for the most part followed English designs, which continued to be reproduced throughout the eighteenth and nineteenth centuries.[10] Impressive gates were at times imported from England, gates, like the still-extant pair at the front entrance of Westover, William Byrd's 1730 Tidewater Virginia plantation, were actually imported from England before 1738 (fig. 84).[11] Governor Spotswood's palace, the most ostentatious setting in Williamsburg, Virginia, is recorded as having flamboyant gates, gatepiers, and finials that may have been imported.[12]

Styles of gates and fencing in colonial America differed radically from country to town settings, with country proprietors selecting agrarian-related barriers and city dwellers choosing decorative boundaries to their property. Westover provides an example of decorative ironwork representing eighteenth-century English fashion as used by an American. William Byrd II spent much of his life abroad, and although he admired the landscape style of Italian villas, he favored the ironwork of England. His plantation's wrought-iron gate

and fence with evenly placed stone finials relates to similar forms at the elegant country seats of England. Westover's simple vertical spike fence gains character from the numerous carved-stone finials of different designs that separate the sections (fig. 85). This level of formality and refinement existed only at the most elaborate country seats in eighteenth-century America.

In the Northeast prior to the Revolution the lawns and gardens of elite city dwellers were elegantly bordered with fencing. The garden of Peter Fanueil, a prominent citizen of Boston, was described in 1738 as ". . . surrounded by a richly wrought iron railing decorated with gilt balls."[13] Even though Boston developed a trade in ironwork in the eighteenth century, a fence of this caliber and sophistication would probably have been imported. Philadelphia also had blacksmiths working in architectural iron before the end of the eighteenth century. In 1760 Joseph Fox, the owner of a property on the northeast corner of Walnut and Sixth Streets, installed a (presumably wood) "ponderous high gate . . . ornamental but heavy" in a substantial brick

FIG. 85
Fence and finials. c. 1730–40. English. Wrought iron and carved stone. Westover, Charles City County, Virginia (see cats. 6.2–6.8).

Situated in front of the Georgian mansion of Westover, this airy wrought-iron fence allows a sense of openness by enclosing the driveway with a minimum of architecture. In spite of William Byrd II's predictably Anglophilic tastes in this case an Italian precedent exists. At the sixteenth-century Villa Orsini, Bomarzo, a garden near Viterbo, Italy, the hippodrome was surrounded by enormous pinecones that alternated with acorn finials, both symbolizing the fruits of the land.[1]

1. Lazzaro, 128–129.

wall. Later, toward the close of the century, Mr. Vaughan, a subsequent owner, replaced the wall with "the present airy and more graceful iron palisade."[14] At about the same time, the Philadelphia house of Isaac Norris, Speaker of the Assembly of Pennsylvania, was reported to have had a garden fence, a distinct sign of status, across the entire front of his property.[15] Around the time of the Revolution the house of Israel Pemberton, another Philadelphian, boasted a formal garden that was bounded by a "low fence . . . [that] never failed to arrest the attention of those who passed that way."[16] No further explanation is given about the appearance of Pemberton's eye-catching barrier. The materials of these fences are not recorded, but it seems likely that wealthy city dwellers would have chosen the durability and status of iron over wood, in spite of the considerable additional cost.

Eighteenth-century Americans also followed the styles of traditional English gateposts and finials. Typical gate piers in seventeenth-century England were topped by stone ball finials or animals holding armorial shields.[17] In Virginia, archaeological excavation in the palace garden at Williamsburg unearthed fragments of a carved stone ball finial as well as some lead globe-shaped finials with swags.[18] At Westover the entrance gates are framed by stone posts surmounted by lead eagles perched on ball finials.[19] In Rhode Island, the house of Godfrey Malbone, a wealthy Newport merchant, was built in 1741. Three years later, Alexander Hamilton mentioned it as "the largest and most magnificent dwelling house I have seen in America.[20] At the entry, the gateposts were capped with carved stone pineapples, a traditional symbol of welcome. These finials also resemble pine cones, which were common Neoclassical ornaments.[21]

After the Revolution and well into the nineteenth century large country estates continued to be built, but there was considerable development of urban and suburban properties. Makers and designers of, and writers about, gardens and garden accoutrements addressed their attention to the burgeoning middle class and their houses. At the end of the eighteenth century, for example, the gardens of the town houses in Salem, Massachusetts, a city known for its beautiful fences, were almost all surrounded with decorative boundaries. Two houses designed by Samuel McIntire, one for Elias Hasket Derby and another for William Orne, both had hand-wrought iron railing edging their yards.[22]

Wrought-iron fencing maintained its popularity for city grounds until the improved production of cast iron — a significantly less costly alternative. The affordability and ease of buying of cast-iron fencing brought about this medium's nearly universal use. As early as 1802, New York City cast-iron furnaces began offering new products that would eventually drive many blacksmith-made fences off the market. An advertisement in the *New York Evening Post* on August 17, 1802, promoted the Cupola Iron Furnace at 104 Front Street in Manhattan, which offered "Cast-Iron Railing of elegant patterns . . . which are handsomer, more durable and much less expensive than wrought-iron."[23] On April 26, 1803, the Phoenix Foundry, making only cast iron at 62 Beekman Street, offered "elegant and Fancy and Plain Cast Iron Railing for Fronts of Houses . . . superior to Wrought Iron."[24]

But even before the introduction of cast iron, wooden gates and fences had been the economical alternative to wrought iron and were often still preferred in rural areas. Almost an art form in themselves, particularly in New England, wooden fences continued to be used in the early nineteenth century in more and more fanciful and intricate patterns. Even an estate as formal as Rosedown in St. Francisville, Louisiana, was furnished with wooden entry gates. In 1857 Calvert Vaux, Andrew Jackson Downing's architect partner, published a design for an intricate gate design combining wood and iron, "a combination which I am led to think may often be used with more advantage in rural architecture than iron alone, which . . . is too suggestive of the town house to be agreeable in the country."[25]

The development of the cast-iron industry encouraged the establishment of foundries in New Orleans, Charleston, Savannah, Boston, Richmond, Philadelphia, and New York City. Homeowners in southern cities particularly embraced cast-iron fencing during the nineteenth century. Handmade wrought iron had been fabricated in New Orleans since the first ironworkers arrived in the 1720s.[26] Following the establishment of the Leeds Iron Foundry at the corner of Foucher and Delord streets in 1825 and the growth of similar businesses over the course of the next decade, New Orleans became a serious competitor in the cast-iron trade.[27] Even there, it did not fully develop until the 1830s, when coal made the industry more cost efficient.

The scale of nineteenth-century cast-iron fencing was selected in proportion to the lawn and garden areas of town properties. The pattern and size of the fence sections, which, in the beginning, mimicked the designs of wrought-iron models, corresponded stylistically with the gates and posts. Both ranged from three to seven feet high and were topped by small finials that were integral to the design of the column. The vertical upright form predominated, with additions and mixtures of numerous recognizable themes: the Greek key pattern and anthemion, the Gothic quatrefoil and pointed arch, classically inspired scrolls, volutes, rinceaux,

urns, tassels, bellflowers, and wreaths. The 1858 catalogue of Janes, Beebe & Co., an early New York founder (1847–59) included in the fence patterns pictured almost all of the above-listed motifs on a single page.[28]

The Victorian love of botanical subjects encouraged naturalistic designs in fencing. Rustic-style branches and twigs were cast into permanent positions to serve as fence components.[29] Wood & Perot, a Philadelphia foundry known for fine castings, showed at least six horticulturally inspired examples of fencing in its 1858 *Portfolio of Original Designs*.[30] In other catalogues flowers, leaves, fruits, and vegetables all appeared in fixed, repeated patterns. Wood, Miltenberger & Co. (1858–61), the short-lived New Orleans representative of Wood & Perot, made the 1858 cast-iron cornstalk fence at Colonel Robert H. Short's villa in New Orleans. This extraordinary fence combines a common agrarian theme with the finest quality casting. Such foundries as Hinderer's Iron

FIG. 86

Fence. Wood, Miltenberger & Co., New Orleans. 1858. Cast iron. Post, 71"; fence, 54". Colonel Robert H. Short Villa, New Orleans, Louisiana.

This whimsical fence incorporates botanical forms to impart a sense of naturalism that was highly desirable during the Victorian era. The vertical posts were fashioned from intertwining cornstalks and morning glory, and crowned by foliate and vegetal finials. Wood, Miltenberger & Co., a subsidiary of the Philadelphia foundry Wood & Perot, was formed in New Orleans in 1858 to satisfy demand for ornamental iron fencing in the city's Garden District.

FIG. 87

Gate. Attributed to John B. Wickersham,
New York. c. 1860. Cast iron and wire. Piers:
7½'. Dunlieth, Natchez, Mississippi.

Composite fencing, an amalgamation of
wire and cast-iron elements, was not only
affordable, but also suitable for lightweight
and airy designs in the nineteenth century.[1] Gates and fences such as this provided a structural barrier that did not
impede a view of the house and gardens.
John B. Wickersham's designs suited the
iron fencing popular in the South during
the nineteenth century almost perfectly.
They may be seen not only in Natchez
but also in Savannah, New Orleans, and
Montgomery, Alabama.

1. Gayle, <4>.

Fence Works in New Orleans, Wood & Perot in Philadelphia,
and Janes, Beebe & Co. in New York produced hundreds
of fence patterns to gratify the Victorian love of diversity.

By the middle of the nineteenth century, cast-iron
fencing had invaded "cemetery plots, dooryard spaces, gardens, open fields, along railroad tracks, bordering sidewalks,
around houses, churches, parks and public buildings,"[31]
but it was not always met with favor. The renowned landscape specialist, Andrew Jackson Downing, had strong
views about the visual impact of introducing fences into
the private landscape, often questioning their artistic value.
Humphrey Repton, the outspoken English garden designer
and one of Downing's many precursors, had disdained
fencing, remarking that "[t]he mind feels a certain disgust
under a sense of confinement in any situation, however
beautiful."[32] In his 1841 *Treatise on The Theory and Practice
of Landscape Gardening,* Downing concurred: "Fences are
often among the most unsightly and offensive objects in our
country seats . . . [t]he close proximity of fences to the house
gives the whole place a confined and mean character."[33]

In 1842 Downing idealized a "light iron fence . . . so
inconspicuous, if painted dark . . . as not to look like a
barrier."[34] John Bartlett Wickersham of New York Wire
Railing Company, invented a fencing style that suited the
discerning Mr. Downing. Wickersham was granted a number of patents, the first in 1847, for a "composite" iron
fence type that interlaced heavy, drawn wire into flowing
loops secured by classically inspired cast-iron components
(fig. 87). The end result was a handsome product that was
both strong enough to be serviceable and simple enough
to be economical. When Downing sought "wire or other
invisible fences" to preserve the natural aspect of a landscape,
it was Wickersham's composite that satisfied him. In June
1851 Downing, as landscape architect to President Millard
Fillmore, chose a Wickersham fence for the White House
grounds.[35] Savannah, Georgia, especially benefited from
Wickersham's occasional sales trips to the South. Such elegant wire fencing as the one surrounding the Forsyth Park
fountain became a popular choice for the borders of town
properties (fig. 6).[36]

Frank J. Scott, the American author of an 1870 work on suburban landscapes, carried on many of Downing's precepts. Where Downing recommended "invisible" fencing, Scott touted "transparent" boundaries. Scott wrote that "For country . . . *that kind of fence is best which is least seen, and best seen through.* But in towns our fences must harmonize with the architecture . . . to be in themselves pleasing objects to the passer-by."[37] Even though cast-iron creations dominated the market for garden fencing, a lesser trade in wrought iron endured until the end of the nineteenth century. A strong voice against all kinds of iron fencing came from an influential source in Great Britain. William Robinson, an English garden expert, wrote in his 1883 book, *The English Flower Garden,* that "the iron fence destroys the beauty of half the country seats in England, and the evil is growing every day."[38] In America around 1900 the critical consensus of opinion went against iron, not in general, but cast iron specifically. By 1913, *The American Architect,* a trade periodical of the day, stated that "the limitations of cast iron are so many that its use in the better class of ornamental work is now nearly extinct."[39]

At the start of the twentieth century wrought-iron gates and fences were accepted not only for their craftsmanship but also as a symbol of good taste and ample resources. Cast-iron foundries continued to offer a few stock fencing patterns to please those customers who bemoaned the built-in additional cost of an architect or designer for wrought-iron installations.[40] The focus of the early twentieth century centered on large country estates where fencing was less important, but where elaborate entrance and garden gates were part of the requisite ornaments for the landed elite.[41] Impressive stone posts and finials embellished the openings to highly architectural gardens. The first significant impression of an estate or garden, the gateway, was expected to rise to the standard of the house. "Tasteful entrance gates are like clothing to a man. . . . the dress of a stranger is our first clue to his character."[42]

In the decades surrounding the turn of the twentieth century, American designers imitated historic precedents from the ironwork of seventeenth- and eighteenth-century England, Germany, and France. Grand Tour excursions

and enterprising antique dealers brought both old and new European objects to the United States, as reverence for European craftsmanship and taste reached an all-time high. The owners of Ringwood Manor, an estate in New Jersey, bounded their courtyard with eighteenth-century antique wrought-iron gates from England.[43] The spectacular gates from Cornelius Vanderbilt II's 58th Street and Fifth Avenue residence were designed by George Browne Post (1837–1913), a Bernardsville, New Jersey, architect. According to prevailing taste for European craftsmanship they were made up in Paris in 1894 by the ironworkers Bergeotte & Dauvillier. In later years they were removed to a location at the entrance of the Conservatory garden on the northeast side of New York's Central Park.

Members of the Vanderbilt family commissioned numerous gates for their respective estates, many of which still exist. One of them, Eagle's Nest, the 1920s Centerport, Long Island, estate of William K. Vanderbilt Jr., claims two imposing pairs, one for the superintendent's cottage and one for the main house, that literally face each other. Huge stone columns at the cottage still support magnificent seated marble lions with shields. Smaller gates were used around the gardens; one example displays the owner's cipher "V." At Eagle's Nest a courtyard gate with perfectly formed wrought-iron scrolls typifies the fine workmanship of the early twentieth century (cat. 6.18).

In the first years of the new century, no one style dominated fencing designs for estate gardens. The wrought-iron uprights characteristic of earlier styles were supplanted by stone balustrades, or, if cost was a consideration, by wooden replicas in place of stone.[44] The Italianate gardens of this period, however, required hedges and walls as dividers, and the introduction of new materials spawned fencing in a multitude of styles. One horrific English fence fashion that was not recorded in America was described in a 1903 book on garden furniture by Charles Thonger: "The garden fence into whose construction barbed wire, broken bottles, and tarred boards largely enter, cannot be otherwise than an eyesore, and however desirable it may be to exclude the neighbors' cats, or even our neighbors themselves, these unclimbable fences should not be allowed anywhere in sight."[45]

In spite of the lack of a single cohesive direction in the design of fencing, the early twentieth century in America produced some exceptional ironwork. In 1906 a young iron craftsman, Samuel Yellin (1885–1940), arrived in Philadelphia from Germany and began a career of extraordinary talent, scope, and achievement.[46] In 1915 Frank Seiberling, the founder of the Goodyear Tire and Rubber Company, ordered a pair of gates from Yellin for his Tudor-style Akron, Ohio home, Stan Hywet (fig. 88). The Seiberlings, who liked to take chances on young artists, requested delivery before their house-warming "Shakespearean Ball" in June 1916. After what seemed to be a hopeless delay, the gates arrived at the last minute. A photograph documents Akron city police officers in Shakespearean costume officiating at the entrance in front of the newly installed gates.[47] Yellin single-handedly put ironworking into the forefront of the crafts of the early twentieth century.[48] His original designs of gates and grills based on traditional ironwork models adorned many American institutions and some private residences as well.

From the early colonial years through the twentieth century, American fencing was adapted to the differing needs of city and country properties. Domestic designers and garden owners embraced a multitude of historic styles, though not always in literal imitation. Indeed, American gates and fences were diverse and inventive, assuming many forms and patterns. The work of Samuel Yellin perhaps best exemplifies the character of American fencing. Yellin designed ironwork for extravagant and humble settings, drawing on the full gamut of historical traditions. Just as his predecessors had in the eighteenth and nineteenth centuries, Yellin responded to the ornamental requirements of a country of great diversity where "fences certainly are nowhere to be found of so many varieties as in America."[49]

FIG. 88

Gates and finials. 1916. Samuel Yellin, Philadelphia. Carved stone and wrought iron. Gate: 8'; posts: 13'. Stan Hywet Hall and Gardens, Akron, Ohio.

These magnificent gates are one of the earliest commissions completed by Samuel Yellin, the most illustrious American wrought-iron craftsman of the twentieth century. Yellin, who despised the repetitive regularity of cast iron, stretched the creative limits of wrought iron to create a look of spontaneity.[1] The stone lion finials with their heraldic shields allude to English tradition, in keeping with the Tudor-style house and walled English garden.

1. Southworth and Southworth, 94.

FIG. 89

Gate. c. 1865. American. Cast iron. Gate: 43";
Posts: 48". Ebenezer Maxwell Mansion,
Philadelphia, Pennsylvania.

This simple gate is lighter and more
informal than many cast-iron fences,
and it is well suited to the suburban
house it surrounds. It is more in tune,
perhaps, with the aesthetics of wrought,
rather than cast, iron work. Its fanciful
treatment, incorporating spears, stars,
crescent moons, and occasional floral
motifs, is dramatized by the light color
with which it is painted; it seems to
glow against the dark foliage behind.

FIG. 90

Gate. c. 1909. American. Wrought iron.
Approx. 8' x 63". Gwinn, Bratenahl, Ohio.

This gate leads from a circular driveway
into Gwinn's formal garden. The tightly
interlaced wrought-iron pattern incorporates the cipher of William Gwinn
Mather, the original owner of the estate.
Although the maker of the gate is not
known definitively, the craftsmanship
bears a strong resemblance to the work
of Samuel Yellin. The gate may have
been designed by Charles Platt, the
architect of the house, and executed
by Yellin, who completed a commission
for nearby Stan Hywet Hall in Akron,
Ohio, in 1916. The lantern, built into
the crest, is a wholly integrated feature
of the gate's design.

FIG. 91

Gates and finials. William H. Jackson & Co., New York. c. 1898. Wrought iron and stone. Approx. 20'. The Breakers, Newport, Rhode Island.

These exceptional gates are some of the most formal residential examples in America. Installed at The Breakers, Cornelius Vanderbilt II's estate designed by Richard Morris Hunt (1827–95), these gates and finials combine the finest wrought-iron work with equally grand carved stone. The gates were produced by William H. Jackson & Co., a firm that completed a large number of architectural ironwork commissions beginning in the mid-1850s. The elaborate central section exhibits a foliate plume surmounting an oval medallion bearing the cypher of Cornelius Vanderbilt and flanked by two urn finials. A similar combination of medallion and plumed ornament can be seen in the gates and screen at Newnham Paddox, Leicestershire, England, which were installed in the first quarter of the eighteenth century and are attributed to Robert Davies.[1] British gates of the eighteenth and nineteenth centuries commonly incorporated a monogram or symbol of heraldry in the overthrow.

1. Lister, facing 101, fig. 12b.

CHAPTER 7

OTHER GARDEN ORNAMENT: OBELISKS, PLANT STANDS, WELLHEADS AND MORE

Elaborate and ornamental, this hexagonal
temple lantern, one of a pair, far exceeds
its simpler granite cousins (see cats. 7.15
and 7.16) in sheer luxury and opulence.
While such lanterns may have originally
provided outdoor lighting, on the grounds
of Kykuit, the John D. Rockefeller estate,
they also serve during the day as spectacular markers at the turn of a garden path.

Historically, the ornaments that Americans chose for their gardens were affected
by technical capabilities and limitations as well as by the tastes of the times. The
selection of outdoor decorations in the eighteenth and early nineteenth centuries
was restricted by limited resources, agricultural priorities, and insular taste. By the
middle of the nineteenth century, however, American Victorians, who revered
home and garden and who loved horticultural and botanical subjects, began to
buy garden ornaments produced by the new domestic industries, as well as pieces
from abroad. By the start of the twentieth century, as travel became easier and
more convenient, landscape designers and homeowners were able to explore new
cultures. Many Americans developed a highly sophisticated, cosmopolitan taste,
selecting accessories with historical and international associations for the grounds
of their estates.

Egyptian in origin, obelisks were often featured in ancient Roman gardens,
where they occasionally functioned as sundials.[1] An obelisk could serve as a single,
vertical gnomon, its shadow marking the approximate time of day.[2] With English
inspiration, eighteenth-century American garden owners developed an interest
in obelisks. For example, the garden at Chiswick, near London, well known to
American visitors, displayed one as a central feature in a small pond.[3] A 1759
English design catalogue, which would have been available in the American colonies,
featured an obelisk in the unlikely Gothic style.[4] An English influence also prevailed

FIG. 93

Obelisk. c. 1930. American. Carved stone. Approx. 38" high. Dumbarton Oaks, Washington, D.C.

In the garden at Dumbarton Oaks, designer Beatrix Farrand (1872–1959) achieved a peaceful and calming effect by designing a series of contained garden spaces that created outdoor rooms.[1] This obelisk is one of a pair placed on a brick wall above and flanking a sculpted bench that divides the Rose Garden and the Fountain Terrace. The openwork style of this piece is nearly identical to that of an obelisk pictured in a 1918 book at Gayhurst, an estate in Buckinghamshire, England.[2]

1. McGuire and Fern, 118–120.
2. Jekyll, 105.

in at least two Philadelphia gardens that are recorded as having obelisks at the termination of walks or avenues: Belfield, the 1815 home of the artist Charles Willson Peale,[5] and Belmont, the 1755 home of Judge Richard Peters, Commissioner of War during the Revolution.[6] Considered part of the essential repertoire of the fashionable eighteenth-century garden, obelisks varied from plain, four-sided, tapering shafts to examples with surface ornamentation of Gothic, classical, or other motifs.[7] Early garden designs made use of obelisks as single focal points. Later, in the early twentieth century, they would appear more often in pairs, flanking an entrance or walkway.

During the nineteenth century, garden designers passed over simple forms like obelisks in favor of complicated rococo or naturalistic shapes. One of the cherished objects of the materialistic Victorian age was the flower stand, which provided a link between house and garden as well as

practical storage space for horticultural specimens. In 1841, Humphrey Repton, the influential English garden designer, and Mrs. Loudon, wife of the landscape expert J. C. Loudon, were each credited with introducing wire flower baskets into the lawns of English gardens.[8] Bent-wire flower stands for porches and verandahs were subsequently manufactured in England, France, and America. Plant holders were fabricated in tiers with easily removable tin liners, and were produced in varied forms: circular, semicircular, elliptical, straight, and arched.[9] The English firm of Coalbrookdale registered a design in 1859 for a pierced cast-iron flower stand.[10] By 1888 the company was offering a number of models.[11] Wood & Perot, the renowned Philadelphia foundry, pictured two elaborate, fixed, multiarmed, cast-iron varieties in its 1858 catalogue (cat. 7.3). An 1871 offering by the Miller Iron Works of Providence, Rhode Island, suggested setting a stone in the ground as a foundation for a flower stand that was to be used in the garden.[12] At times, Victorian plant stand designers in cast iron or metal alloy catered to the taste for the rustic style by decorating legs and pedestals with simulated twigs and branches. Rustic decoration could also be found on such unlikely objects as hitching posts placed by driveway entrances (fig. 95).

Besides flower stands, Miller Iron Works of Providence, Rhode Island, offered a selection of birdhouses that connected architecture and nature in a contrived alliance. The firm recommended these as "adapted to the habitation of . . . various kinds of birds," explaining that they were "made in imitation of cottages, villas and of other fanciful designs . . ."[13] Smaller octagonal versions were reminiscent of minigazebos, while a larger type replicated the Gothic revival gables and attached porches of an actual house in Roslyn, Long Island (cats. 7.20 and 7.20A).[14]

At the end of the nineteenth century in America, designers concentrated less on ornament for smaller gardens and turned their attention to antiquities and other elements for large estate gardens. Stanford White (1853–1906), partner of the prominent architectural firm McKim, Mead & White, forecast the eclectic taste of the early twentieth century. In the 1890s he laid out his own garden at Box Hill in St. James, on the North Shore of Long Island, in a geometric plan enhanced by adept placement of objects drawn from historical sources. His arrangements included "a Greek capital . . . a row of amphorae against a wall, a rich terra-cotta vase, an ancient carved sarcophagus or finely modeled head upon a marble base."[15] Such antiquities as these appealed to American garden furnishers along with pieces adapted from prior use, such as wellheads, cisterns, stone troughs, millstones, and staddle stones or hay armatures.

Acquisitive American collectors avidly tried to assemble assortments of garden ornaments. Seeking innovative ideas, they adapted and converted whatever they could buy into decorative objects for the garden.[16] The relics of Rome

FIG. 94

Flower stand. c. 1860. French. Wirework. 35 x 41 x 28". Rosedown Plantation and Gardens, St. Francisville, Louisiana.

Rococo in its undulating, scrolled supports, this two-tiered flower stand with bent-iron rods supporting woven wire baskets stands on the back porch of the Rosedown Plantation. The stability of the baskets is achieved through the interweaving of wire, which creates a durable holder for plants and flowers.[1] Wire flower baskets such as this were advertised by John Porter of England in an 1839 catalogue.[2] Subsequently, they were manufactured in America by companies such as E. T. Barnum of Detroit.[3]

1. Himmelheber, 61.
2. Himmelheber, 61.
3. Barnum 1881, n.p.

This rustic cast-iron hitching post imitates a heavy tree limb with sawn-off branches. It is appropriately placed along the driveway to the house next to a mounting block. After his horse was tethered to the hitching post, the rider would have descended the stone steps. To ensure stability, these posts always had a large undecorated section intended to be sunk below ground.

and other ancient sites became such status symbols for American gardens that one critic called the artifacts the "second-hand debris from European museums."[17]

In a class by itself, the northern Italian wellhead became practically a requirement for the American villa gardens of the early twentieth century. It has been estimated that Venice had once been home to more than sixty-five hundred public and private wells,[18] most of which were capped with decorative stone wellheads or wellcurbs. Italian wellheads were constructed from blocks of stone that had been hollowed out in the center to accommodate the functions of the well, then decorated on the outside surface with relief designs. Domed, hinged metal lids were attached to the rims for protection. Infinitely more portable than other architectural objects, Italian wellheads were bought and removed by collectors and their agents throughout the nineteenth century (in 1981 it was calculated that only a third of the Venetian examples remained in their original locations). Venice relied on water from wells until late in the nineteenth century, but when they were no longer the city's primary source of water, the merely decorative wellheads were easily sold.[19] When the demand for antique pieces exceeded the supply, enterprising sculptors and unscrupulous art brokers began producing modern replicas that were "executed with dangerous skill,"[20] which passed for authentic medieval examples.[21] The majority of genuine wellheads of Venice and its mainland provinces were carved from the ninth to the sixteenth centuries.[22] They were executed in native Italian stones, including white marble, Rosso di Verona (a red marble), Aurisian limestone, and the sturdy white stone quarried in the former Venetian province of Istria.[23]

Around 1898 in his garden at Blairsden in Peapack, New Jersey, the financier C. Ledyard Blair, along with his architects, Carrère & Hastings and James Greenleaf, his landscape architect and engineer, installed two nineteenth-century Italian wellheads, one behind the tennis pavilion (cat. 7.13) and the other facing the reflecting pool (see pp. 8–9). Both had special piping to enable them to spout

Wellhead. Fourteenth century. Italian. Istrian stone. 34 x 30 x 30". Frederick W. Vanderbilt Mansion National Historic Site, Hyde Park, New York.

Undoubtedly taken from Venice in the late nineteenth century, this early wellhead exhibits many typical features for its type (see fig. 97). Two sides of the wellhead depict amphorae, symbolizing the well's function as a supplier of water. Armorial shields representing family ownership are carved on two other faces of the piece. The upper edge is notched from the rubbing of the rope that would have suspended a container for dipping. The Istrian stone from which the wellhead is made was quarried in the northeast of Italy and was to be used for ornaments in Venice and the surrounding area.

water, exactly in the way suggested by the writer Samuel Swift. Swift's August 1903 article in *House and Garden* recommended "Old well-curbs . . . might often preserve their original functions when transferred to an American country place. . . . Water could be introduced from a spring, or through a pipe, so that garden wanderers might quench their thirst."[24] Besides the two at Blairsden, wellheads, many of them northern Italian, were installed between 1890 and 1930 in the gardens of Biltmore (1888–95) in Asheville, North Carolina; Faulkner Farm (1896) in Brookline, Massachusetts; Bellefontaine (1897) in Stockbridge, Massachusetts; the F. W. Vanderbilt Mansion (1899) in Hyde Park, New York; The Elms (1901) in Newport, Rhode Island; Georgian Court (1901–02) in Lakewood, New Jersey; Longwood Gardens (1907–25) in Kennett Square, Pennsylvania; Villa Turicum (1908–18) in Lake Forest, Illinois; Kykuit (1910) in Pocantico Hills, New York; Huntington Gardens (1912–14) in San Marino, California; and Hearst Castle (1929) in San Simeon, California.

FIG. 97

One traditional form of Venetian wellhead

FIG. 98

Wellhead. c. 1895. Italian. Marble. 46" x 7'7" with base. The Elms, Preservation Society of Newport County, Newport, Rhode Island.

The extraordinary carving on this well-head makes it one of the finest examples of its kind. Its running frieze depicts frolicking putti and baby satyrs carrying grotesque masks and armorial shields. Centrally placed in the sunken garden at The Elms, the wellhead was carved in the nineteenth century after a Renaissance example in the Campo San Giovanni e Paolo in Venice.

Besides purchasing antiquities from abroad, American collectors bought from domestic sources as well. Art galleries imported and retailed objects appropriate for Italianate gardens. A brief list of elite northeast American dealers handling antique and reproduction wellheads and other high-quality antiques such as the example shown here (fig. 102) included: Tiffany Studios, the H. O. Watson Gallery, Eugene Glaenzer, the Adams Gallery, and the H. D. Gardiner Gallery.[25] By 1925 the catalogue of the Howard Studios Collection of New York City offered eight "well-curbs in the Northern Italian style with or without ornate wrought-iron over-throws."[26] Overthrows – decorative wrought-iron arches – are not pictured on any of the medieval Italian wellheads in Alberto Rizzi's 1981 exhaustive study, *The Wellheads of Venice*, and so, in most cases, any wrought-iron frameworks can be assumed to be later additions. Interest in wellheads waned toward 1930, as economic and social changes undoubtedly caused Erkins Studios of New York to offer an Italian and a Spanish wellhead in 1933 at greatly reduced prices from its 1929 catalogue.[27] Even auction galleries sold medieval wellheads. In a 1938 catalogue, the American Art Association of New York City, later Parke-Bernet Galleries, listed three fifteenth- and sixteenth-century examples.[28]

The interest in creating Italianate landscapes in America spearheaded by Charles Platt's and Edith Wharton's writings (see p. 28), led estate owners to embrace the simple, effective forms of the Mediterranean oil jar (see fig. 100). Its application in informal gardens was endorsed by William Robinson in his 1883 *The English Flower Garden,* where a pair of oil jars were pictured framing a marble seat.[29] *House and Garden* in 1901 illustrated two massive terra-cotta jars from the Villa Borghese, a garden which Charles Platt considered the most important in Rome.[30] Not surprisingly, Platt selected a similar unlidded pair of jars to flank a central set of stairs in the garden of Weld, Larz and Isabel Anderson's estate in Brookline, Massachusetts.[31] The terra-cotta jar also made an appearance in Stanford White's garden at Box Hill.[32] It was generally accepted that the Mediterranean oil jar was a standard addition to American gardens of the period done in the Italian style.[33]

Architectural fragments satisfied the desire of garden owners of the early twentieth century to idealize antiquity. The Romans, whose forms inspired centuries of imitation, had originated the practice of displaying ancient objects in gardens. In the mid-sixteenth-century northern Italian Renaissance garden of Villa Brenzone on Punta di San Vigilio on Lake Garda, the owner imitated an ancient Roman custom by placing busts of the caesars and Latin inscriptions in the walls of his rotunda.[34] Charles Platt was aware of these precedents when he incorporated antique marble fragments into the walls of Faulkner Farm, the Sprague house in Brookline.[35] These remnants, generally low reliefs or parts of columns, exhibited the proprietor's knowledge of the ancient world and gave intellectual luster to a garden. The turn-of-the-century garden of Mrs. Montgomery Sears, The Briars, in Bar Harbor, Maine, displayed an antique pedestal fragment with "Latin inscriptions and armorial bearings."[36] In a similar vein, in the 1920s, Caroline Sinkler, a Philadelphia socialite, mounted a Roman plaque inscribed with Latin on the so-called "ancient wall" at The Highlands in Fort Washington, Pennsylvania (cat. 7.18). Freestanding columns, capitals, sarcophagi, keystones — almost any decorative part of a building — constituted the ornamental Italianate repertoire used in early-twentieth-century American gardens.

Less formal, utilitarian objects were swept up by collectors in the decorative enthusiasm of the early 1900s. Lead cisterns from England, originally for collecting water, had functional straight sides and low-relief patterns. Land-scape architects such as Fletcher Steele at Naumkeag in Stockbridge, Massachusetts, found practical applications for these as catch basins for wall fountains (fig. 101). Beatrix Farrand, the landscape architect, added two rectangular cisterns to the top of an ornamental garden at Dumbarton Oaks around 1925 (cat. 7.27). In 1914 John Robinson, a garden designer, chose a granite millstone as a support for a stone urn in a central axial location in the Salem garden of the Ropes Mansion.[37] The most unlikely adapted ornament of all, the mushroom-like staddle stone or hay armature, had been originally used to support hay or corn cribs while protecting the crop from rodents (cat. 7.26). The 1938 auction catalogue of the American Art Association offered one as "medieval English" with the explanation that "these haystacks . . . found on the far-famed Cotswold hills, lend themselves admirably as tables in informal gardens."[38]

The versatility of early-twentieth-century American taste showed itself in an interest in the gardens of other countries. Designers and garden owners were inspired not only by history, but also by international styles as well. During the year 1902, *House and Garden* published articles about Persian, English, Algerian, Dutch, and Spanish gardens. Of particular note was an article by the architect

FIG. 99

Columns. c. 1920. Possibly Italian. Carved stone. 13' x 22" diam. Eagle's Nest, Centerport, New York.

Inspired by such great designers as Stanford White (see p. 115), American garden owners in the early twentieth century made ample use of architectural fragments. The placement of these six columns suggests the ruins of a classical colonnade. One early-twentieth-century writer decried freestanding columns as "much abused in this country," adding that the "American garden is not the place to reproduce ruins or partially restored Pompeian effects."[1] Despite this, William K. Vanderbilt, Jr., clearly liked the instant sophistication conferred on his property by these columns.

1. Holtzoper, 526.

FIG. 100

Oil jar. c. 1850. Italian. Terra cotta. 40 x 30".
Gwinn, Bratenahl, Ohio.

This oil jar is of a type often used in early-twentieth-century gardens. Charles Platt, William Gwinn Mather's architect at Gwinn, probably saw oil jars like this one during his visits to Italy in the 1890s. Originally used to store large quantities of olive oil, these jars were often appropriated for use in Italian gardens. In the early twentieth century, such oil jars were imported to America and used purely ornamentally in formal Italianate settings. Jars of this variety were later retailed by such companies as Erkins Studios.[1]

1. Erkins 1929, 19.

FIG. 101

Wall fountain and cistern. Eighteenth century.
English. Lead. 37 x 70 x 29". Naumkeag,
Stockbridge, Massachusetts. Marked:
E P M 1 7 4 6.

In the early 1900s, eighteenth-century English cisterns were imported to this country to be used as decorative elements in gardens. Cisterns were among the most readily adaptable objects. Originally intended to gather rainwater, they were easily turned into planters, or, as seen here, catch basins for fountains. This early cistern, with its traditional sectioned interior of two vertical dividers, is dated 1746 and bears the letters E P M, probably the initials of the original owner.

Ralph Adams Cram on the temple gardens of Japan.[39] The interest in Japanese gardens and their complement of ornament intensified during the third quarter of the nineteenth century. In the 1880s John Bradstreet, an Art and Crafts cabinetmaker from Minneapolis, returned from Japan with stone lanterns, a dragon head, and two bronze cranes.

According to Henry Saylor in an article for *Country Life in America* in 1909, with these and other ornaments Bradstreet created a small but impressive Japanese garden. Still, the author bemoaned that in its passion for collecting lanterns, bronzes, and dwarf pines, the general public did not comprehend the "Japanese appreciation of beauty – an appreciation that attains unto a deep reverence."[40] E. C. Holtzoper touted the Japanese lantern as a feature of the Japanese garden that could be used "elsewhere if desired" (fig. 92).[41] At Clear Comfort, a 1900 Gothic Revival house and the Staten Island home of Alice Austen, a *kasuge* lantern stood by a walkway as an individual garden element.[42] In the 1901 Brookline garden of Weld, Larz and Isabel Anderson devoted an entire hill to a Japanese garden with stone lanterns and other ornaments.[43] In Ambler, Pennsylvania, Richard V. Mattison, an industrialist who discovered practical uses for asbestos, bordered his long entrance drive in the 1890s with multiple stone *kasuge* lanterns. Eleven of these six-foot-high sentinels remain, guarding the entry to what is now St. Mary's Villa, a children's home.

American garden owners of the early twentieth century were courageous, imaginative, and voracious collectors, who selected a vast array of historical and exotic ornaments for their grounds. The Andersons, for example, laid out ornamental gardens inspired by at least four foreign countries at Weld. Earlier, the eighteenth-century garden makers in America had relied closely on European precedents, replicating ideas and forms from abroad. Changes at the beginning of the nineteenth century, such as the growth of industry and the influx and training of talented craftsmen, established a local trade in American-made metal and stone ornament. However, antiquities from abroad continued to command special appeal for the American elite. Therefore, when American garden ornament blossomed between 1895 and 1940, worldly estate owners embraced a multitude of inspirational sources to decorate their outdoor spaces.

FIG. 102

Wellhead. Sixteenth century. Italian. Marble. 40" x 56" x 6'5". Hearst Castle, San Simeon, California.

Gracing the hilltop home of William Randolph Hearst, this marble wellhead with its unusual boatlike shape was offered for sale by Eugene Glaenzer of New York early in the twentieth century.[1] The rare and unusual shape of this piece does not conform to that of traditional wellheads. Indeed, the writer Samuel Swift said of this exact piece, "And how rare is the shape! One might go far to meet an example of equal distinction."[2] Unique style and masterful carving combined to make it appealing to such a discerning collector as Hearst.

1. Glaenzer, 9.
2. Swift 1903a, 72.

The years from 1895 to 1940 were unquestionably the golden age of garden ornament in America. The ambitions of landowners coalesced with the ideas of their designers, producing magnificent settings decorated with equally lavish objects. The style, selection, and placement of ornaments were intended to reflect the education and enlightenment of the proprietor of the estate. A contemporary description said, "The owner is a man of culture, and possessed of a fine appreciation of art and art values: there was great wealth, without which rare and costly works of art can not be produced or acquired; there was a fine site – for nature had already made the frame that awaited only the creative touch of the designer."[1] To this day, we admire C. Ledyard Blair and his distinguished architects for their vision and accomplishments in creating an ornamental masterpiece on a hillside in New Jersey.

Blairsden and the other historic gardens included in this book represent some of the most valuable artistic resources in this country. In 1904 the American author Barr Ferree wrote that "[o]ld gardens are among the rarest of antiquities, because their survival has meant, in most cases, more years of continuous care and thought....Their survival is hardly short of a miracle."[2] And now, almost a century later, their existence is even more miraculous. Although ornament is infinitely more durable than plantings or the layout of the garden itself, in general the past has shown us that as go the gardens, so go the ornaments. Both are subject not only to the vagaries of fashion, but also to the whims of descendants, financial need, war, weather, neglect, and theft. Thanks to the appreciation and attention given to the preservation of gardens and their ornament in recent years, the richness and breadth of what remains are both extraordinary and reassuring. These historic American houses and gardens give, and shall give, an opportunity for all Americans to study the past through their collections of garden ornament.

POSTSCRIPT

NOTES

1. Ferree, 271.
2. Ferree, 279.

CATALOGUE

1.1

Fountain. c. 1900. Italian. Marble. Rosedown
Plantation and Gardens, St. Francisville, Louisiana.

Incorporating several motifs found in
Renaissance and Baroque Italian sculpture,
this figural marble fountain reflects the
popularity of classical European garden
ornament in America. The three intertwined dolphins are derived from such
sixteenth-century Italian forms as those of
the *Fountain of the Labyrinth* in the garden
of the Villa della Petraia near Florence
designed by Niccolò Tribolo (1485–1550).
The asymmetry and complicated curves
of the shell-shaped basin, however, recall
similar forms in such seventeenth-century
Italian fountains as the *Triton Fountain*
in the Piazza Barberini in Rome by
Gianlorenzo Bernini (1598–1680). While
the Rosedown fountain is not original to
the plantation's garden, its clear European
antecedents would have appealed to the
Turnbulls, the estate's original owners.

CATALOGUE I

FOUNTAINS

1.2

Fountain. Attributed to Wood & Perot,
Philadelphia. c. 1858. American. Cast iron.
The Burn, Natchez, Mississippi.

In the mid-nineteenth century the Mississippi River allowed a special trade relationship to develop between Philadelphia
manufacturers and clients in Natchez.
This fountain may be a product of that
association. Wood & Perot, a Philadelphia
foundry, offered this model in its 1858
catalogue, *Portfolio of Original Designs*.[1]
The Burn, in Natchez, Mississippi, is its
second location, its original site being at
the Wigwam, a house built in Natchez
in the second quarter of the nineteenth
century. The fountainhead, a putto wres-
tling a fish, is ultimately derived from an
antique sculpture in the Vatican collection,
the first-century-A.D. *Boy with a Goose*.

1. Wood & Perot, no. 2.

1.3
Fountain. 1858–60. American. Cast iron. D'Evereaux, Natchez, Mississippi.

Although unmarked, this fountain is identical to a piece offered in the 1875 Robert Wood & Co. catalogue.[1] Southern estate owners often purchased garden ornaments in Philadelphia and shipped them home via the Mississippi River. The fountainhead is of a traditional form while the basin, with its irregular contour, sporadic perforations, and pendulous lobes, strikes a more fanciful note, reminiscent of the fantastic tradition of the grotto. The pan's unusual design testifies to the boundless creativity of nineteenth-century American makers.

1. Wood, 274.

1.4
Fountain. c. 1860. French. Cast iron. Rosedown Plantation and Gardens, St. Francisville, Louisiana.

This elegant, classical, two-tiered fountain was among one of the appropriate additions made to Rosedown in the 1950s by Catherine Underwood, who, out of appreciation for its historic gardens, preserved this antebellum plantation. Having traveled extensively abroad, Martha and Daniel Turnbull, the original owners of the 1835 house and grounds, particularly admired European garden ornament. Not surprisingly, Mrs. Underwood chose a French fountain for the small garden near her toolshed. The 1855 catalogue of C. A. Villard of Lyon, France, pictured the upper section of the bowl, baluster, and spout of this model in Plate 45 and illustrated the lower bowl and putti-caryatid baluster in Plate 24.[1] In the second half of the nineteeenth century it was fairly typical for customers buying cast iron to select and combine components according to their own taste.

1. Villard, 45.

1.5
Fountain. Henry Debiller. c. 1875. American. Cast iron and cast stone. Steves Homestead, San Antonio Conservation Society, San Antonio, Texas. Marked: *MANUFACTURED BY HENRY DEBILLER*.

According to family tradition, this fountain was purchased by Edward Steves at the Philadelphia Centennial Exhibition of 1876 and was installed at the Steves's grand Victorian home in 1878, just one year after the house was completed (see pp. 26–27). The four dolphin spouts at the base of the rock-work baluster are reminiscent of sixteenth-century Italian designs, in which intertwined dolphins formed the stems or pedestals of a variety of objects. Although the piece carries a bronze plaque with the maker's label, the artist is virtually unknown. Henry Debiller may have been a designer or vendor working for a larger foundry. Indeed, the overall style of the fountain is similar to, but perhaps more crude than, pieces produced at the same time by such firms as Robert Wood & Co.[1]

1. See Wood, 274–277, nos. 1, 2, 3, and 4, for examples of cherubs holding fish.

1.6

Fountain. J. L. Mott Iron Works, New York. Ground basin. J. W. Fiske Iron Works, New York. c. 1880–85. American. Cast iron. Private collection. Marked: *J. L. MOTT* (fountain); *J. W. FISKE N.Y.* (ground basin).

This two-tiered fountain illustrates the Victorian taste for the eclectic. In 1905, the J. L. Mott Iron Works catalogue reproduced these same pans, balusters, and base in a number of combinations. The present configuration as a whole, however – a simple tazza-form pan, a "gargoyle octagon pan," and balusters set on a Renaissance base – does not appear in the catalogue.[1] The form shown here resulted from the preferences of the original client and the availability of components. The fountain's present placement in a basin by J. W. Fiske Iron Works, is consistent with its style.

1. Mott c. 1905.

1.7

Font. Early twentieth century. Italian. Marble. Morris Arboretum, Philadelphia, Pennsylvania.

The form of this spectacular, carved marble font, like those of its ecclesiastical cousins, derives from the tazza, a low, shallow bowl. In spite of its liturgical origins, the word "font" is still used informally to refer to a solid shallow bowl, mounted on a tall decorative baluster and set on an ornamented base of square or triangular shape. Fonts of religious origin are rare in American gardens, one exception being the baptismal font at Filoli in Woodside, California, which is used as a garden decoration. The Morris Arboretum at the University of Pennsylvania was originally built in 1887 as Compton, the summer home of John Morris and his sister Lydia Morris. In 1932, it became the Morris Arboretum.

1.8

Fountain. c. 1905. Italian. Marble. Private collection.

This elegant, two-tiered fountain is impressive both for the refinement of its carving and for its unusual height of more than eight feet. The upper tazza is curvilinear and freeform, while the lower tazza is rigidly defined, a combination of styles that gives the whole balance without redundance. A similar union of unlike qualities, equally successful, can be seen in the relationship between the two tiers of the Janes, Beebe & Co. fountain in Savannah's Forsythe Park (fig. 6). Here the putto and fish at the top, the central baluster of intertwined dolphins, and the lower baluster decorated with acanthus leaves are all part of the standard vocabulary of Italianate fountains.

1.9

Fountain. Early twentieth century. Italian.
Marble. Huntington Library Art Collections and
Botanical Gardens, San Marino, California.

This refined tazza-form fountain's wide
mouth, triform base, and tall baluster
recall the form of a liturgical font. Its
location at the center of a fountain
pool, however, lessens its formal impact.
The surface decoration consists of a
variety of fine classical details, including
gadrooning and a guilloche pattern
around the bowl. In 1841, Andrew Jackson
Downing wrote, "[w]eeping, or *Tazza
Fountains,* as they are called, are simple
and highly pleasing objects. . . ."[1]

1. Downing 1841, 471.

1.10

Birdbath. c. 1930. American. Composition
stone. Dumbarton Oaks, Washington, D.C.

The landscape gardener Beatrix Farrand
and her client Mildred Bliss chose this
simple birdbath to stand in the garden
at Dumbarton Oaks. Its unornamented
design leans toward the modern, with
straight, clean lines and only a slight
suggestion of a wave at the basin's lip.
Birdbaths are not a new addition to
gardens by any means, indeed, a second-
century-A.D. fresco in the atrium of the
House of the Vettii in Pompeii depicts
a birdbath.[1] However, the ancients'
intentions toward birds were not always
benign; the Romans netted some varieties
to eat.[2] Nearly two millennia later, garden
owners have relinquished the Roman
taste for lark, and the image of feathered
creatures as pests, and welcome their
presence as another delightful feature
of gardens.

1. Nichols, 399.
2. Masson, 17.

1.11

Fountain. c. 1900–50. American. Lead. Private
collection.

The triple-swan base of this fountain with
a single tazza repeats an earlier Coalbrookdale Company design. In its 1875 catalogue, the English firm offered the same
triform base in cast iron, although paired
with two tiers of bowls and elaborate
balusters.[1] A replica of the fountain shown
here is found in the garden of Caramoor,
the early-twentieth-century home of
Walter Rosen in Katonah, New York.
The same triple-swan base, offered in lead
by the Erkins Studios in its circa 1963
catalogue, was probably also produced
earlier. In that catalogue, the fountain is
pictured in a two-tiered version with a
cupid serving as the uppermost baluster.[2]

1. Coalbrookdale 1875, Section III, 277–279;
nos. 18, 27, 28, and 30.
2. Erkins c. 1963, 9.

1.12

Fountain. 1940–50. English. Cast stone. Private collection.

The playful elements of this two-tiered fountain evoke a lively sense of movement. The lower bowl is supported by three putti – reminiscent of the French rococo paintings of François Boucher – who dance upon the circular stepped base. The rococo theme is continued by the undulating edges of the shell-like bowls, which cause the water to splash unevenly over the sides of the fountain.

1.13

Birdbath. Mid-twentieth century. American. Cast iron. Private collection.

This draped figure supporting a shell is related to a long tradition of fountain decoration in which a figure supports a resevoir to catch or hold water. The birdbath's placement shows its flexibility as a garden decoration. In an informal setting, it may stand attractively on the edge of a carefully groomed landscape, as it does here; it may also be used in a more formal context, for example, at the center of a small geometric garden.

1.14

Wall fountain. c. 1898–1900. American. Carved stone. St. Joseph's Villa (formerly Blairsden), Peapack, New Jersey.

This ram's-head fountain is part of a large semi-circular wall supporting one of the entrance gates to C. Ledyard Blair's spectacular estate. The landscape architect James Greenleaf, originally a civil engineer, is assumed to have collaborated with the architects Carrère & Hastings on the accessing, storage, and piping of water to fountains and pools in remote parts of the clifflike terrain of the more than five-hundred-acre grounds. This particular gate stood at least twenty feet above the bed of the north branch of the Raritan river, which the architects dammed to create a mile-long lake, which provided visual interest, as well as a reliable water supply for the many fountains. The construction of Blairsden took a mere eighteen months, with workers aided by a specially constructed funicular that transported materials up the treacherous hillside.

1.15

Wall fountain. J. L. Mott Iron Works, New York. 1860–80. Cast iron. Collection Elizabeth Street. Marked: *J. L. MOTT IRON WORKS*.

This wall fountain is striking for its use of simple, repeated elements and its radiating lobes set within an architectural framework. The overall aesthetic of the fountain is remarkably reminiscent of vernacular Mexican architecture and plaza fountains. Another correlation can be seen in the wall fountains produced by Walter MacFarlane & Co. at the Saracen Foundry in Glasgow, Scotland. Indeed, a piece nearly identical to this one is pictured in the company's 1882 catalogue.[1]

1. MacFarlane, section 13: Fountains, n.p.

1.16

Wall fountain. Early twentieth century. Italian. Carved stone. Frederick W. Vanderbilt Mansion National Historic Site, Hyde Park, New York.

The water of this three-tiered marble fountain originally flowed from the three masks and the two additional openings in its middle level to fall into the basin below. Set thus along a horizontal axis, the five spouts emphasized the fountain's width, creating the appearance of a gentle waterfall. As with many wall fountains, dramatic and elaborate effects were forfeited here in favor of a subtle aesthetic statement. The use of sphinxes as supports, typical of Roman ornament, and the scrolled palmettes at the apex and at the lower flanks of the arch enliven an otherwise static treatment.

1.17

Wall fountain. Early twentieth century. American. Marble. Eagle's Nest, Centerport, New York.

Located at the William K. Vanderbilt estate on Long Island, this wall fountain is set beneath a large vertical sundial of such size that it dwarfs the substantial water feature below it. The fountain comprises a mask, perhaps representing Zeus or the West Wind, a massive catch basin, and an architectonic pedestal. The mask, which encloses a waterspout, is oddly applied to a partial urn.

1.18

Wall fountain. Early twentieth century. American. Carved stone. Cistern. 1776. English. Lead. Edsel Ford House, Grosse Pointe, Michigan.

In twentieth-century garden decoration, garden planners occasionally found new uses for traditional ornaments and used them without regard to stylistic consistency. The rose garden at the Edsel Ford House, Mrs. Ford's pride and joy, contains this delightful combination of an English lead cistern, which dates to the third quarter of the eighteenth century, and a wall fountain that recalls early-sixteenth-century Italian examples. This style of formal decoration was not in keeping with the work of the landscape architect Jens Jensen, who laid out the plantings on the sixty-five-acre estate. His modernist landscaping concept, known as the Prairie Style, was independent of reference to architecture.[1]

1. Griswold and Weller, 263; and Melanie L. Simo, "Regionalism and Modernism: Some Common Roots," in *Keeping Eden,* 48.

1.19

Fountain. Early twentieth century. Italian. Marble. Private collection.

This fountain, similar in form to a wall fountain but actually freestanding, incorporates a variety of decorative motifs result in a lively concoction. The finely carved lion's mask, the most prominent visual feature, serves as the waterspout. While classical in detail, the piece combines so many elements that its overall impression is one of opulence rather than refinement.

1.20

Wall fountain. c. 1930. American. Lead and carved stone. Dumbarton Oaks, Washington, D.C.

A splendid example of a fountain mask, this work is located in the gardens at Dumbarton Oaks, which were designed by Beatrix Farrand. Although the mask does not strictly conform to traditional images of Poseidon, or Neptune, the cattails, which are echoed at the base of the wall fountain, suggest rivers and wetlands, which fell within the sea god's kingdom. The rays of sunlight, however, may allude to Apollo, the Greek god of music, song, and light, indicating instead a modern representation of that mythological deity.

1.21

Wall fountain. c. 1950–60. Cast stone. Private collection.

This fountain, designed to be placed against a wall, appears to be a combination of individual elements produced by Kenneth Lynch & Sons, Inc. The cherub figure and basin are shown as item no. 2050 in the company's 1974 catalogue,[1] and they have been placed on a pedestal similar, but not identical, to many offered in the same publication. The piece shown here is of cast stone, a medium that can be easily identified by its softened edges.

1. Kenneth Lynch 1974, 180.

1.22

Fountain. J. W. Fiske Iron Works, New York. 1870–1910. American. Cast iron. Private collection. Marked: *J. W. FISKE MANUF. NEW YORK.*

This idyllic representation of two children beneath an umbrella appeared in a J. W. Fiske Iron Works catalogue published between 1908 and 1912.[1] The design undoubtedly dates to four decades earlier, when the Victorian preoccupation with children and other innocent, bucolic subjects greatly affected the styles of statues and fountains. In the catalogue of 1908–12, the fountain was offered in zinc, paired with a "Frog and Turtle Ground Basin," as shown. J. L. Mott Iron Works also produced this fountain, titled "Out of the Rain."[2] Companies such as Fiske and Mott may have been familiar with the works of F. & A. Jacquier of France, who featured a similar figural group in a trade catalogue published around 1900.[3]

1. Fiske c. 1908–1912, pl. 381.
2. Mott c. 1905a, pl. 453–H.
3. Jacquier, pl. 23.

1.23

Fountain. Mathurin Moreau (1822–1912). Barbezat & Cie, Val d'Osne, France. c. 1880. French. Cast iron. Private collection. Marked: *BARBEZAT & CIE/VAL D'OSNE/FRANCE.*

For the design of this group, which is featured in the Val d'Osne trade catalogue of c. 1870, Mathurin Moreau adopted a decorative vocabulary intended to evoke the exotic.[1] The boy wears a "barbaric" headband and heavily beaded necklace, and the goose or bird that such a figure traditionally embraces has been replaced by an alligator, which the boy appears to treat with respect.

1. Société Anonyme des Hauts-Fourneaux, pl. 582, no. 15.

1.24

La Source à L'Enfant. Mathurin Moreau (1822–1912). J. J. Ducel et Fils, Paris, France. c. 1870. French. Cast iron. Private collection. Marked: *J. J. DUCEL ET FILS, PARIS.*

Mathurin Moreau, the creator of many monuments and a number of statues for the garden, was one of France's most distinguished sculptors. His classically inspired standing figure pours liquid into a kylix held up by a child at her feet, a device that immediately declares the function of the group as a fountain piece. J. J. Ducel et Fils, the firm that cast the piece, was one of the preeminent foundries of nineteenth-century France (see drawing below). While working in Paris, Ducel produced numerous cast-iron objects for architectural and interior use, as well as for gardens.[1]

1. Société Anonyme des Hauts-Fourneaux 2, pl. 599, no. 558.

1.25

Unfortunate Boot. J. L. Mott Iron Works, New York. c. 1900. American. Polychromed zinc. Collection The Garden Antiquary. Marked: *J. L. MOTT IRON WORKS.*

Around the turn of the twentieth century American homeowners rediscovered the use of genre figures in gardens.[1] Following a tradition that dated back to ancient Rome, sculptors rendered peasant children, like this fountain figure, with candor, and often, humor. Water for the fountain was intended to spring from the boy's boot while his face reflected fascination with the hole in his worn footwear. A J. L. Mott Iron Works catalogue published in 1905 illustrated this model standing on a naturalistic rock-work base in the center of a ground basin.[2]

1. Lazzaro, 150–151.
2. Mott 1905, pl. 463–H.

1.26

Frog Fountain. Janet Scudder (1875–1940). Roman Bronze Works, New York. 1901. American. Bronze. Private collection. Inscribed: *JANET SCUDDER.* Marked: *ROMAN BRONZE WORKS, N.Y.*

Janet Scudder, along with a number of other early-twentieth-century American sculptors, including her teacher, Frederick MacMonnies, created many statues for garden settings.[1] *Frog Fountain,* perhaps Scudder's best known work, was admired by the architect Stanford White and other American collectors. The statue was available from the Ferargil Galleries in both 30-inch and 37-inch-tall casts – about the size of the version of the work now in The Metropolitan Museum of Art – and in a smaller, around 14-inch, form, like the one illustrated here.[2]

1. Michele H. Bogart, "American Garden Sculpture: A New Perspective," in *Fauns and Fountains,* 13.
2. Ferargil; Bogart, "American Garden Sculpture," in *Fauns and Fountains,* 14.

1.27

Fountain figure. Edward McCartan (1879–1947). Early twentieth century. American. Lead. Private collection.

Many critics have likened Edward McCartan's elegant designs to eighteenth-century French sculpture.[1] This fountain subject, however, may have an Italian heritage. A similar shell-bearing triton, located in the upper garden of the Villa Farnese at Caprarola, was featured in Edith Wharton's 1904 publication, *Italian Villas and Their Gardens.*[2] Since the figure is freestanding and without a catch basin, McCartan probably intended water to fall from the shell's scalloped edge into a basin or pool.

1. *Brookgreen Gardens,* 230.
2. Wharton 1904, <129>.

1.28

Fountain. c. 1905. American. Cast iron. Private collection.

Fountains of this exact type, and other pieces incorporating calla-lily jets, were offered in the catalogue of the J. W. Fiske Iron Works published between 1908 and 1912.[1] The design was certainly used by other firms as well, for similar fountains by a number of foundries are known. For example, several versions of the calla-lily fountain appear in the J. L. Mott Iron Works catalogue of circa 1905, where the "lily group" is variously shown with a "small crane base," a "dolphin base," a "vine and leaf scroll," and other elements in combination.[2] J. L. Mott Iron Works offered this piece alone, or as an ornament for the tops of one-, two-, and three-tiered tazza fountains.

1. Fiske c. 1908–1912, nos. 275, 281, 657, 658, 660.
2. Mott c. 1905a, pls. 316–H, 391–H, 415–H, 437–H, and 443–H.

1.29

Fountain. Rafaello Romanelli (1856–1928). Early twentieth century. Italian. Bronze. Cranbrook House, Bloomfield Hills, Michigan.

The putto on this fountain is raising his hands to protect his face from a jet of water, which would have spouted from the (now lost) figure of a frog crouched on the edge of the bowl. A popular subject, this statue was available at the Barzanti Gallery in Florence, which reproduced traditional sculptures for export.

1.30

Fountain. Attributed to Amerige Brunetti. Early twentieth century. Italian. Marble. Private collection.

Standing only forty inches tall, this small marble fountain is nevertheless remarkably grand in its effect. It was reputedly carved by Amerige Brunetti, a Carrara-born Italian sculptor about whom little is known. Water is piped through the frog's mouth, from which it flows into the shell basin below. The fact that the fountain was discovered in the basement of an estate in New Rochelle, New York, where it had been kept closeted in an unopened crate brought from Italy in the early years of the twentieth century, explains its pristine appearance.

1.31

The Water Goddess. Willard Dryden Paddock (1873–1956). 1916. American. Bronze. Stan Hywet, Akron, Ohio.

This bronze group in Stan Hywet's garden, designed by Ellen Biddle Shipman, is a particularly fine example of early-twentieth-century American fountain sculpture. Many artists, including Janet Scudder, Harriet Frishmuth, and Willard Dryden Paddock, among others, turned their creative energies to ornament for the garden. Paddock's nude goddess pouring water over two babies is a characteristic subject for this period, when sculptors often represented naked figures, many of them female, to express innocence or joyful freedom.[1]

1. Michele Bogart, "American Garden Sculpture: A New Perspective," in *Fauns and Fountains,* 10.

1.32

Fountain. Early twentieth century. American. Carved stone. Private collection.

Three satyrs seated on a rock-work base blow horns that serve as water jets when the fountain operates. Thematically, satyrs are at home in the garden, since they are traditionally associated with the rustic pursuits of woodlands. These half-human, half-animal spirits personify gluttony, revelry, and celebration, and they are also intrinsically linked to the Greek god Pan, a popular subject for fountains throughout the twentieth century both in America and abroad.

1.33

Putto with a Fish. After Andrea del Verrocchio (1435–88). c. 1920. American. Bronze. Private collection.

Around 1470, Andrea del Verrocchio sculpted the original of this widely replicated group for the fountain of Lorenzo de' Medici's villa at Careggi, near Florence. Nearly a century later, Giorgio Vasari reported that Cosimo de' Medici had the figure moved to the fountain, designed by Vasari himself, in the courtyard of the Palazzo della Signoria in Florence, where a modern replacement may still be seen.[1] The figure remains among the most popular modern garden ornaments.

1. Pope-Hennessy, 385.

1.34

Wild Flower. Edward Berge (1876–1924). c. 1920. American. Bronze. Private collection.

Wild Flower, a little girl wearing a lily hat with her head curiously tilted forward, was Edward Berge's signature character. Standing on a flattened fern frond with cattails acting as the waterspouts, Wild Flower emulates the innocent, cherubic pose that was increasingly popular with garden artists in the early 1920s.

I.35

Fountain. J. W. Fiske Iron Works, New York. c. 1927. American. Zinc. Dumbarton Oaks, Washington, D.C. Marked: *J. W. FISKE IRON WORKS, 70–80 PARK PLACE, NEW YORK.*

The twenty-seven-acre garden at Dumbarton Oaks (1922–23) was created for Robert and Mildred Bliss by Beatrix Farrand (1872–1959), a landscape gardener and niece of the writer Edith Wharton. The liberal use of ornament throughout the garden reflects both the Blisses' keen interest in the objects, and Ferrand's gift for appropriate placement.[1] This zinc fountain, made by the J. W. Fiske Iron Works, was offered in the company's 1927 catalogue, *Ornamental Iron and Zinc Fountains,* as a component of a larger piece called "Fish Boy."[2] The fact that zinc does not corrode in harsh weather made it a popular material for fountain figures in the late nineteenth and early twentieth centuries.

1. McGuire and Fern, 122.
2. Fiske c. 1927, 11.

I.36

Fountain. Early to mid-twentieth century. American. Lead. Collection F. J. Carey, III.

This figure of Pan has been produced by a number of American makers since the early decades of the twentieth century. It appeared as a "Piping Boy" in the Kenneth Lynch & Sons, Inc. catalogue of 1979. Pan, a god of green pastures and herdsmen, was thought by the ancient Greeks to wander the countryside beguiling listeners with the sweet notes of his pipe. Such a figure was a logical addition to a garden. The renowned sculptor Frederick William MacMonnies cast his *Pan of Rohallion* (named after the house in New Jersey for which the original version was designed) in 1894,[1] which resembles this piece in its overall positioning of the figure and the attenuated curves of the form. In MacMonnies' fountain, and in the work shown here as well, water flows from Pan's pipes, recalling the ancient god's association with regeneration and fertility.

1. *Fauns and Fountains,* pl. 17.

I.37

Fountain. Mid-twentieth century. American. Cast stone. Private collection.

In classical mythology, the Danaïds (the daughters of Danaus) were doomed to Hades for the murder of their husbands. There they were sentenced to eternally pour water from vases into a broken cistern that could never be filled.[1] This figure is probably an interpretation of this mythological subject. The lack of sharpness in the rendering of the form is characteristic of composition stone of the mid- to late-twentieth century.

1. Murray, 98.

2.2

Statue. Late eighteenth century. English. Lead.
Private collection.

Juno, both wife and sister to Jupiter, was the goddess of wives and childbirth, but was better known as the Queen of Olympus. Her companion is the sacred peacock, who may also be shown pulling the goddess's chariot. The proportions of the female form in this representation – small in the torso and wide through the hips – are those preferred by eighteenth-century figural sculptors.

2.1

River goddess. Pieter van Baurscheit the Elder (1669–1728). c. 1720. Flemish. Gritstone. Private collection. Signed: *PVB.*

The sculptor has defined the volumes of this figure with skillfully carved drapery and has masterfully rendered the visual texture of wet, heavy fabric. The figure's principal attribute, a sheaf of wheat, suggests that she is a river goddess, since riparian divinities such as those in the Piazza del Campidoglio in Rome hold sheaves of grain in addition to their watery attributes. Although it is not entirely certain which river she represents, the ancient barge, the farmer's spade, and the *orbis mundi* – a symbol of the earth – indicate the Nile and the abundance of its delta. The mark "PVB" designates the workshop of the artist, while the mark "PVB I.F." is the signature of van Baurscheit himself. Several of this artist's sculptures decorate the gardens adjacent to the Rijksmuseum in Amsterdam.

CATALOGUE 2

STATUES

2.3

Mercury. c. 1851. Italian. Marble. Rosedown
Plantation and Gardens, St. Francisville,
Louisiana.

According to an 1851 bill of sale and the
diary of Sarah Turnbull, the daughter of
the first proprietors of Rosedown, this figure of Mercury was purchased in August
1851 from F. Leopold Pisani of Florence.
At that time, Sarah and her parents selected
a set of four of the important gods and
goddesses of Mount Olympus, namely
Mercury, Diana, Zeus, and the popular
Venus de Medici. The invoice listed the
statues "per Giardino," a phrase first
interpreted by researchers as meaning "by
Giardino," but which is correctly translated as "for the garden."[1]

1. Rosedown 1 and Rosedown 2.

2.4

Statue. Coade and Sealy, Lambeth, England.
1814. Stoneware. Collection F. J. Carey, III.
Marked: *COADE AND SEALY. 1814.*

This female figure is an allegorical representation of Music. The statue is not fully
finished at the back, which suggests that
it was once joined to a wall, pillar, chim-
neypiece, or perhaps even a concert hall
facade. Coade, established in 1769, made
artificial stone figures that – as the company's advertisements made clear –"FROST
and DAMPS have no effect upon . . ."[1]
Rarely seen in America, Coade figures were,
and still are, considered the finest garden
sculpture ever made of artificial stone.

1. Coade and Sealy, iv.

2.5

Diana de Gabies. c. 1860. English. Stoneware.
65 × 22¾" base. Private collection.

This life-sized figure of the goddess Diana
is a replica of an original excavated in
1792 by an English archaeologist, Gavin
Hamilton. It was one of many finds at
the Borghese estate in Gabii, Italy, where
it remained until 1807, when it was
bought by Napoleon Bonaparte. Since
1820 it has been on display at the Louvre
in Paris. The popularity of this masterpiece was widespread, and by the late
nineteenth century copies in many media
abounded.[1] Wilhelm Fröhner's entry in
the catalogue of the Louvre describes
the Diana as "one of the pearls of the
museum . . . among the most admired
masterpieces of Greek sculpture."[2]

1. Haskell and Penny, 198.
2. Fröhner, 120–121. The text reads, "Cette
statue, une des perles du Musée, compte parmi
les chefs-d'œuvre les plus admirés que la sculpture grecque ait produits." Translation mine.

2.6

Statue. Pasquale Romanelli (1812–87). c. 1860. Italian. Marble. Private collection. Marked: *P. Romanelli.*

Made for export in response to American patriotism, this Italian portrayal of the young George Washington even includes the tool of destruction for the proverbial cherry tree. Pasquale Romanelli was the father of Rafaello Romanelli (cat. 1.29); both sculptors who realized the potential of the expanding export market to America during the mid- to late-nineteenth century.

2.7

Danzatrice. After Antonio Canova (1757–1822). c. 1870. French. Terra cotta. Private collection. Marked: *FONDERIES DE CHOISY-LE-ROI.*

Standing in a classical contrapasto pose, the *Danzatrice,* or dancer, wears a diaphanous dress with a floral wreath resting on her bent wrist. This statue was manufactured by Choisy-Le-Roi, a French firm founded in 1804, which produced pottery wares for architectural, decorative, and utilitarian purposes.[1] Antonio Canova, known also for his *Venus Italica* (cat. 2.16) influenced a generation of sculptors through his dynamic and individualistic interpretations of classical subject matter.

1. Fleming and Honour, 194.

2.8

Diane de Versailles. J. W. Fiske Iron Works, New York. c. 1880. American. Zinc. Private collection. Marked: *J. W. FISKE MANUFACTORY/ 26–28 PARK PLACE/NEW YORK.*

Although similar in form to an antique prototype known in French as the *Diane Chasseresse* (Diana the Huntress), the *Diane de Versailles* portrays the goddess of the hunt with bow and arrow and a canine companion. Giovanni Maria Benzoni (1809–73), an Italian sculptor known for figural monuments and allegorical statues, created a famous version of this piece (present location unknown). A replica of the Benzoni statue was offered by Galloway Terra Cotta Company in its 1905 catalogue.[1] Mrs. Gordon Abbot's garden, Glass Head, in Manchester, Massachusetts, featured a version of this statue that was photographed for the cover of Louise Shelton's 1928 *Beautiful Gardens in America.*[2]

1. Galloway c. 1915, 43, no. 63.
2. Shelton, ix.

2.9

Statue. Gossin Frères, Paris, France. c. 1880. French. Terra cotta. Private collection. Marked: *Gossin Frères, Paris.*

This figure, which probably represents the goddess Ceres, holds her characteristic freshly harvested wheat and wears a headdress of entwined bullrushes. The sensuously draped figure looks down at the ground, the source of nature's bounty. The Gossin brothers, Louis and Etienne, worked in terra cotta and bronze until Etienne died in 1900. Records show an F. Gossin listed as a maker of terra cotta in Philadelphia in 1876, and terra-cotta figures marked *L. Gossin Philadelphia* suggest that Louis worked abroad for a time.

2.10

Statue. J. W. Fiske Iron Works, New York. c. 1880. American. Zinc. Private collection. Marked: *J. W. FISKE MANUFACTURER/26–28 PARK PLACE/NEW YORK.*

One of many renditions of the goddess Venus, this version by Fiske was adapted from a model of antiquity. The head, body, and drapery are exact replicas of those of the Louvre *Venus de Milo*, while the arms bear some resemblance to the lesser-known *Venus d'Arles.* The Fiske statue is often misidentified as Atalanta because of the symbolic apple that she holds in one hand. In this case, however, the appropriate myth tells of Venus holding the apple of the goddess of discord that has been awarded to her by Paris for being the "Fairest of All."[1] By the eighteenth century in England, a virtual craze for statues of Venus led to her occupying nearly every major garden. Reproductions of antique models of Venus were displayed with equal enthusiasm in American gardens during the nineteenth and twentieth centuries.

1. Carr-Gomm, 80; Murray, 283–284.

2.11

Lo Spinario. After the antique. c. 1890. Italian. Bronze. Hearst Castle, San Simeon, California.

The subject of the Capitoline Museum's *Lo Spinario* has often been debated over the years.[1] The figure was thought variously to represent Absalom, Priapus, a shepherd boy removing a thorn from his foot, and a participant in the Greek games. Barbezat et Cie., the noted Paris foundry, offered a cast-iron version of the intent youth in its circa 1858 catalogue.[2] In spite of the confusion about the figure's identity, it was popular with garden owners, including, in this case, William Randolph Hearst, who installed this version in his garden at Hearst Castle.

1. Haskell and Penny, 308–309.
2. Barbezat et Cie, pl. 148.

2.12

Stealing a Kiss. Edouard Maugendre-Villiers. Fonderies L. Gagne de Tussy, France. c. 1890. French. Cast iron. Rosedown Plantation and Gardens, St. Francisville, Louisiana. Marked: *L. GAGNE/ FONDERIES DE TUSSY/FRANCE.*

A suitable addition to the garden at Rosedown in the 1950s by the purchaser and savior of the plantation, Catherine Underwood, this grouping of playful children exemplifies the free-spirited style of French Victorian sculpture. The two putti are locked in a permanent embrace suggestive of the antics of young inhabitants of Mount Olympus.

2.13

Statue. c. 1900. American. Terra cotta. Private collection.

Probably a representation of a pensive Cupid, this statue recalls the pose of the antique statue *Lo Spinario* (cat. 2.11). Although rigidly perched on a stump, the youth seems to be considering some active pursuit. The piece is unascribed, but its discovery in Philadelphia, the home of the Galloway Company, which made distinctive terra-cotta pieces of this type, suggests that it may have been produced by that firm.

2.14

Statue. c. 1900. Italian. Marble. Private collection.

This statue represents Ceres, the Roman corn goddess, and the protectress of the earth's fruits, revered in ancient times for her capacity to nourish. While classical in theme, this statue projects an air of informality not normally associated with the cool and stoic figures of antiquity. Indeed, the intimacy of her communion with the elements of nature makes her an apt choice for a picturesque English landscape garden rather than a formal Italianate setting.

2.15

Spring. c. 1901. French. Marble. The Elms, The Preservation Society of Newport County, Newport, Rhode Island.

Around 1901, Edward J. Berwind, a Philadelphia coal baron, installed a suite of busts representing the four seasons in the interior gallery of the Elms, which were later moved to the formal garden around 1915. Jules Allard & Fils, a prominent Parisian interior decorating firm, provided this and many other objects in the Elms' collection.

2.16

Venus Italica. After Antonio Canova (1757–1822). c. 1920. Italian. Marble. Private collection.

In his book *Nineteenth-Century Sculpture,* H. W. Janson calls the 1812 *Venus Italica* "[p]sychologically . . . Canova's most subtle and complex creation . . ." She has been surprised during her bath and is reacting with a physical response that varies in intensity depending upon one's viewpoint.[1] Better known for her amorous powers, Venus was appropriately the mythological goddess of gardens and flowers.[2] Replicas of this statue have been produced for many years in all sizes and materials. An identical statue is found in the garden of Rosecliff in Newport, Rhode Island.

1. Janson, 55.
2. Murray, 56.

2.17

Crouching Venus. Pietro Barzanti, Florence, Italy. c. 1910. Italian. Marble. Hearst Castle, San Simeon, California. Signed: *P. Barranti.*

The Crouching Venus, a type repeated in variations almost continuously since Antiquity, enjoyed a surge in popularity during the last half of the nineteenth century, along with the revival of Renaissance-style gardens.[1] The architect Stanford White installed a copy in the center of his pond garden at Box Hill, in St. James, Long Island. White's goddess was positioned so as to reflect in the water, as the ancient original may also have been. Pietro Barzanti, whose name has been transcribed in a variety of ways, including Bazzanti and Barranti, established a marble sculpture studio in Florence in 1822, in a prime location on the Arno River. The studio continued operation into the twentieth century, sculpting reproductions of famous statues for export until 1960, when it merged with Antonio Frilli Ltd.

1. Haskell & Penney, 321–323.

2.18

Faun with Pipes. After the antique. c. 1920. American. Lead. Agecroft Hall, Richmond, Virginia.

The illustrious ancestor of this statue was part of the early-seventeenth-century Villa Borghese collection that was purchased by Napoleon Bonaparte in 1807 and subsequently taken to Paris. Currently in the Louvre Museum in Paris, the *Faun with Pipes* is thought to be one of many Roman copies of a Greek bronze original dating from the second half of the fourth century B.C.[1] The languid posture and youthful sensuality of the Louvre example are, however, lacking in this twentieth-century interpretation. Faunus was the Roman version of the lustful Pan, who, in this case, has taken a wholly human form.[2]

1. Haskell and Penny, 212–213.
2. Murray, 138; Carr-Gomm, 92.

2.19

Dancing Faun. After antique model at the Uffizi Gallery, Florence. c. 1930. American. Terra cotta. Virginia House, Richmond, Virginia.

In the late seventeenth century when its existence was first recorded, the Uffizi version of this statue was much admired and frequently copied. Michelangelo was believed to have restored the arms of the Roman original with "modern" replacements.[1] American gardens benefited from their owners' preoccupations with the statues of antiquity. A replica of the *Dancing Faun* was photographed around 1928 in a central location in the garden at Brookside in Great Barrington, Massachusetts.[2] Such terra-cotta statues as this received acclaim in the early twentieth century when cast iron was criticized as an industrial material rather than one suitable for artistic endeavors.

1. Haskell and Penny, 205–207.
2. Shelton, pl. 27.

2.20

Statue. c. 1930. English. Lead. Collection John and Gilda McGarry.

The sentimental subject of children at play was appreciated during the Victorian era, when depictions of innocent youth conjured up such weighty issues as morality or the transience of life. This piece exhibits a feature characteristic of late-nineteenth and twentieth-century lead statues, the lead base. Statue and base are thus an integrated unit, unlike eighteenth-century English lead statues, which were generally mounted on stone bases.

2.21

Clio. Antonio Frilli, Ltd. c. 1938. Italian. Marble. Bayou Bend, Houston, Texas. Marked: *ANTONIO FRILLI LTD. FLORENCE, MADE IN ITALY.*

One of the nine Muses, Clio is portrayed with her scroll half-open. As the muse of history, she inspires humanity with her understanding of the past. At Bayou Bend, an estate in Houston, this serene marble statue sits at the crossing of axial pathways in a small, geometric garden. Now a house museum, Bayou Bend was once the home of Miss Ima Hogg, an inveterate collector of the decorative arts.

2.22

Statues. c. 1930–40. Italy. Carved stone. Private collection.

These costumed figures portray Arcadian types in a lively, anecdotal style that found renewed popularity at the beginning of the twentieth century. They pursue their separate occupations, possibly loosely connected by a hunting theme, defined by their eighteenth-century attire. Ogival pedestals such as these, with inset panels of floral motifs, are often seen supporting twentieth-century statues. Vicenza stone, or *pietra Vicenza,* a popular material in the twentieth century, is a light yellow limestone still quarried in the Veneto region of northern Italy. Soft when first quarried, it grows harder as it ages. The surface is often pitted and embedded with shells, even if cut absolutely straight.

2.23

Four Seasons. c. 1940. English or American. Lead and cast stone bases. Private collection.

In the seventeenth century, Louis XIV's court designer, Charles Le Brun (1619–90), chose subject matter for Versailles' extensive program of garden statuary that was based, in part, upon the sixteenth-century Italian emblemist Cesare Ripa's *Iconologia*. Statues were often chosen in sets of four: the Elements, the Seasons, the Continents, the Humors of Man, the Four Kinds of Poetry, and the Four Times of Day.[1] The practice of placing groups of four related allegorical figures in gardens was continued in eighteenth-century American gardens (see p. 38). Sets of the Four Seasons were popular additions to twentieth-century American gardens. These particular lead representations were produced on both sides of the Atlantic, by H. Crowther Ltd. of England and by The Erkins Studios in America, among others.[2]

1. Pincas, 84–87.
2. J. Davis, 324, pl. 7:50; Erkins c. 1963, 21, LD–114.

2.24

Season. c. 1940. Italian. Carved stone. Private collection.

The much-admired gardener Adele Lovett of Locust Valley, Long Island, whose grounds were illustrated in Rosemary Verey's *The American Woman's Garden Book,* studied in Maine with the renowned landscape designer Beatrix Farrand. Originally in Lovett's collection, this statue cradles grapes in her arms, a fruit that is an attribute of Autumn in many examples. Grapes may also be a symbol of Summer in parts of the world where they ripen in that season.

2.25

Term figure. c. 1910. Italian. Marble. Eagle's Nest, Centerport, New York.

Appropriately situated in the woods that surround the estate of William K. Vanderbilt, Jr., this herm (or term, see p. 58) depicts Pan, the Greek god of pastures and forests. Here Pan is wrapped in fleece and holds a shepherd's pipe, his most recognizable attribute. A remarkably similar figure was offered by the Elmore Studios of New York, a firm carrying many types of garden ornament, in its 1910 catalogue.[1] Elmore also sold term figures of nymphs, probably intended as mates to their satyr or Pan figures.

1. Elmore Studios, 6.

2.26

Sphinx. c. 1910. Italian. Limestone. Private collection.

A lead sphinx at Buckland, an estate in Berkshire, England, published in Gertrude Jekyll's 1918 book *Garden Ornament,* shared many of the characteristics of this example: an elaborate headdress, breastplate, and saddlecloth, in addition to a scrolled mat with a grotesque mask. The form is reminiscent of the grotesque decorations uncovered at the Roman emperor Nero's Golden House in the early sixteenth century. This stone sphinx, one of a pair, was originally in the collection of a Montecito, California, estate. In 1928, Louise Shelton, author of a book on American gardens, characterized the climate of the area around Santa Barbara, California, as "quite similar to Sorrento, Italy, only better."[1] Nearby Montecito was home to many splendid estates in the early twentieth century.

1. Shelton, 494.

2.27

Pair of sphinxes. 1900–1910. Italian. Marble. Collection F. J. Carey, III.

This pair of sphinxes is characterized by Egyptian-style headdresses and decorative breastplates. A strikingly similar model, made in Italy, was retailed through J. P. White's Pyghtle Works of Bedford, England, suppliers of garden furniture and ornament. Featured in the White catalogue, which was first published around 1910, the sphinx was said to be "suitable for use at the foot of terrace steps, entrance steps, porches and a variety of positions."[1] White offered the marble Egyptian sphinx in various sizes while other companies offered the same form in various materials. The J. L. Mott Iron Works catalogue of 1890, for example, featured cast-iron sphinxes in the Egyptian style.[2]

1. J. P. White, 156.
2. Mott 1890, 45.

2.28

Pair of lions. 1855–70. English. Carved stone. Private collection.

Once used as gatehouse guardians in Tudor England, gate pier lions carried Gothic shields bearing the family crests of the estate owners. Reminiscent of the early-sixteenth-century heraldic lions of Henry VIII, these two display a symbolic owl and a suspended fleece to represent the nobility of the family. The fleece refers to the Order of the Golden Fleece, a company of knights founded by Philip the Good, Duke of Burgundy, in 1430. On the other shield, the owl, a companion of Athena, goddess of wisdom, probably signifies the wisdom of the owners.

2.29

Lion. c. 1860–80. American. Cast iron. Belmont Mansion, Nashville, Tennessee.

This noble lion, one of a pair, overlooks the grounds of Belmont. Although this one is unmarked, an identical lion appears in the Robert Wood & Co. catalogue of circa 1875.[1] The lion shown here is indicative of the American preference for reposed, rather than fierce, lion statues.

1. Wood, 144, no. 544.

2.30

Pair of lions. Janes, Beebe, & Co., New York. c. 1860–80. American. Cast iron. Private collection. Marked: *Janes, Beebe & Co.*

These lions, manufactured by Janes, Beebe & Co., achieve a heightened degree of realism by extending their paws beyond their bases. Reminiscent in overall form of the renowned lions by Antonio Canova (1757–1822) on the tomb of Pope Clement XIII in Rome (see pp. 48–49), this pair is striking for its exquisite details, down to the smallest whisker follicles. Similar lions with paws extending over their bases are documented in the catalogues of J.W. Fiske Iron Works and J. L. Mott Iron Works.[1] Replicas of the Janes, Beebe & Co. lions shown here were offered in the Barclay Company Garden Ware Catalogue of 1930.[2]

1. Fiske 1868, 21; and Mott 1890, pl. 45–m.
2. Barclay 1930, no. K7.

2.31

Pair of lions. c. 1930. American. Limestone. Private collection.

Figures of lions have been used to guard the doorsteps of many public buildings and private residences, where they set a tone of strength and majesty. These heavily lichened lions are reputed to have come from the Delano family estate on the Hudson River in New York, where they probably marked an entrance to a mansion or garden.

2.32

Pair of lions. After Bertel Thorvaldsen
(1768/70–1844) c. 1860–80. American.
Cast iron. Private collection.

This pair of lions, cast after an original
group by Bertel Thorvaldsen (see p. 49),
was often reproduced by American manufacturers. The differing poses, one lion
asleep and one awake, used also by Antonio
Canova, make them what is known in the
vocabulary of decorative statuary as a true
pair (see cat. 2.39). These lions were replicated in the late 1850s by Wood & Perot,
for example, and in the 1920s by Howard
Studios.[1]

1. Wood & Perot, figs. H and J; Howard
Studios, no. 340–D.

2.33

Eagle. J. W. Fiske Iron Works, New York.
c. 1874–92. American. Zinc. Collection
The Garden Antiquary. Marked: *J. W. FISKE,
26–28 PARK PLACE, NY.*

In Greek mythology the eagle was an
attribute of the all-powerful Zeus; later,
in Christian iconography, it symbolized
Christ's Resurrection and Ascension. After
1782, the bald eagle was included on the
Great Seal of the United States, thereafter
becoming an American symbol.[1] Traditionally, nineteenth-century American
makers placed zinc or cast-iron eagles on
spheres or rock-work bases. The piece
shown here appears in J. W. Fiske Iron
Works' 1874 catalogue.[2]

1. Hornung, 805.
2. Fiske 1874, no. 289.

2.34

Stag. M. J. Seelig, Brooklyn, New York. c. 1876.
American. Zinc. Private collection. Marked:
M.J. SEELIG 115 & 117 MAUJER WMBURG, NY

Maurice J. Seelig & Co., zinc founders,
was first listed on Maujer Street in the
Brooklyn, New York directories in 1872,
where it remained until 1890. M. J. Seelig's
reclining stag figure was featured in the
company's 1876 trade catalogue.[1] Remarkably similar to a Coade Stone Co. design
published in England in 1784,[2] this popular form was also offered in 1890 by J. L.
Mott Iron Works.[3] The collection of The
Metropolitan Museum of Art boasts an
identical zinc reclining stag marked by
J. W. Fiske Iron Works, also produced in
the last quarter of the nineteenth century.

1. Seelig, No. 84.
2. Coade, n.p.
3. Mott 1890, 54.

2.35

Doe. J. W. Fiske Iron Works, New York. c. 1860. American. Cast iron. Private collection. Marked: *J. W. FISKE*.

J. W. Fiske Iron Works was a leader in the production of high-quality cast animal figures in the nineteenth century. This refined doe is not found in contemporary Fiske trade catalogues, perhaps because it was made for a special commission. The simple grace of this rare form may derive from a bronze deer by an Italian sculptor such as the Neapolitan V. Guccillato, who is known to have copied a Pompeiian-style model. In the second half of the nineteenth century, when the vogue for animal sculpture that accompanied the taste for picturesque gardening was at its height, sculptures of animals were often hidden in groves or set in garden structures.

2.36

Stag. c. 1880. American. Cast iron. Private collection.

2.37

Doe. c. 1880. American. Cast iron. Collection Elizabeth Street, New York.

The standing, cast-iron deer form was a favorite garden figure in the mid- to-late-nineteenth century in America. Doe and stag figures, often sold as pairs, were favored additions to the romantic, pastoral gardens popularized after the 1840s by Andrew Jackson Downing and others. The antlered version shown here, although unmarked, has been incorrectly referred to as a "Fiske" deer because of an assumed association with J. W. Fiske Iron Works of New York. The popular stag figure was, in fact, cast by a variety of makers, including Robert Wood & Co. of Philadelphia[1] and J. L. Mott Iron Works of New York.[2] The doe, less often seen in trade catalogues, is rarer, and thus, at times, more in demand than the stag.

1. Wood, 108.
2. Mott 1890, 53.

2.38

Doe. 1860–80. American. Cast iron. Belmont Mansion, Nashville, Tennessee.

This particular doe is extremely rare and has not been found in any nineteenth-century trade catalogue thus far. A stag, clearly cast from the same mold as the doe shown here, was offered by Wood & Perot in their 1858 catalogue. Perhaps it was not necessary to picture the doe as it could be ordered as an exact duplicate of the stag, only without antlers. Both pieces have the identical body form and leg position, and even exhibit the same detail in the neck fur at the front of the chest (see drawing below).[1]

1. Wood & Perot, no. 477.

2.39

Dog. c. 1860–80. American. Cast iron.
Collection Folly.

Frequently purchased in pairs and used
to flank doorways, greyhounds were a
favorite dog figure in America in the mid-
to-late nineteenth century. The model
shown here was included in several
trade catalogues of that period. Robert
Wood & Co. of Philadelphia, for example,
featured a similar dog in its circa 1875
catalogue,[1] and in the first decade of
the twentieth century, J. W. Fiske Iron
Works of New York offered comparable
greyhounds in zinc, available painted
or bronzed.[2] In order to be a true pair,
the two figures would differ slightly in
details such as carrying their tails in a
dissimilar manner or turning their heads
in opposite directions.

1. Wood, 297.
2. Fiske [1901–1907], 7.

2.40

Pair of dogs. C. Gute. 1860–80. French. Cast
iron. Nemours Mansion, Wilmington, Delaware.
Signed: C. Gute.

The J. W. Fiske Ironworks *Zinc Animals*
catalogue, published 1892–1907, featured
a "French Blood Hound," and a "French
Game Dog,"[1] both faithful copies of
A. Jacquemart's designs, seen in the circa
1870 catalogue of the Val D'Osne foundry
outside of Paris.[2] Not only were French
designs such as these copied by American
foundries, but the actual statues were
purchased by American collectors. Blood-
hounds were retailed by French companies either as pairs, as shown here, or
combined with a gamekeeper figure to
create a more impressive (and costly)
work of art. Such a group made by the
Val D'Osne foundries, called the "Valet
des Limiers," was purchased by the Duke
Gardens of Somerville, New Jersey, in
the early twentieth century.

1. Fiske 1892–1907, 9–10.
2. Société Anonyme des Hauts-Fourneaux,
pl. 651, nos. 67, 68.

2.41

Dog. c. 1860–80. American. Cast iron. Private
collection.

By 1860, zinc and cast-iron dogs, including
greyhounds, terriers, and Newfoundlands,
were popular forms of lawn and garden
statues. The importance of these lawn
animals was noted by a garden writer,
Mrs. Chetwood Smith, in 1949: "Lawn
animals were usually of cast iron. Their
period was roughly from about 1830 to
1890. During their vogue they were a
highly valued part of the outdoor equip-
ment and adornment of American
homes."[1] This particular form has not
been found as yet in any nineteenth-
century trade catalogues.

1. Smith, 89–92.

3.1

Urn. William Adams, Philadelphia. c. 1888–1904. Cast iron. Private collection. Marked: *WM. ADAMS & CO. /960 N. 9TH ST. PHILA.*

Pictured in a William Adams & Co. catalogue produced between 1888 and circa 1890, this urn exhibits certain features that are almost unique to this maker.[1] The peculiar, upturned handles with stylized floral decorations are usually considered to have originated with this firm. However, the urn, which also appears in the Adams 1892 catalogue, was published again in a later catalogue by another Philadelphia maker, F. & E. Aubel.[2] The pedestal is noteworthy for its foliate motif, reminiscent of a traditional fleur-de-lys. This abstracted and schematic feature could owe its inspiration to the Aesthetic Movement, which was flourishing in the United States around the time the urn was cast.

1. W. Adams [1888–1890] b, no. 75.
2. W. Adams 1892, 54, pl. 162; Aubel, no. 27B.

CATALOGUE 3

URNS

3.2

Urn. c. 1850–60. American. Cast iron. Belmont Mansion, Nashville, Tennessee.

This rare vase stands an impressive forty-one inches tall. Mounted on a square plinth, it features a bust of George Washington encircled by laurel leaves on either side of the cup, a testament to the patriotism that proliferated in nineteenth-century America. Sold by several companies in the second half of the nineteenth century, the Washington urn was offered by Chase Brothers of Boston in 1850,[1] and by J. W. Fiske Iron Works of New York in 1868.[2] Most often, such portrait vases depicted George Washington on both sides of the body. Others featurued Benjamin Franklin, and in some rare cases, a single urn will display the images of both men.

1. Chase Brothers, 21.
2. Fiske 1868, 18.

3.3

Urn. c. 1855. Cast iron. Rosedown Plantation and Gardens, St. Francisville, Louisiana.

This urn is one of a pair that flank the staircase on the south portico at Rosedown Plantation. Somewhat distinct in form, it is characterized by a reeded pedestal with a slightly flaring collar, surmounted by a deep body with a wide semi-lobed band and a scalloped rim. In 1858, Daniel Turnbull purchased a pair of "Iron Vases & Pedastles" [*sic*] for $36.00 at S. A. Harrison in Philadelphia.[1] Documentation does not confirm which pair of urns was bought that day. It is interesting to note, however, that there was "no charge for cartage," possibly indicating the ease of delivery by way of the country's internal river system.

1. Rosedown 3.

3.4

Urn. Wood & Perot, Philadelphia. c. 1858–66. American. Cast iron. Private collection. Marked: *WOOD & PEROT MAKERS, PHILADA.*

The variations in the decoration of Victorian urns was almost limitless. In this case, the designer started with the classical shape of a campana-form urn and added a few flourishes to generate visual interest. The scalloped rim with its egg-and-dart pattern invites a comparison of the urn to floral shapes, an effect emphasized by the handles, which are embellished with a touch of foliage. The entire object, like other campana-form urns, recalls the ancient Greek calyx krater, a vessel used to mix wine and water.

3.5

Urn on pedestal. Janes, Beebe & Co., New York. c. 1860. American. Cast iron and terra cotta. Private collection. Marked: *Janes Beebe & Co., N.Y.*

Featured in Janes, Beebe, & Co.'s 1858 trade catalogue,[1] this rustic form was registered by the Coalbrookdale Company of England and offered in its 1875 catalogue.[2] Its production in England may be a result of the lingering fashion for deer ornament popularized by Prince Albert's forays into the countryside. This distinctive urn was offered in 1868 by J. W. Fiske Iron Works as the "Deer Head" urn,[3] and in 1893 the base was identified as the "Stump" pedestal. On the other hand, J. L. Mott Iron Works published it in its 1893 catalogue as the "Staghead Vase."

1. Janes, Beebe & Co., no. 29.
2. Coalbrookdale 1875, Section III, 323, no. 7.
3. Fiske 1868, 18; Fiske c. 1893, 93, no. 313, 93; Mott 1893, 7, pl. 87–L.

3.6

Urn with cover. c. 1860–80. American. Cast iron. Private collection.

The form of this urn may be characterized as a classic campana, or bell-shaped, urn. The egg-and-dart decoration on the rim, the semi-lobed lower bowl, and the ringed stem are hallmarks of many urn designs. Designers sometimes incorporated handles and, in this example, a winter cover to protect the urn from the cold. The cover's austere line and flame-shaped finial recall its heritage as a funerary object. J. W. Fiske Iron Works carried this combination in three sizes in their 1868 catalogue as "Palo Alto, with base and cover."[1]

1. Fiske 1868, 18.

3.7

Urn. c. 1860–80. American. Cast iron. Private collection.

The short, wide bowl of this vessel identifies it as a tazza-form – or cup-shaped – urn. Known as a self-watering urn, it has a special feature that is invisible when the piece is assembled. Small openings protrude from the sides of the vase, allowing water to enter and collect in a reservoir in the bowl. Then, as needed, the plant draws water from this reservoir, lessening the necessity for frequent tending.

3.8

Urn. Walbridge & Company, Buffalo, New York. c. 1860–80. American. Cast iron. Private collection. Marked: *WALBRIDGE AND CO./ BUFFALO*.

An otherwise simple urn is embellished with intricate handles terminating in birds' heads. This urn and pedestal were made in significant numbers by several companies, one of which, Kramer Brothers of Dayton, Ohio called the urn the "Queen" in its circa 1910–20 catalogue.[1] Likenesses can be found between the products of Walbridge and Co. and some Ohio companies, a fact that implies that some trade association or sharing of patterns existed between them.[2]

1. Kramer, 41, Fig. S–60.
2. Stewart; Van Dorn; F. A. Floom & Co., Tiffin, Ohio, advertisement in *House and Garden*, inside back cover, c. 1902.

3.9

Urn. c. 1860–80. American. Cast iron. Private collection.

Many American foundries carried this simple cup-shaped urn. With its semi-lobed form and curved rim, it was used as a basic form that could be made into a formal presentation by the addition of handles and foliate decoration. Although similar to J. W. Fiske's "Victoria" vase, it lacks that model's encircling band and decorative collar.[1]

1. Fiske c. 1893, 46.

3.10

Pair of urns. c. 1860–80. American. Cast iron. Private collection.

The handles on these two urns were found on a variety of tazza-form examples offered by the Phoenix Iron Works of Utica, New York, around 1852. Such elaborate handholds were the signature of many American Victorian urns and were often interchangeable by the removal of a single bolt. The earnestness of salesmen in the mid-nineteenth century is demonstrated by the words of the proprietor of the Utica foundry, C. F. Palmer, who told his customers that he would "strive to merit a continuance of the same [good business] by honorable dealing and small profits."[1]

1. Phoenix, 3, 9, 34, 39, 46.

3.11

Urn. 1860–80. American. Cast iron. Collection Janet and Joseph Shein.

This tazza-form urn, called the "Ivy and Grape Leaf Vase," was offered by many cast-iron foundries during the nineteenth century. J. W. Fiske Iron Works illustrated it in the firm's c. 1893 vase catalogue.[1] It was sold with or without the sweeping, stylized handles shown here, and with either a "slab" pedestal or the more costly and elaborate "pillar" or "crane" pedestals. E. G. Smyser & Sons, among others, also produced the Ivy and Grape Leaf pattern.[2]

1. Fiske c. 1893, 59, no. 311; 60, no. 223; 65, no. 309; 66, no. 308; 72, no. 312; 78, no. 343; 79, no. 345.
2. Smyser, no. 307 1/2, 308, 309.

3.12

Urn. c. 1860–80. American. Cast iron. Private collection.

This tazza-form urn, most likely an American design derived from a French source, is adorned with leonine handles. The Val d'Osne catalogue of c. 1870 pictured a semi-lobed tazza with similar lion-face handles, but surmounted by large C-scroll-shaped handles not seen on this example.[1] The lion masks on this American urn may have held rings in their mouths at one time.

1. Société Anonyme des Hauts-Fourneaux, pl. 478.

3.13

Urn. 1860–80. American. Cast iron. Private collection.

This shallow tazza-form urn is ornamented with a row of putto heads below the rim, a rarely seen decorative feature that gives an exceptional character to an otherwise common form.

3.14

Urn. c. 1860–80. American. Cast iron. Collection Maymont Foundation.

Three cranes backed against a sheaf of cattails form the distinctively American pedestal of this urn. Cranes such as these served as bases for urns as well as aquaria and fountains throughout the nineteenth century. In this piece, the base supports a tazza-form urn adorned with dragon handles, another motif frequently found in the trade catalogues of American cast-iron foundries. In the J. W. Fiske Iron Works vase catalogue this combination was identified as "Flower and Leaf Vase With Handles on Crane Pedestal."[1]

1. Fiske c. 1893, 43, no. 307.

3.15

Urns. J. W. Fiske & Company, New York. c. 1840–80. Cast iron. Private collection. Marked: *J. W. FISKE.*

In its circa 1893 trade catalogue, J. W. Fiske Iron Works referred to these urns as the "Windemere Vase."[1] The exceptional bird handles, reminiscent of Gothic ornament, flank a body encircled with stylized foliage. The unusual bases, marked with the name of the manufacturer, have Renaissance-style cartouches at the corners.

1. Fiske c. 1893, 90.

3.16

Urn (one of a pair now piped as fountains). c. 1860–80. French. Cast iron. Rosedown Plantation and Gardens, St. Francisville, Louisiana.

Located in the formal boxwood garden of Rosedown Plantation, this urn, with its distinctive putto handles, is identical to designs found in a nineteenth-century French trade catalogue.[1] Installed in the 1950s by Catherine Underwood, this urn and its companion are now piped as fountains, as are the urns in the Bassin de Neptune at Versailles.

1. Renard, 100.

3.17

Urn. c. 1860–80. American. Cast iron. Collection Matt and Chris Matthews.

The bowl of this urn sits on the flared collar of its slender, baluster-form pedestal that surmounts a circular stepped base. A similar urn is featured in the Peter Timmes' Son trade catalogue of 1896, where it is called the "jardiniere vase."[1] The morning-glory pattern that encircles the rim exemplifies the American Victorian desire to cover every available surface with naturalistic decoration.

1. Timmes, 70.

3.18

Urn. c. 1860–80. French. Cast iron. Private collection.

The French rococo garden featured enclosed, intimate spaces. At no point could a viewer take in all the separate horticultural domains that made up the entire landscape.[1] The broken profile of the rim and the irregular handles of this urn and its companion are characteristic of rococo ornament.

1. Helmut Reinhardt, "German Gardens in the Eighteenth Century: Classicism, Rococo and Neo-classicism," in Mosser and Teyssot, 298.

3.19

Urn. c. 1870. American. Cast iron. Collection Elizabeth Street.

The diameter of this monumental urn, described as a "Deep Roman Vase" in the J. W. Fiske Iron Works vase catalogue of 1893, is approximately sixty-six inches.[1] J. L. Mott Iron Works identified the same shape as a "Grecian Vase, with Handles."[2] This design incorporates an egg- and-dart motif around the rim, and was sold with or without the scrolling, foliate double handles shown here by a number of manufacturers. A similar vase served as the sole ornament on the grounds of Effingham, the Alexander estate in Dongan Hills, Staten Island, in 1891.[3]

1. Fiske c. 1893, 18.
2. Mott 1893, 9, pl. 52–L.
3. Doell, 64–65.

3.20

Urn. c. 1870. French. Cast iron. Collection Elizabeth Street.

The extraordinary handles on this urn, female figures attached to the body, represent the finest in French design. At Versailles, similar handles on the urns in the Parterre du Nord and Parterre du Midi set a standard of originality and excellence that was continued by French artisans into the twentieth century. The expressive masks on the sides of this urn recall the grotesques so often seen in Italian Renaissance gardens. The Nelson A. Rockefeller Gallery at Kykuit in Pocantico Hills displays an exact replica of this piece, marked by the nineteenth-century French founder, J. J. Ducel of Paris.

3.21

Urn. Val d'Osne, France. c. 1888. French. Cast iron. Private collection. Marked: *FONDERIES DU VAL D'OSNE, 58 BO^{ARD} VOLTAIRE, PARIS.*

The portrait medallions on either side of this striking urn may have derived from similar motifs found on seventeenth-century French urns. A bronze vase designed in 1665 by Claude Ballin, Louis XIV's royal goldsmith, for the Parterre du Nord at Versailles, for example, bears comparable medallions that contain portrait profiles.[1]

1. Pincas, 275.

3.22

Urn. John Wood, Jr. & Co., Philadelphia. c. 1870–80. Cast iron. The Highlands, Fort Washington, Pennsylvania. Marked: *JOHN WOOD, JR. & CO.*

This elegant design is rarely found in the catalogues of American manufacturers. This example was produced by a Philadelphia maker, but was probably inspired by a French model. The overall form, the high relief, and the foliate handles are quintessentially French. Indeed, the urn is quite similar to one produced by the French foundry Barbezat & Cie.[1] Little is known about the maker, John Wood, Jr. & Co., but this firm should not be confused with Robert Wood & Co., also of Philadelphia. The relationship between the two Wood foundries is unknown.

1. Barbezat & Cie, pl. 137, R.

3.23

Jardiniere. c. 1870–80. French. Cast iron. Private collection.

An elegant French-Renaissance-style piece, this jardiniere exhibits a curvilinear contour rising to scrolling upper corners. Low planters with elegant classical decoration like this one were particularly appealing to the French. The Val d'Osne catalogue of c.1870 devoted an entire page to designs of such containers.[1]

1. Société Anonyme des Hauts-Fourneaux, pl. 495.

3.24

Pair of urns. 1850–60. American. Cast iron. Richmond, Natchez, Mississippi.

The "mask-and-loop" handles of these urns are composed of two small classical masks joined by an arched, or looped, member. This style of handle is derived from the Medici vase, a neo-Attic example discovered in Italy in the sixteenth century (see cat. 3.39). Indeed, this vase type is sometimes known as a "mask-and-loop" urn because of the characteristic design of the handles. Recalling a carved ancient marble frieze now in Rome, the wide band of *rinceaux,* or scrolling foliage, was cast separately and applied to the body.[1] A heavy, beaded decorative rim was also made as a separate piece and bolted to the upper edge. When this model is found without the rim, it should be considered incomplete.

1. Speltz, 80–81.

3.25

Urn. c. 1880. Cast iron. Collection Charlotte Inn.

While the shape of this piece is distantly related to the campana-form urn, its design marks a novel departure from the type. Instead of the customary decorative elements, molded rim, and lower lobing, its body is carved with leaflike shapes that rise to form a scalloped rim. The urn's floral appearance and crisp profile have earned it the name "tulip urn."

3.26

Urn. After Claude Ballin (1615–78). c. 1880. French. Cast iron. Private collection.

This urn is based on Claude Ballin's 1665 design for Louis XIV's gardens at Versailles. Ballin's design, with its distinctive satyr masks mounted on the rim, was for a group of twelve planters for the King's orange trees. Around 1870, Napoleon III allowed the fourth Marquess of Hertford to make bronze casts of the Versailles urns for his estate, the Chateau de Bagatelle, located outside Paris.[1] Immediately after these bronze copies were made the leading French foundry Val d'Osne offered replicas in cast iron.[2]

1. J. Davis, 133–139.
2. Société Anonyme des Hauts-Fourneaux, 114, 119, pl. 482, nos. 106–109.

3.27

Urn. c. 1880. French. Cast iron. Private collection.

The overall form of this urn relates closely to many French examples on which there were numerous handle variations used. The Société Anonyme des Hauts-Forneaux & Fonderies du Val d'Osne, a group of designers and founders active during the second half of the nineteenth century in France, illustrated six variations of this urn with and without handles in its circa 1870 trade catalogue.[1] J. W. Fiske Iron Works of New York manufactured a nearly identical urn, also without handles, which the firm called the "Antique" pattern.[2] French urns of this style were often produced with an unpainted, burnished finish.

1. Société Anonyme des Hauts-Fourneaux, pl. 479.
2. Fiske c. 1893, 26.

3.28

Urn. J. W. Fiske and Company, New York. c. 1880. American. Cast iron. Private collection. Marked: *J. W. FISKE.*

The upswept handles of this urn give it a height of almost five feet, which is counterbalanced by its heavy, triple-crane base. Pictured in a J. W. Fiske Iron Works catalogue, it was designated there as the "Shield and Leaf vase."[1] A rare and important piece because of its refined form, impressive size, and the fact that it bears the mark of the renowned Fiske foundry, the urn now stands in a cemetery in New England, where it serves, as it would in a private garden, as a sculptural monument in the midst of natural surroundings.

1. Fiske c. 1893, 42.

3.29

Urn. Abendroth Brothers, New York. c. 1880. American. Cast iron. Collection Matt and Chris Matthews. Marked: *ABENDROTH N. Y.*

Abendroth Brothers was not the only firm to produce this fanciful urn. In 1881, Samuel S. Bent, another New York founder, moved to 72 Beekman Street near Abendroth at 119 Beekman and offered this pattern as the "Rodent" urn.[1] Coincidentally, both companies also had foundries in Portchester, New York. Illustrating some of the stylistic variations among urns, this exceptional design used such standard decorative elements as a molded rim, a lobed lower bowl, and a ringed stem, but added two nibbling squirrels for handles and a medallion representing a rabbit peeking out of an imaginary burrow. The inclusion of such elements lessens the formal impact by adding a note of whimsy.

1. Bent, 11.

3.30

Urn. c. 1880. American. Cast iron. Collection Garden Room.

This particular piece is often termed the "Jenny Lind" urn. Jenny Lind, a talented soprano, came to the United States in the 1850s and toured with P. T. Barnum as "The Swedish Nightingale." The faces on the urn were thought to resemble that of the diva, thus the name. Neither J. W. Fiske Iron Works nor J. L. Mott Iron Works, both founders of New York, have been found to carry this urn in their extensive catalogues of vases. An unusual form in nineteenth-century American cast iron, this piece features four larger classical portrait masks adorning the bowl, with smaller, framed faces set between them. The stepped pedestal is characteristic of the type; at times this urn is seen with four scrolling, foliate handles.

3.31

Urn. c. 1880–90. French. Cast iron. Collection Janet and Joseph Shein.

Figural handles of all types were a favorite design motif of French founders. On this urn, identical to one found in a trade catalogue of the Parisian manufacturer F. A. Villard,[1] graceful female figures form the decorative handles. In addition, an unusual band of abstract vegetal ornament decorates the rim of this broad, tazza-form urn.

1. Villard, pl. 39, item G.

3.32

Urn. c. 1885. French. Cast iron. Collection Janet and Joseph Shein.

This urn is a variation on the standard campana-form shape. The ornamented rim and foot can be found on many urns of American manufacture. However, the vase's exaggerated lobing and figural handles are less common. These features are found in the Val D'Osne catalogue of circa 1870,[1] suggesting a French origin for the piece.

1. Société Anonyme des Hauts-Fourneaux, 480, pl. 477.

3.33

Urn. c. 1885. American. Zinc. Collection F. J. Carey, III.

This urn is an unusual combination of materials and ornaments. First, it is made of zinc, which, while often used as a non-corrosive material for statues or fountain parts in America, has rarely been considered as a material for urns. Second, the otherwise standard campana form is embellished with fanciful, braided handles, a particularly French touch. Another example of braided, or twisted, handles can be seen on a vase design in the Barbezat & Cie. catalogue of circa 1858.[1] This urn exhibits the grace and fluid proportions also associated with the products of Wood & Perot of Philadelphia.

1. Barbezat & Cie., pl. 159, no. 12.

3.34

Pair of urns. c. 1890. American. Cast iron. Private collection.

This unusual pair of urns mounted on atypically scalloped, domelike bases reflects the taste for exoticism that marked the Aesthetic Movement in America during the 1870s and 1880s. Their vasiform shape recalls pieces of early nineteenth-century French Empire porcelain rather than late nineteenth-century cast iron. Their perforated bodies may also have been derived from the delicately pierced Chinese porcelains of the late Ming Dynasty (1368–1644). Unless these urns were lined at one time, they would have been purely ornamental. Neither their form nor their decoration has been found in trade catalogues of the period.

3.35

Pair of urns. Walbridge & Co., Buffalo, New York. c. 1900. Cast iron. Shadyside, Natchez, Mississippi. Marked: *WALBRIDGE & CO. BUFFALO, N.Y.*

These formal, simplified urns were used as markers at the entrance to Shadyside, an addition that dignified the entrance stairway. Barely visible except on close examination, precisely detailed, elongated swallows glide around the belly of the urn. This pair was made by Walbridge & Co., however, Kramer Brothers of Dayton, Ohio, produced similar urns. In the Kramer catalogue they were offered as the "Bell" model, probably referring to the commonly used term for this shape, *campana,* the Italian word for "bell."[1]

1. Kramer 1995, 56.

3.36

Urn. c. 1910–20. Kramer Brothers, Dayton, Ohio. Cast iron. Collection Janet and Joseph Shein. Marked: *KRAMER BROS. DAYTON OHIO.*

Kramer Brothers, a prolific foundry that marked many of its pieces, was first listed in the Dayton city directory in 1890, even though its own official founding date was 1895. The company is still in business today. This urn is one of a pair characterized by elaborately scrolled, rococo-style vine handles and a rim of pointed foliage that is typical of the foundry's work. Featured in a reprint of a Kramer Bros. trade catalogue of circa 1910–20, this form is called "Beauty," and was offered with or without different types of handles. This model, "Beauty No. 2," could be finished in primed aluminum, or painted white or stone gray.[1]

1. Kramer, 59.

3.37

Urn. c. 1900. American. Cast iron. Collection Charlotte Inn.

This urn was one of the most economical, versatile, and common types produced by American cast-iron manufacturers. The circa 1868 catalogue published by J. W. Fiske Iron Works listed this example as the "Fluted Vase," and sold it in six graduated sizes (see drawing).[1] The different sizes made the urn adaptable to both grand and modest architectural and landscape schemes. It was offered with either a simple slab pedestal or the so-called "Grecian" pedestal.

1. Fiske 1868, n.p., no. 1–5.

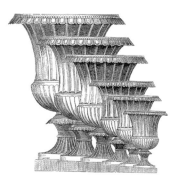

3.38

Urn. Kramer Brothers, Dayton, Ohio. c. 1910–20. American. Cast iron. Collection F. J. Carey, III. Marked: *KRAMER BROS., DAYTON, OHIO.*

One of a group of four, this well-proportioned urn was a standard offering of the Ohio cast-iron manufacturer Kramer Brothers. Known as "Prize" in Kramer's early-twentieth-century catalogue, the vase was offered in three forms: as illustrated here, on a taller pedestal and without handles.[1]

1. Kramer, 50, no. 1, fig. S–83; no. 3, fig. S–85; no. 4, fig. S–86.

3.39

Vase. After the Medici vase. c. 1900. American. Cast iron. Private collection.

The Medici vase, a marble piece accepted as a neo-Attic example of the second half of the first century A.D. and believed to be in the inventory of the Villa Medici in Rome of 1598, was used decoratively as a companion to another marble neo-Attic vase known as the Borghese vase throughout the eighteenth and nineteenth centuries. The Medici vase, a krater-form vessel whose distinctive mask-and-loop handles provided the original archetype for many later ones, is now in the Uffizi Gallery in Florence. Figural processions encircle the exteriors of both the Medici and Borghese vases. The scene on the Medici vase was once thought to represent the story of Iphigenia, although this idea is now disputed. The scene on the Borghese vase represents a Bacchic procession (see drawing).[1] Other characteristics distinguishing the vases are the Medici vase's foliate decoration and the Borghese vase's total lack of handles.

1. Haskell and Penny, 316.

3.40
Urn. c. 1997. Chinese. Cast iron. Private collection.

While this urn appears attractive and normal, *watch out!* Although the form resembles a period nineteenth-century urn on pedestal, it is no more than a recent Chinese-made reproduction. This is one of many new cast-iron urns in a variety of patterns that were imported to America from both China and Mexico in the last decade of the twentieth century. The proportions of this example are proper, but in other cases the imports betray their origins by being larger, narrower, or generally more awkward than their nineteenth-century counterparts. One identifying characteristic is a seamline that runs horizontally through the center of the bowl. While some of these reproductions display crisp lines, the casting is often not as sharp or distinct as that of period examples. Most of all, beware of being misled by a skillful "antique" finish and overpaying for a replica.

3.41
Urns. Bromsgrove Guild of Applied Arts. English. c. 1908. Lead. Cranbrook House, Bloomfield Hills, Michigan.

These urns are situated on the grounds of the Cranbrook Educational Community. Founded by George Booth (1864–1949) in the 1910s, Cranbrook became a preeminent center of design, craft, and architecture that was fundamentally linked to the Arts and Crafts movement in America. In keeping with his dedication to handcraftsmanship, Booth commissioned many of the twentieth century's most esteemed architects, sculptors, and artisans to construct Cranbrook's buildings and ornamental features. The pictured urns were purchased from the Bromsgrove Guild of London, in accord with Booth's sympathies for guild practices and ideals.

3.42
Urn. 1913–18. French. Lead. Planting Fields Arboretum State Historic Park, Oyster Bay, Long Island.

Standing in the so-called Italian Blue Pool Garden adjacent to Coe Hall at Planting Fields, this urn has its roots in French design. Although its maker is not known, an identical form is to be found in the circa 1870 catalogue of the Société Anonyme des Hauts-Fourneaux & Fonderies du Val d'Osne.[1] It is assumed to be original to the garden where it now stands, which was designed by Guy Lowell and A. Robeson Sargent between 1913 and 1918.

1. Société Anonyme des Hauts-Fourneaux, pl. 483, no. 19.

3.43

Pair of urns. Late nineteenth century. English. Lead. Private collection.

These elegant urns follow the design of an antique example from the Villa Albani near Rome. In 1857 J. M. Blashfield of Stamford, England, offered a single terra-cotta model, shown on a finely figured columnar pedestal.[1] Perched ravens overhang the lip of each urn as if drinking from it, a device that adds textural contrast to the simple lines of the vessels.

1. Blashfield, <35>, nos. 190, 315.

3.44

Urn. c. 1930–40. American. Lead. Private collection.

This urn has been manufactured by Erkins Studios of New York City, and Kenneth Lynch & Sons of Wilton, Connecticut, throughout much of the twentieth century.[1] Kenneth Lynch & Sons sold the urn as part of its "Charles II Series," apparently deriving its motifs from those of late-seventeenth-century England. The dramatically curved handles are formed by a fusion of acanthus leaf scrolls with a birdlike head that contributes to the urn's animated character.

1. Erkins 1929, 21, LD 15; Kenneth Lynch 1979, 176, no. 2416–M.

3.45

Lidded urn. c. 1940. American. Lead. Private collection.

This particular urn, notable for its bulging rim and dramatic classical masks, was retailed by Kenneth Lynch & Sons, Inc. of Wilton, Connecticut, and Erkins Studios of New York City.[1] Rendered in the style of eighteenth-century English lead urns, its design is strikingly similar to the lidded-vase finials that stand on eighteenth-century Italianate terrace walls at Powis Castle in Wales.[2] This urn's visible signs of wear and its pronounced spots of dark and light patination are typical for the material; they contribute to the urn's convincing period appearance.

1. Kenneth Lynch, 1979, 177, no. 1530; and Erkins c. 1963, 27, LD–III.

2. For an illustration of these, see Hinde, 31.

3.46

Pair of urns. c. 1790–1810. Italian. Marble. Private collection.

The discoveries at the Roman sites of Pompeii and Herculaneum in 1748 prompted a renewed interest in classically inspired ornament. These sensational excavations guided tastes out of the rococo vernacular, first into Neoclassicism, and later into the Empire and Regency styles. The restrained simplicity of these urns marks them as earlier than those of the Renaissance revival of the mid-nineteenth century, which are more ornate. In 1857 the swag and mask decoration of these urns was said to have originated from an "ancient marble."[1] The marble examples illustrated here exhibit both leonine and human faces. In his 1857 catalogue J. M. Blashfield of England offered a terra-cotta version of the vases, adorned with only human faces.[2]

1. Blashfield, Table of Contents, pl. 9.
2. Blashfield, no. 160.

3.47

Vase. After the Townley vase. c. 1910. Italian. Marble. Huntington Library, Art Collections, and Gardens, San Marino, California.

In 1773, Sir Gavin Hamilton discovered the first-century-B.C. marble original of this vase in Italy. A year later, Charles Townley, a British antiquarian, purchased it for his own collection.[1] Some makers of garden ornament, such as James Blashfield of Stamford, England, took molds from it and produced replicas to sell. On his death in 1804, Townley bequeathed the vase to the British Museum, where it remains on display. The vase itself is a volute krater, on the body of which is carved a procession of bacchantes and satyrs, one of whom holds an amphora, a container for wine. Several early-twentieth-century American garden ornament makers, such as Galloway Terra-Cotta Company in Philadelphia and the Fischer & Jirouch Company in Cleveland, offered reproductions of the Townley vase.[2] During the early twentieth century replicas of antique originals were generally produced in appropriate materials: marble, stone, terra cotta, or even cast stone.

1. J. Davis, 183.
2. Galloway c. 1915, 20, no. 183; Fischer & Jirouch, no. 5052.

3.48

Urns. Early twentieth century. Continental. Marble. Château-sur-Mer, Preservation Society of Newport County, Newport, Rhode Island.

These classical tazza-form urns, arranged in a straight line, give the garden a formal sobriety. An 1821 design for a marble tazza by the German architect Karl Friedrich Schinkel (1781–1841) exhibits precisely the same shape as the urns shown here,[1] and a slightly modified version of this urn is said to have been on display at the 1851 Crystal Palace Exhibition. Another precedent for this basic, refined design is found in the drawings of New York architect Alexander Jackson Davis (1803–92). In one sketch, Davis rendered a semi-lobed tazza-form urn that is nearly identical to the pictured examples.[2] The overall presentation of this group at Château-sur-Mer seems precarious and would benefit from the introduction of proper square plinths.

1. Speltz, 626.
2. Davis Collection, Avery Library, Columbia University, drawing no. 1940.001.00443.

3.49

Urn. c. 1920. Probably French. Marble. Nemours, Wilmington, Delaware.

This urn, with its simply styled volute handles and elegantly proportioned form, is of a type rarely seen in America. A closely related urn appeared in a 1934 catalogue of the Anciens Établissements Gilbert Cuel et Société, a Paris-based manufacturer of "pierre agglomérée," a composite stone.[1]

1. Cuel, fig. 181.

3.50

Urn. c. 1830. English. Bath stone. Private collection.

This lidded urn of ovoid form was probably made near Bath, England. It is carved after a design by Robert Parsons published in the late eighteenth century by his son, Thomas Parsons, in his sketchbook of designs by various artists, entitled *A Collection of Vases, Terms. . . .*[1] The urn is mounted on a pedestal of a later period. The warm beige tone of the vase is characteristic of the stone quarried in the Bath region.

1. J. Davis, 120.

3.51

Urn. c. 1900. Carved stone. John and Mable Ringling Museum of Art, Sarasota, Florida.

The lobed egg-and-dart molding along the rim, the figural drum, and the vegetal decoration on the lower bowl all identify this urn as a work in the Louis XIV-style. The actual inspiration for it may have come from the marble vases adorning the Parterre de Latone at Versailles, especially those made after 1683 by Jean Cornu and Louis Leconte.[1] Although the Versailles vases are carved with bacchanalian processions like the one on the urn shown here, the Ringling urn's handles are composed of naturalistic forms unlike any found at Versailles. These alterations show that makers sometimes deliberately varied the forms of their prototypes, even of the urns at Versailles. In this case, the sculptor has used the Versailles urns as a point of departure for a very personal interpretation of the original form.

1. Pincas, 131.

3.52

Jardiniere. c. 1920. American. Marble. Private collection.

A departure from the ordinary rounded urn, this marble jardiniere was designed to display plants. A creation of the Italian artisans who emigrated to Lee, Massachusetts, around 1900, this box planter rests on classical supports generally seen carrying flat-topped marble benches. Similar Italianate planters were featured in the circa 1925–31 catalogue of the Pompeian Garden-Furniture-Company.[1] These examples incorporated figures and other decoration on the sides.

1. Pompeian, 18, no. 966.

3.53
Lidded urn. c. 1840. English. Carved stone.
Private collection.

Portland stone, a light-colored limestone
quarried on the south coast of England,
takes carving exceptionally well.[1] This urn
attests to its artistic possibilities. Bacchic
devices decorating the body include
impish satyr masks among fruit forms on
the lower bowl and symbolic grapes and
vines on the upper portion. Because the
base has been shortened, the urn in its
present state relies on a large pedestal to
retain its original proportions.

1. J. Davis, 71–73.

3.54
Urn. c. 1940. English. Cast stone. Private
collection.

The soft edges of this urn are one way to
identify it as cast stone. As weather erodes
porous cast stone more quickly than
carved stone, the elements often give cast
stone a smooth, velvety finish. Although
the crispness of the lines of the piece are
diminished, collectors may prefer the
weathered appearance of cast stone to the
harder-edged look of carved stone. The
dark, lichenlike color that develops with
age often gives a cast stone piece and its
surroundings an air of history.

3.55
Pair of planters. c. 1940. English. Cast stone.
Private collection.

These simple square jardinieres are embellished with a Gothic quatrefoil pattern.
This motif, characteristic of medieval
cathedrals and other buildings, was often
appropriated for decorative objects. Designs
incorporating quatrefoils, pointed arches,
and other quintessentially Gothic devices
became especially popular in England
during the first half of the nineteenth century and were championed by the designer
and architect, Augustus Welby Northmore
Pugin (1812–52). The taste for Gothic-
style objects also flourished in America,
although with slightly less fervor than in
England, appearing on furniture, buildings, and silverwork.

3.56

Pair of urns. Doulton & Co., Lambeth, London. c. 1860. English. Stoneware. Private collection. Marked: *DOULTON LTD LAMBETH.*

Of simple, classical shape, these tazza-form urns gain stature from pedestals decorated with egg-and-dart and rope-twist moldings, and inset panels. Doulton & Co., known for stoneware and terra cotta of superb design and quality, produced numerous variations on the semi-lobed shallow urn.[1] Originally a pottery company, Doulton expanded into garden accessories in the 1850s, achieving recognition for their buff and red-colored, unglazed ornaments.

1. Doulton 2, 27.

3.57

Urn. Mark H. Blanchard, London. 1869. Stoneware. Dumbarton House, The National Society of the Colonial Dames of America, Washington, D.C. Marked: *M.H. BLANCHARD. / TERRA / COTTA. / LONDON. / 1869. / BLACKFRIARS RD.*

This urn is one of a pair that has recently had its original finish restored. Once thought to be of Coade stone, the pair was sold as such at a 1932 auction.[1] The attribution was undoubtedly made in part due to the urn's design, which is nearly identical to many offered by Coade in its circa 1784 catalogue, but also to excessive layers of paint that obscured the mark of the actual maker. In fact, the urn is marked Blanchard, one of the preeminent nineteenth-century makers of artificial stoneware, who is believed to have purchased a number of molds from the Coade manufactory. The mark, and the fact that M. H. Blanchard worked at Coade before starting his own company, further explains the similarity between this piece and earlier Coade works. The design of this urn and its companion is derived from the elegant Neoclassical designs of Robert Adam (1728–1792).

1. Anderson Galleries 1, 47–48, no. 188.

3.58

Urn. Mark H. Blanchard, London. 1869. English. Stoneware. Private collection. Marked: *M. H. BLANCHARD. / TERRA COTTA. / BLACKFRIARS RD. / LONDON / 1869.*

Although the maker of this urn is clearly established, its form is perplexing. It may relate to antique examples, but exact antecedents have not been found. The use of faces as part of, or in place of, handles was an ancient practice seen first in the first century A.D. Medici urn's mask-and-loop configuration.[1] The undulating lip and the overtly bulbous profile relate to the styles of the nineteenth-century rococo revival. Blanchard's ties to the Coade firm are well documented, yet these urns bear no stylistic relationship to the rigidly classical products of the earlier firm. Blanchard's wares should be termed "stoneware," in spite of the fact that he referred to them as "terra cotta." Strictly speaking, stoneware is a vitrified, ceramic material fired at high temperatures for long periods of time, as were Blanchard's pieces.[2]

1. Haskell & Penny, 316.
2. I would like to thank Alice Cooney Frelinghuysen, curator of American porcelain and glass at The Metropolitan Museum of Art, for this information.

3.59

Urn. Portland Stone Ware Co., Portland, Maine. c.1880. American. Stoneware. Collection Matt and Chris Matthews. Marked: *PORTLAND STONEWARE CO.*

The Portland Stone Ware Company prided itself on its successful ceramic designs as well as its special finish, which gave its pieces both durability and beauty. Developed especially for the Maine climate, Portland's surface coating was a vitrified salt glaze, an attractive glossy finish that could withstand severe winters. Pictured in Portland's catalogue of circa 1895, the substantial form of this urn is softened by its naturalistic details. It could be displayed on a variety of pedestals according to a customer's taste.[1]

1. Portland, 42.

3.60

Urn (one of six). c.1895. Terra cotta. American. Rosecliff, Preservation Society of Newport County, Newport, Rhode Island.

Attributed to the Perth Amboy Terra Cotta Company, these urns are made of glazed terra cotta, a material revitalized during the Arts and Crafts movement and widely used during the early twentieth century. The overall shape of this vase probably derived from the *vaso,* a type of Italian terra-cotta planter used to contain and transport citrus and other temperature-sensitive plants in and out of doors as the seasons changed. The artist started with this vernacular – and largely unadorned – form, adding three bands of classically-inspired decoration: one of *rinceaux* (scrolled foliage), one of garlands and leonine masks, and one of acanthus leaves. Thus, by lavishing ornament on this usually bare form, the artist produced an object of monumental beauty.

3.61

Pair of urns. c.1904. American. Terra cotta. Private collection.

These unusual, four-foot-high urns have a simple, ovoid form. The bowl, embellished with swags and rams' heads, meets a rising and tapering circular foot to produce a strikingly integrated ensemble. These urns are said to have been exhibited at the 1904 St. Louis World's Fair, one of a series of American expositions that displayed classical architecture and decoration.

4.1
Seat. After Karl Friedrich Schinkel. c. 1860–80.
Possibly German. Cast iron. Private collection.
4.2
Chair. After Karl Friedrich Schinkel. c.1850.
Possibly German. Cast iron. Private collection.

The garden seat shown here as 4.1 is distinguished by its association with a particular designer. Around 1835, Karl Friedrich Schinkel (1781–1841), the Prussian Neoclassical architect, designed this pattern for the Roman baths in Potsdam Park.[1] Its classical decoration and curule legs were based on ancient Roman examples, perhaps inspired by the archaeological discoveries at Pompeii and Herculaneum in the eighteenth century. The openwork decoration on the back of Schinkel's original featured a symmetrical composition of classical winged figures and scrolling foliate ornament flanking a central lyre. Occasionally, other classically inspired frieze motifs, such as the double winged splat in 4.2, were substituted on the back. Unlike Schinkel's other seat designs for royal gardens and parks, this seat was put into general production.[2] Well suited to the casting process, the basic form was multiplied to create two-, three-, and four-seat settees with various degrees of aesthetic success. We know that the seats were made by Prussian foundries, but since they have not been found in any trade catalogues, their actual place of production remains an enigma. The bench shown here has round slats on its seat, while that of the armchair displays a honeycomb pattern.

1. Ostergard 1994, 90.
2. Ostergard 1994, 93.

CATALOGUE 4

FURNITURE

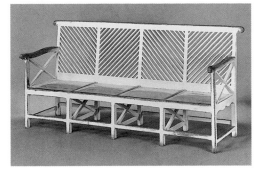

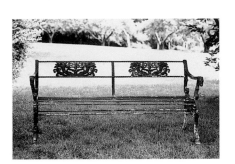

4.3

Almodington Seat. 1760–70. Maryland. Yellow pine. Museum of Early Southern Decorative Art, Winston-Salem, N.C.

This seat, named after the Maryland plantation from which it came, is perhaps the oldest piece of American garden furniture that has come to light thus far. Unlike early pieces made from cast iron, early wooden seats, being made of such a perishable material, rarely survive. The simple design of this seat is characterized by its overall geometric pattern and its lack of ornamentation. The compartmentalized backrest is made up of alternating diagonal slats, which recall a design by the English furniture designer William Halfpenny for "Open Gates with Dutch Battend Pannels and Chinese Barrs" published by him in 1750 (see drawing).[1]

1. W. Halfpenny, "Twenty New Designs of Chinese Lattice," in E. White, 428.

4.4

Seat. c. 1850. German. Cast iron. Private collection.

This seat is an adaptation of the more recognizable one designed by Karl Friedrich Schinkel (see cat. 4.1). Indeed, it is identical to the Schinkel seat, except for the unique cornucopia backsplat. The seat matches an original casting by the Andersen Foundry of Güstrow, in northern Germany, which came under the direction of the sculptor Heinrich Kaehler (1804–78) in 1846. This rarely seen version of Schinkel's design was presumably devised by Kaehler shortly after he took over the foundry.[1] Current research indicates that this version was never made in America. Matching armchairs were produced, although they have seldom appeared on the twentieth-century market.

1. Himmelheber, 24, also see pl. 70.

4.5

Armchair and ottoman. 1840–50. American. Cast iron. Private collection.

The dating of this particular chair has been the source of some confusion. Although unmarked, the piece illustrated here is identical to a large set of cast-iron lyre-back armchairs from the collection of The Highlands, in Fort Washington, Pennsylvania, one of which was pictured in William M. Hornor, Jr.'s *Blue Book Philadelphia Furniture*. In his caption, Hornor assigned a date of 1804 to the chair, which had been cast by the Robert Wood foundry.[1] Since the chairs were marked "Robert Wood," they would indeed date to the earliest part of his forty years in the trade (see Appendix 1). However, Wood's business on Ridge Road in Philadelphia did not begin production until 1839, making the much earlier date an impossibility. Unfortunately, many publications have accepted this erroneous date and have thus compounded what may have been originally a simple reversal of digits – turning 1840 into 1804. Despite this foible, this uniquely American chair, which appears in Wood & Perot's 1858 catalogue,[2] remains an elegant example of the integration of rococo and neoclassical design elements.

1. Hornor, 259.
2. Wood & Perot, no. 89.

4.6

Seat. Carron Company, Falkirk, Scotland. c. 1840–50. Scottish. Cast iron. Private collection. Marked with diamond registration mark for March 1846.

Nineteenth-century British seats can often be identified by the presence of a diamond registration mark behind the central motif on the seat back or inside the side supports. At times these marks are obscured by the build-up of paint over the years. The design of this settee, often termed "Gothic," was patented in England in 1846 by the Carron Company of Scotland, and then later copied and patented in the United States in 1848.[1] The American version of the design with rear cabriole legs differed slightly from the earlier Carron prototype, shown above, which featured an unornamented, straight rear leg. Primarily rococo revival in aesthetic, the pattern was labeled "Gothic" but also "Rococo" in catalogues (see p. 222, Janes, Beebe & Co.). It was published in many American foundry catalogues, including those of J. L. Mott Iron Works, J. W. Fiske Iron Works, and the Stewart Iron Works.[2]

1. MMA, no. 119.
2. Mott 1889, 24, pl. 28; Fiske 1868, 30; Stewart, 95, no. 367.

4.7

Settee. c. 1850. French. Cast iron. Private collection.

Several of the earliest cast-iron furniture types, including this one, displayed elements derived from Gothic architecture, including pointed arches, quatrefoils, and lozenges. Examples of this pattern are found in French trade catalogues, including those published by François Thiollet[1] and J. J. Ducel,[2] both of which date from before 1850. This form is extremely rare in this country, and no American foundries are known to have produced it.

1. Himmelheber, 20.
2. Ducel, fig. 1774.

4.8

Seat. West Point Foundry, Cold Spring, New York. c. 1840. American. Cast iron. Putnam County Historical Society and Foundry School Museum, Cold Spring, New York.

This cast-iron settee is possibly one of the earliest produced in America. Thought to be a housewarming gift from Gouverneur Kemble, owner of the West Point Foundry, to Washington Irving for Sunnyside, Irving's home in Tarrytown, New York, the seat features an unusual backrest with a centered Gothic-style wheel flanked by truncated arches. A letter dated November 14, 1836 from Irving to George Harvey bears, superimposed on its text, two sketches for Gothic seats, one of which resembles this one. Although it has long been assumed that these designs were by Irving himself, the tone of the letter suggests, on the contrary, that the seats were designed by Harvey.[1] Irving wrote: *Mr. Gouverneur Kemble, who was at my cottage a few days since, offered to furnish me with two gothic seats of cast iron for the porch, and to have them cast in the highlands, if I would send him patterns. You were kind enough to say you would give me designs for the seats; I will be much obliged to you if you will do so at your leisure and convenience. . . . "*[2]

1. I would like to thank Kathleen Eagen Johnson, Curator of Historic Hudson Valley, for this information.
2. Letter from Washington Irving to George Harvey, November 14, 1836, Berg Collection, New York Public Library. Quoted in Butler, 42–43.

4.9

Garden seat. Wood & Perot, Philadelphia, Pennsylvania. c. 1860. American. Cast iron. Private collection. Marked: *WOOD & PEROT.*

The Coalbrookdale Company registered this "Gothic" pattern in 1854 and included it in its 1875 catalogue.[1] In America, Wood & Perot published it as early as 1858, revealing the firm's awareness of international design trends.[2] The coat of arms in the raised central medallion on the seat back is an aristocratic element that implies use by titled landholders. It would have been particularly appealing to the socially conscious, recently affluent American middle class of the late nineteenth century.

1. Coalbrookdale 1875, Section III, 253, no. 22.
2. Wood & Perot, no. 302.

4.10

Hall chair. c. 1860. American. Cast iron. Rosedown Plantation and Gardens, St. Francisville, Louisiana.

Suitable for outdoor and indoor use, this three-legged chair was small enough to occupy a narrow passageway such as a hall. The Coalbrookdale Company offered the chair with an option to order it with a "Japanned and gilt" finish and a cane seat, attesting to an indoor, rather than outdoor, use.[1] The chair also appears in the New York Wire Railing Company's 1857 catalogue,[2] and in Wood & Perot's 1858 catalogue.[3]

1. Coalbrookdale 1875, Section III, 273, no. 28.
2. New York Wire Railing, 68.
3. Wood & Perot, no. 291.

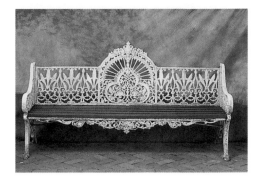

4.11

Seat. 1860–80. English. Cast iron and wood. Private collection.

Although this design is seldom seen on the American market today, it was made by several American foundries in the nineteenth century. Chase Brothers & Co. of Boston offered it in its trade catalogue of circa 1850,[1] and Wood & Perot offered a double-back variation on the design in its 1858 catalogue.[2] Also registered by the Coalbrookdale Company of England in circa 1860, the design is characterized by a central Moorish-style sunburst flanked by stylized plant motifs.

1. Chase Brothers, no. 6.
2. Wood & Perot, no. 295.

4.12
Settee. John McLean, New York. c. 1870. Cast iron. Smithsonian Institution, Washington, D.C. Marked: *JOHN MCLEAN N.Y.*

4.13
Chair. c. 1870. American. Cast iron. Virginia House, Richmond, Virginia.

The so-called "Grape" or "grapevine" pattern had appeared in trade catalogues by 1850, and thereafter became one of the most popular and recognizable patterns of the nineteenth century (see p. 81).[1] The Grape pattern is unusual because it does not incorporate any visible linear structural supports. The charm of this rococo-style pattern was emphasized in an article in the November, 1857, issue of *The Horticulturist*, which suggests that grape chairs are "much used in the open air and for cemetery lots."[2] Nearly every maker of cast-iron furniture offered an interpretation of this design, and

foundries such as Robert Wood & Co. of Philadelphia, and John McLean of New York featured Grape chairs and settees in their trade catalogues. The different leg patterns on the settee and chair shown here exhibit two variations that were available: the chair features splayed leaf legs, while the settee features legs composed of grapes and leaves. The popularity of the Grape pattern in the nineteenth and early twentieth centuries has led to large numbers on the American market today. The survival of the delicate aprons on these two pieces is somewhat rare, and makes them more desirable.

1. Snyder, 231.
2. *The Horticulturist* 9, 498.

4.14
Seat. 1860–80. American. Cast iron. Private collection.

The "Twig," or "Rustic," settee imitates the wooden furniture that was often found in naturalistic gardens of the nineteenth century. Each member of the settee represents an organic element, including bound twigs and branches that compose the back and arms, and serpents that wrap around the legs and intertwine below the seat.[1] Armchairs were made in this pattern as well. Manufactured in England and Scotland by 1850, the Twig, or Rustic, pattern subsequently became one of the most popular cast-iron designs in America. Although it was manufactured well into the 1890s, it reached the height of popularity in the third quarter of the nineteenth century.[2] Janes, Beebe & Co. of New York City, for example, featured the rustic settee in its trade catalogue of 1858.[3]

1. Snyder, 230.
2. Snyder, 230.
3. Janes, Beebe & Co., pl. 141.

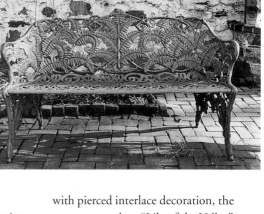

4.15

Chairs. c. 1860–80. American. Cast iron. Private collection.

Reminiscent of the naturalistic "twig" settee, this rustic design features twisted elements that simulate tree limbs and branches. The back is composed of a stylized representation of the tree-of-life motif. Referred to in the 1868 Fiske catalogue as the Cottage chair, this organic pattern evolved from grotto design.[1]

1. Fiske 1868, 27.

4.16

Chair. 1880–90. American. Cast iron. Collection F. J. Carey, III.

4.17

Seat. 1860–80. American. Cast iron. Collection F. J. Carey, III.

The "Fern" seat is one of the best-selling cast-iron furniture patterns. These naturalistic pieces have an allover pierced botanical design not unlike the "Lily of the Valley" and "Grape" patterns. The settee and chair designs originated with the Coalbrookdale Company, and are registered at the London Public Records Office. In the firm's 1875 catalogue, this pattern, called "Fern and Blackberry," was offered in two design variations with either a wooden or iron seat.[1] The "Fern" pattern was also manufactured by most American makers. American interpretations often feature a form-fitting iron seat

with pierced interlace decoration, the same seat used on "Lily of the Valley" settees and chairs. There are three sizes of the "Fern" armchair available on the current market: small, medium, and large. The small size has a plain round crest rail unbroken by any fern fronds. The middle size, which is shown in J. L. Mott's 1875 catalogue[2] and J. W. Fiske's catalogues published between 1919 and 1933, has a single fern frond that extends above the crest rail.[3] The large size chair (cat. 4.16) is wider and has two diamond motifs below the crest rail.

1. Coalbrookdale 1875, Section III, 254, nos. 29, 29A.
2. Mott 1875, n.p., pl. 14.
3. Fiske [1913–33], 4, no. 263.

4.18

Seat. James W. Carr, Richmond, Virginia. 1900–1920. American. Cast iron. Virginia House, Richmond, Virginia. Marked: *JAMES W. CARR. RICHMOND. VA.*

This seat is a variation on the "Fern" pattern. Its two-seater form, a rarity in cast-iron furniture and specific to this maker, resembles two conjoined armchairs. The pad foot is another unusual feature of the Carr seat.

4.19

Seat. c. 1880. American. Cast iron and wood. Private collection. Marked: *J. L. MOTT NEW YORK, PAT. APP. FOR*

This design, often referred to as the "Victoria Settee," was registered circa 1865 by the Dalkeith Ironworks in Dalkeith, Scotland.[1] Although it seldom appeared in American trade catalogues, the J. L. Mott Iron Works featured this pattern in 1875 and in 1897.[2] This extremely rare marked example indicates that Mott applied for a patent in an attempt to prevent other American foundries from using the design.

1. Morris, 172.
2. Mott 1875, pl. 1; Mott 1897, pl. 7–A.

4.20

Chair. c. 1860. American. Cast iron. Collection Cragmoor Designs.

The "Morning Glory" pattern of this chair was probably adapted from the Coalbrookdale Company's "Convolvulus" seat pattern, first cast by that firm around 1855[1] and offered in America soon after by Wood & Perot in 1858.[2] The design was altered and renamed "Morning Glory" by several American manufacturers in the last half of the nineteenth century. One of the earliest references to the design was in the 1857 catalogue of New York Wire Railing Company.[3] The form of the legs in some American versions was changed from a formal paw-footed leg with inset grape motif to the leafy one also used on the "Grape" pattern chair. The design appeared in a catalogue of the Phoenix Iron Works, published between 1880 and 1890.[4] Numerous American firms produced chairs in this style, including Janes, Kirtland & Co., W. A. Snow, J. W. Fiske Iron Works, A. B. & W. T. Westervelt, and J. L. Mott Iron Works.

1. Himmelheber, 33.
2. Wood & Perot, no. 306.
3. New York Wire Railing, 68, fig. 306.
4. Phoenix, fig. 151.

4.21

Armchair. William McHose & Co., Dayton, Ohio. 1871–77. American. Cast iron. Private collection. Marked: *WM McHOSE & C., MFS DAYTON.*

As is the case with many cast-iron seat patterns, the "Lily of the Valley" design originates with the Coalbrookdale Company of England.[1] It was subsequently offered by a number of American iron founders in both chairs and settees. While many English models were made with slatted seats of wood, American examples often feature a form-fitting iron seat bottom with pierced interlacing motifs, similar to the "Fern" seat (see cats. 4.16 and 4.17). It should be noted that this pierced seat is not necessarily an American innovation; Coalbrookdale's "Lily of the Valley" armchair, though not its settee, could also be purchased with a similar pierced seat. Apart from William McHose & Co., such manufacturers as J. L. Mott Iron Works[2] and J. W. Fiske Iron Works[3] offered this pattern in trade catalogues. Mott's version was a variation, rather than a strict copy, of Coalbrookdale's model, substituting a continuous crest rail for Coalbrookdale's scalloped crest rail and diamond motifs (see fig. 65, p. 80).

1. Coalbrookdale 1875, Section III, 255, no. 36.
2. Mott 1875, no. 15.
3. Fiske [1908–1912], 35, no. 266.

4.22

Seat. c. 1860–80. American. Cast iron and wood. Private collection.

A relatively rare form produced by American and British manufacturers, this seat is termed the "Berlin" seat in J. W. Fiske Iron Works' catalogues, but is alternately called the "Rustic" seat in the catalogues of the Coalbrookdale Company. Coalbrookdale registered the design with the London Public Records Office as no. 78766 on April 7, 1851. While Coalbrookdale's example has an iron slatted seat, J. W. Fiske's version has a seat made of wooden slats. Coalbrookdale offered the seat in at least four sizes (measuring 3, 4, 5, and 6 feet), while J. W. Fiske only seems to have sold a 4-foot-3-inch model. The version shown here is unmarked, and could have been made by a number of American makers.

4.23

Seat. c. 1870. English. Cast iron and wood. Private collection.

This "Oak and Ivy" seat, originally designed by John Bell (1811–95) for the Coalbrookdale Company, was registered in 1859.[1] The pattern seems to have been exclusively British, since it has not been found in any American trade catalogues. In the Coalbrookdale Company's 1875 catalogue, the design is offered in one, two, and three-seat versions. It was one of the heaviest and most grand – in terms of overall proportions – of all the seats illustrated in the catalogue. "Oak and Ivy" seats seen today are often missing their front aprons, which distracts considerably from the overall design.

1. Himmelheber, 33.

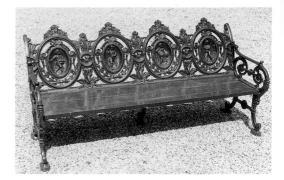

4.24

Seat. 1860–80. American. Cast iron and wood. Private collection.

This seat, often referred to as the "Season Settee," features a backrest illustrating the agrarian labors of the four seasons. A sower, a hower, a reaper, and a harvester are depicted within four medallions that are flanked by lilies and topped with scrolling vines. Although this design was registered in England by the Coalbrookdale Company in 1870,[1] it was also retailed in the United States. The J. L. Mott Iron Works featured the pattern in its 1875 trade catalogue.[2]

1. Himmelheber, pl. 182; p. 228.
2. Mott 1875, pl. 18.

4.25

Seat. c. 1880. American. Cast iron. Collection, The Metropolitan Museum of Art, New York.

This seat pattern, known as "Passion Flower," was first offered by English manufacturers. The design, registered in 1862 by the Coalbrookdale Company, is pictured in its 1875 catalogue[1] and was also retailed by a number of American makers. J. L. Mott Iron Works, for example, included this seat in its 1889 catalogue.[2] The seat also appears in E. T. Barnum Iron and Wire Works' catalogue of circa 1900.[3] This pattern, characterized by a curvilinear silhouette and botanical detail, is similar in form and style to the "Laurel" seat (cat. 4.42). Both were designed without a front apron.

1. Coalbrookdale 1875, Section III, 263, no. 32.
2. Mott 1889, 22, pl. 34.
3. Barnum c. 1900, 23, no. 24–C.

4.26

Seat. c. 1860. American. Cast iron and wood. Smithsonian Institution, Washington, D.C.

This seat type, known as "Serpent and Grapes," was one of the more elaborate nineteenth-century park settees. Dating to 1844, it was one of the Coalbrookdale Company's first registered designs. The pattern was borrowed by several American manufacturers; for example, it appears in the 1858 catalogue of Wood & Perot.[1]

1. Wood & Perot, no. 307.

4.27

Seat. c. 1880. American. Cast iron. Collection Cragmoor Designs.

This type of seat, often referred to as "Versailles," had a matching chair (see cat. 4.29) generally termed a "Hall Chair" or "Piazza Chair."[1] The formal swags on the back are related to Neoclassical design, while the cabriole legs and overall silhouette are strongly rococo in style. A seat of this type stands in the front of the house at Lansdowne, a private residence in Natchez, Mississippi.

1. Westervelt, 16, no. 105; and Fiske [1908–1912], 37, no. 261.

4.28

Seat. c. 1860. American. Cast iron and wood. Private collection.

Embellished with foliate scrolls and snakehead terminals, this park settee exhibits a variation on the "Serpent and Grapes" pattern (cat. 4.26) registered by the Coalbrookdale Company. The seat was retailed in America, along with a variety of benches made for park use, by several cast-iron makers, including Wood & Perot.[1]

1. Wood & Perot, no. 304.

4.29
Chair. c. 1900. American. Cast iron. Private collection.

This chair type is often referred to as a "piazza chair." Similar to a "hall chair" design published in *The Horticulturist* of 1857,[1] it was intended for a piazza or veranda. Like the nineteenth-century hallway, the piazza served as a physical and visual transition space, in this case between the interior of the house and the lawn; transitional furniture such as this chair, therefore, was appropriate.[2] Although the chair shown here is a late model of this particular pattern, it was offered as early as 1858 by Wood & Perot of Philadelphia.[3] (see cat. 4.27)

1. *The Horticulturist* 9, 497.
2. Snyder, 237.
3. Wood & Perot, pl. 315.

4.30
Chair. c. 1860–70. American. Cast iron. Private collection.

This three-legged chair appeared in J. W. Fiske Iron Works' circa 1868 catalogue.[1] By the time of the publication of the same company's catalogue of 1875–79, the pattern had been designated as a "Hall" chair.[2] When J. L. Mott Iron Works offered it in its circa 1875 catalogue, it was called a "Rustic" chair.[3] In fact, the oval back and splayed legs more closely resemble the styles of interior furniture of the period than outdoor rustic forms embellished with branches and twigs. Although produced by a number of nineteenth-century makers, examples of this chair are not often seen on the current market.

1. Fiske 1868, 27, no. 2.
2. Fiske [1875–79], n.p., no. 253.
3. Mott 1875, pl. 24.

4.31
Seat. John F. Riley, Charleston, South Carolina. c. 1890. American. Cast iron. Nathaniel Russel House, Charleston, South Carolina. Marked: *JOHN F. RILEY IRON WORKS CHARLESTON S.C.*

This rococo-style pattern, which features C-scrolls on the apron and naturalistic cross braces, was primarily made in America. Although it is often associated with Hinderer's Iron Works of New Orleans because of the company's prolific production of this design, it was retailed by other American foundries as well. Wood & Perot of Philadelphia, for example, offered a longer variation of this seat in its 1858 trade catalogue.[1] John F. Riley's Foundry and Machine Works was a prosperous business that supplied the South with ornamental wares. The company first appeared in the Charleston city directories in 1886, and continued production until after 1935.

1. Wood & Perot, no. 292.

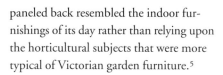

4.32

Seat. North American Iron Works, New York, NY. c. 1895. American. Cast iron. Private collection. Marked: *NORTH AMERICAN IRON WORKS.*

Termed the "Americus Settee,"[1] this seat appears in the J. L. Mott Iron Works catalogue of circa 1870–80.[2] In keeping with the characteristics of the "curtain style," the back of the settee is divided into three panels with correlating decoration. The precedent for this particular design is not entirely clear. The rhythmic horizontality and asymmetry of the scrollwork on the back panels are reminiscent of the traditional decorative arts of Asia. Such design motifs have often surfaced in Western art in the form of *chinoiserie* and *japonisme*. They were especially popular toward the end of the nineteenth century, when the taste for exotic design sources was pervasive.

1. Snyder, 235.
2. Mott 1870–80, pl. 40–A.

4.33

Armchair. Hinderer's Iron Works, New Orleans, Louisiana. c. 1895. American. Cast iron. Monmouth, Natchez, Mississippi. Marked: *HINDERER'S IRON WORKS, NO, LA.*

4.34

Seat. Samuel S. Bent, New York, NY. 1917–20. American. Cast iron. Private collection. Marked: *S. S. BENT.*

The makers of these companion seats were both specialists in producing ornamental castings. Hinderer's Iron Works represented the fine design and historic tradition of New Orleans, a city known for its architectural and ornamental ironwork.[1] In 1868–69, Samuel S. Bent, a New York foundry, advertised their manufactory, the Globe Iron Foundry, as making "Fine Castings."[2] This pattern, the most common of the "curtain" styles, was produced by several makers, including the J. W. Fiske Iron Works.[3] It is often referred to as the "Arlington Settee."[4] The curtain seat was one of the few designs that produced variations on a single theme. The rigid, paneled back resembled the indoor furnishings of its day rather than relying upon the horticultural subjects that were more typical of Victorian garden furniture.[5]

1. Robertson and Robertson, 47.
2. *Wilson's Commercial Register.* New York, 1868–69, 71.
3. Fiske c. 1901, 3, no. 325.
4. Westervelt, 21, no. 75.
5. Snyder, 233.

4.35

Pair of side chairs. North American Iron
Works, New York. c. 1895. American. Cast iron.
Private collection. Marked: *THE NORTH
AMERICAN IRON WORKS, N.Y.*

North American Iron Works was a subsidiary of J. L. Mott Iron Works of New York
City. Organized to manufacture cemetery
ornament, this branch of the business
was first listed in the New York City directory in 1872. The "curtain" design of these
thronelike armchairs is executed in the
Renaissance Revival style, which enjoyed a
renewed popularity in the 1890s; the scrolling crest surmounted by an anthemion
motif, the oval medallion in the back, and
the bosses and strapwork in the apron are
all characteristic of the Renaissance Revival
vocabulary.[1]

1. MMA, pl. 238.

4.36

Pair of armchairs. c. 1895. American. Cast iron.
Private collection.

These curtain-style chairs, termed "Boston
Panel," were offered by a few American
manufacturers. Evident in the seats is a
combination of vegetal arabesques –
relating to Arts and Crafts designs – and
classically inspired floral swags. This
particular pattern always includes a scalloped front apron. M. D. Jones & Co.
of Boston illustrates the armchair, along
with a two- and three-seat settee in its
circa 1903 catalogue.[1] On the same page,
the catalogue states that the chairs were
to be "shipped packed flat, reducing the
cost of freight charges and risk of break-
ages."[2] Such information sheds light on
the manner by which cast-iron garden
furniture was distributed to clients.

1. Jones, 25.
2. Jones, 25.

4.37

Seat. Peter Timmes' Son. c. 1890–1900.
American. Cast iron. Private collection. Marked:
PETER TIMMES' SON, BROOKLYN, N.Y.

Another of the group called "curtain"
garden seats, the Peter Timmes' Son
patented version has the most elaborate
pierced decoration. The typical three-
panel seat back contains Renaissance
motifs within a structured framework.
Known as the "Three-Seat Renaissance
Settee" in Timmes's 1896 catalogue, the
seat displays innumerable foliate patterns.[1] Like a cypher, the central panel's
cresting suggests aristocratic bearing.
The only unlikely element, the row of
hearts forming the apron, adds a touch
of whimsy to an otherwise formal presentation. This pattern is believed to be
unique to the Peter Timmes' Son firm.

1. Timmes, 62, pl. 79.

4.38

Pair of seats. Peter Timmes' Sons, Brooklyn, New York. c. 1890–1900. American. Cast iron. Private collection. Marked: *PETER TIMMES' SONS, BROOKLYN, N.Y.*

John McLean, Philadelphia, Pennsylvania. Cast iron. Marked: *JOHN MCLEAN, PHILA.*

This pair of settees is yet another adaptation of the uniquely American "curtain" seat. In the Peter Timmes' Son 1896 catalogue, a piece of this type is identified as a "two-seat curtain settee."[1] Such classical motifs as the anthemia on the crest rail and the scrolling foliage on the back panels are combined with Moorish-style aprons. This exact cast-iron pattern, minus the apron, is displayed in a brick summer house at the Old Westbury Gardens, built in the early 1900s by Mr. and Mrs. Ogden Phipps.

1. Timmes, 64, pl. 81.

4.39

Seat. c. 1901. American. Cast iron. Collection John and Gilda McGarry, Jr.

A variation on the basic "curtain" style garden seat, this exceedingly rare model was offered by J.W. Fiske Iron Works in its circa 1901 catalogue.[1] The S-scrolls, water plant motifs, and anthemia are Renaissance elements. The resemblance of the Moorish style pierced apron to a curtain apparently gave this seat its name.

1. Fiske c. 1901, n.p.

4.41

Seat. c. 1900. American. Cast iron. Collection Janet and Joseph Shein.

This ornate pattern, a stylistic amalgam of rococo and Renaissance motifs, reflects the complex interiors of the late Victorian period. Believed to be uniquely American, the design is popularly known as "Renaissance Scroll." A settee in this pattern is in the collection of The Metropolitan Museum of Art. The museum's example bears on the back of its apron an otherwise unknown mark, "NAVILLUS," which in the future may help reveal its origin and history.

4.40

Seat. Pequonnock Company, Bridgeport, Connecticut. c. 1910. American. Cast iron. Smithsonian Institution. Marked: *PEQUONNOCK.*

Known as a "Circular Bench" in the Pequonnock catalogue, this form was designed to encircle a tree. The maker included "quality castings" in its logo, and offered a painted finish "in shades of green, with leaves and flowers outlined in natural colors . . ."[1] J. L. Mott Iron Works produced the same seat and identified it as the "Bouquet Settee."[2]

1. Pequonnock, pl. 105.
2. Mott 1875, pl. 2.

4.42

Seat and Chairs. c. 1920. American. Cast iron. Private collection. Marked: *HART*.

The "Laurel" pattern was registered by the Coalbrookdale Company of England and offered with a wooden seat in its 1875 catalogue.[1] Soon after, the J. L. Mott Iron Works published the pattern in its catalogue, apparently lifting the etching from the English firm's catalogue with only minor changes.[2] In both firms' publications, the "Laurel" settee was shown adjacent to the "Passion Flower" settee (see cat. 4.25). Both have similar rounded forms, and both are pictured without aprons. These American "Laurel" seats bear the mark "Hart," which, to this point, has not been identified. Stylistically, the griffin leg relates to French Empire forms, while the back leg, in an eclectic manner typical of the Victorian era, recalls the rustic branches of the Chinese Chippendale style.

1. Coalbrookdale 1875, Section III, 263, no. 31.
2. Mott 1870–1880, 36, pl. 30–A.

4.43

Seat. 1900–25. American. Cast iron. Private collection.

This seat pattern, known as the "Scroll Settee" in many American trade catalogues, was produced in great numbers by Kramer Brothers of Ohio, and is therefore often associated with that firm. However, it was also manufactured by several other American makers, including A. B. & W. T. Westervelt, J. W. Fiske Iron Works, Janes, Kirtland & Co., E. T. Barnum Iron and Wire Works, and Hinderer's Iron Works. It was alternately referred to as the Capital Settee,[1] the Arabesque Settee [2] and the Ornamental Iron Scroll Settee.[3]

1. Kramer, 70, S–164.
2. Hinderer's, no. 28.
3. Barnum c. 1900, 23, no. 33–C.

4.44

Garden seat. c. 1840. English. Wrought iron. Private collection.

Early-nineteenth-century wrought-iron garden seats constructed of reeded strap iron often stemmed from the Neoclassical styles of such designers as George Hepplewhite and Thomas Sheraton. As a writer noted in 1941, this derivation ". . . indicates how much of a real living room the English garden was. . ."[1]

1. Price, 9.

4.45

Seat. c. 1830. English. Wrought iron. Rosedown Plantation and Gardens, St. Francisville, Louisiana.

Produced in England in the late eighteenth and early nineteenth centuries, this type of wrought-iron garden bench, with its scrolling members and reeded seat rails, is often referred to as a "Regency" or "Sheraton" seat. Around 1930, this pattern was retailed by Todhunter of New York City, a firm that advertised inventory brought to the United States from abroad. Not original to the plantation, this ornate seat was installed in the historic gardens of Rosedown during the 1950s restoration.

4.46

Seat. c. 1830–40. English. Wrought iron. Private collection.

Originally intended for English parks, the wrought-iron seats of the early nineteenth century incorporated features of formal furniture design. Even though many companies produced seats of this design, the form retained the name Sheraton, after the English designer, in all its versions.[1] Remarkably modern in appearance, this hand-made creation streamlined the forms of Regency loveseats and chairs to a graphic minimum.

1. Price, 9.

4.47

Armchair. Lalance & Grosjean, New York, NY. 1866–70. American. Wrought Iron. Private Collection. Marked: *LALANCE AND GROSJEAN, 273 PEARL STREET, N.Y., PATENT DATED MAY 15, 1866.*

The Parisian designer François A. Carré was the original patent owner and maker of the spring steel chair. After settling in the United States, the French firm Lalance & Grosjean bought the patent and design from Mr. Carré.[1] The iron frame and ingenious bent-steel seat with back straps allowed flexibility for comfort. A demand for these chairs arose toward the end of the century. In 1892, Schlesinger, Wiessener, & Company of New York published a *Catalogue of Bent Steel Furniture,* which notes a "Boulevard Arm Chair" model.[2] Resembling the Lalance & Grosjean version, the armchair could withstand the elements of nature, including even the salt air of the seashore.

1. Hanks, 80.
2. Hanks, 81.

4.48

Chair. c. 1920. American. Wrought iron. Private collection.

The spring steel chair was created in France in the mid-nineteenth century when the demand for park furniture inspired innovative designs. This example, an adaptation of the original chair (cat. 4.47), reached the height of its popularity in the 1920s. Armchairs, sidechairs, and tables were produced as sets to provide resilient comfort out of doors.

4.49

Chair and table. c. 1900. French. Wrought iron. Private collection.

Tables and chairs such as these were originally used in Paris as park furniture. Similar pieces are illustrated in the circa 1870 catalogue published by the Société Anonyme des Hauts-Fourneaux & Fonderies du Val D'Osne.[1] The chair seat and table top are pierced to allow for easy drainage. Outdoor furniture of this delicacy and practicality was also offered, though not as commonly, by American makers. J. L. Mott Iron Works produced a wrought-iron folding chair that, while less elaborate than the French chair, responded to the demands of functionality and versatility.[2]

1. Société Anonyme des Hauts-Fourneaux, pl. 429.
2. Mott 1889, 33, pl. 44.

4.50

Seat. c. 1900. American. Wrought steel. Collection Janet and Joseph Shein.

The wrought-iron version of this seat is illustrated in the Van Dorn Iron Works catalogue of 1884.[1] The piece was later produced in steel, as in the example seen here. This unadorned piece was also advertised by J. W. Fiske Iron Works as "particularly adapted for parks, porches, lawns and cemeteries."[2]

1. Van Dorn, no. 122.
2. Fiske [1913–1933], 10.

4.51

Pair of side chairs. c. 1880. American. Wirework. Private collection.

Bent-wire seating was a popular feature of American gardens during the second half of the nineteenth century. The strength and flexibility of the material afforded a variety of design possibilities, and many elegant, airy pieces for garden settings were produced in response to the demand for fashionable, lightweight furniture.[1] J. W. Fiske Iron Works offered a chair similar to the pair shown, with a tiered back and scrolled feet, in its trade catalogue produced between 1908 and 1912.[2]

1. Himmelheber, 61.
2. Fiske [1908–1912], 8.

4.52

Seat. c. 1940. American. Wrought iron. Private collection. Armchair. William Adams, Philadelphia, Pennsylvania. 1872. Wrought iron. Private collection. Marked: *WM ADAMS PHILADELPHIA*.

While nearly identical in style, this wrought-iron settee and armchair are an associated pair rather than a matched set. They were produced decades apart by different makers. The chair, an earlier marked example, was finely crafted with a deep seat and elegantly scrolled stretchers. The settee, neither as heavy nor as commodious as the armchair, also lacks the graceful silhouette of the earlier piece. The date of the chair may be deduced from the maker's company name in 1872.

4.53

Armchair. c. 1890. American. Wirework.
Private collection.

The elaborate and fanciful design of this
wirework chair takes its inspiration from
French models. Wirework furniture was
prevalent in Paris, particularly during the
early 1850s and after.[1] In America, several
firms produced pieces from this light,
versatile material, including J. W. Fiske
Iron Works, E. T. Barnum Iron and Wire
Works, F. & E. Aubel, M. Walker and
Sons, and the New York Wire Railing Co.,
the parent company of Hutchinson &
Wickersham. The piece shown here is
one of the finer, more intricate examples
that has come to light.

1. Himmelheber, 60.

4.54

Armchair. c. 1910. American. Wirework.
Private collection.

Around 1900, garden seats and chairs began to resemble their indoor counterparts.
Although constructed of stretched wire,
the rolled edge of this chair suggests the
comfort of upholstery. In the J. W. Fiske
Iron Works catalogue of 1908–12, a wire
settee displays a similar crest rail made up
of a multitude of rolled strands of wire.[1]

1. Fiske [1908–12], 8, no. 326.

4.55

Chair. Trudo Manufacturing Co., Framingham,
Massachusetts. 1930–40. American. Aluminum.
Private collection.

The maker who produced this chair is not
well known. Composed of aluminum,
cast iron's more portable and lightweight
competitor, this chair has a hollow framework, resulting in a sturdy, yet light, piece.
Aluminum, which was introduced in the
United States around 1870, was easily
worked and thus became one of the most
cost-effective materials for the manufacture of garden ornaments. The style of
the chair adheres to a pared-down,
modern aesthetic.

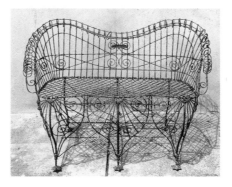

4.56

Seat. Howard & Morse, New York. c. 1890.
American. Wirework. Collection Janet and
Joseph Shein. Marked: *HOWARD & MORSE,
NEW YORK.*

Rarely does wirework furniture bear a
maker's metal label. The label attached to
this garden seat identifies it as a New York
piece, but offers no guidance as to its date
since the maker's address is not given.
The seat is a two-person wire settee constructed of bent rods and finely tightened
wire that was intertwined and tied in
fanciful shapes. A similar form, albeit
with scrolling rather than star-shaped
feet, was offered in the J. W. Fiske Iron
Works 1908–12 catalogue.[1]

1. Fiske [1908–1912], 8.

4.57
Chair. Joseph J. Leinfelder & Sons, La Crosse, Wisconsin. 1930–40. American. Wrought iron. Private collection.

4.58
Seat. Joseph J. Leinfelder & Sons, La Crosse, Wisconsin. 1930–40. American. Wrought iron. Private collection.

This seat and chair were sold exclusively by Mary Ryan of New York and Chicago. The semicircular form takes its stylistic inspiration from the early-nineteenth-century English wrought-iron seats that are known commonly as "Regency" or "Sheraton" benches. Pictured in Leinfelder's 1934 catalogue along with a few other "1933 successes certain to sell as well in 1934," the sweeping curved seat was, according to the retailer, "still as strongly in fashion as ever, and now ranking not as innovations but rather as proved 'repeat sellers.' "[1] Leinfelder also produced a matching quarter-circular model, along with a coordinating table and the chair as shown.

1. Leinfelder, no. CH–37C.

4.59
Chaises and table. c. 1940. American. Wrought iron. Private collection.

These examples are similar to pieces made by the Italian immigrant designer and iron-worker John Salterini, whose work was well received in the 1930s. The collaborative work of Salterini and an unnamed Florentine architect fashioned once hard metal-work into comfortable, decorative pieces. Examples made in imitation of indoor furniture, such as sectional iron sofas with cushions, iron cocktail tables with glass, and iron lamp shades, were instantly popular, bringing about the revitalization of wrought-iron garden furniture.

4.60
Table. c. 1860. American. Cast iron. Virginia House, Richmond, Virginia.

Known as a "Cast Iron Conservatory Table" in the 1875 J. L. Mott Iron Works catalogue, this table was fashioned in the naturalistic, but highly ornate, language of the rococo.[1] A rare tri-footed base that resembles cresting waves supports a pierced honeycomb top elegantly bordered with leaves. The identical base was used on tables made around 1850–60 by two iron founders in The Hague, The Netherlands and one in Stockholm, Sweden.[2]

1. Mott 1875, [30].
2. Himmelheber, 229, pl. 237.

4.61

Table. c. 1860. American. Cast and sheet iron. Collection F. J. Carey, III.

The featherlike supports that rise from the geometric base to carry the rectangular top of this table recall the feathered device of the Prince of Wales that embellishes the splats of late-eighteenth- and early-nineteenth-century English and American Neoclassical chairs. The pierced disk beneath the tabletop, however, is an unusual feature probably intended to offer additional support to the legs. A similar table, albeit with a round top, three legs, and a triangular base, is offered in the Janes, Beebe & Co. trade catalogue of 1858.[1]

1. Janes, Beebe & Co., pl. 160.

4.62

Table. c. 1880. American. Cast iron. Private collection.

This piece, often referred to as a "Zodiac" table, is so named due to the astrological symbols on its top. It is related to a design for the "Zodiac Pattern" table registered by the Falkirk Iron Company of Falkirk, Scotland. The form of the table, with its round, pierced top and ornate baluster, resembles many of the "Conservatory Tables" illustrated in American trade catalogues. While most similar tables are not ornamented with astrological motifs, they do often display the same style of interlaced, pierced decoration seen here. One characteristic of the nineteenth-century American version of this table is a hinged tilting top.

4.63

Table. c. 1880. English. Cast iron and wood. Private collection.

Not originally intended for the garden, tables like this one, topped with iron, wood, or marble, were moved outdoors from the interiors of English public houses. The spandrels were at times decorated with patriotic symbols or commemorative portraits. This particular piece, one of the most common types, was known as a "Britannia" pub table, since it was embellished with a woman in classical dress representing Britannia, holding a shield emblazoned with the Union Jack.[1] The Coalbrookdale Company pictured a version identified as "Victoria" in its 1888 catalogue. The "Victoria" table was ornamented with a medallion of the Queen cast into the spandrels.[2]

1. Morris, 165.
2. Coalbrookdale 1888, 33, no. 72.

4.64

Table. c. 1880. English. Cast iron. Collection
F. J. Carey, III.

Numerous variations of this round cast-
iron table were manufactured by foundries
in Scotland and England in the late nineteenth century.[1] The highly detailed
pierced top and shelf are not only attractive and serviceable, but also perforated
to allow water to drain. The distinctive
cabriole legs terminate in griffinlike heads,
giving the table a classical look. Identical
designs were featured in Wood & Perot's
1858 catalogue[2], and in Coalbrookdale's
1895 catalogue.[3]

1. Himmelheber, 47.
2. Wood & Perot, pl. 303.
3. Coalbrookdale 1875, Section II, 199, no. 50.

4.65

Table. c. 1880. American. Cast iron. Collection
Charlotte Inn.

This type of table, which has an unusual
revolving top above an ornamental baluster,
is relatively rare, although similar tables
can be found in the Coalbrookdale Company's 1888 catalogue.[1] The revolving top
is related in concept to J. L. Mott Iron
Works' "swivel chair," patented in 1847
(see drawing). Both objects are the result
of innovative technology in the cast-iron
industry in the late nineteenth century.

1. Coalbrookdale 1888, 32.

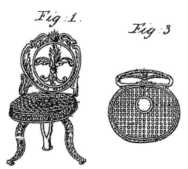

4.66

Table. Late 19th century. American. Cast iron
and marble. Collection Charlotte Inn.

The base and balusters of this table are
nearly identical to a design for a "cast
iron table stand" published in the 1889
catalogue of the J. L. Mott Iron Works.[1]
Marble tops were sold separately. Another
similar table appears in the catalogue of
A. B. & W. T. Westervelt.[2] In the Westervelt publication, the piece is labeled as a
Double Colebrook Table, since it was also
available in a single-baluster form. The
origin of the term "Colebrook" probably
refers to the Coalbrookdale Company
of England. Table stands were available
with or without bronzed, wooden, or
marble tops.

1. Mott 1889, 40, pl. 66.
2. Westervelt, 28.

4.67

Table. c. 1920. American. Cast iron. Collection
Charlotte Inn.

While this table is formally and stylistically related to other oblong rectangular
tables produced by American manufacturers, its double stretcher is rare. In 1858,
Wood & Perot offered a table with similar
scrolled rococo-revival supports, but with
only one stretcher.[1] Two "ornamental iron
table[s]" are illustrated in a later catalogue
published by J. W. Fiske Iron Works in
1924.[2] However, while close in overall appearance to the table shown here, neither
has a second stretcher. This example, which
appropriately serves as a plant stand, has a
pierced top to permit water drainage.

1. Wood & Perot, no. 125.
2. Fiske 1924, 26, nos. 316 and 317.

4.68

Table and seats. c. 1930–40. French. Cast stone.
Private collection.

A precedent for these woodland fantasies
existed in the early nineteenth-century
garden at Redleaf, in Penshurst, England
which contained a set of cast-iron mush-
room seats.[1] Twentieth-century makers
in St. Jean-de-Luz in the Basque region
of France created cast-stone furniture that
replicated logs, branches, and in this case,
mushrooms. These remarkable pieces
could be termed "rustic," as they reflect a
conscious effort to blend art with nature.
The American landscape specialist Andrew
Jackson Downing wrote that ". . . rustic
seats . . . are felt at once to be in unison
with the surrounding objects."[2]

1. Edwards, 78.
2. Downing 1841, 455.

4.69

Seat. Antonio Frilli, Ltd. Florence, Italy. c. 1900.
Marble and wood. Private collection. Marked
A. FRILLI / FIRENZE.

In the early twentieth century elite American garden collectors traveled to Europe,
often to Florence, Italy, to furnish their
gardens with the finest carved marble and
stone ornaments. The firm of Antonio
Frilli, advertised as "the largest and oldest
exporter of marble statuary in Italy," also
offered to reproduce any "famous piece
of work in the museums of Europe . . ."[1]
J. P. White of The Pyghtle Works of
Bedford, England, offered a similar seat
in his circa 1910 publication, but with
sphinx supports in terra cotta called
the Pistoja Design.[2] The rinceaux decoration on the sides of this marble example
recall the flamboyant foliate scrolls of
Roman ornament.[3]

1. Frilli, n.p.
2. J. P. White, 55.
3. O. Jones, pl. XXVI.

4.70

Chairs. c. 1920. Italian. Marble. Private collection.

This pair of rustic chairs was probably intended for the type of romantic, naturalistic garden promoted by Andrew Jackson Downing in the nineteenth century. They are composed of marble supports fashioned in the form of truncated tree branches that carry a slab seat, while the backs are formed of flowers and leaves. The carvings on the chairs vary slightly, emphasizing the organic nature of the pair.

4.71

Bench. c. 1910. Italian. Marble. Private collection.

This copiously ornamented bench exhibits a range of classical motifs. The molding on the flat seat displays the palmette motif seen in ancient Greek art, while the serpentine volutes are also part of the classical vocabulary; the grotesque mask at the center of the apron – the most prominent and animated feature of the bench – is reminiscent of similar masks used on fountains of the Italian Renaissance. This type of ornament was well suited to the large, ornately styled American estates of the early twentieth century. Similar, albeit less decorated, benches flanked the entrance to the forecourt at the Villa Borghese in Rome. Maxfield Parrish illustrated the Villa Borghese benches for Edith Wharton's influential *Italian Villas and Their Gardens,* of 1904.[1]

1. Wharton, pl. opposite 86.

4.72

Seat. c. 1900. Italian. Marble. Rosecliff, Preservation Society of Newport County, Newport, Rhode Island.

Italianate influence can be seen in the deeply carved sides of this piece, which incorporates Roman rosettes, scrolling designs, and winged lions, which often represent Saint Mark, the patron saint of Venice. In keeping with the formal classical style of the Rosecliff garden, a pair of these benches was added to the 1898 plan of the architect, Stanford White. Unfortunately, one of the two was damaged, leaving a single example on the mansion's front lawn.

5.1

5.1

Sundial plate. 1630. English. Brass. Peabody-Essex Museum, Salem, Massachusetts. Marked: *William Bowyer of London, Clockmaker Fecit 1·1630·E.*

This sundial was made for and owned by John Endecott (1588/89–1665) of Salem, Massachusetts (see p. 92). William Bowyer, the dial's English maker, calibrated it for Salem's latitude of forty-two degrees north. From the sixteenth century in England until the nineteenth century in America, clockmakers were one of several professionals who made sundials. The Endecott dial is considered one of the oldest, and best documented examples in America.

5.2

Sundial on pedestal. c. 1750. English. Carved stone and bronze. Private collection. Marked: *T. Heath Fecit.*

This rare sundial plate was made by T. Heath, an eighteenth-century English maker. It is calibrated with hours and compass points for latitude 53° 10' north. This would place its original location just south of the sixteenth-century Chatsworth House in Derbyshire, England. The shaped gnomon is simple and unpierced. The carved stone base, while of massive rather than elegant proportions, can also be dated to the mid-eighteenth century.

CATALOGUE 5

SUNDIALS AND ARMILLARY SPHERES

5.3

Sundial. c. 1750. English. Lead, marble, and stone. Private collection. Inscribed: *Io vado e vengo ogni giorno ma tu andrai senza ritorno* [I go and come everyday. But thou shalt go without returning].

This important figural sundial represents the continent of Africa. Its unique form derives from the early-eighteenth-century example at Dunham Massey House in Cheshire, England, thought to have been executed by John Van Nost, or his assistant, Andres Carpentière. A version identical to this one, also with a marble plate, was pictured at Aldenham House, in Hertfordshire, England, in Gertrude Jekyll's 1918 book, *Garden Ornament*.[1]

1. Jekyll, 261.

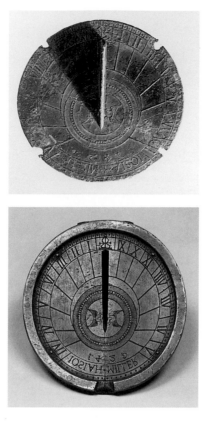

5.4 and **5.5**

Sundial plate and mold. Josiah Miller. 1750–75. American. Pewter and bronze. The Metropolitan Museum of Art, New York.

This pair of objects demonstrates one method of sundial production in eighteenth-century America. The bronze mold could replicate multiple dial plates, suggesting a demand for dials in America. The plate's material, pewter – also known as poor man's silver – implies that it was to be sold to a public that preferred less expensive dials. The lines on the dial lack their original crispness, and the once discreet holes for attachment to a base have broken away, illustrating how poorly pewter resists weathering. The number "42" inscribed in the mold may indicate that the dial was calibrated for a latitude of forty-two degrees north, like the dial shown in figure 5.1.

5.6

Sundial. Goldsmith Chandlee (1751–1821). c. 1800. American. Brass and mahogany. The Metropolitan Museum of Art, New York.

The straightforward design of this sundial underlines its use as an instrument. Goldsmith Chandlee, a Virginia pewterer, fabricated it in brass around the beginning of the nineteenth century. The marking of 38° 20' north latitude corresponds to a location in Northern Virginia. The precise demarcation of hours further subdivided into halves, quarters, and twelfths – indicating intervals of thirty, fifteen, and five minutes, respectively – suggests its use as an actual timepiece rather than as a decoration.

5.7

Sundial on pedestal. c. 1840. English. Bronze and sandstone. Private collection. Marked: *Whitehouse Fecit.*

The design for the pedestal shown here is featured in John Claudius Loudon's *Encyclopedia of Cottage, Farm and Villa Architecture and Furniture* of 1835.[1] Its large scale suggests that it was intended to be the central focal point of a formal or geometric garden. A nearly identical pedestal, termed an "Enriched Grecian Sun Dial," appeared in the English maker Austin's Artificial Stone Works catalogue of 1835.[2] Twentieth-century American incarnations of the pedestal were offered by the Barclay Company of Narberth, Pennsylvania, and the Atlantic Terra Cotta Company of New York.[3] The dial plate, calibrated for the northerly latitude of 52° 48', is not original to the pedestal, and dates to the mid-eighteenth century.

1. Loudon 1835, 994.
2. Austin, 5, no. 8.
3. Barclay 1924, no. 302; Atlantic, 17, no. Z 403.

5.8

Sundial. A. Abraham & Co., Liverpool, England. c. 1800. English. Bronze. Private collection. Marked: *A. ABRAHAM & CO. / 20 LORD ST. LIVERPOOL.*

This dial, calibrated for latitude 53° 23' north, is an exceptional example of an early nineteenth-century English piece. The pierced gnomon, accentuated by a simple C-scroll, is placed at a high angle due to its northerly latitude. Its original location may have been near Morpeth in Northumberland, Scotland. A formula for calculating Greenwich Mean Time is inscribed near the maker's mark.

5.9

Sundial on pedestal. c. 1845. American. Cast iron. Richmond, Natchez, Mississippi. Inscribed: *TIME TAKES ALL BUT MEMORIES.*

Pulham & Son, a manufactory of composition stone in London, made a version of this sundial called the "Winchfield" sundial.[1] This example in cast iron, a rare material for sundials, is probably the product of an American firm. Although it is not the centerpiece of a garden its slender static form lends an air of formality to its surroundings.

1. Pulham, 37, no. 89.

5.10

Sundial on pedestal. c. 1880. English. Bronze and limestone. Private collection. Inscribed: *Horas non numerent nisi serenas [I count only sunny hours]*.

This sundial plate is mounted on a pedestal from the early nineteenth century. The dial was probably produced near the end of the nineteenth century in the Colonial Revival style. The pedestal's bulbous contour and classical swags of fruit and foliage recall eighteenth-century designs for sundial pedestals by James Gibbs.[1]

1. Strange, 47.

5.11

Sundial. Richard Melvyn. c. 1880. English. Bronze and slate. Private collection. Marked: *RICHARD MELVYN, LONDON, MAKER TO . . .* (remainder obscured).

This dial, calibrated for latitude 50° 51' north, was made by Richard Melvyn, who also created a sundial for the 1851 Crystal Palace exhibition hall. The dial face is made of slate, a material well-suited for this purpose, while the multiple gnomons are of bronze. The four smaller dials and gnomons at the corners of the slate, one of which is missing, are calibrated for four different locations around the globe. These are inscribed: "Morning New York," "Afternoon Alexandria," "Evening Island of Borneo," and "Night New Zealand." Also inscribed on the slate are phrases excerpted from the Bible.

5.12

Sundial on pedestal. c. 1900. American. Marble and bronze. Old Westbury Gardens, Old Westbury, New York. Inscribed: *Ye Sunny Tyme Anno Dom 1642*.

This sundial is situated in the Walled Garden at Old Westbury Gardens. Although inscribed with a seventeenth-century date, this dial and its inscription were probably selected and made around the turn of the twentieth century, when the desire to recapture a romanticized colonial past was most pervasive in America. The sundial is likely to be American because marble was not a popular material in England due to the effects of humidity on it. The dial's right-triangle-shaped gnomon is an unusual configuration that, based on its sharp angle, is calibrated for a northerly location.

5.13

Figural group with sundial. c. 1900. Possibly French. Bronze with marble face. Georgian Court College (formerly Georgian Court), Lakewood, New Jersey.

This sculptural sundial, with its three intertwined baby satyrs supporting a round sundial that depicts the twelve signs of the zodiac, is prominently displayed at the center of the formal, elliptical flower garden at Georgian Court.[1] An identical figural group, which supports a shallow basin for fruits and flowers rather than a sundial, was designed by Charles Le Brun and cast in 1669–1670 by the sculptor Pierre Legros the Elder. This piece is after one of seven groups of figures known as the "Marmousets of the Allée d'Eau" in the gardens of Versailles.[2]

1. Geis, 147.
2. Pincas, 59.

5.14

Celestial globe. c. 1900. American. Carved stone. Gwinn, Bratenahl, Ohio.

Celestial globes are fairly unusual in American gardens. In her 1872 compilation *The Book of Sun-Dials,* Mrs. Alfred Gatty calls celestial globes "globe dials." Mrs. Gatty quotes Joseph Moxon's *Tutor to Astronomie* (1659), in which the author described a "Dyal upon a solid Ball or Globe, that shall shew the Hour of the day without a gnomon."[1] The globe shown here, which is indeed without a gnomon, indicates the time by the use of twenty-four hour divisions of the equinoctial circle that circumscribes the sphere. Similar globes are found at Lotusland, the estate of Ganna Walska, in Santa Barbara, California. However, while the celestial globes at Lotusland are mounted on simple, rectilinear stone plinths, the globe at Gwinn is supported by an imaginatively carved curvilinear pedestal. At Gwinn, the globe is set in the formal garden at the end of a vista through a pergola. Such a placement is in accord with Charles Platt's preference for the axial structure of formal Italian villa gardens.

1. Gatty, 106.

5.15

Sundial. c. 1920s–30s. American. Cast iron and composition stone. Maymont Foundation, Richmond, Virginia. Inscribed: *I COUNT ONLY SUNNY HOURS.*

The piece is situated at the center of a geometric floral bed, a typical placement for sundials. The barley-twist pedestal is a traditional form often used in Baroque architecture and decorative arts. The dial itself is characterized by a lack of ornament and the restrained lines associated with twentieth-century modernism. Although Maymont's gardens were completed in 1910, the sundial appears to date at least thirty years later, judging from its style and the quality of its execution. The pedestal, which is almost certainly earlier than the dial itself, can be seen in American trade catalogues from the 1920s and 1930s.[1]

1. Primo, no. 43; Erkins 1933, 4, no. C-50.

5.16

Sundial. Abastenia St. L. Eberle (1878–1942).
c. 1931. American. Bronze. Location unknown;
reprint from Ferargil Galleries catalogue, 1931.

Retailed through the Ferargil Galleries in
New York City,[1] this imaginative and
whimsical sundial is composed of a putto
leading a tortoise by a string, which serves
as the sundial's gnomon. Eberle, a female
sculptor who worked in New York, made
an appropriate choice in her inclusion
of a tortoise; not only does it symbolize
eternity, but it is also associated with the
Chinese belief that the markings on a
tortoise's shell reflect the lunar calendar.[2]

1. Ferargil, 9.
2. Earle 1902, 186.

5.17

Sundial on pedestal. c. 1920–30. American.
Bronze and carved stone. Private collection.
Marked: *T. Nash, Londini.*

This dial and pedestal are in the Colonial
Revival style, which was prevalent in
America from the mid-nineteenth century
onward. The bronze hemispherical, or
half-globe is marked with hour designa-
tions to tell the time when a shadow from
the diagonal bronze band serving as a
gnomon falls on the semicircle. Although
the dial plate is marked "1700," the style
of workmanship dates it to the first decades of the twentieth century. Erroneous
early dates are often found on Colonial
Revival sundials; they are self-conscious
references to a much-romanticized colonial past.

5.18

Sundial and pedestal. c. 1950. American.
Composition stone and cast iron. Maymont
Foundation, Richmond, Virginia. Inscribed:
GROW OLD WITH ME THE BEST IS YET TO BE.

In the Italian Garden at Maymont, this
sundial is a variation on the traditional
baluster; the pedestal takes the form of an
abstracted column with twisted fluting.
Similar pedestals were retailed by F. Barker
& Son, Ltd., of London in the first decade
of the twentieth century,[1] and by the
Hartmann-Sanders Company of New
York and Chicago in 1928.[2]

1. Barker, 14.
2. Hartmann-Sanders, 56.

5.19

Armillary sphere. c. 1920. English. Bronze.
The Highlands, Fort Washington, Pennsylvania.
(Detail)

Simple floral ornaments and a delicately
scrolled arrow give this exemplary armillary
sphere a lively, whimsical character. It was
installed at The Highlands by the estate's
owner, Caroline Sinkler, as part of a vast
reconstruction of the gardens in the 1920s
under the leadership of the landscape architect Wilson Eyre (see p. 96 and fig. 80, p. 97).

5.20

Armillary sphere. c. 1930. American. Bronze
and composition stone. Virginia House,
Richmond, Virginia.

Due to the lack of markings on its rings
and its missing arrow, it may be assumed
that this armillary sphere was meant to be
ornamental rather than functional. The
rings of the sphere represent the paths of
the celestial bodies. The plain, conical
pedestal enhances the simple elegance of
the sphere itself.

5.21

Armillary sphere. Paul Manship (1885–1966).
c. 1928. American. Bronze and granite. Collection
Phillips Academy, Andover, Massachusetts.

This grandly scaled armillary sphere is
perhaps the most complex sculptural
example of this instrument in America
(see pp. 96–97). The artist used several
traditional motifs in his design, including
tortoises and the signs of the zodiac, all
rendered with his characteristic graphic
simplicity. The Andover sphere, not
merely ornamental, gives an accurate
reading of the hour. According to a letter
of December 28, 1927 from Thomas
Cochran, the donor, to James Sawyer,
a school administrator, the cost of this
unique work was $4,576.02, a significant
sum at the time. The same letter also
states that the sculptor had previously
made an identical sphere for a certain
Mrs. Harriman.[1]

1. Letter of 28 December 1927 from Thomas
Cochran, donor, to James Sawyer, Phillips
Academy administrator. Property of the
Archives, Phillips Academy, Andover.

6.1
Gates and finials. c. 1730–40. English. Wrought iron and carved stone. Westover, Charles City County, Virginia.

The ornamental ironwork at Westover includes such fine extant eighteenth-century English examples as these garden gates. The detailing in the side panels and overthrow represent the light, airy work of skilled blacksmiths whose command of the medium exceeded that of most smiths in America at the time. The dog bars at the foot of the gate prevented the entry of canine invaders, while the silhouetted bird at the top of the cresting was, no doubt, to remind the viewer of the name of the landholder himself, William Byrd II. The simple ball finials served to cap the gate piers appropriately while not interfering with the overall visual effect.

CATALOGUE 6

GATES, FENCING, AND FINIALS

6.2, 6.3, 6.4, 6.5, 6.6, 6.7, and 6.8
Finials. c. 1730–40. Carved stone. English. Westover, Charles City County, Virginia.

This extraordinary group of finials laid out along the fence at Westover would have had particular allegorical and moralistic appeal to their owner William Byrd II. The pineapple form (6.2) represented a rare luxury – a delicacy brought back from a Caribbean voyage. During the seventeenth and eighteenth centuries the pineapple, which at the time had not yet been definitively established as a symbol of hospitality, was a sign of Christian sacrifice: a plant that gave its life to bear a single fruit.[1] The Tidewater Virginia plantations, however, attached great value to the pineapple as an ornamental motif. The lobed, lidded urn (6.3) bears a distant resemblance to the finials on the roof and walls of the Italian Baroque Villa Palmieri near

Florence.[2] A similar form with a distinctive overhanging lid and floral terminal appeared in the 1835 Austin's Artificial Stone Ornament catalogue.[3] On the ball finial (6.4), the Greek key fret pattern, an essential element of Greek ornament, symbolizes the key to knowledge.[4] The graduated bell flower or hanging bud motif on a second urn-form example (6.5) may represent beauty, or even Paradise or Eden. Another finial (6.6), an oval-shaped example with cornucopia motifs of overflowing fruit and flowers, is an emblem of bounty or generosity. The cornucopia, or mythological horn of plenty, was said to have come from the head of the mother goat that nursed Zeus.[5] A similarly shaped finial with acanthus leaf decoration is thought to represent a beehive, the symbol of industry (6.7). This sign would have had special meaning for Byrd, whose secret diaries, written in code and not transcribed until the twentieth century by a staff member of the Huntington Library, revealed days filled with hard work and rigid self-discipline. Byrd's recollections show that sadness was also a part of his life.[6] Thus, the smallest finial, an acorn form (6.8), might have cheered him with its message of perseverance – that from little acorns great oaks grow.[7] The stylistic and symbolic combination of these variegated finials enhanced the aesthetic and cultural effect of the Westover garden.

1. Olmert, 47.

2. Shepherd & Jellicoe, 59.

3. Austin, no. 32.

4. Westover Self-Guide. Pamphlet. Charles City County. Virginia [4].

5. Carr-Gomm, 69.

6. Byrd, 354–382.

7. Westover Self-Guide, pamphlet, Charles City, Virginia [4].

6.9

Finials. c. 1808. English. Carved stone. Nathaniel Russel House, Charleston, South Carolina.

Round stone ball finials surmount the simple brick posts that mark the entrance gate to the Nathaniel Russel House, completed in 1808. As Charleston was an extremely active seaport at the time the house was built, the finials were probably imported from England. This type of finial was found not only on seventeenth-century English gates,[1] but in Italian Renaissance architecture, as well. In 1572, the architect Giacomo Vignola incorporated stone ball finials into the design of an entrance gate on the grounds of Villa Mondragone in Frascati, Italy.[2]

1. Edwards, 150.

2. Shepherd & Jellicoe, 87.

6.10

Fence sections and posts. Wood, Miltenberger, & Co., New Orleans. c. 1858. American. Cast iron. New Orleans, Louisiana. Marked: *WOOD, MILTENBERGER, & CO.*

This dramatic fence exhibits a number of Gothic elements. The diamond-shaped lozenges in the middle section and the finials along the top are reminiscent of medieval architecture. The concentration of pointed vertical components gives this heavy fence an upward-reaching lightness that recalls Gothic cathedrals. The shorter vertical members in the lowest register known as "dog bars" are intended to keep small animals off the property. The maker, Wood, Miltenberger & Co., was a short-lived branch of the Philadelphia-based Wood & Perot.

6.11

Gate. c. 1860. American. Cast iron. Myrtle Terrace, Natchez, Mississippi.

The fence and gate of Myrtle Terrace are of distinctly different characters. In general, even Victorian designers, who are notable for their eclectic taste, chose components of corresponding styles. Although this fence is in the Gothic style, the only Gothic features on the gate are the two quatrefoils in the bottom panel. Its classical lyres, antefix cresting, and scrolling, rococo foliage are incongruous adjuncts to the Gothic fence and posts.

6.12

Fence. Attributed to John B. Wickersham, New York. c. 1860. American. Cast iron and wire. Stanton Hall, Natchez, Mississippi.

This openwork fence, composed of cast-iron components within a bent-wire framework, conforms to the dictates of Andrew Jackson Downing, who advocated naturalistic gardens and disapproved of heavy barriers. The pattern and structure of this fence give it a light appearance and do not interrupt the visual continuity of the property.

6.13

Fence. c. 1840. American. Cast iron. Gardner-Pingree House, Salem, Massachusetts.

The whimsical design of this cast-iron barrier adds another dimension to an otherwise ordinary boundary fence. In the 1840s in America, cast iron was still a novel product for ornamental ironwork. Salem, Massachusetts, known for its beautiful fences, soon welcomed newly fashioned cast-iron designs to enhance property boundaries.[1] In some cases they mimicked examples in wrought iron, but in the Gardner-Pingree pattern, the designer chose to interpret forms of Grecian ornament.[2]

1. Lockwood, vol. 1, 432.
2. O. Jones, pl. XVI.

6.14

Fence. c. 1860. American. Cast iron. Myrtle Terrace, Natchez, Mississippi.

The Gothic quatrefoils, crockets, and medieval-style floral ornaments on this fence contrast with the classically inspired lyre motifs of the entrance gate (cat. 6.11). The fence posts, topped by knob terminals, recall the architectural supports of thirteenth-century cathedrals. Gothic motifs such as these were popular among American designers of ornamental cast iron. The Israel P. Morris foundry of Philadelphia produced an important Gothic-style seat at Richmond Plantation, also in Natchez (fig. 67, p. 82), which is similar to the pattern of this fence section.

6.15

Fence. c. 1870. American. Cast iron. New Orleans, Louisiana.

This fence successfully integrates a few seemingly disparate elements. The fanlike floral motifs, called anthemia, or honeysuckle ornaments, are derived from classical Greek and ancient Indian decoration.[1] The allusion to ancient Greek ornament is fitting, considering the Greek Revival architecture of the associated house. The fence's classically inspired motifs are juxtaposed with such Gothic elements as the pattern of quatrefoils compressed into a regular arrangement of square lozenges in the lowest register.

1. O. Jones, pls. XLIX, XVI.

6.16

Fence sections and posts. c. 1870. American. Wrought and cast iron. New Orleans, Louisiana.

The cast-iron posts at the corners of this fence bear ornament related to the classical "candelabra" motifs of Renaissance Italy. These candelabra, continuous vertical arrangements of scrolling, often grotesque, decorative elements, are based on the painted designs on the walls of the *Domus Aurea,* the palace of the Roman emperor, Nero.[1] The use of such motifs in America coincided with a fervent revival of Renaissance ornament in the 1860s and 1870s. The fence itself is made primarily of simple, vertical wrought-iron components. The spearhead finials along the top of the fence are separately cast elements that were fused with the wrought-iron support members.

1. Fleming and Honour, 370–71.

6.17

Gates. c. 1900. Continental, possibly Spanish. Wrought iron. Private collection.

This gate, produced of heavy stock wrought iron, is an example of fine craftsmanship. The gate displays an imaginative array of decorative elements, including stars, scrolls, and abstracted heraldic shields. While not fully explained, such shields imply a heraldic tradition or family lineage. The individual pieces of iron that comprise this gate are noteworthy for their varying widths.

6.18

Gates. c. 1910–12. Spanish. Wrought iron. Eagle's Nest, Centerport, New York.

Eagle's Nest, the hillside home of William K. Vanderbilt, Jr., the president of the New York Central Railroad, was designed by the architects Warren & Wetmore in the Spanish style at the request of the owner. This lyrical, finely wrought gate is silhouetted against a light-colored stucco wall, revealing the perfect symmetry of the scrolling decoration.

6.19

Gate and gateposts. Hinderer's Iron Fence Works, New Orleans. 1912–16. American. Wrought and cast iron. St. Francisville, Louisiana. Marked: *HINDERER'S/IRON FENCE WORKS/304 CAMP ST./NEW ORLEANS, LA.*

The nineteenth-century preference for exotic design sources is still seen in this later gate manufactured by the Hinderer's Iron Fence Works, the company name from 1912 to 1916. Moorish-style ornament is evident on the gateposts in the form of architectonic arches and twisted columns. The gate itself is an eclectic ensemble of abstracted classical rosettes and nearly Gothic tracery, seen on the spearheads. A thin stock of wrought iron comprises the gate's framework, while the gateposts and smaller ornaments are made of cast iron.

6.20

Gates. c. 1915. American. Wrought iron. Henry Ford House, Dearborn, Michigan.

Made with great skill, these elaborate gates could easily have stood at the main entry to Henry Ford's grand residence, rather than at the junction of two simple garden paths. Indeed, gates of such splendor and scale (nine feet across) are not often nestled in American gardens. Even so, these gates, with their profusion of C-scrolls, blend in among the tall lilac bushes that surround them. Grounded by strong, square columns, classical rounded arches, and delineated segments, the gates are a study in formality.

6.21

Gates. c. 1920. American. Wrought iron. Private collection.

The beginning of the twentieth century witnessed the development of elaborate country estates in the Santa Barbara area of California. These stately wrought-iron driveway gates, originally from a Montecito estate, were probably made locally by an artisan trained in the Spanish artistic vernacular.

6.22

Gate. 1940–50. American. Wrought iron. Private collection.

The small size of this gate indicates that it was made for a garden rather than an entrance drive. Its light weight is typical of wrought-iron work executed in the mid-twentieth century. The highly naturalistic design is composed of scrolling, sinuous vines rising from two classical urns, which give stability to the profuse ornamental work.

6.23

Gates and finials. c. 1925–30. Samuel Yellin, Philadelphia. Wrought iron and carved stone. Dumbarton Oaks, Washington, D. C.

The extraordinary resemblance of these gates to the smaller ones at Westover (cat. 6.1) underscores Samuel Yellin's knowledge of historic forms. The gates' design, which may be attributed to the landscape gardener Beatrix Farrand and the owner Mildred Bliss, took advantage of the expertise of the ironworker. The leafy cresting that surrounds Mrs. Bliss's cypher represents nature as skillfully as possible. The pineapple gate-pier finials were probably executed in Indiana limestone by Frederick Coles, who was responsible for the masterful carving of most of the stone ornament at Dumbarton Oaks. The popular symbolism of the pineapple, that of welcome and hospitality, was undoubtedly in the minds of the two ladies who together created this exceptional garden.

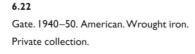

6.24

Finial. c. 1910. American. Terra cotta. Cranbrook House, Bloomfield Hills, Michigan.

This urn-shaped finial, one of a pair, is marked by an exuberant range of classical motifs. Abundant swags of fruit complement the upswept scrolled handles, adding to its successful mixture of whimsy and symmetry. The handles are reminiscent of the French urns at Nemours, in Wilmington, Delaware (see cat. 3.49). The overall shape and decoration of the finial recall similar examples at the Villa Corsi-Salviati, a fanciful country residence in Sesto, Italy, built in the mid-seventeenth century.[1]

1. Shepherd & Jellicoe, pl. 56-E.

6.27
Finial. c. 1930. American. Lead. Planting Fields
Arboretum, Oyster Bay, New York.

The lead finials crowning the gateposts
at Planting Fields owe their form to late-
eighteenth-century English models,
specifically the designs of Robert Adam.
Actually lidded urns, these are identical
to no. 2909 in the 1979 catalogue of
Kenneth Lynch of Wilton, Connecticut.[1]
Planting Fields was the north shore Long
Island home of William Robertson Coe,
an insurance executive, and his second
wife, Mai Rogers.

1. Kenneth Lynch 1979, 491, no. 2909.

6.28
Finial. c. 1930. English. Carved stone. Virginia
House, Richmond, Virginia.

This lion finial, holding a shield dated 1630,
recalls the heraldic stone lions associated
with sixteenth-century Tudor manors. The
lion suggests the earlier history of Virginia
House, which was built from the original
masonry of a twelfth-century monastery
in Warwick, England. The monastery was
active in England until the sixteenth century, when it was remodeled as a house.
All of the building's components were purchased by Alexander and Virginia Weddell
and sent to America in the late 1920s to
be reconstructed as Virginia House.

6.25 and **6.26**
Finials. c. 1916. American. Carved stone.
Gibraltar, Preservation Delaware, Wilmington,
Delaware.

Surmounting the posts leading into
Gibraltar's formal garden, this pair of
figural finials are composed of two putti
supporting fruit-filled cornucopia. The
putti and cornucopia suggest bounty,
renewal, and perhaps Bacchanalian
revelry. These finials, which complement
other classically styled ornaments at
Gibraltar, are similar to examples found
at the late-seventeenth-century Villa
Crivelli, in Inverigo, Italy[1] and the
seventeenth-century French château
Vaux-le-Vicomte.

1. Shepherd and Jellicoe, pl. 78, fig. A.

6.29
Finials. c. 1935. American. Cast stone.
Private collection.

Formerly in the collection of prominent
Long Island attorney Bronson Winthrop,
these small finials are fashioned in the form
of fruit baskets. Probably used at Winthrop's
Long Island country home designed by
Delano and Aldrich in 1909, they may have
crowned small fence posts, flanked doorways, or been placed along terrace walls;
their small size would have made them
inappropriate for gate finials. The flower
basket finial was popular during the 1920s
and 1930s, and retailers such as J. P. White
of England,[1] and Howard Studios of New
York City[2] sold a variety of this form.

1. J. Davis, 301.
2. Howard Studios, 9.

Pair of obelisks. c. 1940. American. Cast stone.
Collection Richard L. Feigen.

In the eighteenth century, single obelisks
were often used in the garden as monumental focal points or as gnomons, creating
an alternative to the traditional sundial.
In the twentieth century, however, obelisks
were frequently purchased in pairs. This
pair may have been made by Kenneth
Lynch & Sons, which offered identical
obelisks in three different sizes in its
twentieth-century catalogue. Lynch suggested that a pair of obelisks could also be
used as "surveyors marks, as turning points
in a walk, and many times used to link
fences made of hedges."[1] This simple
architectural pair is void of ornament,
relying on geometric lines and shapes
to create an overall symmetry.

1. Kenneth Lynch 1974, 516–517, no. 690.

7.2

Flower stand. c. 1870–90. English. Cast iron.
Private collection.

In the second half of the nineteenth
century, a number of multi-tiered plant
stands with circular, pierced shelves to
allow for water drainage were registered
and manufactured by the Coalbrookdale
Company of Shropshire, England. The
company's 1875 catalogue illustrated
stands of a similar form, but with a few
more shelves, than the pictured piece.[1]
Ornamented with foliate motifs, this
example can carry a number of potted
plants; its pierced surfaces make it
effective both in and out of doors. This
plant stand is exceptional both for its
material, cast iron, not often seen in
flower stands, and for its elegant form.

1. Coalbrookdale 1875, Section III, 333, no.117.

CATALOGUE 7

OTHER GARDEN ORNAMENT:

OBELISKS, PLANT STANDS, WELLHEADS, AND MORE

7.3

Flower stand. Wood & Perot, Philadelphia. c. 1858. American. Cast iron. Munson Williams Proctor Institute, Utica, New York. Marked: *WOOD & PEROT*.

The upper section of the catalogue illustration for this elaborate flower stand bears an extraordinary resemblance to chandelier No. 9 in the mid-eighteenth-century design book of Thomas Chippendale.[1] Supported by a clover-leaf-top table edged with a pierced Moorish-style apron,[2] this stand is transformed into a flamboyant, rococo ornament more than six feet high, and was pictured in Wood & Perot's 1858 catalogue (see line drawing).[3] However, the label beneath its illustration reads "Robert Wood, Philadelphia," which reveals that the original design was probably conceived between 1840–58 before Elliston Perot joined the firm.

1. Strange, no. 9, 107,
2. O. Jones, pl. XL.
3. Wood & Perot, n.p., flower stand A.

7.4

Flower stand. c. 1860. English. Cast iron. Collection Charlotte Inn. Marked: *CRICKLEY WRIGHT & CO., BURTON WEIR, SHEFFIELD.*

Typical of mid-nineteenth-century eclecticism, this ornate, finely cast plant stand incorporates both rococo and Renaissance-style ornament. Intended to be placed against a wall, it exhibits three graduated shelves mounted on scrolling supports of fruit and foliage, atop a T-shaped base. Registered in 1860 by Crickley Wright & Co., Burton Weir, Sheffield, England, this rare design provides a striking support for lush plants with overflowing vines, leaves, and flowers.

7.5

Flower stand. c. 1900. English. Wirework. Collection Charlotte Inn.

A rare example of bowed leg supports, this two-tiered plant stand is set on modest feet of twined wire. The scalloped V-edging of the upper level is a common motif on wire stands of the mid- to late-nineteenth century. The near invisibility of the piece would make it an appealing addition to an informal garden as well as to a porch or terrace.

7.6

Flower stand. c. 1860–80. American. Wirework. Private collection.

To create works like this flower stand, makers of wirework furniture drew wires into frames supporting several levels of interwoven strands that were then decorated with loops and whimsical shapes. Many of these models relied on porcelain casters for ease of movement. This semicircular shape, popular with makers and customers alike, was offered in catalogues with a wirework arch that gave it added height.[1]

1. Barnum 1881, <2>, no. 5.

7.7

Flower Stand. c. 1860–80. French. Wrought iron and wirework. Collection Charlotte Inn.

Nineteenth-century French designers of garden ornament excelled in the creation of delicate, graphic wrought-iron furniture. This elegant flower stand relies on wirework to conceal the actual planter, while its tall, scrolling legs refine the silhouette of an otherwise customary presentation.

7.8

Wellhead and overthrow. Sixteenth century. Italian. Stone and marble. Canyon Ranch (formerly Bellefontaine), Lenox, Massachusetts.

This large-waisted wellhead and playfully decorative overthrow evoke the bizarre and nonsensical decorative style of Mannerism, which evolved in Italy during the sixteenth century. Although slightly more exaggerated, the cylindrical, undulating wellhead at Canyon Ranch closely resembles a wellhead of 1568 in the Piazza Baldassare Galuppi on the island of Burano, near Venice.[1] Both pieces exhibit a wide mouth, pedestal-like base, and bulbous contour (see drawing below). The twisted columns, capped by abstracted Corinthian capitals joined by a pediment embellished with ball finials and scrolling volutes, form a baldachinlike structure similar to one at the Villa Marlia near Lucca, Italy.[2]

1. Rizzi, 283.
2. Shepherd & Jellicoe, 45.

7.9

Wellhead. Sixteenth century. Italian. Marble. Private collection.

Smaller than most Venetian wellheads, this example may have originally belonged to a monastery in the Veneto region of Italy.[1] Ornamental wellheads were used as caps for wells and more often than not, fitted with hinged lids. The piece shown here was clearly in actual use, as it exhibits indentations and holes from a now missing lid, and deep vertical wear marks from the ropes that would have suspended a bucket for dipping out the water. These signs of use are important in dating the wellhead, since garden ornament makers in the second half of the nineteenth century produced decorative versions that could pass for medieval originals. It is not unheard-of for these later pieces, however, to show false signs of wear intended to deceive.

1. I would like to thank Mario De Valmarana of the University of Virginia for this information.

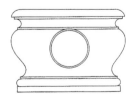

7.10

Wellhead. Sixteenth century. Italian. Istrian stone. Hearst Castle, San Simeon, California.

This impressive wellhead, ornamented with lion heads, acanthus leaves, cornucopiae, palm trees, and winged cherubs, is reputedly from the Palazzo Balbi on the Grand Canal in Venice. In 1925, French and Co. of New York City sold it to William Randolph Hearst for his estate in San Simeon, California. This piece is representative of the American taste for Venetian wellheads, which were often imported from Europe to embellish the gardens of wealthy estate owners.

7.11

Wellhead and overthrow. c. 1915. American. Wrought iron and carved stone. Cranbrook House, Bloomfield Hills, Michigan.

This wellhead has been converted into a drinking fountain and is known at Cranbrook as a "well-wisher's well." The cylindrical body, mounted on a double octagonal base, is decorated with Dionysian imagery in relief; dancing putti carry floral garlands, play musical instruments, and drink wine. Probably inspired by an early-sixteenth-century wellhead in the Campo Ss. Giovanni e Paolo in Venice, which exhibits a similar form, dentilated molding, and ornamental motifs,[1] this piece was purchased at Marshall Field's department store in Chicago. A remarkably similar wellhead and decorative wrought-iron overthrow were offered by the studios of the Pompeian Garden Furniture Company in its trade catalogue of 1925–31.[2]

1. Rizzi, 157.
2. Pompeian, 16.

7.12

Wellhead. c. 1890. Italian. Carved stone and wrought iron. Private collection.

This wellhead was made in Italy and probably exported to America after the turn of the twentieth century. At that time, the demand for medieval Venetian wellheads and the relative paucity of actual examples led sculptors to create new pieces that mimicked the old. The form of the piece, with its high-relief carving of stiff acanthus leaves, rosettes, and scrolled volutes on the upper corners, bears stronger resemblance to classical Corinthian capitals than to standard Venetian wellheads. The attached overthrow, finely wrought with a simple linear form, is original to the piece.

7.13

Wellhead. c. 1890. Italian. Marble. St. Joseph's Villa (formerly Blairsden), Peapack, New Jersey.

This wellhead, placed behind the tennis pavilion in the garden at Blairsden, was fitted with a water jet so that it could either act as a decorative fountain or provide refreshment. The arcaded form with free-standing columns closely imitates an eleventh- or twelfth-century example in the Vendramin palace in Venice.[1] The Blairsden piece replicates Byzantine ornament in both form and surface decoration.

1. Rizzi, 15–17.

7.14

Garden pot. Italian. Mid-sixteenth century. Carved stone. Private collection.

In an article written for *Country Life in America* in 1905, E. C. Holtzoper asserted that "The garden pot is used as a receptacle for shrubs or small decorative trees . . . usually placed directly on the ground or a flat base provided for them."[1] This deep pot exhibits classical imagery such as scrolling *rinceaux,* rosettes, and a lobed band that encircles the bottom of the pot. The armorial shield represents the family for whom the pot, made of Istrian stone from northeastern Italy, was designed. The base was probably added in the late nineteenth century, when such pieces were collected as decorative ornaments.

1. Holtzoper, 526.

7.15

Lantern. c. 1900. Japanese. Granite. Collection Vickie and Steve Morris.

This type of lantern, termed a "storm" or "snow" lantern, resembles a small dwelling or temple structure, and sits relatively close to the ground. Its most important characteristics are four curved legs and an overhung top. In the 1909 article, "The Japanese Garden in America," Henry Saylor referred to these objects both as "legged" and "snow scene" lanterns. According to Saylor, the type "owes its popularity largely to its habit of retaining a covering of snow."[1]

1. Saylor, 484.

7.16

Lantern. c. 1870. Japanese. Granite. Stan Hywet Hall and Gardens, Akron, Ohio.

This lantern, which probably dates to the last decades of the nineteenth century, is of a type known variously as *kasuge*, or "standard."[1] It is characterized by its scrolled cap, ball top, and carved animal figures. Traditionally, the windows were covered with rice paper and it held a candle in its interior. *Kasuge* lanterns, which are constructed in several pieces for portability, enjoyed particular popularity in American gardens of the early twentieth century. This example was given to Stan Hywet by the government of Japan in 1974. In that year, Stan Hywet's Japanese garden, originally conceived by the architect Warren Manning, the owners of the estate, Mr. and Mrs. F. A. Seiberling, and a Mr. Otsuka, was reconstructed by the Japanese landscape architect, Kaneji Domoto.[2]

1. Saylor, 484.
2. For this information I would like to thank Stan Hywet Hall and Gardens.

7.17 and 7.17A

Pair of medallions. Coade Manufactory, Lambeth, England. Late eighteenth century. Stoneware. The Highlands, Fort Washington, Pennsylvania. One marked: *COADE LAMBETH*.

In the 1920s, prevailing taste for historic relics inspired Caroline Sinkler to install antique Coade stone medallions into the "ancient" wall at The Highlands. According to Coade nomenclature, round or oval panels were identified as medallions. Their allegorical subjects probably represent Agriculture (with the leafy branch) and Abundance (with the bowl of fruit). The reclining nymphs repeat the designs for rectangular plaques Nos. 230 and 231 in Coade's 1784 catalogue, with only slight variations.[1] They are presumably the design of the sculptor and Associate of the Royal Academy John Bacon (d. 1799), whose prodigious talents helped to establish the extraordinary reputation of the Coade Manufactory during the last quarter of the eighteenth century.[2]

1. Coade, n.p., nos. 230, 231.
2. Kelly, 40–43, 167.

7.18

Plaque. c. 270 A.D. Roman. Marble. The Highlands, Fort Washington, Pennsylvania.

In his design for the garden at The Highlands, Wilson Eyre decided to replicate the ancient Roman tradition of displaying Latin inscriptions in garden walls (see p. 119). This marble fragment from the garden was a memorial plaque for the Roman emperor Claudius II. The half-masks and twisted columns suggest that it was formerly attached to a wall or other structure. The rather rudimentary low relief carving depicts a man in a short cloak driving a horse, while at the top of the plaque another figure reclines on a couch. The inscription refers to "II CLAUDIUS MARCUS," who was emperor from 268 to 270 A.D. He succeeded to the throne while head of the cavalry, but his reign ended abruptly when he died of the plague.[1]

1. Scarre, 184.

7.19

Architectural panel. c. 1900. Continental. Terra cotta. Private collection.

This relief is reminiscent of the architectural ornament of Renaissance Italy.[1] The arrangement of motifs, with a vase in the center flanked by acanthus scrolls and dolphins, is standard to many such pieces. Although the eagle with spread wings might imply American manufacture, it is more likely that this panel was made in a country closer to its decorative origins, such as Italy. Fragments from buildings have been popular as garden ornaments since the early twentieth century.

1. O. Jones, pl. LXXIV.

7.20

Birdhouse. Miller Iron Company, Providence, Rhode Island. c. 1880. American. Cast iron. Private collection. Marked *MILLER IRON COMPANY, PROVIDENCE.*

This birdhouse is illustrated in the 1871 catalogue of the Miller Iron Company.[1] It was designed after an engraving of a house in Roslyn, Long Island, New York (see below). The birdhouse follows its two-dimensional model as closely as possible; whatever could not be discerned from the engraving was imaginatively created. In the 1871 catalogue, the piece was referred to as an "English cottage, finished in white enamel, with the windows and doors appropriately colored."[2] Both the birdhouse and the actual house are constructed with pointed arches and tracery in the style of the Gothic Revival.

1. Miller Iron, 13, no. 4.
2. Miller Iron, 13, no. 4.

7.20A

House. Roslyn, Long Island, New York.

This house was the model for an engraving from which a birdhouse was manufactured by the Miller Iron Company.

7.21

Birdhouse. c. 1880. American. Cast iron. Collection Janet and Joseph Shein.

This piece is one of several types of architectural birdhouses that were manufactured in America during the nineteenth century. This particular example, resembling a traditional town hall, is very similar to a birdhouse produced by Peter Timmes' Son of Brooklyn, New York. In the firm's catalogue, however, the little dwelling is shown perched on top of a "gipsy pot," a tripod structure with a pot suspended from its center (see line drawing).[1] Traditionally, these cast-iron birdhouses were mounted on posts away from any possibility of interference by humans.

1. Timmes, 85, pl. 103.

7.22

Bootscraper. c. 1850. French. Cast iron. Rosedown Plantation and Gardens, St. Francisville, Louisiana.

This is a rare form, using understated classical motifs: grotesque masks, volutes, lion-paw feet, and a rope-twist handle specifically recalling Greek ornament. An elegant interpretation for a functional object, it is illustrated in J. J. Ducel's catalogue of 1845–1857.[1]

1. Ducel, pls. 31 and 38, no. 2904.

7.23

Bootscraper. c. 1850–60. English. Cast iron. Rosedown Plantation and Gardens, St. Francisville, Louisiana.

This useful adjunct to a doorway incorporates such diminutive architectural elements as cluster column supports and lidded urn finials. Appearing more like an English bridge than a bootscraper, it is set in a quatrefoil-shaped pan that would have been secured to the floor.

7.24

Bootscraper. c. 1880–1900. English or American. Cast iron. Elms Court, Natchez, Mississippi.

Perhaps intended for a ladylike boot, this refined scraper consists of a single post terminating in swirling rococo foliage. Although Natchez homeowners were known to have purchased cast-iron products in Philadelphia, this "pan scraper," as they are sometimes known in England, resembles offerings in some English trade catalogues.[1]

1. Ames, 66. Coalbrookdale 1875, Section II, 243.

7.25

Bootscraper. c. 1860–80. French. Cast iron. Private collection.

The strong graphic decoration on this practical object can be traced to Greek ornament, specifically the reversed antefix, or anthemion, and the volute of the sort used on the Erechtheion and the Parthenon in Athens.[1] Another ancient motif, that of a lion's-paw foot extending from a volute, was used on the bases of marble seats, as C. Thierry in *Klassische Ornamente* noted.[2]

1. Speltz, 48–49, 52–53.
2. Speltz, 57–58, 629.

7.26

Staddle stones. Early nineteenth century. English. Carved stone. Private collection.

These curious objects, called staddle stones, were used over the course of many centuries in England as supports for granaries and corncribs; elevating these structures helped to avoid damage from flooding and rodents. In the twentieth century, staddle stones were adapted as ornaments for the garden. Two staddle stones sold at a 1938 auction were also referred to as "hay armatures." The catalogue for the sale cites them as "lend[ing] themselves admirably as tables in informal gardens."[1]

1. Anderson Galleries 2, 25–26, nos. 55 and 56.

7.27

Cistern. c. 1774. English. Lead. Dumbarton Oaks, Washington, D.C.

Now used decoratively, vessels such as this once originally functioned as water storage tanks. Many of the earliest examples are marked with initials and dates, and they are often decorated with geometrically arranged moldings. Most cisterns are rectangular, with interior sections.[1] The cistern illustrated here is a fine example of this common type. Although this piece probably dates to the eighteenth century – judging from its visible signs of age – it should be noted that many reproductions are marked with false dates, which can be misleading.

1. Weaver, 65.

7.28

Trough. c. 1850. English. Carved stone. Collection Charlotte Inn.

Stone troughs in England were used to store water, not only in the fields for animals, but also in small country villages. Spring water was fed into the troughs, and then held in reserve to be used by the townspeople. At Horbling in Lincolnshire some large troughs still remain, exhibiting evidence of their importance as suppliers of fresh cold water to the village.[1] In America these vessels have been adapted for garden use as rustic planters or, as originally planned, as cisterns.

1. Eve, 1920.

7.29

Aquarium. J. W. Fiske Iron Works, New York. c. 1858. American. Cast iron and glass. Magnolia Hall, Natchez, Mississippi. Marked *J. W. FISKE NY.*

Ornamental aquaria of this type were popularly used in conservatories and parlors of the mid- to late-nineteenth century, serving as fish tanks, or, just as often, as small ornamental fountains. On the cover of an 1868 catalogue, the J. W. Fiske Iron Works claimed to be "the sole proprietor and manufacturer of Hogarty's Patent Parlor Fountains," which were of a type similar to, though more elaborate than, the pictured piece shown here.[1] According to the catalogue, these "[f]ountains purify the air of furnace-heated rooms; make a handsome ornament; a first-class aquarium; bouquet holder, and vase combined . . . they are also desirable for country residences, the water being kept in motion by the aid of mechanism, same as if supplied from a reservoir."[2] This aquarium at Magnolia Hall, now kept in the garden, is also nearly identical to pieces offered by the J. L. Mott Iron Works.[3]

1. Fiske 1868, front cover.
2. Fiske 1868, front cover.
3. Mott 1875, pl. 3.

7.30

Hitching post. c. 1890. American. Cast iron. Collection Charlotte Inn.

The horsehead model is one of the more common types of hitching posts offered by American cast-iron makers. Following the tendency of nineteenth-century manufacturers to embellish utilitarian objects — even those as mundane as pipe-fittings — with decorative motifs, such hitching posts as this one were adorned with a range of ornamental patterns. Similar equine posts were produced by, among others, the New York Wire Railing Co., Janes, Kirtland & Co., Bartlett, Robbins & Co., and Wood & Perot.[1] The pictured example, decorated with swagged foliate motifs and a fluted Doric column, makes use of a classically-inspired ornamental vocabulary.

1. New York Wire Railing, 69, fig. [311]; Janes, Kirtland & Co., no. 135; Barlett, Robbins & Co. in Latrobe, 48; Wood & Perot, no. 92.

7.31

Hitching post. The Rogers Iron Co., Springfield, Ohio. c. 1902. Cast iron. Salem, Massachusetts. Marked: *ROGERS IRON/CO./SPRINGFIELD/OHIO.*

Originally serving as uprights to which horse bridles could be tied, hitching posts in the later twentieth century have become decorative reminders of a simpler past, and are now often adapted as garden ornaments. This example, cast by The Rogers Iron Co., takes the form of a stylized branch or log. A grapevine pattern wraps around it, adding a naturalistic ornament to an otherwise basic form.

7.32

Downspout. c. 1900. American. Carved limestone. St. Joseph's Villa (formerly Blairsden), Peapack, New Jersey.

This imaginative carving, one of a pair, offers an ornamental solution to a functional problem. Serving as a downspout for water drainage, this clever piece takes the form of a gargoyle. Built into the garden wall that supports Blairsden's grand terrace, the fanciful creature adds an unexpected, playful element to the majestic grounds of the estate. A similar sense of humor is reflected in the four satyr statues that guard the entrance to the terrace (fig. 23, p. 43).

7.33

Edging tile. c. 1880. English. Terra cotta. Collection Charlotte Inn.

Edging tiles like these, decorated with classical motifs, were made by French and British manufacturers. The device of a stylized flower on top of a pair of volutes derives from an antefix, an ancient Greek roof ornament. The purpose of such edging was to add a decorative boundary to a flower bed and to contain the spread of plants such as this pachysandra.

7.34

Edging. c. 1910. American. Cast iron. Smithsonian Institution, Washington, D. C.

Lawn and flower bed edging of this type was manufactured by several foundries in the United States. Cast in the form of gnarled branches, this unobtrusive edging is one variety of naturalistic, rusticated ornament that would have satisfied the high standards of the landscape specialist Andrew Jackson Downing. In its catalogue of circa 1900, F. & E. Aubel, a Philadelphia foundry, offered a "garden railing" nearly identical to this example.[1] The same edging was also manufactured by the J. W. Fiske Iron Works.[2]

1. Aubel, no. 33.
2. Fiske 1924, 31, no. 4.

During the nineteenth and twentieth centuries, a vast number of manufacturers made goods suitable for use in the garden. For most of these firms, garden ornament was only a minor aspect of overall production. Utilitarian and industrial wares such as pipes, stoves, and architectural decoration formed the bulk of their output.

For the most part, few specifics are known about the design, manufacture, and retailing of garden ornament. This list, by no means comprehensive, is intended to be a guide to some of the major makers of garden ornament in America. Also included are selected European firms that exported goods to the United States or influenced American manufacturers. The firms' names were collected from both marked objects and trade catalogues, the latter a valuable record of a company's product line. The active dates of each firm are given in as much detail as possible, often with changes of address. In some cases, the changes in address listings may have resulted from changes in zoning rather than from a company's physical relocation. This information, taken from city directories, aids in the dating of marked objects. Further details about nineteenth-century American firms were taken from the R. G. Dun and Company Collection (the precursor of Dun & Bradstreet) at Baker Library, Harvard Business School, an invaluable source for financial statistics and other notes on business operation. The dates of operation given are based on available published information; in some cases, a firm may have been active before the inception date provided here.

ABENDROTH BROTHERS Cast iron
New York
1841–1844 Augustus and William Abendroth, 125 Bowery
1845–1847 Augustus Abendroth, 125 Bowery
1850–1853 Abendroth Brothers, 117 Beekman
1854 Abendroth Brothers, 117 and 119 Beckman
1855–1879 Abendroth Brothers, 109 Beekman
1880–1911 Abendroth Brothers, 109 Beekman and 282 Pearl
1912 Abendroth Brothers, 105 Beekman
1913 Abendroth Brothers, 27 W. 42nd St.

1915 Abendroth Brothers, 33 W. 42nd St.
1916–1918 Abendroth Brothers, 359 W. 42nd St.
1922–1925 Abendroth Brothers, 149 Broadway

William, Augustus, and John Abendroth were German immigrants who owned the eponymous firm. Beginning in 1841, the brothers ran a well-managed factory producing stoves and plumbers' castings, among other wares. They operated a portion of their business under the name Eagle Iron and Stove Works, which, presumably, manufactured stoves. They maintained their foundry in Portchester, New York. In 1865, John D. Fraser entered the partnership. Nine years later, John Abendroth retired, leaving William and Augustus Abendroth and John D. Fraser as the principal partners. Abendroth Brothers maintained an association with another New York stove-making concern, Abendroth and Root Mfg. Co.
  REFERENCE: New York, vol. 316, p. 49; and New York, vol. 406, p. 7 and p. 100 a/79, R. G. Dun & Co. Collection, Baker Library, Harvard University Graduate School of Business Administration.

WILLIAM ADAMS Cast Iron Philadelphia
1872 William Adams, 962 N. 9th
1873 Adams, Gilbert & Storrie, 969 N. 9th
1874–1887 Adams & Storrie, 960 & 961 N. 9th
1888–1904 William Adams & Co., 960 N. 9th
1904–1905 William Adams & Co., Inc., 960 N. 9th
1905–1929 William Adams Foundry Co. Inc., 960 N. 9th

Ornamental ironwork by William Adams was produced at the Hope Iron Foundry. In 1873, the partnership was composed of the short-lived group William Adams, Josiah Gilbert & Griffith O. Storrie. Adams owned a large piece of property that by 1892 encompassed 960 to 981 North 9th Street in Philadelphia.
  REFERENCE: Pennsylvania, vol. 155, p. 84 and p. 411, R. G. Dun & Co. Collection, Baker Library, Harvard University Graduate School of Business Administration

ARCHITECTURAL DECORATING CO.
  Terra cotta Chicago
Active c. 1900–1940

ATLANTIC TERRA COTTA CO.
  Terra cotta New York
Active c. 1885–1930

The self-proclaimed "largest manufacturers of architectural terra cotta in the world," Atlantic also produced a garden pottery line. With four factories in operation as of 1911, Atlantic sold a variety of terra-cotta goods including flower pots, vases, and sundial pedestals. Their terra cotta was available both glazed and unglazed in several colors. According to an Atlantic trade catalogue, the original vases on which their reproductions were based were purchased by the architect Stanford White before the Italian government prohibited exports of antiquities.

F. & E. AUBEL Cast iron Philadelphia
1893 F[rederick] & E[mil] Aubel, 2521 Tyson
1894–1896 Aubel Brothers, 2521 Tyson
1897 F. & E. Aubel, 2521 Tyson & 2520 N. 9th St.
1898–1916 F. & E. Aubel, 2520 N. 9th St. & 2504–2521 Cadwalader
1917–1923 F. & E. Aubel, 2503 Germantown Ave., 2504–2521 Cadwalader
1924–1935 F. & E. Aubel, 2503 Germantown Ave.

The Aubel brothers produced a wide variety of wrought-iron gates and fences, cast-iron furniture and urns, and some wirework.

AUSTIN & SEELY Terra cotta and stoneware
London
Active c. 1826–1875

The year in which Felix Austin founded Austin's Artificial Stone Works is not known. Austin, a sculptor, went into partnership with John Seely, another sculptor, between 1836 and 1843. Austin & Seely was one of England's largest producers of stoneware and terra-cotta goods. It produced garden ornament in a wide variety of styles, including beautiful designs for fountains as well as classically inspired sculptures for use in the garden. It comes as little surprise that Andrew Jackson Downing recommended Austin & Seely in the December 1, 1854 issue of *The Horticulturist* as a supplier of high quality ornament.
REFERENCE: J. Davis, 200.

BADGER WIRE & IRON WORKS
Cast iron, wirework Milwaukee, WI
Active c. 1900–1925 Badger Wire and Iron Works, Cleveland and 25th Avenue

Besides architectural products, Badger manufactured vases, settees, decoration for funerary monuments, fences, gates, and fountains.

BAKEWELL & MULLINS Brass, Copper, Zinc Salem, OH
pre-1880–c. 1886 Bakewell & Mullins
c. 1886–c. 1910 W. H. Mullins

Bakewell and Mullins and its successor manufactured a wide variety of architectural decorations in metal. They also offered sculptures inspired by antique, Renaissance, or more contemporary designs in sheet zinc, copper, or brass. Their stamping department was destroyed by fire on March 5, 1886. Within a year, the firm was reorganized as W. H. Mullins.

BARBEZAT & CIE. Cast iron Paris
See Val D'Osne.

THE BARCLAY COMPANY Cast stone
Narbeth, PA
1920s and 1930s

Barclay Company garden ware was made of crushed white marble or granite, and according to the firm's chairman, Hugh B. Barclay, "closely resembles natural stone." The company also retailed the terra-cotta products of Galloway and Enfield Pottery.
REFERENCE: Letter from Hugh B. Barclay to Harold Hill Blossom, March 15, 1924. Collection, Harold Hill Blossom, landscape architect, Boston, Massachusets. Courtesy of Withington & Wells, York, Maine.

FRANCIS BARKER & SON, LTD.
Sundials London
c. 1840s–twentieth century 12, Clerkenwell Road

The Barkers were specialists in gnomonics, and produced a variety of dials, armillary spheres, and the pedestals necessary to support them. They also sold books on the subjects of dialing and the history of sundials.

E. T. BARNUM IRON & WIRE WORKS
Cast iron, wirework Detroit, MI
1868–1870 E. T. Barnum Iron and Wire Works, 102 Woodward
1871–1875 E. T. Barnum Iron and Wire Works, 118 Woodward
1876–1878 E. T. Barnum Iron and Wire Works, 118–120 Woodward
1879–1883 E. T. Barnum Iron and Wire Works, 29-31 Woodward
1884–1885 E. T. Barnum Iron and Wire Works, corner Howard and Wabash

1888–1894 E. T. Barnum Iron and Wire Works, 721 Grand River Avenue
1895–1904 E. T. Barnum Iron and Wire Works, Champlain Street
1905–1913 E. T. Barnum Iron and Wire Works, 82 Washington Avenue
1914–1919 E. T. Barnum Iron and Wire Works, 864–878 Woodward Avenue
1920–1924 E. T. Barnum Iron and Wire Works, 4612 Woodward Avenue
1925–1931 E. T. Barnum Iron and Wire Works, 511 Cass Street
1932– E. T. Barnum Iron and Wire Works, 6100–6108 Linwood Avenue

Eugene T. Barnum was a leading supplier of ornamental ironwork in the Midwest, working out of Detroit and, starting in 1883, out of branches in Chicago at 110 Lake Street and in Windsor, Ontario, at Sandwich Street. It was a successful business making vases, fountains, and fences.
REFERENCE: Michigan, vol. 81, p. 291, R. G. Dun & Co. Collection, Baker Library, Harvard University Graduate School of Business Administration.

SAMUEL S. BENT Cast iron New York
1843–1848 Thomas Bent, 405 Cherry
1849 Thomas Bent, Bent & Randall, 405 Cherry
1850 Thomas Bent, Bent & Randall, 128 E. 26th Street
1851–1880 Samuel S. Bent, 210-214 (became 414) East 26th Street
1881–1883 Samuel S. Bent, 72 Beekman
1883–1893 Samuel S. Bent, 111 Chambers

According to Samuel Bent, his father, Thomas, began his business in 1840. Samuel took over the foundry in 1865 but continued to create ore iron, stable fixtures, grates, and frames. Bent constructed a foundry in Portchester, New York, as did other New York makers. Samuel did not prove as astute a businessman as his father. He consistently ran into financial problems, some of which resulted from Samuel's use of other designers' patents, for which he probably paid a premium. The 1868–69 *Wilson's New York City Commercial Register* featured an advertisement for "Samuel S. Bent/Stable

Fittings/ Globe Iron Foundry" with images of a chair and a lidded urn.

REFERENCE: New York, Vol. 316A, p. 160, p. 200 a/1, and p. 200 a/29, R. G. Dun & Co. Collection, Baker Library, Harvard University Graduate School of Business Administration

BERGEOTTE et DAUVILLIER
Ornamental Ironwork Paris
Active c. 1894

MARK H. BLANCHARD Stoneware London
1839–1870 Blackfriars Road

Mark H. Blanchard completed an apprenticeship with Coade and Sealy, setting up his own firm in 1839. He allegedly purchased molds from Coade at that time and probably purchased more in the 1843 sale of molds and related materials formerly owned by Coade. The designs of Blanchard's objects and the composition (a vitrified clay) and quality of the material is, in many cases, strikingly similar to those of the Coade manufactory. The tremendous likeness that Blanchard's pieces and Coade's objects share, supports the very probable assertion that Blanchard purchased some of his molds at the 1843 Coade sale. If it were not for Blanchard's recognizable stamp, which often included a precise date of manufacture, many of Blanchard's works could be mistaken for Coade (cat. 3.57). Despite his apparent debt to the older, more celebrated firm, Blanchard established his own reputation for being the next great maker of artificial stoneware. In 1851, Blanchard secured prizes at the Great Exhibition in London. His work also received praise from J. M. Blashfield, another preeminent maker of clay wares, in Blashfield's 1855 publication, *An Account of the History and Manufacture of Ancient and Modern Terracotta and its Use in Architecture as a durable and elegant Material for Decoration*. By 1855, Blanchard reported (in the December 29th issue of *The Builder*) that he was indeed the "successor to [Coade's original works] in the manufacture of this invaluable material."
REFERENCE: Kelly, 51.

JAMES MARRIOT BLASHFIELD
Stoneware Millwall, Stamford, London
1848–1858 J. M. Blashfield, Millwall
c. 1858–1872 J. M. Blashfield, Stamford, Lincolnshire
c. 1872–1875 The Stamford Terracotta Company (Blashfield's) Limited

Blashfield began casting terra cotta (although probably stoneware, the firm called it terra cotta) for architectural uses in 1848, perhaps from the molds he purchased from William Croggan at the time of Coade's closure in 1836. In 1854, Blashfield began making ornamental terra cotta, including sculpture and vases, in addition to his architectural products. Blashfield frequently reproduced antique statues and urns, as well as those designed by Renaissance and contemporary artists. His work, best documented in his 1857 catalogue, continued the tradition of fine terra cotta and pottery produced in England. Blashfield and Blanchard both produced vitrified clay objects. The company was liquidated in 1875.
According to John Davis, the mark "J. M. Blashfield, Stamford" indicates a date between 1858/9 and 1872. Davis also reports that the mark "The Stamford Terracotta Company (Blashfield's) Limited" indicates a date between 1872 and 1875.
REFERENCE: J. Davis, 175.

BRINES, CHASE & CO. Cast iron Philadelphia
1888–1895 Brines, Chase & Co., 437, 439, and 441 N. 12th St.

The three principals of this firm, William H. Brines, Morton Chase, and Robert Pearsall, formed a short-lived iron manufactory in 1888. Their catalogue of the same year illustrates typical wares in ornamental ironwork, including furniture, vases, and several patterns for wrought-iron fences.

BRISTOL WAGON WORKS CO.
Cast iron Bristol, England
Active c. 1876

Bristol Wagon Works offered a selection of garden furniture.

BRITANNIA IRON WORKS
See Andrew Handyside

BROMSGROVE GUILD Lead London
Active 1894–1966

The Bromsgrove Guild of Applied Arts was established in 1894 by Walter Gilbert. Its foundry in Worcestershire also produced iron and bronze, but lead was the mainstay of the firm. Generally unmarked, their urns, vases, and figural statues were contemporary styles, as opposed to imitations of the antique or of 18th-century designs. In 1921 the firm became a limited company; it ceased operation in 1966.
REFERENCE: J. Davis, 313–316.

BUBIER & CO. Cast iron Boston
Active c. 1880. Bubier produced iron-work fountains, vases, and statuary.

N. I. BULL CO. Cast iron Providence, RI

JAMES W. CARR Cast iron Richmond, VA
1888 James W. Carr, 1420 E. Cary
1889 James W. Carr, 2003–2007 E. Main
1890–1941 James W. Carr, 7–17 N. 25th Street

James W. Carr succeeded the firm Sheppard & Carr, which was found at 1511–1513 East Cary in 1886. Sheppard & Carr had originally succeeded E. P. Vial. Carr was a supplier to the South well into the twentieth century, producing many of the most popular patterns of cast-iron furniture and urns. An example of his work may be found at Virginia House, Richmond, Virginia. See cat. 4.18.

CARRON COMPANY Cast iron Falkirk, Stirlingshire, Scotland
Active 1759–early twentieth century

Dr. John Roebuck, Samuel Garbett, and William Cadell founded the ironworks near Falkirk in 1759 and were incorporated by Royal Charter in 1773. James Watt even used the foundry when he was developing the first steam engine. They maintained showrooms in London, Liverpool, Glasgow, and Edinburgh in the early twentieth century, while the mill itself was in the county of Stirlingshire. They also manufactured iron, cast iron, brass, galvanized metal, and all varieties of ironware. Their garden ornaments included benches, dog supplies, sculptures, and umbrella stands.

CHAMPION IRON COMPANY
Cast iron Kenton, OH
Active c. 1880–1900

The Champion Iron Company produced residential and funerary gates, railing, architectural and ornamental iron. Champion also manufactured steel jail cells. The company's principals were James Young, William H. Young, G. J. Carter, and F. S. Bartlett.

CHASE BROTHERS & COMPANY
Cast iron Boston
1849–1850 Chase Brothers, 93 Water
1851–1852 Chase Brothers & Co., 22 Congress
1853–1855 Chase Brothers, 93 Water
1856–1860 Chase Brothers & Co., 383
      Washington
1861–1862 Chase Brothers & Co., 15 Winter
      and 407 Harrison Avenue

Chase Brothers was a co-partnership comprised of Walter Bryant, Irah Chase, and H. Lincoln Chase in 1850. In 1853, Bryant, who had been very successful in stove manufacturing before his involvement with Chase Brothers, left the firm, perhaps to Chase Brothers' detriment. Within the six following years the firm began to lose its financial health.

In 1861–2, the principals were Irah Chase, Jr., H. L. Chase, and William A. Mauran. In 1863, Chase Brothers became insolvent; William A. Mauran assumed control, and changed the name to Mauran & Tuck, Ornamental Iron, Boston. In 1863, Chase Brothers dissolved. H. Lincoln Chase and Henry S. Chase went on to form a bag manufacturing business in 1864, and had improved financial success making burlap products.

REFERENCE: Massachusetts, vol. 68, p. 321 and p. 418; and Massachusetts, vol. 71, p. 200 a/29, R. G. Dun & Co. Collection, Baker Library, Harvard University Graduate School of Business Administration.

COADE'S ARTIFICIAL STONE
MANUFACTORY Stoneware London
1769–1799 Coade's Artificial Stone Manufactory or Lithodipyra, King's Arms Stairs, Narrow Hall, Lambeth, marked "Coade"
1799–1813 Coade & Sealy, still referred to as "Coade" but its products were marked "Coade & Sealy"
1813–1833 Coade Stone, marked "Coade"

George, his wife Eleanor Coade, and their daughter Eleanor founded Coade's Artificial Stone Manufactory in 1769. Assisted by renowned sculptor John Bacon, the Coade's daughter Eleanor became the driving force behind the company. After many years of success, Bacon died in 1799 and Eleanor II made her cousin John Sealy a partner, establishing "Coade & Sealy." By then the factory was being commissioned by royalty as well as doing prestigious work for the St. George Chapel in Windsor. A gallery was opened up on Westminster Bridge Road in 1799 to display the Coade stone in a grand showroom where visitors could pick up a pamphlet and receive a tour. The company itself produced classically inspired architectural features for important British architects, such as Robert Adam. Among Coade's staple products were plaques, urns, sculpture, and architectural decoration.

Coade made the first weather hardy artificial stone. Not only was it technically superb, but it was a cheaper alternative to carved stone. Coade stone was essentially a ball clay, but the true uniqueness of Coade stone came from both its makeup and the firing method of the clay. The factory built oversized kilns which allowed large pieces to be fired at the same time; Coade's rare talent was to control and to maintain a steady four days of firing. Coade led its market, and encouraged the rise of fellow participants, such as Austin and Seely. After its close, Blanchard and Blashfield along with Austin and Seely successfully filled the gap left in the stoneware market. Examples of Coade's work are on the finest structures and in the finest gardens of England. Pieces are marked "Coade Lambeth" and others are marked "Coade & Sealy, Lambeth 18 . . ." Today, one refers to Coade material as "Coade stone." It commands high prices in the market, and it has been counterfeited, with many fakes including appropriate marks and dates.
REFERENCE: Kelly 21–23, 49, 56–58, 66.

THE COALBROOKDALE COMPANY
Cast iron Coalbrookdale, Shropshire, England
1709–1922 The Coalbrookdale Company, Coalbrookdale and Horsehay (until 1881)

Abraham Darby leased a furnace along the Severn in 1708. He founded the firm in 1709, and in the same year Darby successfully smelted iron using coke as a fuel. In 1755, Abraham Darby II built blast furnaces in Horsehay to produce pig iron. During the 18th century, the firm made hollow ware for domestic use, architectural and industrial iron products, and cannon. In 1810, under the influence of the artistically minded Francis Darby, the Coalbrookdale mill began to produce ornamental castings. In 1846, the company was quite large, with a labor force between three and four thousand men. Ornamental products included settees, fountains, sculpture, flower stands, lanterns, lighting, and urns. There is no doubt that Coalbrookdale led the global cast-iron industry in its day. The vast production of the Coalbrookdale Company was noted by countless American cast-iron foundries, who freely copied designs Coalbrookdale had registered in England.

COMPOSITE IRON WORKS CO.
Cast iron Philadelphia
Active c. 1850–1875

GILBERT CUEL et SOCIÉTÉ Cast stone
Paris
Pre-1900–c. 1934 39, Ave. Edouard Vaillant, Billancourt (Seine)
c. 1934–? Charles Schultz, 30, Rue de Pétrograd, Paris

This decorating and upholstery firm succeeded Marchand et Cie and is perhaps best known in this country for decorating Marble House in Newport, Rhode Island, for Alva Vanderbilt and the Metropolitan Club in New York City. Cuel retailed sculpture inspired by antique, Renaissance, and medieval sources and produced vases, finials, reliefs, fountains, and columns in its "pierre agglomérée."

DALKEITH IRONWORKS Cast iron
Dalkieth, Scotland
Active c. 1865

Registered the so-called "Victoria Settee" the 8th of March 1865: "Dalkeith, W & R Mushet, registered 8 March 1865, no. 184619."

DOULTON & CO., LIMITED
Stoneware Lambeth, England
1815 Jones, Watts & Doulton
1826 Doulton & Watts, Lambeth High Street
1854 Doulton & Co.
1956 Lambeth factory closed

J. J. DUCEL et FILS Cast iron Pocé, Paris
1810 J. J. Ducel founded at Pocé in the Pas-de-Clais
1839–1844 J. J. Ducel fils, Pocé, rue des Quatre-Fils, 22
1845–1857 J. J. Ducel fils, rue des Quatre-Fils, 22, Pocé, and Rue du Faubourg Poissonnière, 26, Paris
1858–1877 J. J. Ducel fils, Poisonniere, 26, Paris
1878 Acquired by the Société Anonyme des Fonderies d'Art du Val d'Osne

In 1878 J. J. Ducel et Fils merged with Val d'Osne. Antoine Durenne purchased S. A. d. F. du Val d'Osne in 1888 and begins to list his address at Ducel's former Paris address. See Val D'Osne. J. J. Ducel produced many objects, some of which bear a mark.

ANTOINE DURENNE Cast iron
Sommevoire, Wassy, Paris
1847–1855 A. Durenne, Sommevoire
1855–1888 A. Durenne, Sommevoire, Wassy
1888 Acquires S. A. d. F. du Val D'Osne, Paris address: Rue du Faubourg Poissonnière, 26, Paris (Ducel's address in Paris)
Circa 1930 Société Anonyme des Etablissements Metallurgiques A. Durenne et du Val d'Osne
Currently Générale d'Hydraulique et de Mécanique, 29 rue Cambacérès, 75008 Paris

Durenne acquired Ducel's Paris address in 1888 and is listed at Poissoniere, 26 from 1896-1911.

Antoine Durenne sought new ways of expanding the cast-iron industry. He adapted cast iron to meet the requirements for architectural decoration and produced stairs, balconies, and balustrades, among other objects. He went on to exploit cast iron artistically by reproducing ancient vases and sculptures and by casting groups of animals designed by modern artists. See Val D'Osne.

ELMORE STUDIOS Cast stone, marble, wrought iron New York
Active c. 1920 at 3 and 5 W. 28th Street

Elmore Studios designed, manufactured, and imported garden ornament in marble, terra cotta, cast stone, and wrought iron.

EMPIRE FOUNDRY Cast iron Troy, NY
Active c. 1880?

THE ERKINS COMPANY Cast stone, bronze, lead New York
1910 Erkins Studios, 305 Madison Avenue
1912–1920 Erkins Studios, 227 Lexington Avenue
1921–1924 Erkins Studios, 238 Lexington Avenue
1925–1937 Erkins Studios, 255 Lexington Avenue
1938–1941 Erkins Studios, 121 East 24th Street
1942–1943 Erkins Studios, 6 East 39th Street
1944–1959 Erkins Studios, 40 West 40th Street
1960–1975 Erkins Studios, 8 West 40th Street
1976–1983 Erkins Studios, 14 West 41st Street

Erkins Studios made all varieties of garden ornament. It marketed a line of fountains and urns in "Pompeian stone" that resembled "gray Indiana limestone in color, texture and durability." Erkins Studios also carried some garden antiques. Antique oil jars were a staple, and occasionally the firm offered wellheads.

J. B. EVANS & CO. Cast iron Smyrna, DE

A piazza chair made by Evans & Co., identical to cat. 4.29, is currently in the collection of The White House.

FALKIRK IRON COMPANY Cast iron Falkirk, near Glasgow

Workers from the nearby Carron foundry established the firm in 1819. The foundry was close to Carron Company and Andrew McClaren and Company on the Firth of Forth on the East Coast of Scotland, and maintained warehouses and retailing premises on Upper Thames Street in London along with its Scottish neighbors. Falkirk published a catalog with Carron in 1900, in which it offered decorative iron ranging from benches and urns to hallstands.

FELSTONE COMPANY, INC. Cast stone Biltmore, NC
Active c. 1925.

Felstone offered a selection of garden furniture.

THE FISCHER & JIROUCH CO. Cast stone Cleveland, OH
Active c. 1900–1935. 4821 Superior Ave.

J. W. FISKE IRON WORKS Cast iron, zinc, wirework, wrought iron New York
1858–1867 J. W. Fiske & Co., 120 Nassau
1868–1869 Joseph W. Fiske, 120 Nassau
1870–1874 Joseph W. Fiske, 99 Chambers
1874–1892 Joseph W. Fiske, 21 & 23 Barclay, 26 & 28 Park Place, 38 Vesey
1892–1900 Joseph W. Fiske, 39 Park Place
1901–1907 J. W. Fiske Iron Works, 39 Park Place
1908–1912 J. W. Fiske Iron Works, 56 Park Place
1913–1933 J. W. Fiske Iron Works, 70–80 Park Place

Joseph Winn Fiske established an ornamental ironworks in 1858. He enjoyed a prosperous business, and made all varieties of ornamental iron. Their prolific sculptural production led city directories on occasion to describe their business as "statuary." Fiske marked some of its wares, but it remains unknown whether Fiske marked all of them. Around 1899, his sons John W. Fiske and Joseph W. Fiske II joined the firm.

REFERENCE: New York, Vol. 380, p. 111; and New York, vol. 381, p. 200 a/102, R. G. Dun & Co. Collection, Baker Library, Harvard University Graduate School of Business Administration.

FLORENTINE CRAFTSMEN Wrought and cast iron, lead, bronze, and cast stone Long Island City, NY

The company began in 1918. Vincent Primavera, an Italian immigrant, started out by making hinges and hardware. He soon began to make furniture – mostly of wrought iron, but also of cast iron. Primavera had a full-time blacksmith who hand-forged leaves, tendrils, and berries in his spare time to be used on the firm's signature botanical style furniture. Frederick Sanford, a landscape architect, contributed the original designs for its signature pieces: star, dolphin, seashell, and lyre-back cast-iron seats. Mr. Primavera designed the wrought ironwork. Still in business today, the firm is run by Graham Brown, a descendant of Mr. Primavera, to whom I am grateful for this information.

FOURMENT HOUILLE & CIE
See Val D'Osne.

FONDERIE ARTISTICHE RIUNITE
J. CHIURAZZI E FIL
S. DE ANGELIS E FILS Bronze and
marble Naples
Active mid-nineteenth–twentieth century.
Reale Albergo dei Poveri.

S. De Angelis, a firm founded in 1840, merged with J. Chiurazzi e Fils in the 1900s. According to a 1910 catalogue, the firm produced bronze, marble, and silver works. The firm created reproductions of antique and Renaissance sculpture in bronze and marble. Chiurazzi, like other Italian firms, enjoyed a lively export business.
REFERENCE: Haskell and Penny, 124.

ANTONIO FRILLI, LTD. Bronze and
marble Florence, Italy
1860–Present Via dei Fossi, 4–26 rosso

The firm supplied principally artworks and furniture for export. American tourists on the Grand Tour stayed in nearby hotels in the Piazza Ognissanti and browsed through the workshops on via dei Fossi, where there was, quite wisely, a staff member fluent in English, a Mr. Thompson in the nineteenth century. Named after the sculptor from the first half of the 19th century, the Frilli Gallery became a limited liability corporation after the Second World War. In 1960, the current owner's father conjoined the old sculpture firms of Pietro Bazzanti and Antonio Frilli, but, unfortunately, the flood of 1966 destroyed most of the firm's records. Antonio Frilli, Limited, recently cast reproductions of Ghiberti's *Porta del Paradiso* on the Baptistry in Florence. A sampling of products may be found in the collection of Bayou Bend in Houston, Texas. See cats. 2.21 and 4.69.

WILLIAM GALLOWAY Terra cotta
Philadelphia
1868–1885 Galloway & Graff (William Galloway & John Graff), 1725 Market
1886–1889 Galloway, Graff & Co., 1725 Market
1890–1896 William Galloway, 1711 Chestnut
1896–1911? William Galloway, 3216 Walnut
1911–1941 Galloway Terra-Cotta Company, 3216 Walnut

Reputedly established in 1810, Galloway was a leading manufacturer of ornamental terra cotta throughout the nineteenth century. Galloway produced a wide range of decorative objects and garden ornament, including a line of artistic vases. His ceramic objects earned awards at the 1876, 1893, and 1904 World's fairs.
REFERENCE: Pennsylvania, vol. 149, p. 104 and p. 391, R. G. Dun & Co. Collection, Baker Library, Harvard University Graduate School of Business Administration.

GARNKIRK FIRECLAY WORKS
Terra cotta near Glasgow, Scotland

Established in 1832, Garnkirk fireclay gained a reputation for high quality and an exceptional light color. The factory had originally intended to be a manufactory of firebricks and firebrick products., but by 1833 it was clear that ornamental products for gardens were going to be an important focus of the company. The firm's works were shown at the Great Exhibition of 1851 as well as the Dublin Exhibition of 1853. These showcased examples of ornamental vases and fountains were also published in catalogues. Andrew Jackson Downing spoke of Garnkirk's products to "exhibit pleasing forms and a soft mellow shade of colour, harmoniz[ing] admirably the hue of foliage and turf." The firm closed in 1900 for unexplained reasons. The only known mark for the firm was "GARNKIRK."
REFERENCE: *Horticulturist,* July 1848, vol. III, no. 1.

GAUDILLOT FRÉRES & ROY Wrought
iron Besançon, France
Established c. 1829, Gaudillot was an early French iron working company in Besançon, France.

JOINVILLE GODEFERT Cast iron
France
Active c. 1845

GOSSIN FRÈRES Terra cotta Paris
Active second half of the nineteenth century
Rue de la Roquette, 57

Etienne and Louis Gossin were both sculptors. The Gossin Brothers produced mainly adornments for buildings, gardens, and churches. Their work won medals in a few competitive exhibitions. Louis debuted at the Salon in 1877. His brother Etienne died 23 years later in 1900.

GRASSIN BRAVETE Cast iron
Arras, France
Active c. 1900

THE BRITANNIA IRON WORKS
ANDREW HANDYSIDE AND
COMPANY Cast iron Derby and London
1818–1843 The Britannia Iron Works, Weatherhead & Glover, owners
1843–1848 The Britannia Iron Works, Thomas Wright, owner
1848–1911 The Britannia Iron Works, Andrew Handyside, owner, Andrew Handyside & Co., Britannia Iron Works

Its manufacture of ornamental castings began with Weatherhead and Glover. The business expanded under Wright's direction and started to manufacture railroad-related products. Handyside purchased the firm in 1848 and further increased the scope of the business to include architectural, engineering, and ornamental products. Handyside was well known for his bridge components, but also produced attractive vases, urns, and fountains for the garden.

HARRIS & COMPANY Copper and
cast iron Boston
1868 J. Harris & Son, 130 Lincoln
1869 J. Harris & Son, 76 Kingston
1870 J. Harris & Son, 98 Kingston
1871 J. Harris & Son, 82 Lincoln
1872–1873 Ansel J. Harris & Co., 73 Kingston
1874–1878 Harris & Co., 111 Kingston
1879–1881 Harris & Co., 54 Bromfield

The firm began around 1868 as Josephus Harris and Son (Ansel J.), weathervane makers. Josephus probably died ca. 1871/2, and in 1872 the company became Ansel J. Harris and Company. In 1874, it is listed as Harris and Company. Ansel Harris probably retired in 1882 and moved to Stoneham in 1883.

HART Cast iron United States
Hart is a mark seen on sets of cast-iron furniture in the "laurel" pattern. Little is known about this maker.

HAYWARD, BARTLETT & CO.
  Cast iron Baltimore
1837–1840 Hayward & Friend
1840–1848 Hayward & Company
1848–1866 Hayward, Bartlett & Company
1866–1878 Bartlett, Robbins & Company
1878–1909 Bartlett, Hayward & Company
1909–1936 The Bartlett Hayward Company

Jonas H. Hayward, David L. Bartlett, and, later, Horace W. Robbin were the principal partners in the firm. This large Baltimore foundry produced a full range of ornamental offerings in addition to stoves and architectural ironwork. The Newfoundland dog was the mascot of the company and the firm manufactured replicas of this animal in cast iron. In 1867, Hayward died, and the company reorganized as Bartlett, Robbins and Company. After 1936, The Bartlett Hayward Company became a division of the Koppers Company.
  REFERENCE: Latrobe, 1941; Maryland, vol. 9, p. 5, R. G. Dun & Co. Collection, Baker Library, Harvard University Graduate School of Business Administration.

HECLA IRON WORKS Cast iron
  New York
1878–1879 [Niels] Poulson & [John] Eger, 313 S. 3rd
1880–1884 Poulson & Eger, 3d corner N. 11th
1885 Hecla Iron Works, 102 N. 11th
1886–1887 Hecla Iron Works, N. 11th & Berry
1888–1890 Hecla Iron Works, N. 11th & Berry & 216 W. 23d
1891–1905 Hecla Iron Works, N. 10th to N. 12th from Berry St. to Wythe Ave.
1906–1910 Hecla Iron Works, N. 10th to N. 11th from Berry St. to Wythe Ave.
1912–1913 Hecla Iron Works, N. 10th to N. 13th and from Berry St. to Wythe Ave.

Hecla Iron Works manufactured exotic style wares following the prevailing taste of the Aesthetic Movement. The firm ceased operations between 1913 and 1933. They cast the decorative iron on The Dakota in New York City.

C. HENNECKE & CO. Wirework and
  cast stone Milwaukee
1867 C. Hennecke & Co., 288 East Water
1868–1873 C. Hennecke & Co., 79 & 81 Buffalo
1874 C. Hennecke & Co., 83 Buffalo
1879–1890 C. Hennecke & Co., 79–83 Buffalo
1891–1900 C. Hennecke & Co., 162–164 West Water
1901–1908 C. Hennecke & Co., 378–380 Broadway
1909–1913 C. Hennecke & Co., 1353-1371 North Pierce
1914–1930 C. Hennecke & Co., 1347–89 North Pierce
1931–1962 C. Hennecke & Co., 3225 North Pierce
Caspar Hennecke started a stoneware business with Francis Vollmer (Vollmer & Hennecke) circa 1866. By 1867 the business was called C. Hennecke & Co., and it expanded to include Ohio stoneware, wire, statuary and pottery. Caspar ran the company until his death on Sept 11, 1892, when his wife Katherine took over the firm. Otto Zielsdorf took command of the firm in 1901, changed location and for a short time opened a separate store for "art goods."

HENRY HOPE Lead New York
Active 1930s

HINDERER'S IRON WORKS Cast iron
  New Orleans
1886–1894 Hinderer Iron Works, 302 and 304 Camp St.
1894–1911 Hinderer Iron Works, 1112–1118 Camp St.
1912–1916 Hinderer's Iron Fence Works, 1112 to 1118 Camp St.
1917–1920 Hinderer's Iron Works, 1112 to 1118 Camp St.

Frederick C. A. Hinderer established the firm

in 1886. Around 1913, William Spitz assumed control of the company. Known primarily for their iron fencing, they also made furniture and other ornamental ironwork. Examples of their architectural ironwork are seen throughout New Orleans.

HOWARD & MORSE Wirework New York
1861–1871 Howard & Morse, 63 Fulton
1871–1925 Howard & Morse, 45 Fulton

John W. Howard and David R. Morse were the principle partners of this firm, which produced a small line of ornamental wirework in addition to more utilitarian brass and copper goods (see cat. 4.56). Carried on by their sons Edward S. Howard and William B. Morse, this firm was in business until at least 1925.

HOWARD STUDIOS, INC. Marble
  New York
1916–1917 Howard Studios, 5 West 28th Street
1918 Howard Studios, 4 East 44th Street
1919–1924 Howard Studios, 7 West 47th Street
1925–1928 Howard Studios, 110 East 57th Street, 2nd Floor
1929–1935 Howard Studios, 249 Lexington Avenue
1936–1937 Howard Studios, 222 East 41st Street
1938–1940 Howard Studios, 137 East 57th Street
1941–1943 Howard Studios, 110 East 59th Street
1944 Howard Studios, 37 West 47th Street
1945–1949 Howard Studios, 110 East 59th Street

Francis Howard manufactured all varieties of garden ornament. His catalog offered sundials, fountains, sculptures, urns, and wellheads.

HUTCHINSON & WICKERSHAM
See New York Wire Railing Co.

WILLIAM H. JACKSON & CO.
  Wrought iron New York
1854–1858 William H. Jackson, 891 Broadway and 15 E. 19th Street
1859–1867 William H. Jackson & Co., 891 Broadway and 15 E. 19th Street
1868–1869 William H. Jackson & Co., 31 E. 17th Street
1870–1881 William H. Jackson & Co., 31 E. 17th Street & 36 E. 18th Street
1882–1889 William H. Jackson & Co., 31 E. 17th Street & 315 E. 28th Street
1890 William H. Jackson & Co., 27 and 29 E. 17th. Street
1891 William H. Jackson & Co., 29 E. 17th Street

1892–1893 William H. Jackson & Co., 29 E. 17th Street and 32 E. 18th Street
1894 William H. Jackson & Co., 860 Broadway and 32 E. 18th Street
1895–1900 William H. Jackson & Co., 860 Broadway, 32 E. 18th, 315 E. 28th Street
1901–1902 William H. Jackson & Co., 29 E. 17th, 32 E. 18th, and 315 E. 28th Street
1903–1910 William H. Jackson & Co., 29 E. 17th, 32 E. 18th, and 229 W. 29th Street
1911 William H. Jackson & Co., 29 E. 17th Street
1912–1913 William H. Jackson & Co., 2 W. 47th and 229 W. 28th Street
1915–1933 William H. Jackson & Co., 2 W. 47th Street

William H. Jackson and Company grew out of Jackson and Sons after the death of the patriarch, Nathan Jackson, in 1854. In the 1880s, William H. Jackson and Company also operated a heavy ironworks incorporated under the name Jackson Architectural Iron Works. This company produced work for important American architects such as Richard Morris Hunt (see fig. 91, p. 111), and McKim, Mead & White, and was well-known for its magnificent entry gates. Jackson ran a very profitable business and became quite wealthy.

REFERENCE: New York, vol. 317, p. 256 and p. 300 a/50, R. G. Dun & Co. Collection, Baker Library, Harvard University Graduate School of Business Administration.

F. & A. JACQUIER Terra cotta Caen, France
Active c. 1900. Jacquier offered figural and animal statuary.

JANES, BEEBE & CO./JANES & KIRTLAND Cast iron New York
1847–1850 Janes, Beebe & Co., 120 Fulton
1851–1852 Janes, Beebe & Co., 314 Broadway and Centre
1852–1859 Janes, Beebe & Co., 356 Broadway and 25½ Centre
1859–1864 Janes, Fowler, Kirtland & Co., 356 Broadway and 25½ Centre
1865–1866 Janes, Fowler, Kirtland & Co., 2, 4, 6, 8, 10, & 12 Reade
1867–1870 Janes, Kirtland & Co., 2, 4, 6, 8, 10, & 12 Reade

1871–1873 Janes & Kirtland, 2–12 Reade
1874–1879 Janes & Kirtland, 12 Reade and Westchester Ave.
1879–1881 Janes & Kirtland, 15 Murray and Westchester Ave.
1882–1883 Janes & Kirtland, 19 E. Fifth & 150th Brook Ave.
1883–1884 Janes & Kirtland, 19 E. 17th & 774 Westchester Ave.
1884–1889 Janes & Kirtland, 609 Sixth Ave., 1346 Broadway & 774 Westchester Ave.
1889–1895 Janes & Kirtland, 242 Water, 112 Beekman and 774 Westchester Ave.
1895–1898 Janes & Kirtland, 110 Beekman
1899–1906 Janes & Kirtland, 725 & 727 6th Ave.
1907–1912 Janes & Kirtland, 725 6th Ave.
1913 Janes & Kirtland, 133 W. 44th Street
1915–1925 Janes & Kirtland, 133–135 W. 44th Street
1933 Janes & Kirtland, Inc., 101 Park Ave.

Janes, Beebe & Co. was one of the most important cast-iron foundries in pre-Civil War America. The principals of the firm were Adrian Janes, William Beebe, Charles Fowler, and Rowland A. Rollins. Janes, Beebe & Co. quickly earned high-profile commissions. On October 18, 1852, the White House ordered cast-iron settees in the "Rococo" pattern, and in 1858 the firm produced the splendid fountain found in Forsythe Park in Savannah, Georgia. In the same year, 1858, it also won a sizable contract to provide cast iron for the U.S. Capitol. The company maintained a large foundry on the Hudson River in Melrose, New York. With the death of William Beebe in October 1859, the name of the firm changed to Janes, Fowler & Kirtland. Fowler left the firm in 1867. By the 1890s, the firm was producing "Beebe" ranges and stoves, and seemed to have left ornamental work behind.

REFERENCE: New York, vol. 366, p. 235; and New York, vol. 369, p. 592, R. G. Dun & Co. Collection, Baker Library, Harvard University Graduate School of Business Administration.

M. D. JONES & CO. Cast iron Boston
1870–1876 Melville D. Jones & Co., 52 Sudbury
1877 Melville D. Jones & Co., 115 Washington and 52 Sudbury
1879–1880 Melville D. Jones & Co., 12 Cornhill
1881–1883 Melville D. Jones & Co., 88 Washington

1884–1893 Melville D. Jones & Co., 76 Washington
1894–1897 Melville D. Jones & Co., 368 Washington
1898–1899 Melville D. Jones & Co., 53 Portland
1900–1918 Melville D. Jones & Co., 71–73 Portland

Melville D. Jones, a Boston clerk, probably started his ornamental iron work and copper weathervane business around 1870. The company prospered under Jones's leadership until his death in 1910. The company then moved to nearby Concord in 1919.

KENTON MANUFACTURERS
Cast iron Kenton, OH

KRAMER BROTHERS Cast iron
Dayton, OH
1890–1892 Kramer Brothers (George H. & Joseph F.), 601 E. 3rd Street
1893 Kramer Brothers, 128 E 5th
1894–1903 Kramer Brothers, Michigan Ave.
1904–1916 The Kramer Brothers Foundry, Michigan Ave,
1917–1934 The Kramer Brothers Foundry, 51 E. Dell

Kramer Brothers was a prolific foundry that marked many of its pieces, and is one of the rare companies still to be in business today.

KUNST FOUNDRY Cast iron New York

LALANCE & GROSJEAN Wrought iron
New York
1852 Alfred Lalance, 120 Pearl
1853 Charles Lalance, 120 Pearl
1854–1855 Lalance & Grosjean, 120 Pearl
1856–1862 Lalance & Grosjean, 70 Beekman
1863–1868 Lalance & Grosjean, 273 Pearl Street
1869–1879 Lalance & Grosjean, 89 Beekman and 55 Cliff
1879–1907 Lalance & Grosjean, 19 Cliff
1908–1925 Lalance & Grosjean, 299 Broadway
1933 Lalance & Grosjean, 405 Lexington Ave.

Charles Lalance and Florian Grosjean began as importers, but later produced ironware, agateware, hardware, and stamped tinware. They bought François Carré's patent for the "bent steel" chair and produced it. These chairs are often identified by a marked brass button located in the center of the seat.

REFERENCE: New York, vol. 316, p. 100V, R. G. Dun & Co. Collection, Baker Library, Harvard University Graduate School of Business Administration.

JOSEPH J. LEINFELDER & SONS
Wrought iron Lacrosse, WI
Active c. 1920–40. Joseph J. Leinfelder and Sons

Leinfelder began as a blacksmith shop that made furniture on quiet days (according to Dick and Rita Nelson, whom I thank for this information). Most of their pieces were sent to the East Coast and to Europe. Mary Ryan was the sole agent for their wares in Chicago and New York. From 1934, they offered a wide range of styles in wirework and furniture available in vibrant colors.

LION FOUNDRY Cast iron Kirkintulloch, Northampton

John Bretell and William Roberts operated the Lion Foundry from 1849 to 1851. Roberts ran the foundry from 1851 to 1868. The firm ceased operation in 1929. Marks read "Lion Foundry Northampton, registered by W. Roberts."
REFERENCE: Morris, 165–6.

KENNETH LYNCH Lead, cast stone, bronze Wilton, CT
Active c. 1928–Present

The firm offers a wide range of objects from faucet heads to furniture. It produced many sculptures, some of which were inspired by Western and Eastern sources while others were the original work of the in-house artists Robert Amendola and Anne Jaggard Kopper.

WALTER MACFARLANE & CO., SARACEN FOUNDRY Cast iron Glasgow
Active c. 1830s to the beginning of the twentieth century

The firm registered a number of designs. The Saracen Foundry and a nearby competitor, the Sun Foundry, among other Glaswegian foundries, were large scale suppliers to the architectural iron market.

LA MANIFATTURA DI SIGNA
Terra cotta Florence, Italy
1897 Via Vecchietti, 5, Florence; 17 Mount St. W., London
1898 Via Vecchietti, 2, Florence; Rome, Via del Babuino, 50; Turin, Via Accademia Albertina, 5; Paris, Rue Chaussee D'Antin, 12
1899 Via Vecchietti and Via de' Fossi, 8
1900 Via Vico Stella, 6–8, Genoa
1901 End of business

The company maintained its business headquarters in Florence and its kiln at Signa. Its wares were derived from antique, medieval, and Renaissance sources. Their urns, vases, and sarcophagi may be identified by the firm's characteristic stamp. Most of its very best work was produced before 1928.

E. MARCH-SOHNE Cast iron Charlottenburg, near Berlin, Germany

ANDREW MCCLAREN & CO.
Cast iron London, Scotland
Active second half nineteenth century.

McClaren and Company was situated on the Firth of Forth near the Falkirk Iron and Carron Companies. McClaren was one of the three houses that maintained warehouses on Upper Thames Street where Scottish iron goods were shipped by sea.

McHOSE & LYON Cast iron Dayton, OH
1862–1871 William McHose
1871–1877 William McHose & Co.
1877–1897 McHose & Lyon
1897–1898 William McHose Ironworks

William McHose and Calvin Lyon were partners after 1876. In the 1880s, they were producing both "little novelty machines," ornamental iron, and architectural ironware through their Dayton Architectural Iron Works.
REFERENCE: Ohio, vol. 140, p. 853 and p. 1210, R. G. Dun & Co. Collection, Baker

Library, Harvard University Graduate School of Business Administration.

JOHN McLEAN Cast iron New York
1877–1881 John McLean, machinist
1882–1903 John McLean, 298–300 Monroe
1904 John McLean, 440 Water
1905 John McLean, machinist

From 1873 and 1880, John McLean worked with a partner, William Stevens, making industrial wares. McLean went on by himself after 1880, producing stopcocks and fire hydrants, in addition to consumer goods. He was listed in New York City directories sporadically from 1889 to 1905 as a machinist, engineer, and in 1892, as an ironworker. The year before was significant for McLean, since he received a patent for a cast-iron settee, one of which is at Old Westbury Gardens, Old Westbury, New York.
REFERENCE: New York, Vol. 327, p. 1235 and p. 1287, R. G. Dun & Co. Collection, Baker Library, Harvard University Graduate School of Business Administration

MILLER IRON WORKS Cast iron Providence, RI
1870–1882 Miller Iron Co., 170 Carpenter
1883–1893 Miller Iron Works, 176 Harris Ave.
1894–1895 Miller Iron Works, 316 Harris Ave.
1896–1912 Miller Iron Works, 516 Harris Ave.

Although 1870 is the first instance Miller Iron appears in Providence city directories, dated objects suggest that the firm operated a few years prior to this date. In 1876, George Miller and his son George O. Miller operated the Miller Iron Foundry. By 1880, the name of the firm became Miller Iron Company after forming as a partnership consisting of Henry and George Miller, uncle and nephew, respectively, and Stern Hutchins. They maintained an office in Providence but kept their works in Olneyville. They ran a fairly successful business and manufactured birdhouses among other garden ornaments.
REFERENCE: Rhode Island, vol. 6, p. 250 and p. 251, R. G. Dun & Co. Collection, Baker Library, Harvard University Graduate School of Business Administration.

ISRAEL P. MORRIS Cast iron Philadelphia

1850–1875 Israel P. Morris & Co., 39 Walnut

1876–1886 Israel P. Morris & Co., 1057 Richmond

1887–1893 Israel P. Morris & Co., 2247 Richmond

1894–1916 Israel P. Morris & Co., corner of Beach and Ball

1917 Israel P. Morris & Co., corner of Richmond & Norris

1918–1928 I. P. Morris, Dept. of the William Cramp & Sons Ship and Engine building Co., corner of Richmond and Norris

1929–c. 1934 I. P. Morris & DeLaVargne, Inc., corner of Richmond and Norris

Morris made the Gothic settee in the collection of Richmond in Natchez. A mark identifying the maker and date (1842) suggests that it is an example of some of the earliest cast-iron produced in the United States. See fig. 67, p. 82.

J. L. MOTT IRON WORKS Cast iron, zinc, wrought iron, wirework New York

1828 Business established

1855 Began as J. L. Mott Iron Works

1865–1869 J. L. Mott Iron Works, 264 & 266 Water Street

1870–1897 J. L. Mott Iron Works, 88 & 90 Beekman, 147 W. 35th St., 2411 & 2413 3rd Ave.

1898–1901 J. L. Mott Iron Works, 88 & 90 Beekman, 105 Fifth Ave., and 2411 & 2413 3rd Ave.

1902–1905 J. L. Mott Iron Works, 88 Beekman, 110 Fifth Ave., 221 11th Ave, 2411 3rd Ave.

1906–1907 J. L. Mott Iron Works, 118 Fifth Ave., and E. 137th corner Rider Ave.

1908–1913 J. L. Mott Iron Works, 118 Fifth Ave.

1915–1933 J. L. Mott Iron Works, 525 Fifth Ave.

J. L. Mott & Co. was Mott Iron Works's stove business on Water Street. Jordan L. Mott was the very wealthy principal partner who obtained an 1847 patent for a cast-iron, revolving "Opera chair." The business was worth approximately a million dollars by 1870. Between 1875 and 1878, Mott had a showroom at 549 Sixth Avenue and by 1882 one opened at 1266 Broadway.

In 1883 the firm suffered damage after a fire at its Mott Haven works. Mott also owned the North American Iron Works as his maker of funerary decoration. Mott manufactured all varieties of garden ornament, but, by the 1930s, the firm was producing and selling mainly plumbing fixtures.

REFERENCE: New York, Vol. 326, p. 1134 and p. 1200/p; and New York, Vol. 376, p. 441, R. G. Dun & Co. Collection, Baker Library, Harvard University Graduate School of Business Administration

EMILE MULLER & CIE. Terra cotta Ivry, near Paris

1854–into the twentieth century Rue Nationale, 6; shop: 3 Rue Halevy, Ivry

This firm made adornments for architecture and for the garden in addition to bricks. They manufactured sculptures following the designs of Alexandre Charpentier (1856–1909) such as the advertisement panel, *Boy with a Tile*, in the collection of the Metropolitan Museum of Art.

NEW YORK WIRE RAILING COMPANY Cast iron, wirework New York

1853 J. B. Wickersham's Ornamental Iron Warehouse, 312 Broadway

1855–1860 New York Wire Railing Company, 312 Broadway & 57 Lewis

1861–1865 New York Wire Railing Company, 259 Canal & 57 Lewis

An 1855 catalogue also uses the name New York Wire Railing Works. Ira Hutchinson and John B. Wickersham operated and managed the foundry. Wickersham came to New York from Philadelphia where he had a similar business. He held patents for furniture designs (1847 and 1849) as well as for ornamental railings. It manufactured wares for the garden, such as summerhouses, tree boxes, wire furniture, and animals, as well as objects for domestic use, such as hall stands and fences. The company failed once in 1855 and was briefly under the control of Mrs. Wickersham. In 1857 Hutchinson entered the partnership. It failed for the last time in 1865–66.

REFERENCE: New York, vol. 316, p. 3, R. G. Dun & Co. Collection, Baker Library, Harvard University Graduate School of Business Adminsitration.

NORRISTONE STUDIO Cast stone Rochester, NY

Active c. 1929

Norristone Studio offered benches and Japanese lanterns among other wares.

NORTH AMERICAN IRON WORKS Cast iron New York

1872–1875 North American Iron Works, Walton Street near Mary Ave., Brooklyn

1876 North American Iron Works, 40 & 42 Walton, B'klyn & 90 Beekman

1877–1889 North American Iron Works, 88 Beekman

1890– North American Iron Works, 90 Beekman (for following years see J. L. Mott Iron Works)

North American Iron Works was a subsidiary of J. L. Mott. This branch of the business handled ornaments for cemeteries. It was not uncommon for founders to maintain a differently titled company to handle its funerary wares. For its address, see J. L. Mott.

REFERENCE: New York, Vol. 130, p. 220 and p. 222, R. G. Dun & Co. Collection, Baker Library, Harvard University Graduate School of Business Administration

PEQUONNOCK FOUNDRY INC. Cast iron Bridgeport, CT

1903–1909 Pequonnock Foundry Inc., 31 E. Washington Avenue

1915 Pequonnock Foundry Inc., Fifth Street Extension

1925–1962 Pequonnock Foundry Inc., 335 Fifth Street

Pequonnock produced furniture and urn patterns designed in the mid-nineteenth century. By 1906 Gertrude E. Kirsten was the president of the foundry, a position she continuously held at least until the 1960s. The Foundry probably ceased operations in 1968.

PERTH AMBOY TERRA COTTA CO. Terra cotta Perth Amboy, NJ

Active c. 1890s into the twentieth century.

The firm produced architectural wares

for important American architects such as McKim, Mead, and White. While Perth Amboy produced mainly architectural decoration, it did produce some garden ornament. Samuel Swift mentioned Perth Amboy in his article "Garden Pottery" of 1903.

DAVID PETTIT Cast iron Philadelphia
1874–1878 Hanson & Pettit, N. 12th corner Noble
1879 David & Frank Pettit, N. 12th corner Noble
1880 David Pettit & Co., N. 12th corner Noble
1881 David Pettit & Co., 1130 Ridge Ave. and 1107 Buttonwood
1882 David Pettit & Co., 1126 Ridgeway Ave. and 1219 Callowhill
1887–1888 David Pettit & Co., 1217 Callowhill
1889–1896 David Pettit & Co., 1219 Callowhill
1897 Pettit Ornamental Iron & Fence Co., 1219 Callowhill
1898 Pettit Ornamental Iron & Fence Co., Inc., 1217 Callowhill
1899 Pettit Ornamental Iron & Fence Co., Inc., 46 N. 11th
1900–1903 Pettit Ornamental Iron & Fence Co., 46 N. 11th

REFERENCE: Pennsylvania, vol. 138, p. 326 and p. 329, R. G. Dun & Co. Collection, Baker Library, Harvard University Graduate School of Business Administration.

PHOENIX IRON WORKS Cast iron Utica, NY
1852–1872 Phoenix Iron Works, First corner Blandina
1873–1874 Phoenix Iron Works, 101 and 103 Blandina
1875–1885 Phoenix Iron Works, 97–103 Blandina
1892–1893 Phoenix Iron Works, First corner Blandina
1894 Phoenix Iron Works, 171 to 181 Blandina Street
1899–1900 Phoenix Iron Works, 171–178 Blandina Street
1904–1905 Phoenix Iron Works, 171-183 Blandina Street
1906–1907 Phoenix Iron Works, 179-183 Blandina Street

Chauncey Palmer and his son, Cyrus Palmer, opened the firm. Cyrus took over in 1885, after Chauncey's death. Cyrus died c. 1906 and the company expired with him.

PHOENIX WORKS/JOHN SAVERY'S SONS Cast iron New York
Active c. 1861

The firm offered bronzed, ornamental cast-iron.

PORTLAND STONEWARE COMPANY Glazed stoneware Portland, ME
1879–1886 Portland Stoneware Company, Deering Point
1887–1899 Portland Stoneware Company, rear 35 Forest Ave.
1900–1915 Portland Stoneware Company, rear 253 Forest Ave.
1916–1932 Winslow and Company, Inc., rear 253 Forest Ave.

Portland Stoneware manufactured weather-hardy garden vases along with pipes and other industrial products. Its products are not to be confused with English Portland stone, an artificial stone produced in the United Kingdom.

PRIMO ART GARDEN FURNITURE Cast stone Providence, RI
Active c. 1930

PULHAM'S ARTIFICIAL STONES Cast stone Hoddesdon, London
c. 1840–1843 Pulham's Artificial Stones, at Hoddesdon
1843–1945 Pulham's Artificial Stones, at Broxbourne
1865–1945 Pulham & Son

James Pulham began manufacturing Portland cement and later added ornamental products after the firm's move to Broxbourne. The firm went on to produce architectural products as well as geological follies. Many of the sculptures were reproductions of antique, Renaissance, as well as contemporary subjects. Portland cement is also different from Portland stone. Portland cement is defined as "a hydraulic cement made by heating a mixture of limestone and clay in a kiln and pulverizing the resulting material." It is still used today for building.

T. R PULLIS Cast iron St. Louis, MO
Active 1840–1870

The Missouri Historical Society holds three-legged chairs and a loveseat manufactured by this firm.

WILLIAM F. REMPPIS CO. Cast iron Philadelphia
1898–1906 Wm. F. Remppis & Co., 331 Witherspoon Bldg.
1907–1911 Wm. F. Remppis Co., 1506 Sansom
1912–1916 Wm. F. Remppis Co., 1739 Filbert
1917 Wm. F. Remppis Co., 403 Land

William Remppis, the principal partner, was probably living in Germany – or wherever he was from – and was never listed with a home address in Philadelphia. At times the firm was listed with "(foreign)" next to the name of the company. The other principals were Frank Royer, VP and manager, and Daniel F. Yost, secretary. The firm was listed sometime as "builders iron" and in 1911–13 as "iron fences."

JOHN RILEY FOUNDRY AND MACHINE WORKS Cast iron Charleston, SC
1886–1888 John F. Riley, 8 South
1889–1900 John F. Riley's Machine Works, 6–8 South
1901 Riley's Foundry and Machine Works, 6–8 South
1902–1903 The John F. Riley Foundry and Machine Works, 6–12 South
1904–1927 The John F. Riley Foundry and Machine Works, 2–12 South
1928–1934 The John F. Riley Foundry and Machine Works, 45 Bay

John F. Riley is first listed as a ship's blacksmith in 1886, and seems to have started his business c. 1887–8. The business prospered and he eventually became an alderman of the city of Charleston and president of the Hibernian Insurance Co. The John F. Riley Foundry and Machine Works survived the Great Depression and was in business as of 1934. It was a large supplier of wares for the South.

ROGERS IRON CO. Cast iron Springfield, OH
1885–1887 The Rogers Fence Co., 78 W. North
1888–1889 The Rogers Fence Co., 66–78 W. North

1901–
1903–1904 The Rogers Iron Co., 90 W. North
1905 The Rogers Iron Co., succeeded by The
William Bayley Co., 90 W. North

Rogers manufactured railing and fences as well
as some decorative ornament. The hitching post
in Salem, Massachusetts, pictured as cat. 7.31,
was made by Rogers Iron Co.

DAVIS & WILLIAM ROSE Cast iron
Savannah, GA

SALTERINI Wrought iron New York
Active 1920s–1948–53.

John B. Salterini came to the United States
from Italy in the early 1920s. He operated a
factory in Harlem in the 1940s and 1950s. He
went out of business in the years 1948–53. His
signature treatment of wrought iron which
identifies his work was the distinctive "snake
head twist" of iron with a hammered end. He
competed fiercely with Florentine Craftsmen
and enjoyed some popularity in Philadelphia.

HENRY SANDERS Cast iron Chicago
Active the first quarter of the twentieth century.
Sanders offered sundials and pedestals for their
support in addition to other products.

M. J. SEELIG & CO. Zinc, bronze
Williamsburgh, NY
1855–1865 Morris J. Seelig, Remsen n. Ewen
1866–1870 Morris J. Seelig, Remsen n. Leonard
1871–1913 M. J. Seelig & Co., 115 & 117 Maujer

M. J. Seelig & Co. made zinc statuary for the garden. The firm was composed mainly of German
immigrants, and Seelig himself often ran the
business from his home in Germany. Operations
ceased sometime between 1913 and 1933.
    REFERENCE: New York, vol. 130, p. 20,
p. 380, and p. 431, R. G. Dun & Co. Collection,
Baker Library, Harvard University Graduate
School of Business Administration.

GEORGE SMITH & CO., SUN
FOUNDRY Cast iron Glasgow, Scotland
Active second half of the nineteenth century.

Sun made architectural and ornamental cast
iron that included figural fountains, outdoor
lighting, and benches. George Smith registered
a design for a fountain decorated with griffin
terms on 22 September 1870. Marks may be

"George Smith & Sons, Foundry Co." for
pieces after 1870 and "Geo. Smith & Co., Sun
Foundry, Glasgow" for earlier pieces.

E. G. SMYSER & SONS Cast iron York, PA
c. 1840–1907 E. G. Smyser & Sons, w. North
    se cor. Beaver
1907–c. 1935? Smyser-Royer, 32 W. North,
    se cor. N. Beaver

In 1907 the firm merged to form Smyser-Royer
Company. It endured at least until 1935, manufacturing grates, railings, and architectural iron.

W. A. SNOW Cast iron Boston
1885–1887 William A. Snow & Co., 16
    Devonshire
1888–1904 William A. Snow & Co.,
    19 Portland
1905–1907 W. A. Snow Iron Works,
    19 Portland
1908–1916 W. A. Snow Iron Works, Inc.,
    19 Portland
1917–1933 W. A. Snow Iron Works, Inc.,
    32 Portland
(1922 W. A. Snow Iron Works, Inc., 75
    Portland)
1934–

SPICERS & PECKHAM Cast iron
Providence, RI
1862–1865 Spicer & Peckham, 28 Westminster
1866–1870 Spicers & Peckham, 32 Westminster
1871–1891 Spicers & Peckham, 22 Exchange
    Place

George T. Spicer and Charles H. Peckham
founded the firm in 1862. Around 1866, W. A.
Spicer joined the firm (hence the plurality of
Spicers). Providence was an important center
for cast iron in New England during the nine-
teenth century.
    REFERENCE: Rhode Island, Vol. 10, p. 45,
R. G. Dun & Co. Collection, Baker Library,
Harvard University Graduate School of
Business Administration

E. C. STEARNS & CO. Cast iron
Syracuse, NY

STEVENSON & CASSEL Terra cotta
Philadelphia
1876–1877 Stevenson & Cassel, 2341 N 7th
1878–1881 Henry C. Cassel, then H. C. Cassel
    & Bro., 2341 N. 7th

Stevenson & Cassel produced a line of decorative terra-cotta work. Henry C. Cassel maintained the business after his partner's departure
from the firm.

STEWART IRON WORKS CO.
    Ornamental metal work Cincinnati, OH
1886 Possible date of foundation
1895 Stewart Iron Works, Sycamore between
    7th and 8th
1896–1897 Stewart Iron Works, 710–716
    Sycamore
1898–1903 Stewart Iron Works, Northeast cor-
    ner of 3d and Culvert
1904–1906 Stewart Iron Works, 17th and
    Madison in Covington, KY; branch at 716
    East 3d
1907–1913 Stewart Iron Works, branch in
    Cincinnati Southwest corner of Colerain
    Avenue and Sassafras
1914 Colerain Ave. branch closes.
1915–1961 Stewart Iron Works, 17th and
    Madison in Convington, KY

Stewart Iron produced ornamental railing,
gates, and residential fencing in addition to
urns and garden furniture. Stewart also produced objects for the funerary market.

PETER TIMMES SON BROOKLYN N.Y.

PETER TIMMES' SON Cast iron
    Brooklyn, NY
Pre–1860 Address unknown
1860–1866 Peter Timmes, 1st n. N. 11th
1867 P[eter] & J[ohn] Timmes, 1st n. N. 11th
1868 P. & J. Timmes, 131 N. 5th
1870–1872 Peter Timmes, 283 N. 6th
1874 Peter Timmes, 281 N. 6th
1875 Peter Timmes & Son, 281 N. 6th
1876–1887 Peter Timmes' Son, 281 to
    285 N. 6th
1888–1891 Peter Timmes' Son, 281 N. 6th &
    304 N. 7th
1892–1901 Peter Timmes' Son, 281– 285 N. 6th
1902 Timmes & Hecht, 281 N. 6th

The elder Timmes began in 1840 as a nail merchant. The junior Timmes assumed control in
1875 and was a member of the firm until its

waning in 1903. The Timmes's firm held five design patents for gates and one for a settee. Timmes produced elegant gates for cemeteries and for residences along with urns and furniture.

G. C. TIMPE Cast iron New Orleans, LA
1866 G. C. Timpe, machinist, 419 Jackson
1867 G. C. Timpe, machinist, 441 Julia
1868–1872 G. C. Timpe, machinist, 300 Camp
1873–1875 G. C. Timpe, iron works, 194 Magazine

Before Hinderer's began production, Timpe was an early supplier of architectural ironwork to New Orleans and the South.

TRUDO MANUFACTURING CO.
  Aluminum Framingham, MA
Active c. 1950

Trudo produced Modernist chairs and probably other furniture.

FONDERIES DU VAL D'OSNE Cast iron Osne-le-Val, Haute-Marne and Paris, France
1833–1855 J. P. V. André, Val d'Osne. 8, rue Neuve-Menilmontant, Paris (1847)
1855–1867 Barbezat et Cie./Maitres des Forges. 10, rue Neuve-Menilmontant, Paris (1859–1864)
1867–1870 Société Fourment, Houille, et Cie.
1870–20th c. Société Anonyme des Hauts-Fourneaux & Fonderies du Val d'Osne
1878 J. J. Ducel merged with Val D'Osne group.
1888 Fonderies d'Art du Val D'Osne acquired by Antoine Durenne and became part of the group G. H. M. Boulevards Voltaire, 58 et Richard-Lenoir, 95 and 97, Paris.
Circa 1930 Société Anonyme des Etablissements Metallurgiques A. Durenne et du Val d'Osne. Currently Générale d'Hydraulique et de Mécanique, 29 rue Cambacérès, 75008 Paris

A large and long-lived French manufacturers of cast iron. The firm was known for its fine quality sculptures, urns, and furniture, among other products. It marked its pieces. An urn is illustrated in the catalog (see cat. 3.21, p. 155).

VAN DORN IRON WORKS Cast iron Cleveland, OH
1872–1883 Cleveland Wrought Iron Fence Works, C. & P. R. R. nr. Woodland Avenue
1884–1891 Van Dorn Iron Works, C. & P. R. R. nr Woodland Avenue
1892–1894 Van Dorn Iron, Works, 157 Euclid Avenue
1895–1896 Van Dorn Iron Works, Woodland Ave. and C. & P. R. R.
1897–1906 Van Dorn Iron Works, 1793 E. Madison Avenue
1907–1920 Van Dorn Iron Works, 2685 E. 79th Street
1921–1930 The Van Dorn Iron Works, 2685 E. 79th Street
1930–1957 The Van Dorn Iron Works, Co., 2685 79th Street

James H. Van Dorn started the Cleveland Wrought Iron Works circa 1874, which specialized in producing his patented fence design. The firm changed its name to the Van Dorn Iron Works some time shortly before June of 1884. (The 1921 directory states that Van Dorn Iron Works was incorporated in 1872, but the 1930 directory gives the date as 1891.) The company seems to have survived the Depression by focusing on the manufacture of steel and iron for prisons and railroads.

VERMONT MARBLE COMPANY
  Marble Rutland, VT
Active 1856–post 1950

All products, such as sundials, birdbaths, gazing globes, fountains, and benches, were made of Rutland white marble in a simple, structural almost modernist style.

C. A. VILLARD Cast iron Lyon, France
Active middle nineteenth century. Quai St. Antoine, 34

Villard won various medals for its pieces, and was admitted to the Exposition Universelle in 1855. They manufactured articles for buildings, churches, and gardens.

WALBRIDGE & CO. Cast iron Buffalo, NY
1869–1872 Charles E. Walbridge, 271 Main
1873–1878 Charles E. Walbridge, 297, 299, 301 Washington
1879–1884 Charles E. Walbridge, 317, 319, 321 Washington
1885–1897 Walbridge and Co., 317 to 321 Washington
1898–1900 Walbridge and Co., 317 to 325 Washington
1901–
1916–1922 Walbridge and Co., 392-394 Main, with branches at 2213 Seneca, 1071 Grant, 310 W. Ferry and 1033 Broadway
1922–1925 Walbridge and Co., 392-394 Main, with branches at 2213 Seneca, 1071 Grant, 310 W. Ferry, 1033 Broadway, and 1421 Hertel

By 1920, the Walbridge family left the cast-iron and hardware business and became a general or department store.

M. WALKER & SONS Wrought iron Philadelphia, PA
Active c. 1850s

M. Walker and Sons offered a selection of wrought iron garden furniture.

WASHINGTON IRON WORKS
  Cast iron Buffalo, NY
Active twentieth century

Washington Iron Works produced the "bird & flower" handleless urn and often marked their products.

WEST POINT FOUNDRY Cast iron Cold Spring, NY
1818–1911

After studying founding in Europe, in 1818 Gouverneur Kemble returned to New York and incorporated his West Point Foundry in Cold Spring, New York. The foundry was located in the heart of the Hudson River valley, an area rich with the natural resources needed to supply such an industry. Kemble's manufactory produced primarily cannon and other weapons for the military installations along the Hudson River, and later, in the 1830s, the foundry earned commissions to make steam engines and iron-hulled ships. Cast-iron building façades, including many in SoHo in New York City, were also produced in Cold Spring. This state-of-the-art operation also produced a small number of ornamental iron wares. Most notable among these were the cast-iron settees the foundry manufactured for author Washington Irving and his home Sunnyside, down the Hudson River in Tarrytown, New York (see cat. 4.8). Urns and elaborate halls stands can also be documented to this foundry. In 1898, Cornell & Co. took over operation of the West Point Foundry and eventually the firm went out of business in 1911.

My thanks to Charlotte Eaton, Curator of the Putnam County Historical Society and Foundry School Museum, who generously provided this information.

A. B. & W. T. WESTERVELT & CO.
  Cast iron New York
1880–

Adrian B. Westervelt began as an importer and branched into the iron business with a relative, Walter T. Westervelt.

J. FRANKLIN WHITMAN CO.
  Cast stone Philadelphia
Active c. 1903.

Whitman produced statues and vases.

JOHN B. WICKERSHAM
See New York Wire Railing Company.

WICKWIRE BROTHERS MFG.
  Wirework Cortland, NY
Active c. 1890.

This firm produced wire goods, figures, and sieves.

WIESSNER, SCHLESINGER & CO.
  Cast iron New York
Active c. 1892

Wiessner, Schlesinger, & Company produced round iron-rod chairs & benches and "spring steel" chairs, among other products.

E. C. WILLSON Marble Boston

W. W. WILSON Clockmakers Pittsburgh
1844–1856 W. W. Wilson, corner of Market

and Fourth (nos. 57, 71, or 67 Market)
1861–1886 William Wilson, 54 Fourth Ave.
1887–1891 William Wilson, 61 Fourth Ave.
1893 William Wilson, 22 Diamond

Wilson manufactured the sundial that may be found at Rosedown Plantation. See fig. 78.

JOHN A. WINN & CO. Cast iron Boston
Active c. 1870

John A. Winn offered a selection of ornamental ironwork.

WINSLOW BROS. Cast iron Boston
Active c. 1880–1910

WIRE GOODS CO. Wirework Worcester, MA
Active c. 1893

Wire Goods created novelties and specialties in wire.

JOHN WOOD JR. & CO. Cast iron
  Philadelphia
1904–1910 John Wood, Jr. & Co., 718 Pennsylvania Building
1911 John Wood, Jr. & Co., 605 Crozer Building
1912 John Wood, Jr. & Co., Iron & Steel, 1420 Chestnut
1913–1915 John Wood, Jr. & Co., Iron & Steel, 605 Crozer Building
This foundry produced a small line of ornamental iron work (see cat. 3.22). It is not known if John Wood Jr.'s foundry was related with the works of the successful Robert Wood, also in Philadelphia.

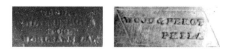

ROBERT WOOD/WOOD & PEROT
  Cast Iron Philadelphia
1840–1858 Robert Wood, Ridge Road
1858–1866 Wood & Perot, 1136 Ridge Avenue
1858–1861 Wood, Miltenberger & Co., 57 Camp Street, New Orleans, LA
1866–1879 Robert Wood & Co., 1136 Ridge Avenue

Robert Wood, an early Philadelphia blacksmith and iron founder, formed a partnership with

Elliston Perot in 1858. Wood & Perot enjoyed great success and exported their goods all over the eastern seaboard. Together, the two men created a short-lived New Orleans branch with coal merchant C. A. Miltenberger. Wood, Miltenberger & Co. made ornamental cast-iron fences for several homes in the Garden District of New Orleans (see fig. 86 and cat. 6.10). After the Civil War, Elliston Perot moved to Brooklyn, NY, and Robert Wood continued production as Robert Wood & Co. with new partners Irah Case and Thomas S. Root. Many of the ornamental pieces made by this firm are marked with their names.

REFERENCE: Pennsylvania, vol. 133, p. 106; Pennsylvania, vol. 137, p. 540; and Louisiana, vol. 11, p. 319, R. G. Dun & Co. Collection, Baker Library, Harvard University Graduate School of Business Administration.

WOODWARD AND SONS Wrought iron
  Owosso, MI
1880–present

Woodward and Sons started in Owosson, Michigan in 1880 and is still in business today. It produces wrought iron furniture, and during the 1930s and 1940s, produced excellent fine wrought-iron work. I thank Joni Lima for this information.

JAMES YATES, EFFINGHAM WORKS
  Cast iron Rotherham, England
1830s–40s James Yates, Effingham Works
1848–1852 Yates, Hayward, & Co. Rotherham
1852– Yates, Hayward & Drabble, Rotherham

Yates registered a Gothic pattern bench that enjoyed widespread success. James Yates was a very active designer and registered 66 designs by 1883.

APPENDIX 2

MAINTENANCE, IDENTIFICATION, AND SECURITY

MAINTENANCE OF GARDEN
ORNAMENT: SURFACE, STRUCTURAL,
AND WEATHER PROTECTION

Fountains and Birdbaths

Empty all water out of fountains and bird-baths before the first winter frost. If the container does not have drainage holes, cover and protect from water all winter. Cover smaller fountains and birdbaths of any material with clear, heavy-duty plastic sheeting and secure tightly. Put evergreen branches in their reservoirs on top of the plastic.[1] Smaller pieces should be taken inside for the winter. The tops of birdbaths should be removed and placed upside down on the ground.

For a large fountain it may be necessary to have a special structure built of wood or PVC and stretched with plastic sheeting, but beware of winter winds causing severe damage if the temporary supports blow over. If a cast-iron fountain figure is rusting, consult a professional and consider having him apply three coats of epoxy primer as a sealant.

Statues

Less prone to damage from snow, statues are endangered by ice and wind. If they do not seem securely placed, lower them from their pedestals early in the winter. In windy cities, statues on terraces should be secured to a permanent structure with cords or placed lying down on a cushioned support. Portable statues should be taken indoors.

Any unsealed cracks in a statue can collect water that may freeze and thaw, causing further cracking. Unglazed terra-cotta statues should be protected with canvas or plastic sheeting in areas with extreme weather. In Great Britain, reusable wooden sentry boxes are built to house valuable, fragile statues during the winter. Alternatively, British collectors wrap statues in hay to absorb dampness and cover them in canvas to keep them dry.[2]

Marble statues weather rapidly in humid climates due to acid deposits (acid rain) and should be watched carefully for sugaring. Sugaring is the fine sandy surface resulting from acidic deterioration of marble.

Urns

The procedure for urns is similar to that of fountains and birdbaths. Planted containers are *not* protected by having a reservoir filled with dirt. Water can still enter, collect, freeze, and thaw. Cast-iron urns with drainage holes do not need protection, but those without should be tipped over or covered. Finishes on cast iron can be protected from oxidation with a coat of paste wax, unbuffed for a matte surface or buffed for a shiny finish. Apply late fall and mid-spring. Consult a professional for applications of other, more permanent sealants.

Furniture

With very few exceptions, wooden furniture should never be left outdoors. If painted or stained regularly it will last longer in the elements. Cast-iron seats, chairs, and tables require little other than the brushing off of deep snow. Marble or stone post-and-lintel style benches need to be watched carefully to anticipate trouble in case the ground underneath their legs heaves from frost. I have heard of fine marble benches literally "knocked over" by frost heaves, resulting in clean breaks right through the entire top section. Do not attempt to move any garden seats that have frozen to the ground. Cast iron is very brittle and should never be dragged or pulled out of the ice. Legs can snap off easily. Lawn mower blades have been known to break the legs of cast-iron furniture.

Sundials

Sundials and armillary spheres are, for the most part, impervious to the weather. An antique bronze dial or sphere that detaches from the base can be taken inside for the winter. If your garden is in a windy location it would be wise to have a professional permanently attach your armillary sphere to its base.

Gates and Fencing

Wooden fencing, like furniture, needs regular maintenance. Wrought and cast iron are durable as long as their painted finishes are maintainted to avoid corrosion. Consult a professional to consider all available options before restoring a prized old surface.

Other Garden Ornament

Wellheads should be wrapped with canvas or plastic sheeting or covered with plywood. As with statues, any cracks should be protected from collecting water. If rust from the iron overthrow migrates onto the upper surface of a stone or marble wellhead, acting promptly will keep any staining to a minimum. Hire a professional to reseal the surface of the wrought-iron framework. Rust can irretrievably stain marble. Marble is an extremely porous material into which water or stains can seep deeply. To wash marble, use distilled water; to remove organic matter from the surface, use a mild abrasive detergent that contains no bleach. Consult a professional to clean stubborn stains out of marble.

Terra-cotta oil jars need special treatment in winter. Even if they have drainage holes, they should still be reversed or brought indoors. One small leaf can fall on a drainage hole and freeze into place, causing water to collect. Consider having a custom-made wooden lid constructed to fit securely into the mouth of the jar to prevent the entry or accumulation of water in the bottom. Otherwise, there is no way to leave terra-cotta jars outdoors safely where there is a threat of frost or snow. Someone once told me to roll an oil jar on its side in order to move it. Sadly, my enormous oil jar split in half like a giant egg.

GENERAL SURFACE MAINTENANCE OF CAST IRON

Protect an old, valued surface by keeping the object indoors. For the most part, a series of applications of paste wax will arrest the rusting process on surfaces of outdoor pieces. Keep an eye on an unprotected, partially painted, rusty finish, and consult a professional immediately if it seems to be rusting too far and losing its attractiveness.

A build-up of paint over the years sometimes obscures details of design. Consult a professional to consider the different options available to correct this, as some popular methods of paint removal may damage the piece.

PROFESSIONAL CONSERVATION

If an object needs restoration, or if you desire to know more about maintenance, you should consider contacting a professional conservator. Make sure that the professional you choose is familiar with the material you need restored or repaired. The value of your piece will be protected if you have skillful repairs done. A free referral system is available if you wish to locate a conservation professional in a particular area. FAIC (Free Conservation Services Referral Service) lists a phone: (202) 452-9545, a fax (202) 452-9328, or e-mail: vny@aol.com. Its address is: 1717 K Street NW, Suite 301, Washington, D.C. 20006

IDENTIFICATION OF CARVED OBJECTS

Detecting the difference between carved and cast stone objects can be extremely difficult. There are very few written words that can substitute for the experience of seeing the two side by side. Cast stone is also called composition, "compo" in Great Britain, aggregate, concrete, or cement. Carved stone generally commands significantly higher prices than cast stone.

1. Carved stone has stiffer, more rigid lines and a rough, uneven surface.
2. Genuine stone has veins and fissures.
3. The relief is higher on carved pieces. A mold can only partially replicate the depth that a stone carver's tool can create. As a result, cast stone pieces may have flatter sculptural detail. To add to the confusion, some cast pieces are drilled or carved after casting, particularly on their bases, to give them a "carved" look.
4. Cast stone often has bubbles in its surface and seam lines from the mold.
5. Cast stone can have marble chips or marble dust mixed into the composite material. There can be many textural and color variations in cast stone.
6. Carved stone is hard to the touch, as well as denser and heavier than cast stone. But do not be fooled by Bath stone, a soft limestone from the west of England that, like cast stone, is soft and powdery to the touch, or by Bordeaux limestone, an equally soft stone from France. Both of these are remarkably hard to differentiate from cast stone, but they are only occasionally seen in America.
7. Some limestones have shells or fossilized material in them. The presence of these inclusions is not necessarily an indication that the material is a composition mixture.

IDENTIFICATION OF NINETEENTH- OR EARLY-TWENTIETH-CENTURY CAST IRON

Cast-iron reproductions with antiqued finishes are seen throughout the garden ornament market, making authentication of a period piece more difficult. If a cast-iron piece is unmarked, it can only be *attributed* to a maker. Unless there is indisputable proof, such as an ironclad provenance, a maker's name should not be assigned to a piece unless it is marked. Many foundries produced identical models.

Weight

Old cast-iron pieces tend to be heavier than their modern counterparts.

Magnetism

Hold a magnet up to the surface of a piece. If the magnet sticks, the piece is of ferrous metal, i.e. made of iron. If it does not hold, the piece is a nonferrous metal, probably aluminum, bronze, or zinc. In certain rare cases a very thick coat of paint will keep a magnet from sticking.

Nuts and Bolts

In nineteenth-century seats, arms and legs were joined to the back or seat by iron bolts and square nuts. Hexagonal nuts were in use by 1905, developed so that there were more bearing surfaces available for more secure tightening.[3] If all the nuts in a piece are hexagonal, the likelihood is that it is mid- to late-twentieth century. Square nuts do not prove that a piece is early, however, as it would be possible to put square nuts on a brand-new piece. In certain circumstances, also, all the nuts of a period piece may have been replaced after restoration. In that case, it will be necessary to evaluate other features of the object to determine its age.

A single hexagonal nut among square nuts probably indicates a recent replacement of a single older nut. Pieces with no visible nuts and bolts indicate joints that have been welded together. This may or may not signal a later date. Some 1930–40 American garden seats have had welded joints, but some joints on nineteenth-century objects were also welded. Replaced bolts on urns are fairly common, as the long, central original bolts have often corroded and broken.

Grind Marks

Late-twentieth-century pieces are likely to have grind marks on their surfaces. These are marks made by a die grinder, which is used to level out joints where pieces fit together. Nineteenth-century molds for cast iron were somewhat more precise, yielding pieces that fit together better. Moreover, cast pieces were finished more carefully, obliterating most traces of marks on the surface. Many nineteenth-century molds were melted down for scrap metal in World War II. Newer molds produced less precise-fitting pieces, and often required grinding to even out seams. Be on the lookout for grind marks, and, judging from other information as well, try to understand whether the marks indicate a recent restoration or an entirely new piece.

Edges

A piece may have jagged edges after it is removed from a mold. In the nineteenth century rough spots were hand filed to an even edge. Although today's techniques of mass production may be superior to nineteenth-century methods, they often omit the "fine finishing" which typically characterized nineteenth-century workmanship.[4]

Repairs

Finding welded repairs on an object means that the piece was once broken. This may or may not be a sign of age, inasmuch as an unrepaired example might signal a reproduction. If a structural member has been repaired, it is a sign of weakness that should be reflected in the price, if you are evaluating it for purchase.

Surface

A build-up of paint can be an indication that a piece is not new. Inspecting the interior and underside of an object often reveals nuts or bolts with a thick covering of paint that has clearly been there for many years. Old rust on period pieces is dark in color, while new rust is bright orange. Pieces that have no rust at all cannot be cast iron.

The authenticity of a piece must be determined by a careful, thorough compilation of many pieces of information.

SECURITY MEASURES FOR OUTDOOR ORNAMENT

Theft is a concern for some garden ornament owners. Due to the nature of their placements, outdoor ornaments are vulnerable. There is no one perfect solution to the problem of keeping garden ornaments secure, but certain measures can be taken. For example, very valuable pieces can be hard-wired to your alarm system.

List important objects on your fine arts policy. Keep a photographic record of all pieces, whether insured or not, to assist in recovery if anything is stolen.

Ornaments can be marked with serial numbers for future identification. In England, a system called Smart Water is coming into use. A homeowner or collector pays both a registration and an annual fee to receive an amount of a one-of-a-kind liquid, which is coded, like DNA, specifically for him or her. The collector then paints the liquid onto a protected, interior surface of a piece, to identify it exclusively as his own.

My thanks to Scott Merritt, conservator and Head of Collections Management at the Smithsonian Institution's National Museum of the American Indian, who assisted with this appendix.

Notes
1. For this suggestion I thank the Caramoor Garden Guild in Katonah, New York.
2. Schmerler, 106.
3. For this information I thank James Grundy, antique car specialist.
4. For the information here and above I thank Rocco De Angelo, specialist in cast-iron restoration.

APPENDIX 3
SELECTED
HISTORIC
GARDENS IN
AMERICA

Open to the public unless otherwise noted

Agecroft Hall
4305 Sulgrave Road
Richmond, VA 23211
(804) 353–4241

Belcourt Castle
657 Bellevue Ave.
Newport, RI 02840
(401) 846–0669

Bellefontaine (presently Canyon Ranch)
165 Kemble Street
Lenox, MA 01240
(413) 637–4400

Belmont Mansion (Belmont Mansion
Association)
1900 Belmont Blvd.
Nashville, TN 37212
(615) 460–5459

Biltmore Estate
One North Pack Square
Asheville, NC 28801
(800) 543–2961

Blairsden (presently St. Joseph's Villa)
Not open to public
Peapack, NJ 07977
No telephone

The Breakers (Preservation Society of
Newport County)
Bellevue Avenue
Newport, RI 02840
(401) 846–0813

Ca d' Zan (John and Mable Ringling
Museum of Art)
5401 Bay Shore Road
Sarasota, FL 34243
(941) 359–5700

Casa del Herrero
1387 East Valley Road
Montecito, CA 93108
(805) 565–5653

Château-sur-Mer (Preservation Society of
Newport County)
Bellevue Ave.
Newport, RI 02840
(401) 846–0813

Cliveden
6401 Germantown Ave.
Philadelphia, PA 19144
(215) 848–1777

Cranbrook House and Gardens
1221 North Woodward Ave.
Bloomfield Hills, MI 48303–0801
(248) 645–3323

Isaiah Davenport House Museum
324 East State Street
Savannah, GA 31401
(912) 236-8097

D'Evereaux
Private Residence, Historic Natchez
Foundation
108 Commerce Street
Natchez, MS 39120
(601) 442–2500

Dumbarton House
2715 Que Street, NW
Washington, DC 20007
(202) 337–2288

Dumbarton Oaks
1703 32nd Street, NW
Washington, DC 20007
(202) 339–6460

Dunlieth
Private Residence, Historic Natchez
Foundation
108 Commerce Street
Natchez, MS 39120
(601) 442–2500

Ebenezer Maxwell Mansion
200 W. Tulpehocken St.
Philadelphia, PA 19144
(215) 438–1861

Edsel Ford House
1100 Lake Shore Road
Grosse Point Shores, MI 48236
(313) 884–4222

The Elms (Preservation Society of Newport
County)
Bellevue Avenue
Newport, RI 02840
(401) 846–0813

Fair Lane / Henry Ford House
4901 Evergreen Road
Dearborn, MI 48128
(313) 593–5590

Ganna Walska Lotusland
695 Ashley Road
Santa Barbara, CA 93108
(805) 969–3767

Georgian Court (Georgian Court College)
900 Lakewood Ave.
Lakewood, NJ 08701
(732) 364–2200

Gibraltar
2600 Pennsylvania Ave.
Wilmington, DE 19806
(302) 651–9617

Gwinn
Open to nonprofit organizations for
meetings and receptions only.
12407 Lakeshore Blvd.
Bratenahl, OH 44108
(216) 541–1407

Hearst Castle
750 Hearst Castle Road
San Simeon, CA 93452
(805) 927–2020

The Highlands
7001 Sheaff Lane
Fort Washington, PA 19034
(215) 641–2687

The Huntington Library, Art Collections,
and Botanical Gardens
1151 Oxford Road
San Marino, CA 91108
(626) 405–2100

Kykuit (Historic Hudson Valley)
150 White Plains Road
Tarrytown, NY 10591
(914) 631–8200

Lansdowne
Private Residence, Historic Natchez
Foundation
108 Commerce Street
Natchez, MS 39120
(601) 442–2500

Longwood Gardens
Route 1 South
Kennett Square, PA 19348
(610) 388–1000

Maymont
1700 Hampton Street
Richmond, VA 23220
(804) 358–7166

Melrose (National Parks Service)
1 Melrose-Montebello Parkway
Natchez, MS 39120
(601) 442–7047

Middleton Place
Ashley River Road/ Route 61
Charleston, SC 29414–7206
(803) 556–6020

Moffatt-Ladd House
154 Market Street
Portsmouth, NH 03801
(603) 436–8221

Morris Arboretum of the University of
Pennsylvania
100 Northwestern Ave.
Philadelphia, PA 19118
(215) 247–5777

Mount Vernon (Mount Vernon Ladies'
Association of the Union)
End of George Washington Parkway South
Mount Vernon, VA 22210
(703) 799–8650

Nathaniel Russell House (Historic
Charleston Foundation)
51 Meeting Street
Charleston, SC 29401
(803) 724–8481

Naumkeag (The Trustees of Reservations,
Western Regional Office)
Prospect Hill Road
Stockbridge, MA 01262
(413) 298–3239

Nemours Mansion and Gardens
Rockland Road
Wilmington, DE 19899
(302) 651–6919

Old Westbury Gardens
71 Old Westbury Road
Old Westbury, NY 11568
(516) 333–0048

Planting Fields Arboretum
Planting Fields Road
Oyster Bay, NY 11711
(516) 922–9206

Richmond
Private Residence, Historic Natchez
Foundation
108 Commerce Street
Natchez, MS 39120
(601) 442–2500

Rosecliff (Preservation Society of Newport
County)
Bellevue Ave.
Newport, RI 02840
(401) 847–1000

Rosedown Plantation
12501 Highway 10
St. Francisville, LA 70775
(504) 635–3332

Stan Hywet Hall and Gardens
714 North Portage Path
Akron, OH 44303–1399
(330) 836–5533

Vanderbilt Mansion National Historic Site
(F. W. Vanderbilt Mansion)
Route 9
Hyde Park, NY 12538
(914) 229–2067

Eagle's Nest (W.K. Vanderbilt, Jr. Mansion)
180 Little Neck Road
Centerport, NY 11721
(516) 854–5508

Virginia House
4301 Sulgrave Road
Richmond, VA 23221
(804) 363–4251

Vizcaya Museum and Gardens
3251 S. Miami Avenue
Miami, FL 33129
(305) 250–9133

Westover
7000 Westover Road
Charles City, VA 23030
(804) 829–2882

Figures in brackets refer to sequential pages in an unpaginated text.

Chapter 1: Fountains

1 Elisabeth B. MacDougall, "L'Ingegnoso Artifizio: Sixteenth-Century Garden Fountains in Rome," in MacDougall, 101.

2 Lablaude, 75.

3 Lazzaro, 57–61, see for a discussion of Italian grottoes.

4 Barnum c. 1900, 27; Wood, 296; Mott c. 1905a, 128.

5 P. Martin, 150.

6 Robert Wheelwright, "Gardens and Places of Colonial Philadelphia," in ASLA, 27.

7 Sarudy, 109, 136.

8 Sellers, 368–369.

9 Lockwood, vol. 1, 38, 64.

10 Bentley, vol. 1, 272.

11 Bentley, vol. 1, 280.

12 See "Introduction," in Ostergard 1994, 11; Elisabeth Schmuttermeier, "The Central European Cast-Iron Industries," in Ostergard 1994, 81–84.

13 Water, 505.

14 It was reported that Great Britain's iron trade had grown from 25,000 tons in 1740 to 2,000,000 tons in 1852. See AMM 3 (Sept. 1853): 199.

15 For this information, I thank Bill Gustafson, historian at the Museum of Anthracite Mining in Ashland, Pennsylvania.

16 Snyder, 226.

17 AMM 3 (Sept. 1853): 199.

18 Wood, 283.

19 Hinckley, 12.

20 Downing 1841, 466.

21 Wardin, 15, 20–22; for this information, I thank Mark Brown, director of the Belmont Mansion Association.

22 Humphreys 1851, 134–136.

23 Downing 1848, 503–504.

24 *Godey's* 1, 251.

25 Elliott, 131.

26 Elliott, 132.

27 Humphreys 1850, 208–9.

28 *Godey's* 2, 282.

29 Doell, 62–63.

30 *New York State Mechanic,* 101.

31 London, 103, 235, 600, 709–710, 852, 1061–1062, 1205, 1229.

32 Philadelphia, 38, 44. Also see: Symmes, 106.

33 For this information, I thank Eva Milstead, the librarian of the San Antonio Conservation Society.

34 J. Patrick, 3.

35 Morgan, 75–92.

36 Wharton 1904, 11.

37 Michele Bogart, "American Garden Sculpture: A New Perspective," in *Fauns and Fountains,* <3>.

38 For a complete discussion of this period see Bogart, "American Garden Sculpture," in *Fauns and Fountains.*

39 Rehmann, 106.

40 Bogart, "American Garden Sculpture," in *Fauns and Fountains,* <6–10>.

41 For this information, I thank S. Marinelli, the octogenarian owner of the A. Frilli Gallery in Florence.

42 Renwick, 40–50.

43 Renwick, 151–153.

44 Favretti and Favretti, 52.

45 Swift 1902, 150–162; Swift 1902a, 416–428.

46 For a discussion of this period, see Donn Barber's introduction in Baker.

47 Van Valkenburgh, 33–34.

Chapter 2: Statues

1 Richardson Wright, "The History of Garden Architecture," in SFMA, 27.

2 C. Allan Brown, "Eighteenth-Century Virginia Plantation Gardens: Translating an Ancient Idyll," in O'Malley and Treib, 131.

3 Letter from William Byrd II to Charles Boyle, Earl of Orrery, 5 July 1726, Tinling, *Correspondence,* 355–56. Cited in C. Allan Brown, "Eighteenth-Century Virginia Plantation Gardens," in O'Malley and Treib, 135.

4 M. Acomb, ed. & trans. *The Revolutionary Journal of Baron Ludwig Von Closen, 1780–1788.* Chapel Hill, N.C., 1958, 188. Cited in Brown, "Eighteenth-Century Virginia Plantation Gardens," in O'Malley and Treib, 137.

5 Farish, 126.

6 J. Davis, 219.

7 For this information I thank Elizabeth Laurent, curator of Cliveden.

8 McGuire, 63, 66, 90–91, 110.

9 Vermeule, 207.

10 Lionello Puppi, "Nature and Artifice in the Sixteenth-Century Italian Garden," in Mosser and Teyssot, 53.

11 Margherita Azzi Visentini, "A Model

NOTES

Humanist Garden: Villa Brenzone at Punta San Vigilio," in Mosser and Teyssot, 107.

12 Sarudy, 134–5.

13 For a complete discussion see Aghion et al.

14 Byrd, 168–169, 198–199.

15 Peter Martin, "Introduction," in Maccubbin and Martin, 2.

16 Diary of Hannah Callender, quoted by Elizabeth McLean in "Town and Country Gardens in Eighteenth-Century Philadelphia," in Maccubbin and Martin, 141, 147.

17 J. Davis, 58–60.

18 J. Davis, 163.

19 J. Davis, 168; 173.

20 Kelly, 443–444.

21 Kelly, 444.

22 *Pennsylvania Packet*, Sept. 12, 1796. Published in *The Arts & Crafts in Philadelphia*, 310.

23 Rosedown 1, n.p.

24 Rosedown 2, 1–2. For these documents we thank Gene Slivka, owner of Rosedown.

25 *Federal Gazette* (Philadelphia), March 22, 1796. Published in *The Arts and Crafts in Philadelphia,* 309.

26 Leighton 1976, 375.

27 Lockwood, vol. 1, 359.

28 Haskell and Penny, 90–91.

29 Proske, vol. 1, xix.

30 *New York Evening Post* (Jan. 15, 1852): 1.

31 *New York Evening Post* (Jan. 16, 1852): 4.

32 *The Independent* (June 26, 1856): 205.

33 *New York Evening Post* (Jan. 16, 1852): 2.

34 Emmet 1996, 98.

35 "Hints to Beginners in Ornamental Planting," *The Horticulturist* 10 (Dec., 1855): 545. Quoted in Doell, 70.

36 Lichten, 27.

37 Lichten, 27–28.

38 *The Albion* 35 (Apr. 25, 1857): n.p.

39 Holtzoper, 526.

40 For a full discussion of these see Symes, 26–27.

41 Janson, 51. Also see, for example, Pompeian, nos. 803, 804.

42 Fairbanks and Reynolds, 702–703.

43 Janson, 72–73.

44 See: Wood & Perot; Elmore Studios; Howard Studios; Barclay 1930.

45 Haskell and Penny, 247–249. See also Shepherd & Jellicoe, 878.

46 Coade, Design No. 55; Austin, 12.

47 Braithwaite, 74.

48 Smith, 89.

49 J. Davis, 105.

50 Fiske 1892–1907, 10.

51 Janson, 76–77.

52 Mott 1875, 59.

53 Latrobe, 33.

54 Swift 1903, 29.

55 Proske, vol. 1, xxvi.

56 Van Rensselaer, 356.

57 R. Wright, 44.

58 Eglington, 19.

59 Renwick, 152–153.

60 Radice, 144.

61 Radice, 131, 234; and Murray, 126, 134–135.

62 A. Adams, 172.

63 Lowell, pls. XIV, XLVIII, and CIX.

64 Proske, vol. 1, xxxii.

65 See *House and Garden*, Jan.–Dec. 1902.

66 Proske, vol. 1, xxxii–xxxiii.

67 J. P. White, preface, 156.

68 Symes, 21.

69 Lockwood vol. 1, 354; and Kenworthy, 235.

70 Ruckstuhl, 484.

Chapter 3: Urns

1 G. Richter, 320–322.

2 Haskell and Penny, 315–316.

3 For research on this subject the following were consulted: Leighton 1976; Lockwood, vols. 1 and 2; Maccubbin and Martin; P. Martin; O'Malley and Treib (especially C. Allan Brown's "Eighteenth-Century Virginia Plantation Gardens: Translating an Ancient Idyll"); and Sarudy.

4 James D. Kornwolf, "The Picturesque in the American Garden and Landscape before 1800," in Maccubbin and Martin, 100.

5 Weaver, 199.

6 Weaver, 199.

7 Leighton 1976, 365.

8 As cited in L. Martin, 78.

9 Lidded urns were often used in architectural settings as decoration at the edge of the roof; examples seen in the Samuel McIntire design for the Elias Hasket Derby house in Salem, Massachusetts, and at Benjamin Chew's residence, Cliveden, in Philadelphia. See Lockwood, vol. 1, 67, 79.

10 Kocher and Dearstyne, 42.

11 Eliza Southgate, letter of July 6, 1802, quoted in Kimball 1940, 88.

12 Sarudy, frontispiece preceding 125.

13 Ring, 69, no. 113.

14 Strange, 44–46, 263.

15 Lockwood, vol. 1, 101.

16 Lockwood, vol. 1, 314.

17 Greiff, 2, 52.

18 For commentary on the Victorian predilection toward aesthetic pursuits, see Lichten, 41.

19 *The Horticulturist* 2, 43.

20 *The Horticulturist* 2, 40.

21 Doell, 58.

22 Doell, 64–65.

23 Favretti and Favretti, 49.

24 For this information I thank Rocco De Angelo, cast-iron restorer and specialist.

25 *The Horticulturist* 2, 40.

26 *The Horticulturist* 2, 40.

27 *The Horticulturist* 2, 41.

28 Snyder, 227.

29 Favretti and Favretti, 37.

30 Société Anonyme des Hauts-Fourneaux, nos. 62, 70, 81, 98, 99, 100, 115, 116, 117, pl. 499, H, I; Fiske c. 1893, 89, 90, 91, 92, 97; no. 264 (antique); nos. 43, 44 (jardinieres).

31 *The Horticulturist* 2, 40.

32 Swift 1903, 29.

33 Tolkwsky, 186.

34 *H & G* 1, 442.

35 Geis, 145–6.

36 Downing 1841, 423.

37 Downing 1841, 423.

Chapter 4: Furniture

1 Masson, 21; and Pliny, vol. 1, Book 5, Letter 6, to Domitius Apollinaris, 351.

2 Paul, 4.

3 Della Pergola, figures 41, 54. Also see Masson, 153.

4 For examples, see E. White, 129–146.

5 Sarudy, 146.

6 Its dimensions are: height 45 ½", width 28¼", length 96 ¼". For a complete discussion of the seat see Rauschenberg.

7 Illustrated in E. White, 428.

8 Evans, 45–53, 246, 272; Dietz, 980–983.

9 Watson, vol. 1, 397.

10 Hornor, 299.

11 Hornor, 303, pl. 484, facing 306.

12 C. Allan Brown, "Eighteenth-Century Virginia Plantation Gardens: Translating an Ancient Idyll," in O'Malley and Treib, 129.

13 Henry Wansey, *An Excursion to the United*

States of North America, in the Summer of 1794, 2nd ed. Salisbury, England, 1798, 34, cited in Abbott Lowell Cummings, "Eighteenth-Century New England Design: The Pictorial Evidence," in Maccubbin and Martin, 134.

14 Kimball 1917, 185.

15 McMahon, 77.

16 Heckscher, 59–62.

17 Himmelheber, 53.

18 Lockwood, vol. 1, 351.

19 For this information I thank Ann P. Moye of Davenport House.

20 Mt. Auburn is itself inspired by the influential Père Lachaise cemetery in Paris. See Keith N. Morgan, "Garden and Forest: Nineteenth-Century Developments in Landscape Architecture" in *Keeping Eden*, 32–33.

21 *The Horticulturist* 6, 208.

22 Ellen Marie Snyder, "At Rest: Victorian Death Furniture," in Ward, 263.

23 Morgan, "Garden and Forest," in *Keeping Eden*, 33.

24 Georg Himmelheber, "The Beginnings of Cast-Iron Garden Furniture," in Ostergard 1994, 90–93.

25 Société Anonyme des Hauts-Forneaux; J. Davis, 275.

26 Lawley, 3–4. Courtesy of the Library at the Ironbridge Gorge Trust, and John Powell, librarian.

27 Himmelheber, "The Beginnings of Cast-Iron," in Ostergard 1994, 96.

28 For a description of the British registration mark system see Ames, 130–32; Robertson & Robertson, 25–26.

29 See Wood & Perot. For further commentary on Wood & Perot see Mitchell, 20–21; Lichten, 89.

30 Coalbrookdale 1875, section 3: Garden and Park Embellishments.

31 Fiske [1913–1933].

32 Sarudy, illustration facing 125.

33 Himmelheber, 31, pl. 114.

34 I would like to thank Mimi Miller, director of Historic Natchez, who explained that shipping via northern canals and the Mississippi enabled businesses to ship easily to the Louisiana and Mississippi areas.

35 McIntosh, vol. 1, 634.

36 McIntosh, vol. 1, 649.

37 McIntosh, vol. 1, 674.

38 McIntosh, vol. 1, 696.

39 London, 660.

40 London, 732.

41 London, 597, fig. 13; and Himmelheber, 61, illustrated on 64; referred to as Joseph Reynolds in Edwards, 75, fig. 33.

42 Wickersham, 29.

43 Gaudillot Frères & Roy, n.p.; also illustrated in Himmelheber, 50.

44 Himmelheber, 55.

45 Hanks, 60, 62. A patent on an object did not guarantee its exclusive production by one firm.

46 Fiske 1868, 29.

47 Hanks, 60.

48 I would like to thank Richard Nelson, a Leinfelder collector and resident of La Crosse, Wisconsin, for this information.

49 I would like to thank Graham Brown, the grandson of Vincent Primavera, the founder of Florentine Craftsmen, for this information.

50 I would like to thank Joni Lima, wrought-iron specialist, for this information.

51 For more see Edwards, Frary, and Jeffries.

52 Renwick, 151–53.

53 Swift 1903a, 76.

54 *H & G* 1, 438, 443.

55 A. Hill, 81.

56 Davison, 144.

57 Robinson, 275.

58 Robinson, 232.

59 Robinson, 233.

60 A. Hill, 83.

Chapter 5: Sundials and Armillary Spheres

1 Letter from Thomas Jefferson to Mr. Clay, 23 August 1811. See Earle 1901, 91.

2 Gatty, 6.

3 For a discussion of their history, see Rohr.

4 Gatty, 11, 35, 42–43, 94–95.

5 Gatty, 23.

6 Earle 1902, 3.

7 Watson, vol. 1, 218.

8 Rohr, 70–81.

9 Rohr, 14.

10 Daniel, 25, 27.

11 A. Hill, 82.

12 Daniel, 5, 9, 10.

13 Dolan, 123.

14 Fennimore, 198.

15 Dolan, 124.

16 Lockwood, vol. 1, 62–64.

17 Daniel, 3.

18 Bentley, vol. 2, 197–198.

19 Lockwood, vol. 1, 49.

20 I would like to thank Donald Fennimore, Curator of Metalwork at the Winterthur Museum, a specialist and scholar in the field of early American metalwork, for this information.

21 I wish to thank King Laughlin, Manager of Special Projects at Mount Vernon, for this information. It is further substantiated by the presence of a horizontal sundial in a 1792 painting, cited by Fennimore, 199.

22 Earle 1901, 369–370.

23 Dolan, 127.

24 Dyer, 541.

25 Emmet 1996, 51, from a description made after 1854 by Maud Howe Elliot, a friend of the owners of Vaucluse.

26 Lockwood, vol. 1, 231.

27 Favretti and Favretti, 18.

28 For this information, I thank Jeff Meyer, Curator of Ashland.

29 Loudon 1835, 995.

30 Sanford, 22.

31 *The Horticulturist* 4, 23.

32 The painting, *A Morning Rainbow, A Composition on the Grounds of R. Donaldson, Esq.,* by George Harvey, is reproduced in HHV, pl. 11.

33 See Downing 1841, frontispiece.

34 Doell, 70.

35 *The Horticulturist* 5a, 305.

36 Doell, 149.

37 Emmet, 183.

38 Holtzoper, 526.

39 A. Hill, 82–83.

40 I would like to thank Emily Croll, Project Director at Morven, for this information. Also, see Bill, 17, 151.

41 Jekyll, 251.

42 Reisem, 92.

43 Dyer, 538.

44 Thonger, 67.

45 See Lowell, Osborne and Day, R. Wright, and Shelton. For examples of formal placements, see Shelton: Welwyn, Glen Cove, Long Island (pl. 119); Mrs. Charles Henry's in Chestnut Hill, Pennsylvania, pl. 164; Radnor Valley Farm in Radnor, Pennsylvania (pl. 180); and Piranhurst in Montecito, California (pl. 246). For further examples, see Lowell: Drumthwacket, Princeton, New Jersey, pl. LIV; The Garth in Strafford, Pennsylvania, pl. XLII; and

Villa Narcault, Montclair, New Jersey, pl. LXX.

46 A. Hill, 82.

47 Dyer, 538.

48 I would like to thank Patty Glumac, acting Curator of The Highlands, for this information.

49 In a letter of 28 December 1927 from Tom Cochran, donor, to James Sawyer, Phillips Academy administrator. Property of the Archives, Phillips Academy, Andover, Massachusetts. I am grateful to David Chase for this information.

50 Ferargil, 3.

51 Dyer, 538.

52 Letter from Thomas Jefferson to Mr. Clay, 23 August 1811. See Earle 1902, 91.

53 Edwards, 91.

54 Kauffman 1978, 235.

55 Fennimore, 203.

56 Meyrowitz, 6–14.

57 For a listing of old sayings, see Cross.

58 Rohr, 127.

59 Earle 1902, 186.

60 Earle 1901, 375–377.

61 Rohr, 27.

62 Earle 1902, 211–212.

63 Strange, 47, 320.

64 Dyer, 540.

65 Robie, 558.

66 Dyer, 537, 541.

Chapter 6: Gates, Fencing, and Finials

1 Richardson Wright, "The History of Garden Architecture," in SFMA, 26.

2 Lockwood, vol. 1, 423–424; Favretti and Favretti, 16; and V. Patrick, 100.

3 David Johann Schoeff, *Travels in the Confederation* (1783). Quoted in Lockwood, vol. 1, 427.

4 Fletcher Steele, "The Colonial Garden Today," in ASLA, 64.

5 Lockwood, vol. 1, 423.

6 Brinkley and Chappell, 4.

7 Kauffman 1966, 21–28.

8 Southworth and Southworth, 27. Also see Kauffman 1966, 75–79.

9 Edwards, 151–52; Southworth and Southworth, 18.

10 Southworth and Southworth, 29–30.

11 Sale, 139.

12 Brinkley and Chappell, 4.

13 Bushman, 135.

14 Watson, vol. 1, 397.

15 Watson, vol. 1, 408.

16 Watson, vol. 1, 375.

17 Edwards, 150.

18 I would like to thank M. Kent Brinkley, the landscape architect of the Colonial Williamsburg Foundation, for this information.

19 P. Martin, 72–73.

20 Lockwood, vol. 1, 209.

21 Lockwood, vol. 1, 211; and Olmert, 46–50.

22 Kimball 1940, 87, and Fig. 153. For further commentary on the houses of Salem, see Lockwood, vol. 1, 432.

23 Gottesman, 225.

24 Gottesman, 228.

25 Vaux, 274.

26 Wilson, 214–215.

27 Masson and Owen, 3.

28 Janes, Beebe & Co., nos. 260, 261, 263–265.

29 Southworth and Southworth, 44–45.

30 Wood & Perot, nos. 197–200, 202, 203.

31 Gayle, Introduction, 3.

32 Repton, 127.

33 Downing 1841, 343.

34 Downing 1842, 237.

35 Gayle, Introduction, 6.

36 Southworth and Southworth, 64. Also see Gayle, n.p., near fig. 4.

37 Scott, 51.

38 Robinson, 232.

39 *American Architect*, 99.

40 Fisher, 647.

41 Favretti and Favretti, 56.

42 Doell, 72.

43 *H & G* 2, 400.

44 Holtzoper, 524–525.

45 Thonger, 59.

46 Southworth and Southworth, 93–109.

47 I would like to thank Laura Strauss, Public Relations, Stan Hywet Hall and Gardens, for this information.

48 Tachau, 440.

49 See note 3.

Chapter 7: Other Garden Ornament

1 Masson, 21.

2 Gatty, 9.

3 Pieter Andrea Rysbrack painting of 1728–30, illustrated in Linda Cabe Halpern, "The Uses of Paintings in Garden History," in Hunt, 193; also see James D. Kornwolf, "The Picturesque in the American Garden and Landscape Before 1800," in Maccubbin and Martin, 101.

4 Paul Decker's designs illustrated in E. White, 138.

5 Lockwood, vol. 1, 372.

6 Robert Wheelwright, "Gardens and Places of Colonial Philadelphia," in ASLA, 24, 27.

7 Leighton 1976, 377.

8 Edwards, 113.

9 Barnum 1881, 2; M. D. Jones, 47.

10 Sotheby's, 94–95.

11 Coalbrookdale 1888, 24–26.

12 Miller Iron, 12.

13 Miller Iron, 4–5.

14 Miller Iron, 13–14.

15 Gade, 206.

16 Swift 1903a, 69–70.

17 Prior, 174.

18 Rizzi, 7.

19 Hetherington 1995, 162.

20 Swift 1903a, 76.

21 Two of the wellheads in the Budapest Museum of Fine Art collection are suspected of being just such forgeries. See Rizzi, 55–57.

22 Hetherington 1980, 13–14.

23 Rizzi, 374–377.

24 Swift 1903a, 72.

25 Swift 1903a, 69–77.

26 Howard Studios, 16–17.

27 Erkins 1929, 19; Erkins 1933, 7.

28 Anderson Galleries 2, 58–61.

29 Robinson, 233.

30 Dawson, 7; Platt 1894, 27.

31 Shelton, pl. 30.

32 Doell, 166.

33 See Lowell, pls. XVIII, XXV, LXIV, LXXXVI, CVI, and CVIII; Shelton, pls. 151, 170; and Swift 1903, 30.

34 Margherita Azzi Visentini, "A Model Humanist Garden: Villa Benzani at Punta San Vigilio," in Mosser and Teyssot, 106–7.

35 Emmet 1996, 202.

36 *H & G* 1, 443.

37 P. Richter, 56.

38 Anderson Galleries 2, 25.

39 See Cram.

40 Saylor, 481–2.

41 Holtzoper, 526.

42 Doell, 54–55.

43 Kenworthy, 232.

BIBLIOGRAPHY

ABN 1929: "Garden Sculpture." *Architect and Building News* 122 (1929): 150–151, 177–178.

A&D 1923: "One of the Great Show-Places of Long Island." *Arts & Decoration* 19 (May 1923): 24–25.

A&D 1924 a: "Garden Furniture of Individuality and Grace." *Arts & Decoration* 20 (Apr. 1924): 29.

A&D 1924 b: "Garden Sculpture: From a Recent Exhibition of the Garden Club of America." *Arts & Decoration* 20 (Apr. 1924): 22.

A. Adams: Adeline Adams. *The Spirit of American Sculpture*. New York: National Sculpture Society, 1923.

W. Adams [1888–1890] a: William Adams & Co. *Park, Garden and Cemetery Chairs, Settees, Vases & Gypsy Pots*. Trade catalogue. Philadelphia: William Adams & Co. [1888–1890].

W. Adams [1888–1890] b: William Adams & Co. *Park, Garden and Cemetery Vases, Urns and Gypsy Pots*. Trade catalogue. (Hope Iron Foundry) Philadelphia: William Adams & Co., [1888–1890].

W. Adams 1892: William Adams & Co. *1892 Illustrated Catalogue and Price List of the Hope Iron Foundry: Cast and Wrought Iron Stable. Fittings, Water Troughs, Hitching Posts, Vases, Cemetery Chairs, and Settees, Builders Cast and Wrought Iron Work*. Trade catalogue. Philadelphia: William Adams & Co., 1892.

Aghion et al.: Irène Aghion, Claire Barbillon and François Lissarrague. *Gods and Heroes of Classical Antiquity*. Paris and New York: Flammarion, 1996.

AJ 1853: The Art Journal. *Exhibition of Art Industry in Dublin, 1853*. London: Virtue & Co., 1853.

AJ 1855: The Art Journal. *The Exhibition of Art Industry in Paris, 1855*. London: Virtue & Co., 1855.

AJ 1868: The Art Journal. *The Illustrated Catalogue of the Universal Exhibition*, London and NY: Virtue & Co., 1868.

AJ 1878: The Art Journal. *The Illustrated Catalogue of the Paris International Exhibition, 1878*. London: Virtue & Co., 1878.

AJ 1901: The Art Journal. *The Paris Exhibition, 1900*. London, 1901.

American Architect: "Wrought Iron Fences." *The American Architect* 104 (Sept. 10, 1913): 97–100.

Ames: Alex Ames. *Collecting Cast Iron*. Ashbourne, Derbyshire, England: Moorland Publishing, Co. Ltd., 1980.

AMM: *Appleton's Mechanics' Magazine*

Anderson Galleries 1: American Art Association Anderson Galleries, Inc. "Rare Wrought Iron Furniture and Objects of Art in Many Media." Auction catalogue. Sale 3979. New York, 1932.

Anderson Galleries 2: American Art Association Anderson Galleries, Inc. "Art for the Garden." Auction catalogue. Sale 4375. New York, 1938.

AR 1912: "The Renaissance Villa of Italy Developed into a Complete Residential Type for Use in America," *The Architectural Record* 31 (Mar. 1912): 201–225.

Arts and Crafts in Philadelphia: The Arts and Crafts in Philadelphia, Maryland, and South Carolina, 1780–1800. Series Two. Gleanings from Newspapers. Collected by Alfred Coxe Prime. The Walpole Society, 1932.

ASLA: American Society of Landscape Architects. *Colonial Gardens: The Landscape Architecture of George Washington's Time*. Washington, D.C.: United States George Washington Bicentennial Commission, 1932.

Atlantic: Atlantic Terra Cotta Company. *Garden Pottery*. Trade catalogue. New York: Atlantic Terra Cotta Company, 1911.

Aubel: F. & E. Aubel. *F. & E. Aubel's Industrial Plain and Ornamental Wire and Iron Railing Works*. Trade catalogue. Philadelphia: c. 1900.

Austin: Austin's Artificial Stone Works. Trade catalogue. 1835.

Axelrod: Alan Axelrod. *The Colonial Revival in America*. New York: W. W. Norton & Company for The Henry Francis du Pont Winterthur Museum, Winterthur, Delaware, 1985.

Ayrton and Silcock: Maxwell Ayrton and Arnold Silcock. *Wrought Iron and Its Decorative Use*. London: Country Life, Ltd., 1929.

Badger: Badger Wire and Iron Works. *Badger Wire and Iron Works, Catalogue 9*. Trade catalogue. Milwaukee, WI: Badger Wire and Iron Works, c. 1900.

Baker: John Cordis Baker. *American Country Homes and Their Gardens*. With an introduction by Donn Barber. Philadelphia:

House & Garden, The John C. Winston Company, 1906.

Barbezat & Cie.: Barbezat & Cie. *Ornements en Fonte de Fer.* Trade catalogue. Paris: Barbezat & Cie., c. 1858.

Barclay 1924: The Barclay Company. *Garden Ware: Catalog No. 24.* Trade catalogue. Narberth, P.A.: The Barclay Co., [1924].

Barclay 1930: The Barclay Company. *Garden Ware: Catalog No. 26.* Trade catalogue. Narberth, P.A.: The Barclay Co., [1930].

Barker: F. Barker & Son, Limited. *Descriptive Booklet and Price List of Sundials, etc.* Trade catalogue. London: F. Barker & Son, Limited, c. 1902.

Barnum 1881: E. T. Barnum Iron and Wire Works. *Special Catalogue of E.T. Barnum's Wire Goods, Wire and Iron Work.* Trade catalogue. Detroit: E. T. Barnum Iron and Wire Works, 1881.

Barnum c. 1900: E. T. Barnum Iron and Wire Works. *Vases, Settees, Fountains and Other Lawn Furniture.* Trade catalogue. Detroit: E.T. Barnum Iron and Wire Works, c. 1900.

Beiswanger: William Beiswanger. "Jefferson's Designs for Garden Structures at Monticello." *Journal of the Society of Architectural Historians* 35 (1976): 310–312.

Bent: Samuel S. Bent & Son. *Illustrated Catalogue & Price List of Settees, Chairs, Vases, Summer Houses . . .* Trade catalogue. New York: Samuel S. Bent & Son, c. 1890.

Bentley: William Bentley, D.D. *The Diary of William Bentley, D.D.: Pastor of the East Church, Salem, Massachusetts.* 3 vols. Salem, MA: The Essex Institute, 1905; Reprint, Gloucester, MA: Peter Smith, 1962.

Bibb: Arthur Burnley Bibb. "The Gardens and Grounds of Mount Vernon, Virgina." *House and Garden* 2 (Oct. 1902): 459–473.

Bill: Alfred Hoyt Bill. *A House Called Morven.* Revised ed. Princeton: Princeton University Press, 1978.

Blashfield: J. M. Blashfield. *Terra cottas by J. M. Blashfield: A Selection of Vases, Statues, Busts, &c.* Trade catalogue. London: J. M. Blashfield, 1857.

Blomfield and Thomas: R. Blomfield and F. I. Thomas. *The Formal Garden of England.* London, 1892.

Brady: George S. Brady. *Materials Handbook: An Encyclopedia for Purchasing Managers, Engineers, Executives, and Foremen.* New York: McGraw-Hill Company, 1971.

Braithwaite: H. T. Braithwaite. "A Historical Essay on Taste." *The Horticulturist* 6 (Feb. 1851): 73–78.

Brinkley and Chappell: M. Kent Brinkley and Gordon W. Chappell. *The Gardens of Colonial Williamsburg.* Williamsburg, VA: The Colonial Williamsburg Foundation, 1996.

Brizzi: Bruno Brizzi. *Le fontane di Roma.* Rome: Editore Colombo, 1988.

Brooke: E. Adveno Brooke. *The Gardens of England.* London: T. McLean, 1857.

Brookgreen Gardens: A Century of American Sculpture: Treasures from Brookgreen Gardens. New York: Abbeville Press, c. 1981.

Bushman: Richard L. Bushman. *The Refinement of America: Persons, Houses, Cities.* New York: Alfred A. Knopf, 1992.

Butler: Joseph T. Butler. *Washington Irving's Sunnyside.* Tarrytown, NY: Sleepy Hollow Restorations, 1974.

Byne and Byne: Arthur Byne and Mildred Stapley Byne. *Spanish Gardens and Patios.* New York, 1924.

Byrd: William Byrd. *The Secret Diary of William Byrd of Westover, 1709–1712.* Edited by Louis B. Wright and Marion Tinling. Richmond, VA: The Dietz Press, 1941.

Campbell: Marian Campbell. *Decorative Ironwork.* New York: Harry N. Abrams, Inc., 1997.

Cane: Percy S. Cane. "Modern Gardens British and Foreign." *The Studio* (Special Issue, Winter 1926–1927).

Carr-Gomm: Sarah Carr-Gomm. *The Dictionary of Symbols in Western Art.* New York: Facts-On-File, Inc., 1995.

Chase Brothers: Chase Brothers & Co. *Illustrated Catalogue of Useful and Ornamental Bronzed Iron Goods.* Trade catalogue. Boston: Chase Brothers & Co., c. 1859.

Chew: Chew Family Papers. Collection Historical Society of Pennsylvania.

Close: Leslie Rose Close. *Portrait of an Era in Landscape Architecture: The Photographs of Mattie Edwards Hewitt.* Exhibition catalogue. Bronx, NY: Wave Hill, 1983.

Coade: Coade Artificial Stone Manufactory. Trade catalogue. Lambeth, England: Coade Artificial Stone Manufactory, c. 1784.

Coade and Sealy: Coade and Sealy. *Description of Ornamental Stone in the Gallery of Coade and Sealy.* Trade catalogue. Lambeth, England: Coade and Sealy, 1799.

Coalbrookdale 1875: Coalbrookdale Co. *The Coalbrookdale Illustrated Catalogue.* Trade catalogue. London, Bristol, and Coalbrookdale: Coalbrookdale Co., 1875.

Coalbrookdale 1888: Coalbrookdale Company Limited. *The Coalbrookdale Illustrated Spring Catalogue.* Trade catalogue. London, Bristol, and Coalbrookdale: Coalbrookdale Company Limited, 1888.

Coats: Peter Coats. *Great Gardens of the Western World.* With an introduction by Harold Nicolson. New York: G. P. Putnam's Sons, 1963.

Codman: Henry Sargent Codman. "A List of Works on the Art of Landscape Gardening." *Garden and Forest: A Journal of Horticulture, Landscape Art and Forestry* 3 (Mar. 12, 1890): 131–135.

Conner: Janis C. Conner. "American Women Sculptors Break the Mold." *Art & Antiques* 1 (May/June 1980): 80–88.

Cram: Ralph Adams Cram. "Japanese Temple Gardens." *House & Garden* 2 (Mar. 1902): 76–90.

Crawford: Sharon Crawford. *Ganna Walska, Lotusland: The Garden and Its Creators.* Santa Barbara, CA: Companion Press for Ganna Walska Lotusland Foundation, 1996.

Cross: Launcelot Cross. *The Book of Old Sundials & Their Mottoes.* London: T. N. Foulis, 1917.

Cuel: Anciens Établissements Cuel Gilbert et Société. *Leur Pierre Agglomérée, Leur Décorations: Parcs, Jardins, Intérieurs, Façades.* Trade catalogue. Paris: Anciens Établissements Cuel Gilbert et Société, 1934.

Daniel: Christopher St. J. H. Daniel. *Sundials.* Buckinghamshire: Shire Publications Ltd., 1997.

Davidson: Rebecca Warren Davidson. "Past as Present: Villa Vizcaya and the 'Italian Garden' in the United States." *Journal of Garden History* 12 (1992): 1–28.

A. J. Davis: Alexander J. Davis. *The Fountain, with Jets of New Meaning.* New York: American News Co., 1870.

J. Davis: John P. S. Davis. *Antique Garden Ornament: 300 Years of Creativity: Artists, Manufacturers & Materials.* Woodbridge, Suffolk, England: The Antique Collectors' Club, 1991.

Davison: Ralph C. Davison. *Concrete Pottery*

and Garden Furniture. Trade catalogue. New York: Munn & Co., 1917.

Dawson: George Walter Dawson. "Minor Features of Italian Gardens." *House & Garden* 1 (July 1901): 1–8.

Decker: Paul Decker. *Gothic Architecture.* 1759. Reprint, London: Finborough, Gregg, 1968.

Della Pergola: Paola Della Pergola. *Villa Borghese.* Rome: Istituto Poligrafico Dello Stato Liberia, 1962.

Devaux: Yves Devaux. *L'Univers des Bronzes et des Fontes Ornamentales (chefs d'oeuvre et curiosités, 1850–1920).* Paris: Éditions Pygmalion, 1978.

Dietz: Paula Dietz. "Sitting in the Garden." *The Magazine Antiques.* (June 1992): 979–989.

Doell: M. Christine Klim Doell. *Gardens of the Gilded Age: Nineteenth-Century Gardens and Homegrounds of New York State.* Syracuse, NY: Syracuse University Press, 1986.

Dolan: Winthrop W. Dolan. *A Choice of Sundials.* Brattleboro, VT: The Stephen Greene Press, 1975.

Doulton: Doulton Co. *Price List of Architectural, Decorative, and Sanitary Materials.* Trade catalogue. London: Doulton Co., 1887.

Doulton 2: The Royal Doulton Co. *Terra Cotta Garden Ornaments.* Trade catalogue. London: The Royal Doulton Co., 1928.

Downing 1841: Andrew Jackson Downing. *A Treatise on the Theory and Practice of Landscape Gardening, adapted to North America, with a view to improvement of country residences . . . with remarks on rural architecture.* 1841. Reprint, New York: Wiley and Putnam, 1852.

Downing 1842: Andrew Jackson Downing. *Victorian Cottage Residences.* 1842. Reprint, with a new preface by Adolf K. Placzek, New York: Dover Publications, 1981. Originally published as *Cottage Residences.*

Downing 1847: Andrew Jackson Downing. "Impressions of Chatsworth." *The Horticulturist* 1 (Jan. 1847): 296–302.

Downing 1848: Andrew Jackson Downing. "Design for a Small Flower Garden." *The Horticulturist* 2 (May 1848): 503–505.

Downing 1851: Andrew Jackson Downing. "Mr. Downing's Letters From England." *The Horticulturist* 6 (Feb. 1851): 83–86.

Downing 1853: Andrew Jackson Downing. *Rural Essays.* 1853. Edited by George William Curtis. With a Memoir of the Author by George William Curtis and a Letter to his Friends by Frederika Bremer. Reprint, with a new introduction by George B. Tatum, New York: Da Capo Press, 1974.

Drury: John Drury. *The Heritage of Early American Houses..* New York: Coward-McCann, 1969.

Ducel: J. J. Ducel, & fils. Trade catalogue. Paris: J. J. Ducel & fils, 1845–1857.

Dunne: Dunne & Company. *Catalog of Rustic Work.* Trade catalogue. New York: Dunne & Company, 1902.

Dyer: Walter Dyer. "Sundials in Modern Gardens." *Country Life in America* 9 (Mar. 1906): 537–541.

Earle 1901: Alice Morse Earle. *Old-Time Gardens.* New York: The Macmillan Company, 1901.

Earle 1902: Alice Morse Earle. *Sun-Dials and Roses of Yesterday: Garden Delights Which Are Here Displayed in Very Truth and Are Moreover Regarded as Emblems.* New York: The Macmillan Co., 1902.

Edwards: Paul Francis Edwards. *English Garden Ornament.* London: G. Bell & Sons, 1965.

Edwards, Frary, and Jeffries: Junius David Edwards, Francis C. Frary, and Zay Jeffries. *The Aluminum Industry.* 1st ed. 2 vols. New York: McGraw-Hill, 1930.

Eglington: Guy Eglington. "Sculpture in the Gardens of the World." *Arts & Decoration* 20 (Mar. 1924): 18–19.

Elder: Paul Elder, ed. *The Architecture and Landscape Gardening of the Expo: A Pictorial Survey of the Most Beautiful Architectural Composition of the Panama-Pacific International Exposition.* San Francisco: P. Elder & Co., 1915.

Elliott: F. R. Elliott. "Landscape of Home Adornment." *The Horticulturist* 23 (May 1868): 129–135.

Elmore Studios: Elmore Studios. *Garden Ornaments, Antique and Modern.* Trade catalogue. New York: Elmore Studios, c. 1910.

Elwood: P. H. Elwood, Jr., ed. *American Landscape Architecture.* New York: The Architectural Book Publishing Co., 1924.

Emmet 1986: Alan Emmet. "Faulkner Farm: An Italian Garden in Massachusetts." *Journal of Garden History* 6 (Apr.–June 1986): 162–178.

Emmet 1996: Alan Emmet. *So Fine a Prospect: Historic New England Gardens.* Hanover, NH: University Press of New England, 1996.

Erkins c. 1909: Erkins Company. *Garden and Hall Furniture: Vases, Pedestals, Sundials, Fonts . . . and Pergolas in Marble, Stone and Pompeian Stone.* Trade catalogue. New York: Erkins Co., c. 1909.

Erkins 1929: Erkins Studios. *Garden Furniture.* Trade catalogue. New York: Erkins Studios, 1929.

Erkins 1933: Erkins Studios. *Thirtieth Anniversary Sale.* Trade catalogue. New York: Erkins Studios, 1933.

Erkins c. 1963: Erkins Studios. *Catalogue # 84.* Trade catalogue. New York: Erkins Studios, c. 1963.

Esdaille: K. A. Esdaille. "Coade Stone." *Architect and Building News* 161 (1940): 94–96, 112–114.

Evans: Nancy Goyne Evans. *American Windsor Chairs.* New York: Hudson Hills Press, 1996.

Eve: F. A. Eve. *Adam's Ale From a Spring.* Letter to the Editor. *Country Life* (London) 154 (December 6, 1973): 1920.

Fairbanks and Reynolds: Jonathan L. Fairbanks and Rebecca Gay Reynolds. "The Art of Forest Hills Cemetery." *The Magazine Antiques* 154 (Nov. 1998): 702–703.

Farish: Hunter Dickinson Farish, ed. *Journal & Letters of Philip Vickers Fithian, 1773–1774: A Plantation Tutor of The Old Dominion.* Williamsburg, VA: Colonial Williamsburg, Inc., 1945.

Farrington: Frank Farrington. "Iron Garden Furniture," *Hobbies* (Aug. 1942): 45–47.

Fauns and Fountains: The Parrish Art Museum. *Fauns and Fountains: American Garden Statuary, 1890–1930.* Southampton, NY: The Parrish Art Museum, 1985.

Favretti and Favretti: Rudy J. Favretti and Joy P. Favretti. *Landscapes and Gardens for Historic Buildings.* Nashville: American Association for State and Local History, 1978.

Felton: S. Felton. *Gleanings on Gardens, Chiefly Regarding Those of the Ancient Style in England.* London: A. L. Humphreys, 1897.

Fennimore: Donald L. Fennimore. "The Sundial in America." *The Magazine Antiques* 142 (Aug. 1992): 196–203.

Ferargil: Ferargil Galleries. "Sculpture for the Garden." Catalogue. 5 (Apr. 1931).

Ferree: Barr Ferree. *American Estates and Gardens.* New York: Munn and Company, 1904.

Fischer & Jirouch: Fischer & Jirouch Co. *Catalogue of Garden, Conservatory and Hall Furniture in Art Stone and Caen Stone Cement.* Trade catalogue. Cleveland: Fischer & Jirouch Co., c. 1910.

Fisher: Russell Fisher. "Decorative Ironwork on the Country Place." *Country Life in America* 12 (Oct. 1907): 645–647.

Fiske 1868: J. W. Fiske Iron Works. *Illustrated Catalogue and Price List of Settees, Chairs, Tables, Etc.* Trade catalogue. New York: J. W. Fiske, 1868.

Fiske c. 1870: J. W. Fiske Iron Works. *Illustrated Catalogue of Iron Vases.* Trade catalogue. New York: J. W. Fiske Iron Works, c. 1870.

Fiske 1874: J. W. Fiske Iron Works. *Illustrated Catalogue of Zinc Statuary, Supplement, 1874.* Trade catalogue. New York: J. W. Fiske Iron Works, 1874.

Fiske c. 1875: J. W. Fiske Iron Works. *Illustrated Catalogue of Statuary, Fountains, Vases, Settees, etc.* Trade catalogue. New York: J. W. Fiske Iron Works, c. 1875.

Fiske c. 1875–1879: J. W. Fiske Iron Works. *Illustrated Catalogue and Price List of Settees, Chairs, Tables, etc.* Trade catalogue. New York: J. W. Fiske Iron Works, c. 1875–79.

Fiske c. 1891: J. W. Fiske Iron Works. *Illustrated Catalogue of Artistic Wrought Iron, Brass and Bronze Work, Area Gates, Window Guards, Transoms, Grilles, Railing Posts, &c.,* Trade catalogue. New York: J. W. Fiske Iron Works, c. 1891.

Fiske 1892–1907: J. W. Fiske Iron Works. *Illustrated Catalogue and Price List of Zinc Animals, Deer, Dogs, Lions, Etc..* Trade catalogue. New York: J. W. Fiske, 1892–1907.

Fiske c. 1893: J. W. Fiske Iron Works. *Illustrated Catalogue and Price List of Ornamental Iron and Zinc Vases.* Trade catalogue. New York: J. W. Fiske Iron Works, c. 1893.

Fiske 1897: J. W. Fiske Iron Works. *Catalogue A, Cast Iron Settees, Chairs, etc.* Trade catalogue. New York: J. W. Fiske Iron Works, 1897.

Fiske c. 1901: J. W. Fiske Iron Works. *Illustrated Catalogue and Price List of Ornamental Iron Settees, Chairs, Tables, Archways . . .* Trade catalogue. New York: J. W. Fiske Iron Works, c. 1901.

Fiske [1901–1907]: J. W. Fiske Iron Works. *Illustrated Catalogue and Price List of Zinc Animals, Deer, Dogs, Lions, Etc.* Trade catalogue. New York: J.W. Fiske, [1901–1907].

Fiske [1908–1912]: J. W. Fiske Iron Works. *Illustrated Catalogue and Price List of Ornamental Iron Settees, Chairs, etc.* Trade catalogue. New York: J. W. Fiske Iron Works, [1908–1912].

Fiske c. 1908–1912: J. W. Fiske Iron Works. *Fountains.* Trade catalogue. New York: J.W. Fiske Iron Works, c. 1908–1912.

Fiske [1913–1933]: J. W. Fiske Iron Works. *Illustrated Catalogue of Ornamental Iron Settees, Chairs, Tables, etc.* Trade catalogue. New York: J. W. Fiske Iron Works, [1913–1933].

Fiske 1924: J. W. Fiske Iron Works. *Illustrated Catalogue of Ornamental Iron: Settees, Chairs, etc.* Trade catalogue. New York: J. W. Fiske Iron Works, 1924.

Fiske c. 1927: J. W. Fiske Iron Works. *Ornamental Iron and Zinc Fountains.* Trade catalogue. New York: J. W. Fiske Iron Works, c. 1927.

Fleming and Honour: John Fleming and Hugh Honour. *The Penguin Dictionary of Decorative Arts.* Great Britain: Viking Books, 1989.

Fox: Helen M. Fox. *André Le Nôtre Garden Architect to Kings.* New York: Crown Publishers, 1962.

Friedley & Voshardt: Friedley & Voshardt. *Statuary Catalogue.* Trade catalogue. Chicago: Friedley & Voshardt, 1900.

Friedman: Ann Friedman. "What John Locke Saw at Versailles." *Journal of Garden History* 9 (1989): 177–198.

Frilli: Antonio Frilli. *Marble Statuary, Interior & Garden Decorations.* Trade catalogue. Florence: Antonio Frilli, c. 1915.

Fröhner: Wilhelm Fröhner. *Notice de la Sculpture Antique du Musée National du Louvre.* Vol. 1. Paris, 1889.

Gade: John A. Gade. "Mr. Stanford White's Home at St. James." *House & Garden* 3 (Feb. 1903): 198–207.

Galloway c. 1915: Galloway Terra Cotta Co. *Terra Cotta and Pottery for Garden, Terrace and Interior Decoration: Flower Pots, Vases, Pedestals . . . Fountains.* Trade catalogue. Philadelphia: Galloway Terra Cotta Co., c. 1915.

Galloway c. 1917: Galloway Terra Cotta Company. *Galloway Pottery for Garden and Interior.* Catalogue no. 24. Trade catalogue. Philadelphia: Galloway Terra Cotta Company, c. 1917.

Galloway c. 1920: Galloway Terra Cotta Co. *Galloway Pottery for Garden and Interior.* Catalogue no. 27. Trade catalogue. Philadelphia: Galloway Terra Cotta Co., c. 1920.

Gatty: Mrs. Alfred Gatty. *The Book of Sun-Dials.* 1872. Enlarged and Re-Edited by H.K.F. Eden and Eleanor Lloyd. London: George Bell and Sons, 1900.

Gaudillot Frères : [Gaudillot Frères & Roy]. *Meubles de Jardin.* Trade catalogue. Paris: [Gaudillot Frères & Roy], 1834.

Gayle: Margot Gayle. Introduction to *Victorian Ironwork, A Catalogue by J. B. Wickersham.* Philadelphia: Athenaeum Library of Nineteenth-Century America, 1977.

Gebhard: David Gebhard. "The Spanish Colonial Revival in Southern California (1895–1930)," *Journal of the Society of Architectural Historians* (May 1967): 131–147.

Geis: M. Christina Geis, R.S.M. *Georgian Court: An Estate of the Gilded Age.* Philadelphia: The Art Alliance Press, 1982.

Girard: Jacques Girard. *Versailles Gardens: Sculpture and Mythology.* New York: Vendome Press, 1985.

Glaenzer: Eugene Glaenzer. *Renaissance of Art in America.* New York, c. 1890.

Godey's 1: "Garden Decorations." *Godey's Lady's Book* 42 (Apr. 1851): 251.

Godey's 2: "Garden Ornaments." *Godey's Lady's Book* 42 (May 1851): 282.

Gottesman: Rita Susswein Gottesman, comp. *The Arts and Crafts in New York, 1800–1804.* New York: New York Historical Society, 1965.

Greeley: Horace Greeley et al. "Ornamental Iron and Bronze Work." *The Great Industries of the United States: Being An Historical Summary of the Origin, Growth, and Perfection of the Chief Industrial Arts of this Country.* Hartford: J. B. Burr & Hyde, 1872.

Greiff: Constance M. Greiff. *Morven: A Documentary History.* vol. 1. Heritage Studios, Inc., July 1989.

Greiff 2: Constance M. Greiff. *Early Victorian.* New York: Abbeville Press, n.d.

Griswold and Weller: Mac Griswold and Eleanor Weller. *The Golden Age of American Gardens: Proud Owners, Private Estates 1890–1940.* New York: Harry N. Abrams in association with the Garden Club of America, 1991.

Guettier: Andre Victor Guettier. *De la Fonderie, telle qu'elle existe aujourd'hui en France, et de ses nombreuses applications a l'industrie . . .* Paris: Carilian-Coeury et Dalmont, 1844.

Haley: Jacquetta M. Haley, ed. *Pleasure Grounds: Andrew Jackson Downing and Montgomery Place.* Tarrytown, NY: Sleepy Hollow Press, 1988.

Handyside: Andrew Handyside & Co. *Works in Iron,* Trade catalogue. London: E. & F. N. Spon, 1868.

Hanks: David A. Hanks, ed. *Innovative Furniture in America from 1800 to the Present.* With an introduction by Russell Lynes. Essays by Rodris Roth and Page Talbot. New York: Horizon Press, 1981.

Hartmann-Sanders: Hartmann-Sanders Company. *Art Stone Furniture and Garden Accessories: Catalogue #39.* Trade catalogue. Chicago: Hartmann-Sanders Company, 1928.

Haskell and Penny : Francis Haskell and Nicolas Penny. *Taste and the Antique: The Lure of Classical Sculpture 1500–1900.* London: Yale University Press, 1981.

Headly & Edwards: Headly & Edwards, Ltd. *Ornamental Weather Vanes, Garden Chairs, Arches and Tents.* Trade catalogue. [London?]: n.p., c. 1907.

Hecla: Hecla Iron Works. *Metal Statues.* Trade catalogue. New York: Hecla Iron Works, [between 1870 and 1900].

Heckscher: Morrison Heckscher. "Eighteenth-Century Rustic Furniture Designs." *Furniture History* 11 (1975): 59–65 & plates.

Hennecke: C. Hennecke & Co. *Hennecke's Florentine Statuary.* Trade catalogue. Milwaukee: C. Hennecke & Co., 1886.

Hetherington 1980: Paul Hetherington. "Two Medieval Venetian Well-Heads in England." *Arte Veneta* 34 (1980): 9–17.

Hetherington 1995: Paul Hetherington. "The Venetian Well-Heads at Hever Castle, Kent." *Apollo* (Mar. 1995): 162–167.

Hewitt: Mark Alan Hewitt. *The Architect and the American Country House 1890–1940.* New Haven: Yale University Press, 1990.

H & G 1: "'The Briars,' Bar Harbor, Maine: The Garden of Mrs. Montgomery Sears." *House & Garden* 2 (Sept. 1902): 438–443.

H & G 2: "Ringwood Manor and Its Gardens." *House & Garden* 2 (Sept. 1902): 398–409.

HHV: Historic Hudson Valley. *Visions of Washington Irving: Selected Works from the Collection of Historic Hudson Valley.* Exhibition catalogue. Tarrytown, NY: Historic Hudson Valley, 1991.

A. Hill: Amelia Leavitt Hill. "When Art and Nature Meet: Garden Accessories Humanize the Garden." *Arts & Decoration* 15 (June 1921): 81–83.

M. Hill: May Brawley Hill. *Grandmother's Garden: The Old-Fashioned American Garden, 1865–1915.* New York: Harry N. Abrams, 1995.

Himmelheber: Georg Himmelheber. *Cast-Iron Furniture: And All Other Forms of Iron Furniture.* Translated by Judith Hayward. London: Philip Wilson Publishers Ltd., 1996.

Hinckley: C. T. Hinckley. "A Day at the Ornamental Ironworks of Robert Wood." *Godey's Lady's Book* (July 1853): 5–12.

Hinde: Thomas Hinde. *Stately Gardens of Britain.* London: Ebury Press, 1983.

Hinderer's: Hinderer's Iron Works Inc. *Ornamental Cast Iron.* Trade Catalogue. New Orleans: c. 1930.

Holtzoper: E. C. Holtzoper. "Garden Accessories: Hints on Pergolas, Arbors, Trellises, Summer Houses, Fences, Walls, Steps, Seats, Fountains, Statuary, Pots, Urns and Columns." *Country Life in America* 8 (Sept. 1905): 523–526.

Hood: Davyd Foard Hood. "The Renaissance of Southern Gardening in the Early Twentieth Century." *Journal of Garden History* 16 (Summer 1996): 129–152.

Hornung: Clarence P. Hornung. *Treasury of American Design.* vol. 2. New York: Harry N. Abrams, n.d.

Hornor: William MacPherson Hornor, Jr. *Blue Book Philadelphia Furniture: William Penn to George Washington with Special Reference to the Philadelphia-Chippendale School.* Philadelphia, 1935.

Horticulturist 1: "Paradise in the Country." *The Horticulturist* 1 (June 1847): 551–557.

Horticulturist 2: "Ornamental Vases and Chimney Tops." *The Horticulturist* 3 (July 1848): 37–43.

Horticulturist 3: "Horticultural Exhibitions: Their Influence Upon Cultivation and Taste." From John Claudius Loudon's *Gardener's Magazine of Botany. The Horticulturist* 5 (Feb. 1851): 59–62.

Horticulturist 4: "A Visit to the House and Garden of the Late A. J. Downing." *The Horticulturist* 3, New Series (Jan. 1853): 21–28.

Horticulturist 5: "The Use of Ornaments in Landscape Gardening – No. I." *The Horticulturist* 19 (Aug. 1864): 246–247.

Horticulturist 5a: "The Use of Ornaments in Landscape Gardening – No. II." *The Horticulturist* 19 (Aug. 1864): 303–305.

Horticulturist 6: "Garden Furniture." *The Horticulturist* 3, New Series (July 1853): 801–804.

Horticulturist 7: "Garden Furniture." *The Horticulturist* 3, New Series (Aug. 1853): 855–859.

Horticulturist 8: "Iron Vases." *The Horticulturist* 6, New Series (Jan. 1856): 90.

Horticulturist 9: "Ornamental Iron Work." *The Horticulturist* 7 (Nov. 1957): 496–498.

Howard Studios : Howard Studios. *Howard Studios Collection.* Trade catalogue. New York: Howard Studios [1925–1928].

Humphreys 1850: H. Noel Humphreys, Esq. "Notes on Decorative Gardening: Fountains." *The Horticulturist* 5 (Nov. 1850): 208–211.

Humphreys 1851: H. Noel Humphreys, Esq. "Notes on Decorative Gardening: Architectural Terraces." *The Horticulturist* 5 (Mar. 1851): 134–137.

Hunt: John Dixon Hunt, ed. *Garden History: Issues, Approaches, Methods.* Washington, D.C.: Dumbarton Oaks Research Library & Collection, 1995.

Jacquier: F. & A. Jacquier. Trade Catalogue. Caen, France: F. & A. Jacquier, c. 1900.

Janes, Beebe, & Co.: Janes, Beebe, & Co. *Illustrated Catalogue of Ornamental Ironwork.* Trade Catalogue. New York: Janes, Beebe, & Co., 1858.

Janes, Kirtland & Co.: Janes, Kirtland & Co. *Illustrated Catalogue of Ornamental Ironwork.* Trade Catalogue. New York: Janes, Kirtland & Co., 1870.

Janson : Janson, H. W. *19th-Century Sculpture.* New York: Harry N. Abrams, 1985.

Jekyll: Gertrude Jekyll. *Garden Ornament.* 1918. Reprint, Woodbridge, Suffolk, England: Antique Collectors' Club, 1982.

Johnson: Johnson, Kathleen Eagen and Timothy Steinhoff. *Art of the Landscape: Sunnyside, Montgomery Place and Romanticism.* Exhibition catalogue. Sleepy Hollow, NY: Philipsburg Manor Gallery, 1997.

M. D. Jones: M. D. Jones & Co. *Garden, Lawn, Cemetery and Park Adornments: Illustrated Catalogue.* Trade catalogue. Boston: M. D. Jones & Co., (c. 1903).

O. Jones: O. Jones. *The Grammar of Ornament.* Ontario, Canada: Dover Publications, 1987.

Karson: Robin Karson. *The Muses of Gwinn: Art and Nature in a Garden Designed by Warren H. Manning, Charles A. Platt, & Ellen Biddle Shipman.* Sagaponack, NY: Sagapress in association with The Library of American Landscape History, Inc., 1995; distributed by Harry N. Abrams, Inc.

Karson 2: Robin Karson. *Fletcher Steele, Landscape Architect: An Account of the Gardenmaker's Life, 1885–1971.* New York: Ngaere Macray, 1989.

Kauffman 1966: Henry J. Kauffman. *Early American Ironware: Cast and Wrought.* New York: Weathervane Books, 1966.

Kauffman 1978: Henry J. Kauffman. *American Copper and Brass.* New York: Bonanza Books, 1978.

Keeping Eden: Massachusetts Horticultural Society. *Keeping Eden: A History of Gardening in America.* Edited by Walter T. Punch. Boston: Little, Brown & Co., 1992.

Kelly: Alison Kelly. *Mrs. Coade's Stone.* Upton-upon-Severn, England: The Self Publishing Association, 1990.

Kenneth Lynch 1974: Kenneth Lynch & Sons, Inc. *Garden Ornament: An Encyclopedia.* Trade catalogue. Wilton, CT: Kenneth Lynch & Sons, Inc., 1974.

Kenneth Lynch 1979: Kenneth Lynch & Sons, Inc. *The Book of Garden Ornament.* Trade catalogue. Wilton, CT: Kenneth Lynch & Sons, Inc., 1979.

Kenworthy: Richard G. Kenworthy. "Bringing the World to Brookline: the Gardens of Larz and Isabel Anderson." *Journal of Garden History* 11 (Oct.–Dec. 1991): 224–241.

Kimball 1917: Fiske Kimball. "The Beginnings of Landscape Architecture Gardening in America." *Landscape Architecture* 7 (1917): 181–187.

Kimball 1940: Fiske Kimball. *Mr. Samuel McIntire, Carver: The Architect of Salem.* Salem, MA: The Essex Institute, 1940; Reprint, Gloucester, MA: Peter Smith, 1966.

Klein: William M. Klein, Jr. *Gardens of Philadelphia and the Delaware Valley.*

Philadelphia: Temple University Press, 1995.

Kocher and Dearstyne: A. Lawrence Kocher and Howard Dearstyne. *Colonial Williamsburg: Its Buildings and Gardens.* Williamsburg, VA: Colonial Williamsburg, Inc., 1949.

Kramer: Kramer Brothers Foundry Co. *Metal Vases & Settees: Catalogue no. 12.* Trade catalogue. Reprint of c. 1910 catalogue. Dayton, OH: Kramer Brothers Foundry Co., 1995.

Lablaude: Lablaude, Pierre-André. *The Gardens of Versailles.* Translated from the French by Fiona Bioddulph. London: Zwemmer, 1995.

Lalance & Grosjean: Lalance & Grosjean Mfg. Co. Trade catalogue. New York: Lalance & Grosjean Mfg. Co., 1881.

Latrobe: Latrobe, Ferdinand C. *Iron Men and Their Dogs.* Baltimore: Ivan R. Drechsler, 1941.

Lawley: Ian Lawley, "Art and Ornament in Iron: Design and the Coalbrookdale Company." Ironbridge Gorge, Shropshire, England: The Ironbridge Gorge Trust, 1979.

Lazzaro: Claudia Lazzaro. *The Italian Renaissance Garden: From the Conventions of Planting, Design, and Ornament to the Grand Gardens of Sixteenth-Century Central Italy.* New Haven and London: Yale University Press, 1990.

Leighton 1976: Ann Leighton. *American Gardens in the Eighteenth Century: "For Use or for Delight."* Boston: Houghton Mifflin Company, 1976.

Leighton 1987: Ann Leighton. *American Gardens of the Nineteenth Century: "For Comfort and Affluence."* Amherst: University of Massachusetts Press, 1987.

Leinfelder: Leinfelder & Company. *Fine Wrought Iron & Wire Furniture for Garden . . . Terrace . . . Solarium.* Trade catalogue. Lacrosse, WI: 1934.

Lester: Charles Lester. *Glances at the Metropolis.* New York: Isaac D. Guyer, 1854.

Lichten: Frances Lichten. *Decorative Art of Victoria's Era.* New York: Charles Scribner's Sons, 1950.

Lister: Raymond Lister. *Decorative Wrought Ironwork in Great Britain.* 2nd Edition. Devon, England: David & Charles Limited, 1970.

Listri and Cunaccia: Massimo Listri and

Cesare M. Cunaccia. *Italian Parks and Gardens.* New York: Rizzoli, 1996.

Lockwood : Alice G. B. Lockwood. *Gardens of Colony and State: Gardens and Gardeners of the American Colonies and of the Republic Before 1840.* 2 vols. New York: Charles Scribner's Sons, for The Garden Club of America, 1931–1934.

London: *Official Descriptive and Illustrated Catalogue of the Great Exhibition of the Works of Industry of All Nations.* London, 1851.

Long : Elias A. Long. *Ornamental Gardening for Americans.* New York, 1891.

Loudon 1835: John Claudius Loudon. *An Encyclopedia of Cottage, Farm and Villa Architecture and Furniture.* 1835. Edited by Mrs. Loudon. New edition. London: Longman, Brown, Green and Longmans, 1853.

Loudon 1844: John Claudius Loudon. *Arboretum et Fruticetum Britannicum, or, The Trees and Shrubs of Britain.* 8 volumes. London: Longman, Brown, Green and Longmans, 1844.

Low: James F. Low & Co., Ltd. *The Foundry by the Sea.* Monifieth, Scotland: n.p.,c. 1930.

Lowell: Guy Lowell, ed. *American Gardens.* Boston: Bates & Guild Company, 1901.

Maccubbin and Martin: Robert P. Maccubbin and Peter Martin, eds. *British and American Gardens in the Eighteenth Century.* Williamsburg, VA: The Colonial Williamsburg Foundation, 1984.

MacDougall 1978: Elisabeth MacDougall, ed. *Fons Sapientiae: Renaissance Garden Fountains.* Dumbarton Oaks Colloquium on the History of Landscape Architecture V. Washington, D.C.: Dumbarton Oaks, 1978.

MacDougall 1981: Elisabeth B. MacDougall and Wilhelmina F. Jashemski. *Dumbarton Oaks Colloquium on the History of Landscape Architecture Gardens.* Washington, D.C.: Dumbarton Oaks Trustees for Harvard University, 1981.

MacFarlane: Walter MacFarlane & Co. *Illustrated Catalogue of MacFarlane's Castings.* 6th ed. vol. 1. Trade Catalogue. Glasgow, Scotland: Walter MacFarlane & Company, 1882.

MacKay: Alex MacKay, Esq. *The Western World; Or, Travels in the United States in 1846–47: Exhibiting Them in Their Latest Development, Social, Political, and Industrial; Including a Chapter on*

California. 5th ed. 3 vols. London: Richard Bentley, 1851.

MacKay, Baker, and Traynor: Robert B. MacKay, Anthony K. Baker, and Carol A. Traynor, eds. *Long Island Country Houses and Their Architects, 1860–1940.* With a foreword by Brendan Gill. New York and London: Society for the Preservation of Long Island Antiquities in association with W. W. Norton & Company, 1997.

Magnus: G. E. Magnus at the Pimlico Slate Works. *Illustrated Catalogue: Useful and Ornamental Articles.* Trade catalogue. London: Ashbee & Dangerfield, 1857.

Major: Judith K. Major. *To Live in the New World: A.J. Downing and American Landscape Gardening.* Cambridge, MA: The MIT Press, 1997.

MAMC: Munich Art Metallic Company. Trade catalogue. Cincinnati, OH: Munich Art Metallic Company, c. 1900.

G. Martin: George A. Martin. *Fences, Gates, and Bridges.* New York, 1892.

L. Martin: Laura C. Martin. *Southern Gardens: A Gracious History and Traveler's Guide.* New York: Abbeville Press, 1993.

P. Martin : Peter Martin. *The Pleasure Gardens of Virginia from Jamestown to Jefferson.* Princeton, NJ: Princeton University Press, 1991.

Masson: Georgina Masson. *Italian Gardens.* New York: Harry N. Abrams, 1961.

Masson and Owen: Ann W. Masson and Lydia J. Owen. *Cast Iron and the Crescent City.* Exhibition catalogue. New Orleans: Gallier House, 1975.

Mayall and Mayall: R. Newton Mayall and Margaret L. Mayall. *Sundials: How to Know, Use, and Make Them.* Boston: Charles T. Branford Company, 1962.

McCormick: William B. McCormick. "Samuel Yellin – Artist in Iron." *The International Studio* 75 (1922): 431–434.

McGuire: Thomas J. McGuire. *The Surprise of Germantown.* Gettysburg, PA: Cliveden of the National Trust for Historic Preservation and Thomas Publications, 1994.

McGuire and Fern: Diane K. McGuire and Lois Fern, eds. *Beatrix Jones Ferrand: Fifty Years of American Landscape Architecture.* Washington, D.C.: 1980.

McIntosh: Charles McIntosh. *The Book of the Garden.* 2 vols. Edinburgh and London: Wm. Blackwood & Sons, 1853.

McMahon: McMahon, Bernard. *The American Gardener's Calendar.* New York: Funk & Wagnalls, 1806.

Meyrowitz: E. B. Meyrowitz. *Sun Dials for the Garden.* Trade catalogue. New York: E. B. Meyrowitz, c. 1925.

Middleton: C. Middleton. *Decorations for Parks and Gardens, Designs for Gates, Garden Seats, Alcoves, Temples, Baths, &c.* London: J. Taylor, c. 1800.

Miller Iron: Miller Iron Company. *Illustrated Catalogue of Ornamental Iron Work.* Trade catalogue. Providence, RI: 1871.

W. Miller: Wilhelm Miller. *What England Can Teach Us About Gardening.* Garden City, NY: Doubleday, Page & Company, 1911.

Mitchell : James R. Mitchell. *Antique Metalware.* New York: Macmillan, 1976.

MMA: The Metropolitan Museum of Art. *Nineteenth-Century America: Furniture and Other Decorative Arts.* New York: New York Graphic Society Ltd., 1970.

Morgan: Keith N. Morgan. *Shaping An American Landscape: The Art and Architecture of Charles A. Platt.* Exhibition catalogue, Hood Museum of Art, Dartmouth College. Hanover and London: University Press of New England, 1995.

Morris: Alistair Morris. *Antiques from the Garden.* Suffolk, England: Garden Art Press, a division of Antique Collectors Club, Ltd., 1996.

Mosser and Teyssot: Monique Mosser and Georges Teyssot, eds. *The Architecture of Western Gardens.* Milan: Elemond Editori Associati, 1990. Originally published as *L'Architectura dei Giardini d'Occidente.*

Mott 1870–1880: J. L. Mott Iron Works. [Illustrated Catalogue and Price List of Furniture]. Trade catalogue. New York: J. L. Mott Iron Works, 1870–1880.

Mott 1875: J. L. Mott Iron Works. *Illustrated Catalog of Statuary, Fountains, Vases. Settees, etc., for Parks, Gardens and Conservatories.* Trade catalogue. New York: J. L. Mott Iron Works, 1875.

Mott 1889: J. L. Mott Iron Works. *Wrought Iron Folding Tables and Chairs for Home and Export Trade.* Trade catalogue. New York: J. L. Mott Iron Works, 1889.

Mott 1890: J. L. Mott IronWorks. *'M' Illustrated Catalog and Price List of Statuary and Animals.* Trade catalogue. New York: J. L. Mott Iron Works, 1890.

Mott 1893: J. L. Mott IronWorks. *Illustrated Catalogue and Price List "L" of Cast Iron Vases.* Trade catalogue. New York: J. L. Mott Iron Works, 1893.

Mott 1897: J. L. Mott IronWorks. *Catalogue A: Cast Iron Settees, Chairs, & Table Stands . . .* Trade catalogue. New York: J. L. Mott Iron Works, 1897.

Mott c. 1905: J. L. Mott Iron Works. *Iron vases . . .* Trade catalogue. New York: J. L. Mott Iron Works, c. 1905.

Mott c. 1905a: J. L. Mott Iron Works. *Fountains, Ground Basins, and Basin Rims.* Section 1, Catalogue H. Trade catalogue. New York: J. L. Mott Iron Works, c. 1905.

Mott c. 1919: J. L. Mott Iron Works. *Statuary in Metal.* Trade catalogue. New York: J. L. Mott Iron Works, c. 1919.

Moulton : Robert H. Moulton. "Mellody Farm – The Country Home of Mr. J. Ogden Armour." *House Beautiful* (July 1920): 32–33.

Muller: Emile Muller &c. *Catalogue de l'Execution en Gres d'un Choix d'oeuvres des Maitres de la Sculpture Contemporaine Salon d'Exposition et de Vente, 3 Rue Halevy, Paris.* Paris: Imprimerie Georges Petit, n.d.

Murray: Alexander S. Murray. *Who's Who in Mythology: A Classic Guide to the Ancient World.* 2nd ed. New York: Wings Books, 1989.

Musée des arts décoratifs: Musée des arts décoratifs. *Exposition retrospective de l'art jardins en France du XVI siècle à la fin du XVIII.* Exhibition catalogue. Paris: Palais du Louvre, 1913.

Nevins: Deborah Nevins. "The Triumph of Flora: Women and the American Landscape, 1890–1935." *The Magazine Antiques* (Apr. 1985): 904–922.

New York State Mechanic: *New York State Mechanic* (Albany). Vol. 1, Part 2 (Aug. 20, 1842).

New York Wire Railing: New York Wire Railing Company. *A New Phase in the Iron Manufacture. Important Inventions and Improvements; Historical Sketch of Iron; Descriptive Catalogue of the Manufactures of the New York Wire Railing Company. Hutchinson & Wickersham.* Trade Catalogue. New York: New York Wire Railing Company, 1857.

Nichols: Rose Standish Nichols. "Pompeian Gardens: Constant Excavations Make

These Gardens of Renewed Interest," *House Beautiful* 64 (Oct. 1928): 398–399, 444–449.

Northend: Mary Harwood Northend. *Garden Ornaments*. New York: Duffield & Co., 1916.

O'Brien: W. K. O'Brien & Co. *Illustrated Catalogue of O'Brien Bro.'s Inimitable & Superior Designs, Rustic Work in All its Branches for the Ornamenting of Public and Private Parks, Pleasure Resorts, etc.* Trade catalogue. New York: The Graphic Co., 1874.

Olmert: Michael Olmert. "The Hospitable Pineapple." *Colonial Williamsburg* (Winter 1997–1998): 46–50.

Olmsted: Frederick Law Olmsted, Jr. and Theodora Kimball. *Frederick Law Olmsted: Landscape Architect, 1822–1903: 40 years of Landscape Architecture, Being the Professional Papers of F. L. Olmsted, Sr.* 2 vols. New York: G. P. Putnam's Sons, 1922–1928.

O'Malley and Treib: Therese O'Malley and Marc Treib, eds. *Regional Garden Design i»n the United States.* Dumbarton Oaks Colloquium on the History of Landscape Architecture, XV. Washington, D.C.: Dumbarton Oaks Research Library and Collection, 1995.

Osborne and Day: Charles Francis Osborne and Frank Miles Day. *Historic Houses and Their Gardens*. Philadelphia: The John C. Winston Company in association with House & Garden, 1908.

Ostergard 1987: Derek E. Ostergard, ed. *Bentwood and Metal Furniture, 1850–1946.* Text by Alessandro Alverà, et al. New York: American Federation of Arts, 1987.

Ostergard 1994: Derek E. Ostergard, ed. *Cast Iron from Central Europe, 1800–1850.* New York: Bard Graduate Center for Studies in the Decorative Arts, 1994.

Outing: "Where We Get Our Ideas of Country Places in America." Prepared from an interview with Charles A. Platt. *Outing* 44 (June 1904): 349–355.

Papworth: John Buonarotti Papworth. *Hints on Ornamental Gardening: Consisting of a Series of Designs for Garden Buildings Useful and Decorative Gates, Fences, Railings. &c. . . .* London: R. Ackermann, 1823.

J. Patrick: James B. Patrick, ed. *Longwood Gardens*. Kennett Square, Pa.: Longwood Gardens, Inc., 1995.

V. Patrick: Vanessa E. Patrick. "Partitioning the Landscape: Fences in Colonial Virginia." *The Magazine Antiques* 154 (July 1998): 96–105.

Paul: Martine Paul. "Turf Seats in French Gardens of the Middle Ages (12th–16th Centuries)." *Journal of Garden History* 5 (Jan.–Mar. 1985): 3–14.

Pean: A. Pean. *L'Architecte paysagiste: théorie et pratique de la création et décoration des parcs et jardins; cours d'aquarelle en quatre leçons, notions usuelles de droit; comptabilité des travauses.* Paris: A. Goin, 1886.

Pentecost: George F. Pentecost. "The Formal and the Natural Style." *The Architectural Record* 12 (June 1902): 174–194.

Pequonnock: Pequonnock Foundry, Inc. *Antique Lawn and Garden Furniture.* Trade catalogue. Bridgeport, Conn.: Pequonnock Foundry, Inc., N.d. (Twentieth century).

Philadelphia: *International Exhibition 1876 Catalogue.* Philadelphia: John R. Nagle and Company, 1876.

Phoenix: Phoenix Iron Works. Trade Catalogue. Utica, NY: c. 1882.

Pincas: Stéphane Pincas. *Versailles: The History of the Gardens and Their Sculpture.* Translated from the French by Fiona Cowell. New York: Thames and Hudson, 1996. Originally published by Editions de la Martinière, 1995.

Platt 1894: Charles A. Platt. *Italian Gardens.* New York: Harper & Brothers, 1894.

Platt 1913: Platt, Charles A. *Monograph of the Work of Charles A. Platt.* New York: Tile Architectural Book Publishing Co., 1913.

Pliny: Pliny. *Letters and Panegyricus.* 2 vols. Translated by Betty Radice. London: William Heinemann Ltd., 1972.

Plumptre: George Plumptre. *Garden Ornament: Five Hundred Years of Nature, Art, and Artifice.* New York: Doubleday, 1990.

Pompeian: Studios of the Pompeian Garden Furniture Company. *Garden Furniture.* Trade catalogue. New York: Studios of the Pompeian Garden Furniture Company [1925–1931].

Pope-Hennessy: John Pope-Hennessy. *An Introduction to Italian Sculpture.* 4th ed. 3 vols. London: Phaidon Press, 1996.

Portland: Portland Stone Ware Company. *Illustrated Catalogue of the Portland Stone Ware Co.* Trade Catalogue. Portland, ME: Portland Stone Ware Co., 1895.

Price: F. Newlin Price. "Wrought-Iron Furniture for English Gardens." *American Collector* (June 1941): 8–9.

Primo: Primo Art Studios. *Primo Art Garden Furniture.* Catalogue 28. Trade Catalogue. Providence, RI: Primo Art Studios, c. 1925.

Prior: Edward S. Prior. "American Garden Craft from an English Point of View." *House and Garden* 4 (Nov. 1903): 201–215.

Proske: Beatrice Gilman Proske. *Brookgreen Gardens: Sculpture.* 2 vols. Brookgreen, S.C.: Printed by Order of the Trustees, 1943.

Pulham: Pulham & Son. *Price List of Vases, Tazzae, Pedestals, Balustrades, Fountains, Finials, Terminals, Garden Seats, etc., in "Pulhamite" Stone.* 3rd ed. Trade catalogue. London: Pulham & Son, c. 1905.

Radice: Betty Radice. *Who's Who in the Ancient World.* Reprint, Harmondsworth, Middlesex, England: Penguin Books Ltd., 1985.

Raistrick: Arthur Raistrick. *Dynasty of Iron Founders: the Darbys and Coalbrookdale.* London and New York: Longmans, Green, 1953.

Rauschenberg: Bradford L. Rauschenberg. "An American Eighteenth-Century Garden Seat in the 'Chinese Taste'." *The Luminary: The Newsletter of the Museum of Early Southern Decorative Arts* 18 (Spring 1997): 1, 4, 5, 8.

Rehmann: Elsa Rehmann. "Sculpture in the Garden." *House and Garden* 47 (June 1925): 58–61, 104, 106.

Reisem: Richard O. Reisem. *200 Years of Architecture and Gardens Rochester* [Rochester]: Landmark Society of Western New York, c. 1994.

Renard: Jean-Claude Renard. *L'Age De La Font, un art, une industrie, 1800–1914.* Paris: Les éditions de l'Amateur, 1985.

Renwick: W. G. Renwick. *Marble and Marble Working: A Handbook for Architects, Sculptors, Marble Quarry Owners and Workers, and All Engaged in the Building and Decorative Industries.* London: Crosby Lockwood and Son, 1909.

Repton: Humphrey Repton. *The Art of Landscape Gardening.* Edited by John Nolen, A.M. Boston: Houghton Mifflin Company, 1907.

Ricauti: T. J. Ricauti. *Sketches for Rustic Work, Including Bridges, Park, and Garden Buildings, Seats and Furniture . . . with Descriptions and Estimates of the Buildings.* Trade catalogue. Exeter: P. A. Hannaford, 1842. Reprint, London: H. G. Bohn, 1848.

Richards: Nancy E. Richards. "Cliveden: The Chew Mansion in Germantown." Philadelphia: Cliveden, 1993.

G. Richter: Gisella Richter. *Handbook of Greek Art.* 9th ed. Oxford: Phaidon Press, 1987.

P. Richter: Paula Bradstreet Richter. "A Rediscovered Gardener's Legacy." *Journal of the New England Garden History Society* 4 (Spring 1996): 49–57.

Ring: Betty Ring. *American Needlework Treasures: Samplers and Silk Embroideries from the Collection of Betty Ring.* New York: E.P. Dutton, 1987.

Ripa: Cesare Ripa. *Baroque and Rococo Pictorial Imagery: The 1758–60 Hertel Edition of Ripa's 'Iconologia'. With Introduction, Translations, and 200 Commentaries by Edward A Maser.* New York: Dover Publications, c. 1971.

Rizzi: Alberto Rizzi. *Vere da Pozzo di Venezia: I Puteali Pubblici di Venezia e della sua Laguna.* Venice: La Stamperia di Venezia Editrice, 1981.

Robertson and Robertson: E. Graeme Robertson and Joan Robertson. *Cast-Iron Decoration: A World Survey.* London: Thames & Hudson, 1977.

Robie: Virginia Robie. *By-Paths in Collecting.* New York: The Century Company, 1912.

Robinson: William Robinson. *The English Flower Garden.* 1883. Reprint of 1933 edition, New York: The Amaryllis Press, 1984.

Rohr: René R. J Rohr. *Sundials: History, Theory, and Practice.* Translated by Gabriel Godin. Toronto: University of Toronto Press, 1970; New York: Dover Publications, 1996.

Romaine: Lawrence B. Romaine. *A Guide to American Trade Catalogs, 1744–1900.* New York: R. R. Bowker Company, 1960.

Roscoe: Ingrid Roscoe. "'Of Statues, Obelisks, Dyals, and other invegetative Ornaments': Sources and Meanings for English Garden Statues." *Apollo* (Jan. 1995): 38–42.

Rosedown 1: Sculpture List and Invoice from F. Leopold Pisani, Florence, August 18, 1851. Rosedown Plantation Archives.

Rosedown 2: Sarah Turnbull's Notes on Trip to Europe, April 15, 1851–October 26, 1851. Rosedown Plantation Archives.

Rosedown 3: Invoice from S. A. Harrison for Two Iron Vases & Pedestals. Rosedown Plantation Archives.

Ruckstuhl: F. W. Ruckstuhl. "The Proper Functions of Open-Air Statuary." *House & Garden* 2 (Oct. 1902): 481–494.

Ruskin: John Ruskin. *The Stones of Venice.* 1853. J. G. Links, ed. Reprint, New York: Da Capo Press, 1960.

Saint Pancras: Saint Pancras Iron Work Company. *Synopsis of Manufactures.* Trade catalogue. [London?]: n.p., c. 1863.

Sale: Edith Tunis Sale. *Manors of Virginia in Colonial Times.* Philadelphia and London: J. B. Lippincott Company, 1909.

Sanfilippo: Mario Sanfilippo. *Fountains of Rome.* Translated from the Italian by Andrew Ellis. New York: The Vendome Press, 1996.

Sanford: Juliet Sanford. "Ornaments for Modern Gardens." *Arts & Decoration* (June 1931): 22–23, 68.

Sarudy: Barbara Wells Sarudy. "Eighteenth-Century Gardens of the Chesapeake," *Journal of Garden History* 9 (July/Sept. 1989): 104–159.

Sarudy 2: Barbara Wells Sarudy. *Gardens and Gardening in the Chesapeake, 1700–1805.* Baltimore and London: The Johns Hopkins University Press, 1998.

Saylor: Henry H. Saylor. "The Japanese Garden in America." *Country Life in America* 15 (Mar. 1909): 481–484.

Scarre: Chris Scarre. *Chronicle of the Roman Emperors: The Reign-by-Reign Record of the Rulers of Imperial Rome.* London: Thames and Hudson, 1995.

Schmerler: Sarah Schmerler. "Under the Weather." *Art & Auction* 11 (May 1998): 106.

Scott: Frank J. Scott. *The Art of Beautifying Suburban Home Grounds of Small Extent.* 1870. Reprinted as *Victorian Gardens: The Art of Beautifying Suburban Home Grounds, A Victorian Guidebook of 1870 by Frank J. Scott,* with a foreword by David Schuyler, Watkins Glen, NY: Library of Victorian Culture, American Life Foundation, 1982.

Seelig: M. J. Seelig & Co., *Fine Art Bronze and Zinc Foundry.* Trade catalogue. Williamsburgh, NY, 1876.

Sellers: Charles Coleman Sellers. *Charles Willson Peale.* New York: Charles Scribner's Sons, 1969.

SFMA: *Contemporary Landscape Architecture and Its Sources.* Exhibition catalogue. [San Francisco]: San Francisco Museum of Art, 1937.

Shelton: Louise Shelton. *Beautiful Gardens in America.* Revised edition. New York: Charles Scribner's Sons, 1928.

Shepherd & Jellicoe: J. C. Shepherd and G. A. Jellicoe. *Italian Gardens of the Renaissance.* 1925. Reprint, London: Academy Editions, 1994.

Slade: D. D. Slade. "The Artificial Fountain." *The Horticulturist* 22 (May 1867): 135–137.

Smith: Mrs. Chetwood Smith. "Lawn Animals." *Old-Time New England, The Bulletin of the Society for the Preservation of New England Antiquities* 39 (Apr. 1949): 89–92.

Smyser: E. G. Smyser's Sons Co. *Illustrated Catalogue of Ornamental Iron Vases.* Trade catalogue. York, Pa.: E. G. Smyser's Sons Co., c. 1870.

Snyder: Ellen Marie Snyder. "Victory over Nature: Victorian Cast-Iron Seating Furniture." *Winterthur Portfolio* 20 (Winter 1985): 221–242.

Société Anonyme des Hauts-Fourneaux: Société Anonyme des Hauts-Fourneaux du Val d'Osne. Trade catalogue. Paris: Magasins, c. 1870.

Société Anonyme des Hauts-Fourneaux 2: Société Anonyme des Hauts-Fourneaux du Val d'Osne. Trade catalogue. Paris: Magasins, c. 1880.

Sotheby's: Sotheby's Sussex. *Garden Statuary and Architectural Items: May 27, 1992.* Auction catalogue. Summers Place, Billingshurst, West Sussex, England: Sotheby's Sussex, 1992.

Southworth and Southworth: Susan Southworth and Michael Southworth. *Ornamental Ironwork: An Illustrated Guide to its Design, History & Use in American Architecture.* New York: McGraw-Hill, 1992.

Speltz: Alexander Speltz. *The Styles of Ornament.* Translated from the German by David O'Connor. New York: Dover Publications, 1959.

Sproule: John Sproule, ed. *The Irish Industrial Exhibition of 1853.* Dublin: James McGlashan, 1854.

Stewart: Stewart Iron Works. *No. 35 B Catalogue.* Trade catalogue. Cincinnati, OH: Stewart Iron Works, c. 1908.

Stowe: *Stowe: The Gardens of Lord Viscount Cobham.* London: B. Steely, 1750.

Strange: Thomas Arthur Strange. *English Furniture Decoration, Woodwork and Allied Arts.* New York: Bonanza Books, 1950.

Sutherland: Harvey Sutherland. "The Gardens of the Rich." *Munsey's Magazine*

29 (July 1903): 481–490.

Swift 1902: Samuel Swift. "The Ornamental Movement of Water in City Streets: I." *House & Garden* 2 (Apr. 1902): 150–162.

Swift 1902a: Samuel Swift. "The Ornamental Movement of Water in City Streets: III." *House & Garden* 2 (Sept. 1902): 416–428.

Swift 1903: Samuel Swift. "American Garden Pottery." *House & Garden.* 3 (July 1903): 28–40.

Swift 1903a: Samuel Swift. "Garden Marbles from Abroad." *House & Garden* 4 (Aug. 1903): 68–77.

Symes: Michael Symes. *Garden Sculpture.* Princes Risborough, England: Shire Publications Ltd., 1996.

Symmes: Marilyn Symmes, ed. *Fountains: Splash and Spectacle: Water and Design from the Renaissance to the Present.* New York: Rizzoli, in association with Cooper-Hewitt, National Design Museum, Smithsonian Institution, 1998.

Tachau: Hanna Tachau. "An Awakening Appreciation of Wrought Iron in America: The Work of Mr. Samuel Yellin." *The Art World* 3 (Feb. 1918): 440–442.

Teague: Edward H. Teague. *Sculpture Gardens: A Bibliography of Periodical Literature.* Monticello, Ill.: Vance Bibliographies, 1985.

Thonger: Charles Thonger. *The Book of Garden Furniture.* London and New York: John Lane: The Bodley, 1903.

Thornton: Tamara Plakins Thornton. *Cultivating Gentlemen, The Meaning of Country Life Among the Boston Elite, 1785–1860.* New Haven: Yale University Press, 1990.

Timmes: Peter Timmes' Son. *Illustrated Catalogue of Peter Timmes' Son.* Trade catalogue. Brooklyn, NY: Peter Timmes' Son, 1896.

Tolkwsky: Samuel Tolkwsky. *Hesperides: A History of the Culture and Use of Citrus Fruits.* London: J. Bale, Sons & Curnow, Ltd., 1938.

Toole: Robert M. Toole. "An American cottage ornée: Washington Irving's Sunnyside, 1835–1859." *Journal of Garden History* 12 (1992): 52–72.

Turner: Tom Turner. *English Garden Design: History & Styles Since 1650.* Woodbridge, Suffolk, UK: Antique Collectors' Club, 1986.

Underwood: Loring Underwood. *The Garden and Its Accessories.* Boston: Little, Brown, and Company, 1907.

Vance: Mary Vance. *Garden Ornaments and Furniture: Monographs.* Vance Bibliographies, Architecture Series: Bibliography #A 1268, 1984.

Van Dorn: Van Dorn Iron Works. *13th Annual Circular.* Trade catalogue. Cleveland, OH: Van Dorn Iron Works, 1884.

Van Rensselaer: Mariana Griswold Van Rensselaer. *Art Out-of-Doors: Hints on Good Taste in Gardening.* New York: Charles Scribner's Sons, 1925.

Van Valkenburgh: Michael Van Valkenburgh. *Built Landscapes: Gardens in the Northeast.* Brattleboro, VT: Brattleboro Museum & Art Center, 1984.

Vaux: Calvert Vaux. *Villas and Cottages.* New York: Harper Brothers, 1857.

Vermeule: Cornelius C. Vermeule. *Greek and Roman Sculpture in America: Masterpieces in Public Collections in the United States and Canada.* Berkeley and Los Angeles: University of California Press, 1981.

Villard: C. A. Villard. *Ornements en fonte de fer de la Hte. Marne & de la Meuse.* Trade catalogue. Lyon, France, c. 1855

Walbridge: Walbridge & Company. *Iron Reservoir Vases.* Trade catalogue. Buffalo: Walbridge & Company, c. 1900.

Ward: Gerald W. R. Ward, ed. *Perspectives in American Furniture.* New York: Norton, 1988.

Wardin: Albert W. Wardin, Jr. *Belmont Mansion: The Home of Joseph and Adelicia Acklen.* Revised edition. Nashville, TN: Belmont Mansion Association, 1997.

Warwick Castle: The Warwick Castle Estate Office. *Warwick Castle: A Brief Account of the Earls of Warwick, Together with a Description of the Castle and Some of the More Notable Works of Art Therein.* Warwickshire, England: The Warwick Castle Estate Office, 1954.

Water: Stephen J. Water. *The Oxford History of England: The Age of George III, 1976–1815.* Oxford, 1960.

Watson: John F. Watson. *Annals of Philadelphia and Pennsylvania in the Olden Time.* 3 vols. 1846. Reprint, Philadelphia, 1927.

Weaver: Lawrence Weaver. *English Leadwork: Its Art and History.* London: B.T. Batsford, 1909.

Wells: F. M. Wells. *The Garden Decorative.* London: The Cable Printing and Publishing Co., Ltd., 1903.

Westervelt: A. B. & W. T. Westervelt. *Illustrated catalogue and Price List; Settees, Chairs, Tables, Archways, Ornamental Iron Work of Every Description; Fountains, Vases, Statuary, Deer, Dogs. Lions, etc., and Other Lawn and Garden Adornments.* Trade catalogue. New York: A. B. & W. T. Westervelt, c. 1900.

Wharton 1904: Edith Wharton. *Italian Villas and Their Gardens.* New York: The Century Company, 1904.

Wharton 1995: Edith Wharton. *Edith Wharton Abroad: Selected Travel Writings, 1888–1920.* Edited by Sarah Bird Wright. New York: St. Martin's Press, 1995.

E. White: Elizabeth White. *Pictoral Dictionary of British 18th Century Furniture Design: The Printed Sources.* Woodbridge, Suffolk, UK: Antique Collectors' Club, 1990.

J. P. White: John P. White. *A Complete Catalog of Garden Furniture and Garden Ornament.* Trade catalogue. Bedford, England: The Pyghtle Works, 1906.

Wickersham: John B. Wickersham. *A New Phase in Iron Manufacture.* Trade catalogue. New York: John B. Wickersham, 1853.

Wilkinson and Henderson: Elizabeth Wilkinson and Marjorie Henderson. *House of Boughs: Decorating Eden.* San Francisco: Chronicle Books, 1992.

Wilson: Samuel Wilson, Jr. "New Orleans Ironwork." *Magazine of Art* (Oct. 1948): 214–217.

Wood: Robert Wood & Co. *Portfolio of Original Designs of Ornamental Iron Work.* Trade catalogue. Philadelphia: Robert Wood & Co., c. 1875.

Wood & Perot: Wood & Perot. *Portfolio of Original Designs of Iron Railings, Verandahs, Settees, Chairs, Tables, and Other Ornamental Iron Work.* Trade catalogue. Philadelphia: Wood & Perot, 1858.

M. O. Wright: Mabel Osgood Wright. *The Garden of a Commuter's Wife.* New York: Macmillan Co., 1901.

R. Wright: Richardson Wright, ed. *House & Garden's Book of Gardens.* New York: Condé Nast, 1921.

Yamin and Metheny: Rebecca Yamin and Karen Bescherer Metheny, eds. *Landscape Archaeology: Reading and Interpreting the American Historical Landscape.* Knoxville: The University of Tennessee Press, 1996.

Young: Charles D. Young & Co. *Designs of Vases, Fountains, Dial Stands &c..* Trade catalogue. Liverpool: Liverpool, 1850.

decorative motifs, 64, 69; *49, 54, 57, 58, 60, 3.1, 3.4, 3.13, 3.17, 3.20, 3.24, 3.31, 3.44, 3.60, 3.61.* See also specific motifs

as finials, *49, 91, 6.3, 6.24*

in formal garden style, 63–67, 70, 75; *3.48*

as fountains, 64; *3.16*

functions of, 63–64, 65, 68, 75; *3.28*

Gothic style, *3.55*

granite, 2

handles, 63, 67, 68; *52, 54–56, 58, 61, 3.1, 3.4, 3.8, 3.10–3.12, 3.14–3.16, 3.18–3.20, 3.22, 3.24, 3.28, 3.31–3.33, 3.36, 6.24*

Istrian stone, 70; *45, 55*

Italian garden influence on, 69–70

lead, 64, 65; *3.41, 3.42, 3.43, 3.44, 3.45*

lidded, 66, 70–75; *58–60, 3.45, 3.50, 3.53, 6.3, 6.27*

marble, *50, 58, 3.46–3.49*

mask-and-loop, *3.24, 3.39, 3.58*

materials for, 63, 67, 69; *3.47*

Medici vase, *3.24, 3.39*

neo-Attic style, *3.24, 3.39*

ovoid form, *3.50, 3.61*

pedestals, 66–68, 119; *48, 51, 55, 60, 3.1, 3.3, 3.5, 3.11, 3.14, 3.30, 3.37*

in picturesque garden style, 63–66

placement of, 65–67, 75; *49, 52–53, 59, 3.48*

as planters, 67, 68; *48, 50, 52, 53, 56*

reproductions, *3.40*

rococo style, *57, 3.18, 3.36, 3.58*

rustic style, 13–14; *3.5*

as sculptural ornament, 64, 67

self-watering, *3.7*

as static form, 75

stoneware, *3.56–3.59*

symbolism of, 64–65, 66; *3.6*

terra cotta, 69–70; *53, 54, 3.5, 3.60–3.61*

Townley vase, *3.47*

tulip urn, *3.25*

types of, 63. See also specific types

vasiform shape, *3.34*

Victorian influence on, 67, 68; *52, 3.17*

Warwick vase, *45*

Windemere Vase, *3.15*

Woodbury Vase, *51*

zinc, *45, 3.33*

See also jardinieres

V

Fonderies du Val d'Osne, 69; *67, 2.40, 3.12, 3.21, 3.23, 3.26, 3.27, 3.32, 3.42, 4.49*

Vanderbilt, Cornelius II, 108

See also Breakers, The

Vanderbilt Mansion National Historic Site, 117; *96, 1.16*

vases. See urns

vaso, defined, *3.60*

Vatican Gardens, 39; *20, 36, 55, 70*

Venus motif, 44; *37, 2.10, 2.16, 2.17*

Versailles, 13, 17, 44; *28, 2.23, 5.13*

urns, 64; *56, 3.16, 3.20–3.21, 3.26, 3.51*

Versailles seat, *4.27*

Virginia House, *2.19, 4.18, 4.60, 5.20, 6.28*

Vizcaya Museum and Gardens, 31; *2, 3, 7, 21–22, 27, 39, 75*

W

wall-mounted fountains, 18, 19, 31

baroque style, *4*

carved stone, 10–11; *13, 1.14, 1.16, 1.18, 1.20*

cast iron, *1.15*

cast stone, *1.21*

lead, *101, 1.20*

marble, *4, 1.17*

niche, *13*

tiered, *1.16*

Washington, George, 38, 40, 44, 78, 93; *77, 2.6, 3.2*

Weld (Brookline), 28, 60, 96, 118, 121

wellheads, 118

decorative motifs, *98, 7.10, 7.12*

as fountains, *9*

Istrian stone, *96, 7.10*

Italian, 116–18; *9, 96, 97, 7.8, 7.9, 7.10, 7.12, 7.13*

marble, *98, 102, 7.8, 7.9, 7.13*

materials for, 116

overthrows, 118; *7.8, 7.11*

Westover, 37–38, 40, 78

fence, 40, 104, 105; *84–85, 6.2–6.8*

West Point Foundry, *4.8*

Wharton, Edith, 28, 54, 118; *1.27, 4.71*

wheat motif, *2.1, 2.9*

White, J. P., *72, 2.27, 4.69*

White, Stanford, *99, 4.72*

Box Hill garden, 58, 115, 118; *2.17*

J. P. White, 60; *50, 6.29*

John B. Wickersham, 107; *87, 6.12*

See also New York Wire Railing Company

Windsor chairs, 78

women sculptors, ornament and, 28, 52

Wood, Miltenberger & Co., 81, 106; *86, 6.10*

See also Wood & Perot; Robert Wood

Wood & Perot, 81, 106, 107; *1.2, 3.4, 3.33, 7.30*

flower stands, 114; *7.3*

furniture, *4.5, 4.9–4.11, 4.20, 4.26, 4.28–4.29, 4.31, 4.64, 4.67*

statues, *2.32, 2.38*

See also Wood, Miltenberger & Co.; Robert Wood

Robert Wood & Co., 23; *51, 1.3, 1.5*

furniture, 81; *68, 4.5, 4.12, 4.13*

statues, *31, 2.29, 2.37, 2.39*

See also Wood, Miltenberger & Co.; Wood & Perot

Y

Yellin, Samuel, 109; *88, 90, 101, 6.23*

Z

Zeus motif, 44; *17, 2.33*

Zodiac table, *4.62*

ACKNOWLEDGMENTS

The idea for this book came to me after the 1991 publication of *Antique Garden Ornament* by the English dealer and garden ornament authority John Davis. Received with great anticipation by those of us in the field, Davis's book was one of the first comprehensive books on the subject in many years, and before long it became an important reference on English garden ornament. Soon after, I began to think seriously about writing a similar book from an American point of view, and in 1995 I began the project. Although the approach of my book is quite different from Davis's, and focused on American ornament, I consider myself fortunate to have had his fine model to lead me through many otherwise uncharted waters.

I am forever indebted to the late Mark Hampton for his extraordinary generosity in honoring a promise to me that he would write the Preface to this book. Astonishingly, he persevered through the worst of health and completed his work at a time when he was dangerously ill. I will always remember Mark for this truly noble gesture. I am also immeasurably grateful to Mark's wife, Duane Hampton, and her sister, my great friend, Paula Perlini, both of whom were of enormous help at this difficult time.

During the early stages of this book, several very important people believed in the project and were immensely helpful. I owe thanks to Joan Gers of Archivia Books, and to Heidi Nasstrom, my first research assistant, whose scholarly methods and friendly urging led to the compilation of a bibliography that convinced me that a book on this subject was feasible. I also want to thank Louis Webre for his timely referral to my subsequent editor.

In the initial stages of conceiving the format of the book I was fortunate in having the advice and support of the legendary Margaret Kaplan, Senior Vice President and Executive Editor at Harry N. Abrams, Inc. I cannot sufficiently express my gratitude to my editor and friend, Elaine Banks Stainton, with whom I have worked from the planning stage to the final editing, and whose superb guidance, limitless patience, and amiable leadership transformed a green work into a solid document. And my thanks also to Judy Hudson for her exceptionally beautiful design for the book, for her appreciation of the subject, and for her endurance through all of my revisions.

I am grateful to my agent Alice Fried Martell for her early enthusiasm and steady hand through a long year and a half of preparations.

The quality of the images in a book are of the utmost importance in the representation of the subject matter. I am grateful to a number of individuals for the exceptional photography in this volume, especially to Mick Hales for his patience and energy over many months in a multitude of locations. His superb work in color truly captures the essence of the ornament in historic gardens and properties across America. In addition, I want to applaud the work in the black-and-white catalogue, not only the tireless efforts and superior photographs of Fran Collin but also the excellent images taken by Sharyn Peavey.

I owe an enormous debt of gratitude to Alexandra Truitt, the photo research editor of this book. She has been my guide and savior from beginning to end, particularly for her appreciation of my early objectives, her astute contributions to the visual content of the book, and her patience and good nature through the vast assignment of gathering permissions, arranging for shooting, and obtaining four hundred original photographs. My thanks also to Jerry Marshall for his miraculous photography lists.

In any endeavor such as this there are people who are central to the project. In this case I was extremely fortunate to have four, a true Dream Team, who worked closely with me for months on end.

The first of these was Jeni L. Sandberg, whose contributions to this book were inestimable. The book benefited from her research, her tireless visits to historic properties, her arrangements for photography, her ingenious approach to finding information for the manufacturers' list, and, above all, her high academic standards. I cannot sufficiently express my gratitude to Eva Schwartz, my second team member, for her on-target advice, assistance, and encouragement on the writing and editing of the book from beginning to end; for her sustained work through four hundred captions, of which she is responsible for at least a third; and for her painstaking, laborious, and ingenious formatting of the notes and bibliography. I offer a particular salute of thanks to my third team member, William Andrew Haluska, who tackled seemingly endless tasks with unfailing good nature. His contributions to the research, development, and final format of the manufacturers' list are incalculable. I am grateful also for his lively captions, his computer wizardry, and his willingness and ability to track down information on virtually any subject. Finally, none of this would have been possible without one person managing the business end of the project. The unflappable Sharyn Peavey maintained control during calm or quandary while continuing to provide creative suggestions, schedules and formats, artistic backgrounds, photographic and computer expertise, as well as devising complicated archival systems.

I am also grateful to a number of scholars whose work elevated the standards of the book: Serena Tottman Bechtel in putting together the first proposal of the book; Cornelia Barnwell Spruill in providing remarkable research that truly served as the backbone for the book; Laura Handlin, an intern from the Cooper-Hewitt/Parsons Masters Program in the History of Decorative Arts; Monica Cheslak; Sara Olshin; Grace Williams Kaynor; and Barbara Veith.

Four others were extremely helpful in the last months before the deadline. My thanks go to Robert La France for his scholarly talents and dogged persistence. I am exceedingly grateful to Jennifer Milliken Downs for many hours spent on revisions, on captions, on the historic garden list, and on city directory research; to my nephew, David Kurzman, for his astute computer skills and admirable endurance through hundreds of footnotes; and to Willa Rogers for her energetic determination and shrewd observations. In addition, I would like to thank Barbara Gerrity for arranging numerous trips, and Helen Kiernan for providing sustenance beyond anyone's expectations.

I would particularly like to thank those authors and professionals who generously offered advice, resources, and counsel from their own experiences: most particularly Connie and Bill Hershey for invaluable editing, also Zeynep Çelik, Cynthia Conigliaro, Bill Connington, Madison Cox, Elissa Cullman, Page Dickey, Alice Cooney Frelinghuysen, Enid Glass, Allen Green, May Brawley Hill, Susan Klein, my niece Katherine Kurzman, my brother-in-law Paul Kurzman, Kathryn Meehan, Deborah Nevins, Hugh Palmer, Philip Pfeiffer, Roxana Robinson, Cynthia V. A. Schaffner, Nancy Schiffer, Michael van Valkenburgh, and Bunny Williams.

I gratefully acknowledge the staff and professionals of the Cooper-Hewitt, National Design Museum, Smithsonian Institution, for their constant assistance, good nature, and scholarly advice. Claire Gunning, Reference Librarian, was exceedingly helpful and continuously answered questions and provided information. I would also like to thank Dr. Maria Ann Conelli, Chair, and Janna Eggebeen, Assistant Chair, of the Cooper-Hewitt/Parsons Masters Program in the History of Decorative Arts for the Cooper-Hewitt students and graduates whose impeccable literary and research training assisted in the preparation of this book.

I am deeply grateful for research assistance that I received throughout the project from scholars at a number of institutions. My thanks to Barry Harwood, Associate Curator at the Brooklyn Museum of Art; Morrison H. Heckscher, Curator, and Catherine Hoover Voorsanger, Associate Curator, at the Metropolitan Museum of Art; Donald L. Fennimore, Curator, the Henry Francis Du Pont Winterthur Museum; Mario De Valmarana, Professor, School of Architecture, University of Virginia; Martha Rowe, Research Associate, Museum of Early Southern Decorative Arts; Elizabeth Agro, Curatorial Assistant, Carnegie Museum of Art; Pat and Barbara Bacot, Louisiana State Museum; Bill Gustafson, Historian, Museum of Anthracite Mining; Carolyn Ellis, Reference Librarian, San Antonio Public Library; Robin Karson, Director, Library of American Landscape History; Eva Milstead, Librarian, San Antonio Conservation Society; John Powell, Librarian and Information Officer, Ironbridge Gorge Museum Trust; James Rothwell, Assistant Historic Buildings Representative of the National Trust of England; James Rylands and Jackie Rees, Sotheby's Billingshurst; Chapin Carson, Lisa Alaimo, and Elaine Whitmire, Sotheby's New York; and Stephen Lash, Christie's New York.

Others to whom I am grateful for their help with various research projects are: Luis Badillo, Florie Boice, Graham Brown, Justin L. Cobb, Rocco De Angelo, Margot Gayle, Mark Alan Hewitt, Jim Hinck, N. Pendergast Jones, Ruth Kerridge, Joni Lima, Scott Merritt, Aileen Minor, Dick, Rita, and Laurie Nelson, Charles W. Newhall, Elizabeth Page, Joanne Papachristos, Barry Perry, Dolf Sweerts de Landas, Catherine Valentour, Nancy Wells, and Bob Withington.

Without the help of a few very knowledgeable and helpful people I would not have been able to piece together the history of the ornaments and gardens of Blairsden (St. Joseph's Villa). I offer my thanks to the Sisters of St. John the Baptist, the Mother Superior Mary Cecile Swanton, Sister Angelita, and Sister Lois, and also to Ann Casey van den Berg, Mac Griswold, Georgie Schley, and particularly to Ania Baas, who contributed so much of the landscape history.

I owe a debt of gratitude to John and Samuel Chew, the descendants of Benjamin Chew, for their help in directing my research on the statues at Cliveden. My thanks also to the staff of Cliveden, particularly to Elizabeth Laurent, Curator, and to Ann Roller, staff member. The work of two scholars contributed to my conclusions, namely that of Nancy E. Richards, author of *Cliveden: The Chew Mansion in Germantown,* and Mark Reinberger of the University of Georgia.

Rosedown is a very special historic property deserving of national attention. For information, photography, and historic documents, I thank the director, Gene Slivka. My heartfelt thanks also to David Underwood, the son of Catherine Underwood and himself owner of Rosedown for twenty-eight years, for his insights, enthusiasm, and assistance in so many ways.

To shoot and assemble more than four hundred original photographs, I relied on a great many friends, dealers, and collectors. I thank them one and all for their help and hospitality, namely: Tim Brennan of Webb and Brennan, Moshe Bronstein of the Garden Antiquary, Jay Carey of F. J. Carey, III, Geret Conover of the Charlotte Inn, Michael Garden of Elizabeth Street, Marilyn Gentile of Cragmoor Designs, Susan Lyall of Folly, Michael McCarty of the Garden Room, Anne Rowe of the Sugar Plum, Grazia Bardi, Massimo Giani, and S. Marinelli of Antonio Frilli, Ltd., Michael Bloomberg, Jeffrey and Joanne Klein, Chris and Matt Matthews, John and Gilda McGarry, Vickie and Steve Morris, Janet and Joseph Shein, Gail Ahern, Leigh Keno, Donald Landsman, William Louis-Dreyfus, Melissa Orme, and Carol Prisant.

An essential part of the book, the photographs and stories of the historic houses and properties of America, was made possible by the assistance of many individuals and the staffs of their institutions. For this I owe an enormous debt of gratitude to Cynthia Bronson Altman, Curator, Kykuit, Historic Hudson Valley; Mark Baer, Historic Resource Manager, Naumkeag, The Trustees of Reservations; Linda Bass, Public Relations, Stan Hywet; M. Kent Brinkley, Landscape Architect, Colonial Williamsburg; Mark Brown, Executive Director, Belmont Mansion Association; Charles Burns, Associate Curator, Preservation Society of Newport County; Scott F. Burrell, Director, Virginia House; Deidre Cantrell, Executive Assistant, Ganna Walska Lotusland; David Chase, Historian, Phillips Academy, Andover; Mark Coir, Archivist, Cranbrook; Mary Cranwell, Director of Special Events, Georgian Court; Emily Croll, Project Director, Historic Morven; Frances Diesu, Events Manager, Old Westbury Gardens; Paddy Dietz, Curator, Nemours Mansion; Barbara Doyle, Historian, Middleton Place; Lisa M. Blackburn, Communications Coordinator, and Jacqueline Dugas, Registrar, The Huntington Library, Arts Collections, and Botanical Gardens; Anna D'Ambrosio, Curator, Munson-Williams-Proctor Institute; Dee Durham, Executive Director, Preservation Delaware, Inc.; Charlotte Eaton, Curator, Putnam County Historical Society and Foundry School Museum; Ben Feiman, Landscape Architect of Canyon Ranch (Bellefontaine); Hoyt Fields, Chief Curator, Hearst Castle; Patricia C. Glumac, Curator of Programs, The Highlands; Cynthia Schroeder Gray, Executive Director, Casa del Herrero Foundation; Nadja Gutowski, Public Relations Director, Virginia Historical Society; Kelly Hoysington, Marketing, Biltmore Estate; Kathleen Eagen Johnson, Curator of Historic Hudson Valley; Bill Justice, Chief Ranger, Melrose, National Parks Service; John Lancaster, Belmont Mansion Association; King Laughlin, Manager of Special Projects, Mount Vernon; Michelle A. MacDonald, Curator, Vizcaya; George Marshall IV, Lansdowne; John Miller, Director, Edsel Ford House; Ronald Miller, Executive Director, and Mimi Miller, Director of Programs, Historic Natchez Foundation; Ann P. Moye, Volunteer, Isaiah Davenport House Museum; Cindy Nielsen, Deputy Superintendent, Roosevelt-Vanderbilt National Historic Sites; Florence Ogg, Curator, Vanderbilt Museum; Burns Patterson, Director of Public Relations, Historic Hudson Valley; Laurie Ossman, Curator, Cà d' Zan, and Aaron Degroft, the John and Mable Ringling Museum; Jeff Payne, Registrar, Hearst Castle; Josephine Osbun, Past Chairman, Dumbarton House Board, Dumbarton House; Paula Richter, Assistant Curator, Peabody-Essex Institute; Janet Robinson, Public Relations Director, Magnolia Plantation; Kimberly D. Saulnier, Historic Site Administrator, Naumkeag, Trustees of Reservations; Thomas Savage, Director, Historic Charleston Foundation; Laura Strauss, Public Relations, Stan Hywet; Elizabeth Sullivan, Public Relations Assistant, Longwood Gardens; Kate Sullivan, Director of Marketing, Morris Arboretum; Claudia Thiel, Curatorial Assistant, Preservation Society of Newport County; Harley Tinney, Curator, Belcourt Castle; Lucy Tolmack, Director of Horticulture, Filoli; David B. Warren, Director, Bayou Bend Collection and Gardens, the Museum of Fine Arts, Houston; and Lucy Weller, Director, Gwinn.

I would like to thank the staff of the libraries at the institutions where we have done most of our research: the Historical Society of Pennsylvania; the Winterthur Library; the Library of Congress; Hagley Museum and Library; Special Collections Department, University of Delaware; the Watson Library and the Print Study Room at the Metropolitan Museum of Art; the Avery Library at Columbia University; the New-York Historical Society; the New York Society Library; the New York Public Library, where the major part of the city directory work was done; and the Baker Library of the Harvard University Graduate School of Business Administration.

I am forever grateful to the late William Doyle, who in 1985 led me down the garden ornament path. I am indebted also to my friends and members of my family, whose assistance and support have been unremitting: Denise and Robert Froelich, Naomi Josepher, Nancy Rome, Susan Solomon, Ellen and David Stein, my sisters Margaret Kurzman and Susan van Roijen, my brother Joe Frelinghuysen, and my parents Emily and Joseph Frelinghuysen.

Finally, I cannot sufficiently thank my husband and my children for their patience and forbearance throughout this undertaking. Their lives have been disrupted for what must have seemed an interminable length of time. My most affectionate thanks to my husband, Tom, and to our three children, Peter, Emily, and Wendy, for their constant thoughtfulness, support, and encouragement.

Barbara Israel
New York, 1998

PHOTO AND PROPERTY CREDITS

Access for photographing ornaments kindly provided by:

Agecroft Association: 141 right; Courtesy of Belcourt Castle, Newport, RI: 12; Belmont Mansion: 24, 52, 145 left, 147 right, 149 right; Used with permission from The Biltmore Company: 31, 48; The Breakers, a property of The Preservation Society of Newport County, Newport, RI: 56, 70, 72 top, 111; The Burn c. 1832: 124 right; Courtesy of Canyon Ranch in the Berkshires: 25, 66, 206 center; Collection of F. J. Carey, III: 135 center, 137 center, 144 center, 158 bottom center, 160 center, 173 top center and right, 186 left, 187 left; Furniture designed and made by George F. Steedman for Casa del Herrero, c. 1932-35, and © 1997 by Casa del Herrero Foundation: 84; Charlotte Inn: 156 center, 187 center and right, 188 left, 205 top center and right, 206 left, 213 center, 214 center; Chateau-sur-Mer, a property of The Preservation Society of Newport County, Newport, RI: 163 right; Cliveden of The National Trust, Inc.: 38, 39; Cragmoor Design: 174 center, 176 right; Cranbrook: 16, 133 center, 161 center, 202 bottom left, 207 center; Davenport House Museum: 79; D'Everaux, Natchez, MS: 116; Dellwood Cemetery, Manchester, VT: 157 center; Courtesy, Dumbarton House Collection, Headquarters of The National Society of The Colonial Dames of America, Washington, D.C.: 166 center; Dumbarton Oaks, Washington, D.C.: Page 114, 127 center, 130 center, 135 left, 202 right, 212 center; Dunleith Natchez, MS: 107; Mr. and Mrs. Richard M. Durkin: 199 center, 200 left; Courtesy of Elizabeth Street Gallery: 128 bottom left, 147 bottom center, 154 center and right; The Elms, a property of The Preservation Society of Newport County, Newport, RI: 86, 118, 140 bottom center; Richard L. Feigen, Bedford, NY: 204 left; From the collection of Mr. and Mrs. Lawrence Flinn, Jr.: 150 center; Folly/New York: 148 left; Rose Garden fountain, Edsel and Eleanor Ford House, Grosse Pointe Shores, Michigan: 129 right; Henry Ford Estate - Fair Lane - University of Michigan - Dearborn: 201 bottom left; Moshe Bronstein/The Garden Antiquary: 132 left, 146 center; Photographed at the Gardens of Georgian Court College: 21, 49, 71 top, 85, 194 left; Gwinn: 29, 69, 110 bottom, 120 top, 194 center; Hearst Castle™/Hearst San Simeon State Historical Monument™: 121, 139 right, 141 center, 207 left; Courtesy, The Highlands Mansion and Gardens, Fort Washington, PA: 97, 155 center, 196 left, 209 center and right; Courtesy of Historic Hudson Valley: 32, 55, bottom, 61 bottom, 62, 112; Courtesy The Huntington Library, Art Collections and Botanical Gardens: 30, 54, 61 top, 72 bottom, 76, 127 left, 163 center; Acknowledges the Assistance of Stan Hywet Hall and Gardens in Akron, OH: 89 bottom, 90, 100, 109, 134 left, 209

left; Lansdowne Plantation, Natchez, MS: 83; Longwood Gardens, Kennett Square, PA: 33, 53, 59 top, 73 both; Ganna Walska Lotusland Foundation - Santa Barbara, CA: 59 bottom; Matt and Chris Matthews: 153 bottom center, 157 right, 167 left; Ebenezer Maxwell Mansion, Philadelphia, PA: 68, 110 top; Maymont Foundation: 153 left, 194 right, 195 right; Mr. and Mrs. John P. McGarry, Jr.: 142 top center, 180 top center; Collection of Mr. and Mrs. Thomas M. McNeely, Shadyside, Natchez, MS: 159 center; Middleton Place, Charleston, SC: 6, 46, 57; Moffatt-Ladd House, Portsmouth, NH: jacket front and 96; Monmouth Plantation c. 1818: 178 center; Morris Arboretum of the University of Pennsylvania: 126 center; Vickie and Steve Morris: 208 right; Courtesy of the Mount Vernon Ladies' Association: 93; Property of the Natchez Garden Club: 213 left; Courtesy Natchez National Historic Park: 67; National Park Service: 117, 129 left; Nemours Mansion and Gardens: 27, 71 bottom, 148 center; Northeast Auctions: 138 right; Old Westbury Gardens Inc.: 50, 60, 98, 193 right; Phillips Academy, Andover, MA: 196 right; Courtesy of the Putnam County Historical Society & Foundry School Museum: 170 right; Preservation Delaware, Inc.: 74, 102, 203 top and bottom left; Ownership - Richmond, Inc.: 82, 156 left, 192 right; The John and Mable Ringling Museum of Art: 20, 34, 41, 65, 164 right; Rosecliff, a property of The Preservation Society of Newport County, Newport, RI: 167 center, 189 right; Rosedown Plantation & Historic Gardens, St. Francisville, LA: jacket back and 44, 45, 51, 64, 94, 115, 124 left, 137 left, 140 left, 150 left, 153 right, 171 center, 181 bottom right, 211 left and top center; Susan W. Rotenstreich - Bedford, NY: 147 top center; Nathaniel Russel House, Charleston, SC: 177 right, 198 right; Photo Courtesy of San Antonio Conservation Society Foundation: 125 right; Janet and Joseph Shein: 152 top center, 158 top center and right, 159 right, 180 bottom center, 183 top center, 184 bottom center, 210 right; Sisters of St. John the Baptist: 2, 8–9, 10–11, 43, 55 top, 78, 128 right, 208 left, 214 left; Horticulture Services Division collection, Smithsonian Institution: 172 left, 176 top center, 180 right, 214 right; Stanton Hall: 199 top right; The Trustees of Reservations: 87, 120 bottom; The Suffolk County Vanderbilt Museum: 88, 119, 129 center, 143 right, 201 center; Photographed at Virginia House, an American Country place historic house museum, in Richmond, VA. Virginia House is owned and operated by the Virginia Historical Society: 142 left, 172 center, 173 bottom center, 185 right, 196 center, 203 top right; Vizcaya Museum: 18, 19, 36, 42 both, 47, 58, 89 top; Westover: 103, 104, 197 all, 198 all left; Withington/Wells: 174 left, 195 left. All others from private collections

All Photographs © Mick Hales other than:

Vincent Aiosa: 134 top center, 180 left; Fran Collin: 127 right, 130 left and right, 133 left, 135 right, 136 left, 139 left and center, 142 top center, 143 left, 144 left, 146 center and right, 147 top center, 148 right, 149 left, 150 center, 151 left, center and right, 152 right, 153 bottom right, 156 right, 157 right, 162 right, 164 center, 166 right, 167 left, 168 top, 169 center, 170 center and right, 171 left, 174 center, 176 right, 177 center, 180 top center, 182 left and right, 183 left and bottom center, 184 left, 185 top left, 188 center, 191 left, 192 left, 193 left, 195 center, 201 center, 202 top left and center, 203 bottom right, 205 bottom center, 206 right, 207 right, 208 center, 210 left, top and bottom center; Daniel Delaney: 138 center, 152 left and bottom center, 153 top center, 155 left, 159 left, 162 left, 163 left, 165 right, 167 right, 170 left, 173 left, 176 bottom center, 179 left and center, 181 right, 182 center, 201 top left, 212 left; Richard Goodbody: 147 left; Elise Irving: 156 center, 160 left, 187 center and right, 188 left, 205 top center and right, 206 left, 212 right, 213 center, 214 center; Barbara Israel: 128 center, 142 right, 157 center, 166 left; The Metropolitan Museum of Art, Purchase, Anonymous Gift, 1968. (68.140.2): 176 left; The Metropolitan Museum of Art, Purchase, Anna Glen B. Vietor Gift, in memory of her husband, Alexander Orr Vietor, 1986. (1986.9): 191 right; The Metropolitan Museum of Art, Purchase, Anna Glen B. Vietor Gift, in memory of her husband, Alexander Orr Vietor, 1987. (1987.339): 191 bottom center; The Metropolitan Museum of Art, Gift of Mrs. Stephen S. Fitzgerald, 1962. (62.89.14.): 191 top center; Munson-Williams-Proctor Institute Museum of Art, Utica, NY; Purchase, by Exchange, with Gifts from Jane B. Sayre Bryant and David E. Bryant in Memory of the Sayre Family: 205 left; Collection of the Museum of Early Southern Decorative Arts: 169 left; Hugh Palmer: 164 top left; Courtesy, Peabody Essex Museum, Salem, MA: 190 left; Sharyn Peavey: 126 left, 128 left and bottom left, 131 center and right, 132 center and right, 133 right, 134 right, 143 center, 147 bottom center, 148 left, 154 center and right, 155 right, 157 left, 158 left, 160 right, 165 left and center, 169 right, 172 left, 174 left and right, 175 left and right, 176 top center, 177 left, 178 left and right, 179 left and right, 180 right, 181 center, 183 right, 185 bottom left and center, 186 right, 188 right, 189 left and center, 192 center, 195 left, 204 right, 214 right, all line drawings; Betsy Pinover: 140 top center, 142 bottom center; Rob Rinaldi: 151 bottom left, 154 left, 162 center, 171 right, 181 left, 184 right; Susan van Roijen: 184 top center; Catherine Valentour: 166 center